The Gospel of
JOHN

Also by James Montgomery Boice

Witness and Revelation in the Gospel of John
Philippians: An Expositional Commentary
The Sermon on the Mount
How to Live the Christian Life (originally, *How to Live It Up*)
Ordinary Men Called by God (originally, *How God Can Use Nobodies*)
The Last and Future World
John: An Expositional Commentary (5 volumes)
"Galatians" in the *Expositor's Bible Commentary*
Can You Run Away from God?
Our Sovereign God, editor
Our Savior God: Studies on Man, Christ and the Atonement, editor
Does Inerrancy Matter?
The Foundation of Biblical Authority, editor
Making God's Word Plain, editor
The Epistles of John
Genesis: An Expositional Commentary (3 volumes)
The Parables of Jesus
The Christ of Christmas
The Minor Prophets: An Expositional Commentary (2 volumes)
Standing on the Rock
The Christ of the Open Tomb
Foundations of the Christian Faith (4 volumes in one)
Christ's Call to Discipleship
Transforming Our World: A Call to Action, editor
Ephesians: An Expositional Commentary
Daniel: An Expositional Commentary
Joshua: We Will Serve the Lord
Nehemiah: Learning to Lead
The King Has Come
Romans: An Expositional Commentary (4 volumes)
Mind Renewal in a Mindless Age
Amazing Grace
Psalms: An Expositional Commentary (3 volumes)
Sure I Believe, So What!
Hearing God When It Hurts
Two Cities, Two Loves
Here We Stand: A Call from Confessing Evangelicals, editor
    with Benjamin E. Sasse
Living by the Book
Acts: An Expositional Commentary
The Heart of the Cross, with Philip G. Ryken
What Makes a Church Evangelical?

The Gospel of

JOHN

Volume 4
Peace in Storm
John 13–17

JAMES
MONTGOMERY
BOICE

Baker Books

A Division of Baker Book House Co
Grand Rapids, Michigan 49516

© 1985, 1999 by James Montgomery Boice

Published by Baker Books
a division of Baker Book House Company
P.O. Box 6287, Grand Rapids, MI 49516-6287

Previously published by Zondervan Publishing Company

Second printing, December 2001

Printed in the United States of America

Library of Congress Cataloging-in-Publication Data

Boice, James Montgomery, 1938–
    [Gospel of John]
    The Gospel of John / James Montgomery Boice.
      p.   cm.
    Includes bibliographical references and indexes.
    Contents: v. 4. Peace in Storm, John 13–17.
    ISBN 0-8010-1106-X (hardcover)
    1. Bible. N. T. John Commentaries. I. Title.
BS2615.3.B55   1999
226.5'077—dc21   99-22764

For current information about all releases from Baker Book House, visit our web site:
http://www.bakerbooks.com

To him who,
having loved his own,
loved them unto the end

Contents

Preface

The lengthy section of John's Gospel beginning with 13:1 and concluding with 17:26 contains probably the best-known and most-loved words of religious instruction ever uttered by any religious teacher. It is not hard to see why. For here, on the verge of his own horrible suffering and death by crucifixion, this one, who claimed to be God, speaks out of the peace he possessed to tell his disciples how to experience peace in tribulation.

It is not that Jesus was unaware of what lay before him or that he was unmoved by it. On the contrary, he had repeatedly foretold his crucifixion, saying that "the Son of man will be betrayed to the chief priests and teachers of the law. They will condemn him to death and hand him over to the Gentiles, who will mock him and spit on him, flog him and kill him. Three days later he will rise" (Mark 10:33–34). Again, Jesus had said of his pending death, "Now my heart is troubled, and what shall I say? 'Father, save me from this hour'? No, it was for this very reason I came to this hour" (John 12:27). No, Jesus was not unaware of the suffering that was to come, nor was he unmoved by it. It is simply that he had found the secret of peace in storm, or rather that he was himself the peace in whose shelter those who believed in him might cluster.

This is the message of these famous and final discourses of Jesus of Nazareth, and hence also of this, the fourth volume in my five-volume expository commentary on John's Gospel. The questions it asks are: "Do you want peace?" and "Are you willing to receive it at the point where alone Jesus indicates it may truly be found?"

As has been my pattern in the other volumes in this series, I have occasionally deviated from a strict exposition of these chapters to deal at somewhat greater length with a subject suggested by them. In earlier volumes this procedure has been followed by a study of witnessing, baptism, the Sunday-versus-Sabbath question, the Scriptures, Christ our Good Shepherd, and death. In this volume I devote three special studies to the doctrine of heaven, eight studies to the doctrine of the Holy Spirit, and seven studies to the marks of the church enumerated by Jesus in his great high-priestly prayer recorded in chapter 17.

For those who have purchased the earlier studies, I point out that the five-fold division of the Gospel introduced in volume 1 is still being followed. Volume 1 deals with the coming of the light of the Lord Jesus Christ into this world (chapters 1–4). Volume 2 deals with the growth of hostility toward him on the part of the religious leaders of the day (chapters 5–8). Volume 3 deals with the words of the Lord in beginning to call out a people to himself from among Israel, beginning with his call of the man who had been born blind (chapters 9–12). This volume, volume 4, deals with the final discourses of Jesus and their message of peace in storm, as has been indicated (chapters 13–17). The final volume, number 5, deals with the last events of Christ's earthly life, culminating in his resurrection (chapters 18–21).

One of the much-appreciated blessings that I have experienced in the course of my ministry is the active support of the congregation of Tenth Presbyterian Church in Philadelphia, to whom these messages were originally preached. These dear people encourage me to spend a significant amount of my time in serious Bible study and exposition in order to prepare such messages. Also, Miss Caecilie M. Foelster, my secretary, has assisted me in the editing and proofing of this material, as she has in the preparation of the numerous other books I have written. I am especially thankful to her.

The book bears the dedication: "To him who, having loved his own, loved them unto the end." May this work serve to glorify him, and may he alone be glorified. Amen and Amen.

James Montgomery Boice
Philadelphia, Pennsylvania

Peace in Storm

164

Love Letters from the Lord

John 13:1

It was just before the Passover Feast. Jesus knew that the time had come for him to leave this world and go to the Father. Having loved his own who were in the world, he now showed them the full extent of his love.

In 2 Timothy 3:16–17 the apostle Paul writes that "All Scripture is God-breathed and is useful for instruction, for teaching, rebuking, correcting and training in righteousness, so that the man of God may be thoroughly equipped for every good work." But having acknowledged that this is indeed true, that all Scripture is God's gift to us and is of inestimable value, we nevertheless recognize that for one reason or another some sections of the Bible are particularly valuable and are therefore especially prized and loved by God's people. We come to such a section in this volume.

To many persons the Gospel of John, as the most intense and spiritual of the Gospels, is the "holy place" of Scripture. But if this is so, then these chapters, 13 through 17, which contain the final discourses of the Lord with his disciples just before his crucifixion and which conclude with his great high-priestly prayer on their behalf, are the "holy of holies." Nowhere in the entire Bible does the child of God feel that he is walking on more holy ground. For here, more than in many other portions of Scripture, he hears the voice of Jesus leading him into a greater understanding of his new place before the Father and consequently also of his new position in the world. These chapters contain teaching about heaven, the new commandment, the person and work of the Holy Spirit, the mutual union of Christ with the disciples and the disciples with Christ, and prayer.

To what can we compare these chapters? They can only be compared to love letters, in this case love letters from the Lord. For here the One who is the great and faithful Bridegroom of the church speaks to those who are themselves the church and assures them of his special and enduring love for them.

Not for Everyone

This means that the truths contained in these chapters are not for everyone. They are for the Lord's people only. We have one evidence for this in the fact that they were spoken only to the Twelve in the upper room and not more widely. This irritates some people, of course, for it suggests partiality on the part of God, and in their view partiality is both unjust and despicable. But such people do not recognize the nature of the partiality that is found here, nor do they recognize how much they practice partiality themselves, in some cases even with justification.

We can immediately see the justice of these chapters not being for everyone if we simply extend the idea of these being the Lord's love letters. What would we think of a man who, for instance, is married to one woman but who writes intimate and endearing letters to many other women whom he knows? We would call that man a philanderer, a hypocrite, a liar. We recognize at once that while he may rightly have friendly contacts with many persons, including other women, nevertheless the most intimate things, those that belong in a marriage, deserve to be spoken only between husband and wife. Marriage is a private relationship. Consequently, it must be partial. In the same way Jesus has taken unto himself a special people, the church. These are his bride. It is entirely fitting and even expected that he should have special, loving, and touchingly tender words for them only.

Is this partiality? Not at all! It is grace. For it is God, of his own sovereign will, choosing those whom he thus determines to save and bless abundantly. This has nothing to do with any supposed merit in God's people, for there is none. It is simply that when men had rejected God, choosing to go their own way, God out of infinite mercy still elected to save and bless some. If he had not done so, not one soul would have been saved. That he has done so, is tremendous.

The World

It is not surprising in view of the special nature of these chapters that the verse that begins them makes the contrast between those who are Christ's own and those who are not, sharper than any other comparable passage in the Word of God. It is true that Paul does much the same thing in Romans 9 and 10. A similar contrast is found in Ephesians 2, and many times in the

Old Testament. But nowhere is the contrast clearer and the categories involved more absolute. For here, in the first verse of John 13, we are at once introduced to those who are Christ's own, whom he loved faithfully until the end.

The verse says, "It was just before the Passover Feast. Jesus knew that the time had come for him to leave this world and go to the Father. Having loved his own who were in the world, he now showed them the full extent of his love."

Who are Christ's own? The answer has already been given many times in John's Gospel. They are those who have been given to Christ by the Father (6:37, 44). They are those for whom Christ was about to die (10:11, 15). They are those who were born, "not of natural descent, nor of human decision or of a husband's will, but born of God" (1:13). They are those to whom Christ gives eternal life, who shall never perish, and who therefore shall never be plucked from Christ's hand (10:28–29). What is the world? The world is the human race out of which Christ called them.

It is worth considering this term "world," for, as we pointed out in one of the studies toward the end of John 4, this is one of the most important concepts in the fourth Gospel. There are several Greek words that are translated "world" in our Bibles, but the one we are interested in is *kosmos*, from which we get our word "cosmopolitan." *Kosmos* means "world." *Politēs* means "citizen." So a citizen of the world is a cosmopolitan. The Greek word *kosmos* occurs 185 times in the New Testament. But what is extremely interesting is that of these 185 occurrences of the word *kosmos*, 105 are in the books traditionally ascribed to John. There are 78 occurrences of the word in the Gospel, 24 in the Epistles, and 3 in the Book of Revelation. Moreover, the importance of the word in John's Gospel is made even more obvious when we compare its 78 occurrences to the 8 times it occurs in Matthew and the merely 3 times each it occurs in Mark and Luke.

What does *kosmos* mean? The answer to the question is a complex one, for the word is old and therefore in time has acquired multiple meanings. The word originally meant "an ornament," that is, a decorative object, the unique feature of which was its fine proportions or beauty. This meaning is preserved in our English word "cosmetic," though in this case the meaning has shifted from what is beautiful in itself to that which is used to improve features that perhaps are not. In time the word was applied to the universe or world globe, as the well-proportioned ornament of God. This meaning occurs in John 1:9 and 10, which tell us that the Light "that gives light to every man was coming into the world" and that "the world was made by him." Even here another meaning is also present, however, for verse 10 goes on to say that "the world [that is, the people in the world] did not recognize him."

Since *kosmos* was used to describe the "world globe," it was natural that it next came to denote "the world of human beings." In this second sense we might also translate it as "the human race." It is said of the world in this sense that God loved it and gave his only Son for it (John 3:16), that it is the object of his saving purposes (John 3:17), that Jesus died for it (1 John 2:2), that he is its Savior (John 4:42; 1 John 4:14). It must be understood of this use of the word that it refers to the human race collectively and not necessarily to each individual, otherwise the verses cited would imply a universal salvation of all men that is clearly repudiated elsewhere.

The third and major use of the word *kosmos* is the one that occurs in our text and that comes to dominate the remaining chapters of John's Gospel. This usage also signifies the world of human beings, but with the additional thought that this world stands in rebellion against God. At times we may translate this use of *kosmos* as "the world system," including the world's values, pleasures, pastimes, and aspirations. It is said of the world in this sense that the world does not know God (1 John 3:1), that it rejected Jesus (John 1:10–11), and consequently that it also does not know and therefore also hates his followers (15:18–21; 17:14). This sense of the word is involved in every instance in which Christ's own are distinguished from the world. For example, "If the world hates you, keep in mind that it hated me first" (15:18). Or again, "I have given them your words and the world has hated them, for they are not of the world any more than I am of the world" (17:14).

In summary we may say that, in the first sense, Christians are to receive the world and be thankful for it, for it is God's gift. In the second sense, they are to love the world and seek to evangelize it, for God also loves the human race. In the third sense, however, believers in Christ are to reject the world and then by God's grace also order their lives according to an entirely different set of values.

All Things for Some

The difference between God's relationship to the world and his relationship to his own has sometimes been stated in this way. God has done *some things for all men,* that is, everyone in the world. He has created them, sustained them, kept them from the worst that is possible, even tolerated them and thus kept them for a time from hell. On the other hand, God has done *all things for some men.* These are his own. They do not lack and will never lack any good thing.

What has God done for his own? In one sense the chapters we are to study are themselves the full answer to that question. The answer will come in fullness only as we study them. But as we stand at the threshold of these chapters cannot avoid at least a partial answer by way of expectation. The answer has at least six parts.

1. The first and greatest teaching of these chapters is that Jesus specifically loved those who are his own. This is how the section begins: "Jesus . . . having loved his own who were in the world . . . showed them the

full extent of his love" (13:1). It ends with: "I have made you known to them and will continue to make you known in order that the love you have for me may be in them and that I myself may be in them" (17:26). It is not necessary to say at this point that there is no love of God for the world in general. There is a sense in which the love of God extends to all people. It is only necessary to say that the love of which we are speaking here is a special, saving love as a result of which those who are Christ's own become his own and are kept by him. For having loved *them,* "he showed [and continues to show] *them* the full extent of his love."

While this undoubtedly gives some special privileges to those who are his own, it also gives them equally special obligations. For if they are loved, they also are to love. In this lies the basis for Christ's new commandment. "A new command I give unto you: Love one another. As I have loved you, so you must love one another" (13:34).

2. The second great teaching of these chapters is that Jesus has gone to prepare a place known as heaven for his people. We are not told a great deal about heaven or what awaits us there. But we are told that in it there is a place for us who believe in him, and we are also promised that he will return one day to guarantee that we get there. "In my Father's house are many rooms; if it were not so, I would have told you. I am going there to prepare a place for you. And if I go and prepare a place for you, I will come back and take you to be with me, that you also may be where I am" (14:2–3). Even if heaven did not exist, the love of the Lord that we have come to experience here on earth would be wonderful in itself. But, in addition to this, there is heaven. In this promise we learn that the fact that the Lord loved his own "to the end" does not merely mean "to the end of Christ's life" or even "to the end of our lives." Rather, it means "to the very end," "to the uttermost." His love for us will never end; it is eternal.

3. During these last discourses, the disciples were naturally troubled, for they had been told that the Lord, whom they loved, would be leaving them in order to return to the Father. In this context, Jesus' words about heaven were a source of great comfort. But there is another source also, and in this is found the third of Jesus' teachings. He tells the disciples, and therefore also tells us, that he is going to send a replacement for himself; that replacement, the Holy Spirit, would come and dwell within those who belong to Jesus. "And I will ask the Father, and he will give you another Counselor to be with you forever—the Spirit of truth. The world cannot accept him, because it does not see him or know him. But you know him; for he dwells with you, and will be in you" (14:16–17).

It is also the work of the Holy Spirit to lead the apostles into all the truth concerning Jesus, bringing it to their remembrance (14:26; 16:13), and to convict the world of sin, righteousness, and judgment (16:8–11).

4. The fourth teaching of the Lord concerns his commissioning of the disciples to a special work, indeed a different work in each individual case. We find it in the fifteenth chapter. "You did not choose me, but I chose you and appointed you to go and bear fruit—fruit that will last" (v. 16). According to this verse, each of us has a spiritually fruitful work to perform. The promise of the Lord is that all we will accomplish in this area will remain.

5. We are told in these chapters that the Lord intercedes or prays for us. Here the seventeenth chapter is itself one long example. It is encouraging; for in these verses the Lord prays that his own might be kept from the evil that is in the world, that they might have his joy fulfilled in them, that they might be sanctified by means of the Word of God, that they might be one, and finally that they might be with Jesus in heaven. Can God turn his back on a request made by his own dear Son? Of course not! We rightly sing,

> The Father hears him pray,
> His dear anointed One;
> He cannot turn away
> The presence of his Son.

So these requests are already fulfilled or are in the process of being fulfilled. They carry the same weight as direct promises. We shall be kept from evil. We shall have joy. We shall be one. We shall be with Jesus in heaven.

6. Finally, just as Jesus has prayed for us, so he invites us to pray, describing this as a new and blessed privilege. "I tell you the truth, my Father will give you whatever you ask in my name. Until now you have not asked for anything in my name. Ask and you will receive, and your joy will be complete" (16:23–24).

These are the themes that are developed fully in this important fourth section of John's Gospel. Perhaps the best comment about them is that of Paul in the great eighth chapter of Romans: "What, then, shall we say in response to this? If God is for us, who can be against us? He did not spare his own Son, but gave him up for us all—how will he not also, along with him, graciously give us all things?" (vv. 31–32). God has indeed given us all things. But to whom much has been given, much shall also be required. May God use our study of John 13–17 to help us become increasingly his obedient and therefore also his exceedingly joyous children.

165

Having Loved, He Loved

John 13:1

It was just before the Passover Feast. Jesus knew that the time had come for him to leave this world and go to the Father. Having loved his own who were in the world, he now showed them the full extent of his love.

In the previous study of the first verse of John 13 we saw that, while God has done some things for all men, he has, in addition to this, done all things for some. This is a tremendous truth. But, like all great truths, it almost cries out for an explanation. Fortunately the explanation is in our text also. For having distinguished between those who are of the world and those who are Christ's own, the verse goes on to say, "Having *loved* his own who were in the world, he showed them the *full extent of his love.*" Love is the explanation. Jesus loves his own; he loves us. This is the entire explanation of why God has done all things for those who are his spiritual people.

No Explanation

When we say this, however, we must immediately recognize that love itself is unexplainable. For if we go on to ask, "But why did God love us? Why does Jesus love us?" there is just no answer to be given.

Obviously we are not loved because we are lovable, for we are not. It is true that some of us may be lovable to some others of us, but this is only when we look at the matter from a human perspective. From God's perspective there is nothing in us to make us even remotely desirable. He is holy; we are unholy. He is just; we are unjust. He is loving; we are filled with hatred and all forms of sin. In short, we are sinful and in willful rebellion against him. Yet he loves us. In fact, this is so great a marvel that God even uses it to commend his love to us. He says, "You see, at just the right time, when we were still powerless, Christ died for the ungodly. Very rarely will anyone die for a righteous man, though for a good man someone might possibly dare to die. But God demonstrated his own love for us in this: While we were still sinners, Christ died for us" (Rom. 5:6–8).

God has not loved us because we first loved him; he is not merely returning our love. We did *not* love him. On this point the apostle John writes clearly, "This is love, not that we loved God, but that he loved us and sent his Son as an atoning sacrifice for our sins" (1 John 4:10).

Again, the Lord did not love us because of anything that we could do for him, for we had nothing to offer. He does not need praise; the angels praise him. He does not even need spiritual children; for, as Jesus said, he is able of stones to raise up children to Abraham. Even our numbers are not an asset. So why does God love us? The only answer is the one he gave Moses concerning the children of Israel. "The LORD did not set his affection on you and choose you because you were more numerous than other peoples, for you were the fewest of all peoples. But it was because the LORD loved you and kept the oath he swore to your forefathers" (Deut. 7:7–8). The reason God loves us is that he loves us. Beyond that, his love is unexplainable. It is without reason, at least without reason known to us.

Empirical Data

If we were to stop at this point, I suppose that in that thought alone we would have enough to keep us pondering on the love of God for eternity. But there is more. For the verse that tells us that God loves without reason also tells us that God loves without variation and without end. His love is eternal. The verse says, "Having loved his own who were in the world, he showed them *the full extent of his love.*"

We want to come back to that phrase, "the full extent." But before we do so we need to see the reasons God gives why we should believe that his love is eternal. We cannot see into the future; therefore, rationally at least, the future lends no evidence. Why should we believe in this everlasting quality of God's love? The answer is an empirical one. It has to do with observable data, particularly data from the past and present. First, there is the past: "Having loved." Second, there is the present: "he showed." This second occurrence is a past tense (an aorist); but the sense is present, for it refers to what Jesus was then doing and was about to do.

In other words, the verse calls our attention to the observable past and present love of Christ, and it is asking us to reason on that basis. Is not love his nature? Will not he who loved in the past and loves in the present also love in the future? If he loved his disciples to the end, will he not love us similarly?

Past and Present Love

What do we know about the love of God the Father and of the Lord Jesus Christ in the past? Obviously that is a big question, the answer to which can never fully be given. But we can suggest some areas in which the answer can be seen.

First, we can see the love of God in the creation of ourselves and other human beings. We refer at this point, not merely to the fact of our existence, for our existence in itself might prove nothing. We refer rather to the fact that in creating us God created us with a spiritual vacuum within that can be filled only by himself. In other words, he created us, not to a meaningless existence but to an existence that is the highest existence possible for any created object, namely, communion with the One who created it. So it is as Augustine said, "Thou hast made us for Thyself, and our hearts are restless until they rest in Thee." The fact that we can know God and are restless until we do know him is proof of his love.

Second, God's love is seen in the fact that he, by the Holy Spirit's regenerating power has called us to himself. We have seen this several times in John's Gospel. We are told, on the one hand, that no one can come to God unless God draws him. In this fatal inability we measure the extent of our depravity. But then, on the other hand, we are told that God does draw some to himself and that none of these can be lost. In this we see God's love, for apart from the sweet drawing of that love, no one would ever come to him.

Third, we see God's love in Jesus' death for his people. This, if you will, completes the trinitarian formula, for in creation we see the love of the Father. In the effectual calling of God's people we see the love of the Holy Spirit. In the act of redemption we see the love of Jesus Christ, the Son.

The love of the Lord Jesus Christ in dying for us may be illustrated by the following story as told by Harry Ironside. Many years ago, Czar Nicholas I of Russia knew a young man for whom he cared a great deal. He was the son of a good friend of his. Because of his interest in this young man, Nicholas had him assigned to a border fortress of the Russian army and caused him to be given charge of the money used for paying the soldiers. The young man started well. But he fell into bad habits, took to gambling, and eventually gambled away not only his own wealth but also a great fortune taken from government funds. He had taken just a few rubles at a time, but these had mounted up and become prodigious. One day he received notice that on the following day an official would be coming to inspect the books. The young man knew he was in trouble. So he took out the records to find out how great his debt was. He totaled the amount. Then he went to the safe, took out his own small amount of money, and counted it carefully. He subtracted the lesser from the greater. The debt was astronomical. As he sat looking at the final figure, the young officer picked up his pen and wrote in large letters, "A great debt; who can pay?" Then, because he did not see how he could face the terrible dishonor the next day held, he determined to kill himself with his revolver at the stroke of twelve.

The night was warm and drowsy. So as he waited for the midnight hour, in spite of himself the young man's head dropped lower and lower and he fell asleep.

It happened that Nicholas, who was in the habit of sometimes putting on the uniform of a common soldier and visiting the troops to see how they were getting on, did so this night, coming around to the halls of the very fortress in which the young officer was sleeping. Most of the lights were out, as they should have been. But when Nicholas got to the door of this one room he noticed a light shining under it. He knocked. No answer! He tried the latch and opened the door. There was the young officer, whom he recognized, asleep. He saw also the books and the money. The whole thing became clear in a moment. His first thought was to awaken his young friend and place him under arrest. But as he read the young man's note, his heart went out to him. "A great debt; who can pay?" Moved by a generous impulse, the Czar leaned over, picked up the pen that had fallen from the hand of the sleeping officer, wrote just one word, and tiptoed out.

For an hour or so the young man slept. Then he suddenly awoke and, seeing that it was long past midnight, reached for the revolver. As he did so his eye caught sight of his note—"A great debt; who can pay?"—and under it the one word that had not been there before: "Nicholas." He was astonished. Dropping his gun, he raced to the files where the signature of the Czar was available. He pulled this out and carefully compared it with the signature on his note. It was the real signature. He said to himself, "The Czar has been here tonight and knows all my guilt; yet he has undertaken to pay my debt; I need not die." So instead of taking his life, he rested upon the word of Nicholas and was not surprised when, early the next morning, a messenger came from the palace bearing precisely the amount of money needed to satisfy the deficit. Later, when the inspector came, everything was found to be in order.[1]

Thus did Jesus love us and pay our great debt. We are sinners. There is no possible way for us to atone for that sin. But Jesus has paid that debt. He has signed his name to our bankrupt account. No wonder we sing:

> Jesus paid it all,
>   All to him I owe;
> Sin had left a crimson stain—
>   He washed it white as snow.

That is the love of the Lord Jesus Christ for us as seen in the past. It is that to which God points us and directs our eyes. Thus has he loved. Who then can doubt that he will continue to love us unto the end?

Full Extent . . . unto the End

The phrase "the full extent" brings us to the second half of our text. The King James Version says "unto the end." It raises the question: Unto the end of what? There are several answers.

First, it means "unto the end of the earthly life of Jesus Christ." Even the context suggests this, for the verse is given to us at the start of those chapters that tell of Christ's final ministry to his disciples prior to his crucifixion. We must admit that we are not always appreciative of this, for we take Christ's love for granted. Yet, if we would think of the possible hindrances to love both on his part and on the part of the disciples during these days, we would be more sensitive.

On his part there were great hindrances, as the verse indicates. It says, "Jesus knew that the time had come for him to leave this world and go to the Father," thereby indicating that Jesus knew clearly that he was about to die. So if we were to read that in those moments his thoughts turned from his own to himself so that, at least for a time, he ceased to love them or think about them, who could blame him? Yet knowledge of his impending death did not deter him. There were also hindrances on the part of the disciples. They were worldly, for instance. He thought spiritually. But every time he tried to teach them spiritual things, they interpreted his words on a wordly level. Moreover, they were dull. He explained great truths to them, and they did not understand. In fact, he had been explaining that he was to leave them to go to the Father, but they could not understand even this. Not one of the disciples was a fit companion for the Lord Jesus Christ. So if he had said to himself, "I have thought about these men long enough; I have done everything for them that I know how to do; it is time I thought of myself," who could blame him? No one! Yet he loved them, fully and unselfishly, to the end of his life.

Second, he obviously also loved them to the end of their lives. True, he was to be the first to die. He died before Peter, James, John, or any of the others. But then he rose, and as the risen Lord he returned to bestow his own Spirit upon the disciples and then guide them and preserve them until the time when each would go to be with him in glory.

Finally, the phrase also means "to the very end," that is, "to the end of ends" or "without end," "forever." In Greek the word is *telos*, which literally means "perfection." Jesus, having loved his own who were in the world, loved them perfectly. So we sing:

> The love of God is greater far
> Than tongue or pen can ever tell;

> It goes beyond the highest star,
> And reaches to the lowest hell.
>
> Oh, love of God, how rich and pure!
>   How measureless and strong!
> It shall forevermore endure—
>   The saints' and angels' song.

Such love is indeed forever. Having loved his own who were in the world, he loves them to the end.

Love Others, Love Him

How shall we apply these truths? On the one hand, we must apply them to believers, and, on the other, to those who are not yet believers. The word to those who believe on Christ is this: If this is the way in which God has loved us, then should we not love one another, and also fervently love him? We will never in this life love as he loved, but we can begin to try to love as he loved—unselfishly, without discrimination, without wavering. We should also serve him. For, as the hymn declares:

> Love so amazing, so divine,
> Demands my soul, my life, my all.

Again, there is a word for those who have still not become true Christians. If you are not yet a believer in the Lord Jesus Christ, let me ask you a question that flows from everything I have been saying. If God loves like this, how can you afford to be without such a great love? There is no love on earth like it. Your husband or wife will not love you like this. Your children and parents will not love you like this. Your neighbors and friends will not love you like this. Only Jesus Christ loves with a perfect and everlasting love! Moreover, one day you must stand before the judgment seat of his Father, whom you have offended by your ungodly conduct and by your rejection of his great grace. What will you do in that day—if you refuse the love of the Lord Jesus Christ? What will you do without having him to stand by you and say, "This is one of my own; this is one for whom I died; this is one whose debt I undertook to pay; this is one I love unto the end"? Without such love you will be lost forever. Fortunately, the day of God's grace is still present; you may yet come to Jesus Christ as your Savior.

166

Love on Its Knees

John 13:2-15

The evening meal was being served, and the devil had already prompted Judas Iscariot, son of Simon, to betray Jesus. Jesus knew that the Father had put all things under his power, and that he had come from God and was returning to God; so he got up from the meal, took off his outer clothing, and wrapped a towel around his waist. After that, he poured water into a basin and began to wash his disciples' feet, drying them with the towel that was wrapped around him.

He came to Simon Peter, who said to him, "Lord, are you going to wash my feet?"

Jesus replied, "You do not realize now what I am doing, but later you will understand."

"No," said Peter, "you shall never wash my feet."

Jesus answered, "Unless I wash you, you have no part with me."

"Then, Lord," Simon Peter replied, "not just my feet but my hands and my head as well!"

Jesus answered, "A person who has had a bath needs only to wash his feet; his whole body is clean. And you are clean, though not every one of you." For he knew who was going to betray him, and that was why he said not every one was clean.

When he had finished washing their feet, he put on his clothes and returned to his place. "Do you understand what I have done for you?" he asked them. "You call me 'Teacher' and 'Lord,' and rightly so, for that is what I am. Now that I, your Lord and Teacher, have washed your feet, you also should wash one another's feet. I have set you an example that you should do as I have done for you."

Actions speak louder than words." This expression is not always true, but it is sometimes true. And in some instances it is only actions that speak at all. The need for action in some instances reminds me of the farmer who was stuck in the middle of the road with his donkey. The donkey had planted his feet firmly on the ground and would not move no matter what the farmer did. So the man stood there shouting at the donkey, kicking him and getting angrier all the time. While this was going on another farmer came down the road and immediately sized up the problem. "Do you want help?" he asked.

"I sure could use it," the first farmer answered. "But I don't think it will do any good. I've been shouting at this stupid donkey for half an hour, and he just won't budge."

"I can fix that," the second man answered. He went over to the side of the road, picked up a club, and then came back and hit the donkey between the eyes. After that he stood back and said "Gee haw!" in a normal tone of voice, and the donkey started off.

"I don't understand it," said the owner. "I yelled at him, and he acted as if he didn't even hear me. You spoke in a normal tone of voice, and he moved off."

"That's true," said the second man, "but first I got his attention."

The right action is valuable in many circumstances, of course. It applies in child rearing, for instance. I have saved many useless words with my children by a well-timed use of a related attention-getting mechanism. Or again, it applies in teaching. Sometimes a gesture or an object lesson gets the point across faster and better than any number of words. True, on his last full night with his disciples just before his crucifixion, when he wanted to teach them many things, Jesus began his teaching, not with words that might have been missed by them but with two significant actions. The first was the washing of the disciples' feet, recorded in John 13:2–11. The second was the giving of the bread to Judas, recorded in John 13:21–30.

Why did Jesus perform these actions? The answer is that the disciples were preoccupied. We have already been told that they were terrified of the Jewish leaders; they suspected that Jesus was about to be arrested, and they were afraid that he would die and that they would die with him. Or, even if that were not the case, it might be that he would be taken and they be left. Nothing in their present circumstances had prepared them to hear his teaching. So Jesus acted boldly in order to get their attention.

Judas and Jesus

The first action we have in John 13 is that of Jesus washing the feet of the disciples. But as John tells the story, he draws our attention, first of all, to the contrast between Judas, who was moved by Satan, and Jesus, who was motivated solely by love and by his knowledge of God the Father and his unique relationship to him. John writes, "The evening meal was being served and the devil had already prompted Judas Iscariot, son of Simon, to betray Jesus . . ." (vv. 2–3).

As we read these verses, stopping at that point, we can hardly miss the fact that John wishes to contrast the action of Jesus, who gave himself for his disciples, with that of Judas. We have here the humility of Christ, who washed the disciples' feet, versus the pride of Judas. There is faithfulness to the end, versus treachery and betrayal. Then, lest we miss the most important point, John also mentions the devil so we will see that the basic contrast is between Satan and God.

Satan's way, described vividly in Isaiah 14:12–14, is simply personal advancement at the expense of others, in this case at the expense of God. "How you have fallen from heaven, O morning star! You have been cast down to the earth, you who once laid low the nations! You said in your heart, 'I will ascend to heaven; I will raise my throne above the stars of God; I will sit enthroned on the mount of assembly, on the utmost heights of the sacred mountain. I will ascend above the tops of the clouds; I will make myself like the Most High.'" The consequence of this satanic desire is destruction. For the passage goes on to say, "But you are brought down to the grave, to the depths of the pit" (v. 15).

On the other hand, there is the way of God, which is described in the case of Jesus in Philippians 2:5–8. "Your attitude should be the same as Christ Jesus: Who, being in very nature God, did not consider equality with God something to be grasped, but made himself nothing, taking the very nature of a servant, bring made in human likeness. And being found in appearance as a man, he humbled himself and became obedient to death—even death on a cross." The result of this course of action is honor for Jesus and blessing for those who are his own. "Therefore, God exalted him to the highest place and gave him the name that is above every name, that at the name of Jesus every knee should bow, in heaven and on earth and under the earth, and every tongue confess that Jesus Christ is Lord, to the glory of God the Father" (vv. 9–11).

Satan, like Judas after him, said, "I will think first of myself; and the first thing I will seek is my aggrandizement." God says, "You will actually go down to defeat." Jesus said, "I will surrender my life for my brethren." God says, "Therefore, you will be honored and will be a great blessing."

Christ's Motivation

The second thing we notice is Christ's motivation in washing the disciples' feet. Verse 3 goes on to say, "Jesus knew that the Father had put all things under his power, and that he had come from God and was returning to God. . . ." Here we are told three things about Jesus' state of mind as he performed this action. First, he knew that "the Father had put all things under his power." This speaks of Christ's *authority*. Second, he knew that "he had come from God." This speaks of his *divine origin*. Third, he knew that he was even then on the verge of returning "to God." This speaks of his *future glory*.

We notice that it was not in forgetfulness of who he was and where he was going, then, that Jesus washed the disciples' feet, but rather in full consciousness of it. It was not that he forgot he was God and so humbled himself. It was because he was God and wished to act as God that he did it.

A Parable

At this point we can begin to appreciate the significance of what Jesus did when he washed the disciples' feet, for he was obviously not giving just an example of humility. Still less was he instituting an additional sacrament, as some have imagined. What he was doing was giving a dramatic illustration of his entire ministry. In a recent book, entitled *Secrets of the Spirit*, Ray C. Stedman spells this out clearly. He writes, "There can be little doubt that here Jesus was deliberately working out a parable for the instruction of his disciples. He was dramatizing for them the character of his ministry. He was showing them by this means what he had come into the world to do, and what he would send them out to do."[1]

We can easily follow the meaning of the parable by comparing the verses from Philippians that I cited earlier with the events that John records. First, John tells us that Jesus *rose* from supper. This had already been done in a far greater way when he rose from his throne of glory prior to his coming into this world. Second, he *laid aside his garments*. Paul in Philippians says that when he came into the world he laid aside that glory which was his so that he could appear as a true man and not blind with his celestial glory those who looked upon him. Next, he took a towel and *girded himself*. This was the garb of a servant, a role that, Paul says, he took upon himself. Finally, he *poured water into a basin* and began to wash the disciples' feet, just as in a few short hours he was to pour out his blood for the washing away of human sin by the atonement.

To see the end of the parable we need only skip over to verse 12, as Stedman notes. For there we read, "When he had finished washing their feet, he put on his clothes and returned to his place. . . ." In the same way, Christ is even now highly exalted. Or again, as the author of Hebrews writes, "After he had provided purification for sins, he sat down at the right hand of the Majesty in heaven" (1:3).

There is another way in which the spiritual nature of this parable is evident, and that is in the exchange between the Lord and Peter. Jesus had laid aside His clothes and had begun to go around the table washing the disciples' feet, presumably in an atmosphere of stunned silence, for this was the work of a slave and not that of a distinguished rabbi. However, when Jesus came to Peter, the impulsive Peter could stand it no longer so he blurted out, "Lord, are you going to wash my feet?"

Jesus replied, "You do not realize now what I am doing, but later you will understand."

Peter, who was humble enough to feel the incongruity of having his feet washed by Jesus but not humble enough to refrain from telling his master what not to do, replied, "You shall never wash my feet."

Jesus said, "Unless I wash you, you have no part with me."

At this, Peter did an about-face and declared that in that case he wanted to be washed all over: "Then, Lord, not just my feet but my hands and my head as well!"

Jesus replied in conclusion, "A person who has had a bath needs only to wash his feet; his whole body is clean. And you are clean, though not every one of you." Here the somewhat confusing dialogue clears up, at least partially; for it is evident that Jesus is talking, not about physical dirt but about sin and the need to be cleansed from it. He is explaining that Peter (not Judas) is a justified person and therefore needs only cleansing from the contaminating effects of sin, not pardon from sin's penalty.

The image involved is of an oriental who would bathe completely before going to another person's home for dinner. On the way, because he would be shod in sandals and because the streets would be dirty, his feet would be contaminated. When he arrived at his friend's home, his feet would need to be washed, not his whole body. In a parallel way, those who are Christ's are totally justified men and women, but they do need constant cleansing from their repeated defilement by sin in order that the fellowship they have with the Father and with the Son might not be broken.

Jesus is telling Peter that he does not need to be born again and again and again. To be born again once is enough. Nevertheless, as regenerated people, we do need to come to Christ for cleansing.

Our Example

After the conversation with Peter, Jesus, we are told, resumed his place at the head of the table and began to explain to the disciples what he had done. He said, "Do you understand what I have done for you? You call me 'Teacher' and 'Lord,' and rightly so, for that is what I am. Now that I, your Lord and Teacher, have washed your feet, you also should wash one another's feet. I have set you an example that you should do as I have done for you" (vv. 12–15).

What does this mean? Does it mean that we should go out and institute a new sacrament to be known as the sacrament of foot washing? Not at all, though some have done this. What Jesus is talking about is humility and the need for God's people to take a servant role. He is simply saying, "If I, your Master, have played the servant role, you who are my servants should certainly play the servant role with one another." We are to care for those who can no longer care for themselves—our aged parents, the poor, orphans. We are to get close to those who are suffering and do everything in our power to alleviate their suffering. We are to open our homes to the lonely.

Above all, we are not to take the first place in Christian gatherings but are to take a lower place that someone else might be honored.

Moreover, we are even to fulfill Christ's example in regard to spiritual defilement and cleansing, for this is what the parable is about. According to Christ's words to Peter, the cleansing of the feet symbolized the spiritual cleansing of Christians who have, nevertheless, fallen into specific sin. So if we are to follow Christ's example at this point, we must do as Paul admonished in writing to the Galatians: "Brothers, if someone is caught in a sin, you who are spiritual should restore him gently. But watch yourself, or you also may be tempted" (6:1).

How do we seek to restore a brother who has fallen into some sin? How do we seek to wash the feet of such a person? We are to take the Word of God, with which we are all to cleanse our ways, and then gently, ever so gently, apply it to our brother that he might respond to it by the grace of God.

Notice the word "gently." In his commentary on these verses Harry Ironside points out that if we are going to wash another's feet, we ought to be careful of the temperature of the water. You would not go to anyone and say, "Here, put your feet into this bucket of scalding water." Nor would you ask him to place his feet in a bucket of ice water. It is just as bad to be too hot in approaching another person as it is to be too cold and formal. Stedman points out that in trying to cleanse others, some Christians do without water at all. They try to dry-clean feet. They scrape them free of dirt and unfortunately sometimes take the skin with it.[2] Instead of this, we who are spiritual are to approach the other person meekly and in love.

167

A Clue for Finding Happiness

John 13:16–17

"I tell you the truth, no servant is greater than his master, nor is a messenger greater than the one who sent him. Now that you know these things, you will be blessed if you do them."

I do not know what you consider to be the number-one desire of most people today, but I suspect that if I were to conduct a poll, in one form or another the answer that would come highest on the list would be "happiness." Above all else most people want to be happy. It is true that they do not always see this clearly; they even express it in different terms. Some might say that most of all they would like to be rich. Others might wish to be famous. Some might want to be loved. But basic to all these replies would be the desire to find happiness, however it might be supposed to come.

The difficulty, however, is that happiness is not easily attainable. We seek for it. Indeed, in this country the privilege of seeking for happiness is even declared to be one of our inalienable rights. But no one can guarantee happiness itself. So our founding fathers wrote wisely when they defined those rights as "life, liberty, and the *pursuit* of happiness." Liberty can be guaranteed. So can life, up to a point. But not happiness. Only the right to pursue happiness can be guaranteed to any individual.

But how do we pursue happiness, and in what direction? One man thinks that he will be happy if he can save ten thousand dollars. So he saves all he can; he gets his ten thousand. But he still is not happy. He thinks in terms of fifty thousand, then a hundred thousand. If he is able, he earns a million dollars, but still happiness eludes him. Why? Because happiness does not come through amassing a fortune. A Texas millionaire once said, "I thought money could buy happiness. I have been miserably disillusioned."

Some persons try to find happiness through fame, but fame does not guarantee happiness either. If it did, we would not hear of so many of the world's famous people committing suicide. Still other persons think that they will be happy with power. They run for a local political office and win. Next they aspire to the mayor's chair. If they become mayor, they want to be state senator. After this they think in terms of national politics. But still they are not happy. One of the world's greatest statesmen once said to Billy Graham, "I am an old man. Life has lost all meaning. I am ready to take a fateful leap into the unknown."

Knowing and Doing

If you are one who desires to find happiness (as most of us do) and if you have not been able to find it in any of the ways I have just listed, or others, then you should be interested in these words spoken by the Lord Jesus Christ nearly two thousand years ago. They are our text, and they contain a clue for finding happiness. "I tell you the truth, no servant is greater than his master, nor is a messenger greater than the one who sent him. Now that you know these things, you will be blessed if you do them" (13:16–17).

As we read these verses we notice at once that Christ's clue for finding happiness has two parts. The first part consists in knowing certain things. The second part consists in doing them. Obviously both are important.

Several years ago I was talking to a man who has approximately half a million dollars invested in the stock market. I asked him, "Did the recent market decline affect you greatly?"

"It surely did," he answered.

"Did you have any idea that the market might go down?"

"That's the funny thing," he said. "About two months before the market tumbled, when the Dow Jones average was still high, we were having a meeting of a number of us who sometimes invested together. I remember saying in that meeting that the market simply could not continue as it was. I said that it would have to go back down. Surprisingly, everyone agreed. When I said that we ought to sell now, they agreed to that too. But, you know, nobody did it. None of us sold. So when the bottom dropped out, all of us were left with losses."

Obviously it is the combination of knowing and doing that makes for success. Or, to put this in spiritual terms once again, it is the combination of knowing and doing certain spiritual things that leads to true happiness.

Jesus Is Lord

So what is it that the one who would truly be happy should know? These are short verses, but in spite of their length they suggest a number of important things. The first is that *Jesus Christ is Lord*. Jesus alludes to this when he says, "No servant is greater than his *master* (lord), nor is a messenger greater than the one who sent him."

The problem that most of us have in finding happiness begins right here, for if we are honest, even as Christians, we must acknowledge that we frequently have the whole thing inverted. Jesus says that he is Lord and that we are his servants, but in actual fact, we act as if we are the Lord and he is the servant. Examine your prayers sometime and see if the greater part of your prayers does not consist of your telling Jesus what he should do for you and the far lesser part your asking what you can do for him. We say that Jesus is Lord. But in practical terms we want to make our decisions, choose our own way of life, and set our own courses of action.

When we do this, what we are actually doing is setting ourselves in the center of our own spiritual universe. And the difficulty is that we are not adequate as the center. Take this example from astronomy. In the early days of astronomy, before Copernicus, all work was done on the basis of the Ptolemaic system according to which theory all things revolved around the earth. The earth was the center of the system. The Ptolemaic system was not all bad. In fact, it was better than most people living today imagine. It could predict sunrise and sunset. It could predict new moons. To some extent it could even predict the course of the planets. But the difficulty with the Ptolemaic system is that it was not always accurate, particularly in charting the course of the planets. In attempting to provide numerous adjustments for the erratic planetary movements the system eventually broke down. Besides, the Ptolemaic system did not allow for progress. New discoveries always went against it, and certain other discoveries were not even possible. What was wrong? The difficulty was not in the conclusions, for some of these were right. The difficulty was at the heart of the theory; for the sun, not the earth, was at the center of the solar system.

There is a close parallel in spiritual terms. Those who make themselves the center of the spiritual universe do get certain results. If they are selfish enough, they get most of what they want. If they are ruthless enough, they can keep others from taking it away from them or taking advantage of them. But in spite of such apparent success, the system is never quite accurate. Therefore, the happiness that is supposed to follow these devices eludes them. Moreover, there is no progress. In fact, things get worse and worse. Life gets straightened out only when by the grace of God we get ourselves out of the center and the Lord Jesus Christ in. For he is Lord, and it is only he who can give order to the system.

The second truth we find in these verses is that Jesus took *a servant role*. He is Lord, the Lord of glory. Still he divested himself of his lordly prerogatives in order to be made like his brethren and serve them, even to death. This is what the episode of the foot-washing is all about, of course. On the one hand, it shows Jesus in a servant role. On the other, it is a parable of his entire ministry in which the dominating thought is service. "The Son of Man came not to be served, but to serve, and to give his life as a ransom for many," Jesus said (Matt. 20:28).

Ourselves, His Servants

The first two truths that the man who would be happy must know pertain to Christ: his position as Lord, and his role as servant. The next three truths pertain to ourselves.

To begin with *we are not greater than Jesus.* We acknowledge this verbally, but in actuality we often deny it by our actions. We say, "Of course we are not greater than Jesus." But we act out the opposite belief whenever we prefer our judgment to his judgment or think that we can manage without him. Jesus reminds us of the true nature of things when he declares, "*No servant is greater than his master, nor is a messenger greater than the one who sent him.*" We need to learn that we can do nothing without him.

The fourth truth in these verses is that *what is proper for Jesus is proper also for us.* How shall I live? What shall I do with my life? What shall my values be? Where shall I place my energies? We find the answers to these questions by looking to Jesus to see how he lived, what he did with his life, what his values were, and where he placed his energies. In other words, he is our example, as he said in the previous verse.

The fifth point is the climax of this argument. We have seen that Jesus is Lord, that he took a servant role, that we are not greater than Jesus, that what is proper for him is proper also for us. It follows, therefore, that *we also should be servants.* That is, we should all be ministers, for that is what the word "minister" means. It is the word *diakonos,* from which we get our word "deacon"—"servant." This is the clue for finding happiness.

As we read the other Gospel accounts of these last hours in which Jesus and his disciples were together, we soon discover that service was the issue of the moment. To begin with, in Matthew 20, which tells of the events of just a day or two before this, we read of the mother of James and John going to Jesus with the request that when Jesus came into his kingdom he would choose her sons to sit closest to him, one on his right hand and the other on his left. Obviously, these two disciples wanted the most prominent positions. But Jesus had to reply that this was not the nature of his ministry. He spoke of the cup that he was to drink and the baptism that he was to be baptized with. Then he said, "You know that the rulers of the Gentiles lord it over them, and their high officials exercise authority over them. Not so with you. Whoever wants to become great among you must be your servant, and whoever want to be first must be your slave—just as the Son of Man came not to be served, but to serve and to give his life as a ransom for many" (Matt. 20:25–28).

We would think perhaps that after that episode and lecture the disciples would have learned the lesson, and that the desire for the chief place among them might be forgotten. But this was not so. Apparently the conflict intensified and continued even into the upper room. For, if Luke is giving us an accurate chronology of this evening, we learn that even after the institution of the Lord's Supper "a dispute arose among them as to which of them was considered to be the greatest" (Luke 22:24). It was at this point perhaps that the Lord divested himself of his clothing and performed the foot washing.

If we can learn from the disciples, we should learn that the desire to be foremost is so great in us that we can be maneuvering for prominence even as we come to the communion service. We should learn that taking the servant role is a great clue for finding happiness.

Our Commission

There is one more thing that we should know; it too is suggested in these verses. It is that *we are sent to be servants.* That is, so far as God is concerned, the servant role for us is not optional. It is our assignment, just as it was also the task of the Lord Jesus Christ. Notice that in the second half of verse 16 the Lord uses the verb "send" twice. In Greek these are different words: *apostolos,* from which we get the word "apostle" (it denotes a specially commissioned spokesman and representative of the Lord) and *pempsantos,* which is the word Jesus uses of his own commissioning by the Father. Both words occur in John's version of the Great Commission, in which Jesus says, "As my Father has sent me, I am sending you" (20:21). We are to be servants primarily because it is for this that God has called us, just as he called Jesus. If he has done this, we will not be fully happy in any other role.

Amen and Amen

We now come to the most neglected part of all. Up to now we have been talking about the first part of Christ's clue for finding happiness: knowing certain things. We have looked at six of them: (1) Jesus is Lord, (2) he took a servant role, (3) we are not greater than Jesus, (4) what is proper for him is proper also for us, (5) we also should be servants, and (6) we are sent to be servants. The second part, which is based upon these things, is that we should do them. "Now that you know these things," said Jesus, "you will be blessed if you do them" (v. 17).

We notice, of course, that this is more than mere knowing. Knowing is important, as we have seen. You cannot do unless you know. You must begin with knowing. Nevertheless, knowing is not enough; for many people know how to succeed and yet fail just because they do not exercise their knowledge.

Moreover, the second part of this clue for finding happiness is not knowing these truths in order that others might do them. Some of us use our knowledge in this way, that is, as a club or lever to get others to measure up to our standards and serve us. Husbands know just what their wives should do to make them happy. Wives know exactly what is wrong with their husbands. Young people are sure they know what their parents and everyone else should be doing. But this is not what Jesus says. In fact, in one sense it is even the opposite of what he says. For if this is the way you are thinking, I can guarantee that the results will be the opposite of what you want. The other person will not conform to your wishes, and you will not find happiness. Happiness comes not from knowing alone or from getting the other person to do what you know he or she should do but rather from knowing these truths and then doing them yourself.

Why is this so? Because in taking this role you will inevitably develop the kind of character that God himself can bless. We find such character in the Beatitudes of Matthew 5:3–12. Jesus said, "Blessed are the poor in spirit . . . blessed are those who mourn . . . blessed are the meek . . . blessed are they who hunger and thirst for righteousness . . . blessed are the merciful . . . blessed are the pure in heart . . . blessed are the peacemakers . . . blessed are those who are persecuted for righteousness' sake."

We say, "But that does not make sense." Everything within us tells us that it is not the poor in spirit, the meek, the merciful, the peacemakers, or any similar type who is happy. We say, "Happy are the winners, the dominant, those who are waited upon." But we are wrong. Our way does not work. It is the words of the Lord Jesus Christ that should be trusted.

These verses begin with the words. "I tell you the truth." These words are translations of the words, "Amen, amen," and they mean "Truly, truly." They mean, "Pay attention to this; it is true." The interesting thing about these words is that we frequently find them on the lips of Jesus, and every time we find them on his lips they precede the statement. That is, Jesus first calls attention to the truth of what he is about to say and then says it. On the other hand, we also frequently find these words on the lips of normal men and women. But in this case the words always come at the end of the statement, as they do, for instance, in our prayers. In our usage the words are therefore an acknowledgment of the truth of God. They are our way of saying, "So be it; let God be true and every man a liar." Jesus says, "I tell you the truth, no servant is greater than his master, nor is a messenger greater than the one who sent him. Now that you know these things, you will be blessed if you do them." Can your heart add, "Amen, amen," and then do them?

168

A Classic Prophecy

John 13:18-20

"I am not referring to all of you; I know those I have chosen. But this is to fulfill the scripture: 'He who shares my bread has lifted up his heel against me.'

"I am telling you now before it happens, so that when it does happen you will believe that I am He. I tell you the truth, whoever accepts anyone I send accepts me; and whoever accepts me accepts the one who sent me."

In the Reformation period of church history it was common to speak of the ministry of the Lord Jesus Christ under a threefold division of prophet, priest, and king. The word "prophet" referred to Christ's role in speaking for God and as God. It dealt with revelation. The word "priest" referred to Christ's role in giving himself as the perfect sacrifice for sin, and also in interceding for his own with the Father. "King" referred to his rule both in heaven and in his church through the Holy Spirit.

This is a particularly interesting division in light of the functions of the Lord during his last days upon earth. Within twenty-four hours after the events recorded in John 13, which we are studying, Jesus was to die. That is, he was to exercise his priestly role by offering up himself as a perfect sacrifice for human sin. Within another three days he was to be raised from the dead and then ascend into heaven, from which he was to rule his church as King. In this chapter, as if to make the trilogy complete, Jesus speaks as a prophet. Moreover, this is not just in the sense of speaking for God, as he had indeed been doing all along, but in the full sense of the word; that is, by actually foretelling what was to come to pass. In these verses he says that one who for three years had been a member of the apostolic band was to betray him.

This is a classic prophecy. It takes only three verses, verses 18–20, but within these three verses is found all for which prophecy is given and what it normally does. The verses have three parts: (1) the prophecy itself, (2) the explanation of why the prophecy is given, and (3) an encouragement lest those who heard the prophecy should be discouraged by it.

The Prophecy

The prophecy concerning Judas is given to qualify what had been said a bit earlier. Several verses before this, after Jesus had told Peter, "And you are clean," he hastened to add, "though not every one of you." In this section, having spoken of the man who can be happy through knowing and obeying Christ's commandments, Jesus in a similar way qualifies his remark by adding that he does not speak of each one. His actual words are, "I am not referring to all of you; I know those I have chosen. But this is to fulfill the scripture: 'He who shares my bread has lifted up his heel against me'" (v. 18). The quotation is from Psalm 41:9. "Even my close friend, whom I trusted, he who shared my bread, has lifted up his heel against me."

Nothing in this psalm identifies the person about whom the author, David, was speaking. But it seems most likely that he was referring to Ahithophel, his most faithful counselor, who nevertheless sided with Absalom at the time of Absalom's rebellion. It is a tragic story as it unfolds in 2 Samuel 15–17. The revolt of Absalom had caught David unaware, and he and his mighty men had been forced to flee from Jerusalem. Ahithophel remained behind. When David heard that Ahithophel was with Absalom, David was greatly concerned, for Ahithophel gave wise counsel. David prayed, "O LORD, turn Ahithophel's counsel into foolishness" (2 Sam. 15:31). God answered David's prayer, not by causing Ahithophel to give bad counsel to Absalom, for Ahithophel continued to speak wisely, but by causing his good counsel to be disregarded. The story concludes by saying, "When Ahithophel saw that his advice had not been followed, he saddled his donkey and set out for his house in his hometown. He put his house in order, and then hanged himself. So he died and was buried in his father's sepulcher" (2 Sam. 17:23).

The fact that Ahithophel hanged himself is excellent evidence that it is probably to him that Christ (and therefore also David) is referring in the forty-first psalm, for Judas also went and hanged himself. But the point of the story is not in Ahithophel's or Judas's end but in the fact that one who had been close to Jesus would betray him. Ahithophel had eaten at David's own table. So had Judas eaten with Jesus. Ahithophel had betrayed David. So Judas would betray the Lord of glory.

In his commentary, William Barclay stresses the sheer cruelty of Judas's betrayal, noting that "in the east to eat bread with a person was a sign of friendship and an act of loyalty. Second Samuel 9:7, 13 tell how David granted it to Mephibosheth to eat bread at his table, when he might well have eliminated him as a descendant of Saul. First Kings 18:19 tells how the prophets of Baal ate bread at the table of Jezebel. For one who had eaten bread at someone's table to turn against the person to whom by that very act he had pledged his friendship was a bitter thing. This disloyalty of friends is for the Psalmist the sorest of all hurts. 'For it was not an enemy that reproached me; then I could have borne it; neither was it he that hated me that did magnify himself against me; then I would have hid myself from him: but it was thou, a man mine equal, my guide, and mine acquaintance. We took sweet counsel together, and walked unto the house of God in company' (Ps. 55:12–14)."[1]

Jesus was prophesying that one who had been with him for the entire three years of his earthly ministry would betray him, and that is sobering. It is sobering because we reason that if one could have been among the company of the Twelve for all those years, during which time he not only heard the Lord Jesus Christ but also witnessed the miracles he did, if one who had experienced all that could betray him, then it is certainly possible for a person to be in the company of God's people today, in a context in which the Word of God is faithfully preached, and yet not actually be a child of God.

We should stop at that point and ask the question: Am I really a child of God or am I just in the company of God's people? If the latter is true of you, if you are just in the company of Christians, then this passage should have a special urgency for you, and you should not rest until you have actually come to believe in him whom to know is life eternal.

Faith in Himself

In the second of these three verses the Lord gives the reason for his prophecy. It is, he says, "that when it does happen you may believe that I am he" (v. 19). The prophecy is given so that the fulfillment, when it comes to pass, might be received as evidence that Jesus really is who he claims to be—the unique Son of God, Jehovah.

I am impressed with the fact that in the Old Testament, particularly in Isaiah, this is the primary reason offered for the giving of prophecy. We usually think of prophecy being given to satisfy our curiosity or, at the very least, being given to warn us and allow us to prepare for what is coming. But the reason the Bible gives is that, when the prophecy comes to pass, we might know that God, who gives the prophecy, is the true God, for only he can see the future and guarantee its outcome. This is clear in the central chapters of Isaiah, for instance. In chapter 40, which begins this discussion, God contrasts himself with the idols of the pagans who, he says, cannot even stand upright by themselves, let alone move about. "To whom, then, will you compare God?" he asks. "What image will you compare him to? As for an idol, a craftsman casts it, a goldsmith overlays it with gold and fashions silver chains for it. A man too poor to present such an offering selects wood that will not rot. He looks for a skilled craftsman to set up an idol that will not topple" (vv. 18–20).

Then, in chapter 41, the argument continues. "'Present your case,' says the LORD. 'Set forth your arguments,' says Jacob's King. 'Bring in your idols to tell us what is going to happen. Tell us what the former things were, that we may consider them and know their final outcome. Or declare to us things to come, tell us what the future holds that we may know that you are gods. Do something, whether good or bad, so that we will be dismayed and filled with fear. But you are of nothing and your works are utterly worthless; he who chooses you is detestable'" (vv. 21–24).

By contrast God can tell the future and therefore should be believed. "I foretold the former things long ago, my mouth announced them and I made them known; then suddenly I acted, and they came to pass" (Isa. 48:3).

This is the same argument employed by the Lord Jesus when he says, "I am telling you now before it happens, so that when it does happen, you may believe that I am he." Just as God argues in the Book of Isaiah, so also does Christ argue in John 13. And the conclusion is the same. Jehovah is the true God. Jesus is the true God. Jesus is Jehovah. Jesus argues that he is not just a spokesman for God, though he is that also. He argues that he is God. Whatever he has prophesied he brings to pass.

Faith in the Scriptures

The clearest reason why Christ gives the prophecy concerning Judas is that the disciples might find their faith in him strengthened. But as we read this in the context of the quotation from Psalm 41, we can hardly miss the truth that the same knowledge will also strengthen faith in the Scriptures. How? By showing us that they, no less than the Lord himself, may be trusted. Why? Because, like the Lord himself, they are eternal. Jesus said, "Heaven and earth will pass away, but my words will never pass away" (Matt. 24:35). Or again, "Until heaven and earth disappear, not the smallest letter, not the least stroke of a pen, will by any means disappear from the Law until everything is accomplished" (Matt. 5:18). The fulfillment of prophecy helps us to believe this and to alter our lives accordingly.

Why do we cherish the Scriptures? Why do we memorize them? It is because these words, having come to us from God and therefore also bearing his nature, are eternal and so will not pass away. Everything else that we know will pass away, sometimes well within our lifetimes. The ideas and viewpoints that your children are being taught today in grade school will be changed before they reach high school. What they are taught in high school will be altered by college. College outlooks will change by the time the young man or woman enters his or her profession. Even then professions change so quickly that unless the person reads to keep up he or she will soon be behind in the field. Nothing we learn is permanent, nothing we see is eternal—except the Scriptures! They *are* permanent; they are absolutely trustworthy. That is why we memorize them and teach them to our children.

If you are a parent, have you ever thought that there is nothing you can leave your children that will not pass away in time except the truths found in this Book? Some parents think they have served their children well if they have left money to them. But money can disappear overnight. Sometimes the children even reject it. Other parents think their legacy to their children will be a fine education or, perhaps, their own values. But these change also, and even education is not valued as highly by many as it was formerly. Only the Word of God remains valuable and without change.

Do not be foolish enough to neglect this Book when you are trying to give your children the best. Do not neglect it yourself when you are sorting out your priorities.

In his youth John Newton had been brought up in a Christian home in England. But his parents died when he was only six years old, and he was sent to live with an unbelieving relative. In the relative's home he suffered great abuse. At last, to escape this ill treatment, Newton ran away to sea, as boys often did in those days, and joined the navy. Unfortunately, he fell into gross sin and eventually abandoned the navy and fled to Africa. In Africa sin gained a terrible hold on him, and he sank to utter degradation and misery. At last he left Africa and got on a ship going back to England. On the return journey the ship ran into a terrible storm, and Newton, who was part of the ship's crew, was sent down into the hold of the ship to pump water. Newton was terrified. The ship seemed to be sinking, and he knew that, if it sank, he would most certainly go down with it. For days and nights he pumped, thinking himself to be abandoned both by God and man. But as he pumped water out of that hold and began to cry to God to save him, verses that he had learned in the home of his parents before he was six years old came back to his memory. The Holy Spirit showed him what those verses meant. He believed on Christ, and was born again. Later, when the storm had passed and he was again safe in England, he went on to become a highly gifted preacher and teacher of the Word of God.

What had happened? The Word of the living God had remained with him and had become the vehicle by which the Holy Spirit brought forth new life.

I would like to insert one more word here for parents. It concerns two great principles for communicating the Bible's content. First, the Word must be communicated a bit at a time, so that what is learned at one time may be added to and built upon in later lessons. Isaiah expresses it best when he writes, "For it is: Do and do, do and do, rule on rule, rule on rule, a little here, a little there" (28:10). In other words, do not think that you have taught your child or even yourself when you have been to church just once or even a dozen times, or when you have read the Bible just once. Learning is a lifetime process. So you must keep at it. It must be a precept here and a precept there, here a little and there a little.

Second, you must memorize the Bible. We have a great resistance to memorizing anything today, but David tells us what is needed when he declares, "I have hidden your word in my heart, that I might not sin against you" (Ps. 119:11). It is the memorized word that stays with us and is available when we need it.

An Encouragement

We come finally to the third of these verses. It is a verse of encouragement. It says, "I tell you the truth, whoever accepts anyone I send accepts me; and whoever accepts me accepts the one who sent me" (v. 20). When we first read that verse it seems disconnected from what has gone before, but a little thought soon shows the connection. In the previous verses Jesus had been encouraging his disciples to follow the example he had given them through the foot washing, but as he had done that he had begun to speak of Judas and of the fact that he would betray him. Were they discouraged at this point? We do not know. But if they were, we could certainly have understood their dismay. They may have thought that if these things were so, then none of them would ever be capable of serving the Lord. They would have thought that they were all a total loss and that any possibility of future usefulness to Jesus was ended.

But this was not so. One would betray him. Yet in spite of this, Jesus had chosen them, the others, to be his representatives in an ungodly world. And they would *be* his representatives, so much so that whoever received them would be accounted as having received Jesus, and whoever received Jesus would receive God.

This is a great encouragement, for ourselves as well as for the first apostles. There is much to discourage us in the Christian life. There really are betrayals. We see it within our churches. We see it in our seminaries, in professors who deny the God who bought them. "But," says Jesus, "I know that. It is not new. It has always been that way. Nevertheless, in the midst of betrayals I still have my ambassadors, whom I will use and who will be a blessing." We are such ambassadors, if we believe on Jesus and speak for him as we are instructed to do.

169

Journey into Night

John 13:21–30

After he had said this, Jesus was troubled in spirit and testified, "I tell you the truth, one of you is going to betray me."

His disciples stared at one another, at a loss to know which of them he meant. One of them, the disciple whom Jesus loved, was reclining next to him. Simon Peter motioned to this disciple and said, "Ask him which one he means."

Leaning back against Jesus, he asked him, "Lord, who is it?"

Jesus answered, "It is the one to whom I will give this piece of bread when I have dipped it in the dish." Then, dipping the piece of bread, he gave it to Judas Iscariot, son of Simon. As soon as Judas took the bread, Satan entered into him.

"What you are about to do, do quickly," Jesus told him, but no one at the meal understood why Jesus said this to him. Since Judas had charge of the money, some thought Jesus was telling him to buy what was needed for the Feast, or to give something to the poor. As soon as Judas had taken the bread, he went out. And it was night.

In a book that is in some sense an autobiography, Eugene O'Neill writes of his *Long Day's Journey into Night*. It is a story of increasing despair and darkness. The same title may be chosen for the incident recorded in John 13:21–30, for these verses record the departure of Judas from the company of him who is the light of the world so that he could go out into eternal darkness. The passage begins with the announcement of the traitor: "I tell you the truth, one of you is going to betray me." It ends with the somber sentence: "And it was night."

These verses may also be introduced by pointing out that within them the Lord Jesus Christ performs the second symbolic action of this chapter. The first was the foot washing in which he vividly illustrated the nature of his ministry and admonished those who followed him to assume a servant role. That action was visible to all the disciples and was remembered with clarity, as the great number of references to that event, both direct and indirect, throughout the New Testament, would indicate. The second symbolic action, the one recorded in these verses, was the giving of the bread to Judas, by which he was identified as the traitor. Unlike the foot washing, this act was not made clear to everyone. True, they all saw it, but the nature of the act was such that only John and possibly Peter understood it, and even they did not realize the betrayal was imminent. The incident ends when Judas, leaving the little band, goes to carry out his betrayal, an action that would eventually end in the deaths of both himself and his master.

There are three parts to this section. First, there is the announcement of the betrayer. Second, there is a contrast between Judas, who was reclining on one side of the Lord, and John, who was reclining on the other side. Finally, there is a disclosure of Judas's fate.

A Troubling Announcement

"After he said this, Jesus was troubled in spirit and testified, 'I tell you the truth, one of you is going to betray me.' His disciples stared at one another at a loss to know which of them he meant."

These verses tell us that Jesus was deeply disturbed. Sometimes, as we look upon Christ in his deity and forget his humanity, we assume that he was unbothered by the things that bother us. We assume that he had resources that we do not have and, therefore, was above life and untroubled by it. But this is not the teaching of the Word of God. The teaching of Scripture is that he was "tempted in every way, just as we are—yet was without sin" (Heb. 4:15). So if we know discouragement, we may know that he knew discouragement. If we know distress, we may know that he knew distress. If we know sorrow, we may know that he knew sorrow. Here in the upper room, during the last hours he had to spend with his disciples before his crucifixion, Jesus was increasingly troubled by all that was coming.

We know that by the time the Lord got to Gethsemane he was troubled, so much so, we are told, that he sweat as it were great drops of blood. He was troubled by the fact that he was about to go to the cross and would be separated from the Father as a judicial punishment for our sins. Here he was undoubtedly also troubled by the thought of the impending betrayal and of the one who would prove traitorous, one who had lived with him in the closest communion for three years. Yet at the end of that time was willing to sell his master for the price of a slave.

Three Lessons

There are great lessons in the fact that Judas was among the disciples and yet was not a born-again man.

First, the situation teaches us that *fallen man needs more than an example* if he is to be saved. What better example could Judas have had than the Lord Jesus Christ? Jesus had chosen Judas three years earlier. Judas had been in the company of the Twelve and had been instructed by Jesus. He had heard the Beatitudes. He had heard the Sermon on the Mount and the parables. Judas had heard all the other teachings. Indeed, he had been given on-the-field experience, because when the Twelve and the seventy were sent out, Judas was undoubtedly among them. Besides all that, Judas had seen a perfect example of all the Lord was teaching during the three-year ministry. When the Lord said, "Blessed are the meek," Judas saw perfect meekness in him. When Jesus said, "Blessed are the peacemakers," he saw the perfect peacemaker. When the Lord said, "Be holy as your Father in heaven is holy," he saw that holiness. Above all, Jesus was filled with the love of God. Judas saw all that, and yet was unsaved.

That is why we must pray and ask the Holy Spirit to do the work of regeneration in the lives of men and women. Examples are not enough. Even the example of the Lord Jesus Christ is not enough. If we think that men and women are going to be converted by the way we live, we are going to be disappointed. If we think that they are going to be converted even by bringing them into our congregations and exposing them to the teachings of Scripture and allowing them to see who Jesus Christ is and what he did, we are going to be disappointed. That is not enough. What is required is regeneration, and that is the work by which the Holy Spirit brings forth new life in the heart of an individual so that these things become real to him and he becomes able to respond to the Lord Jesus Christ as Savior.

There is a second lesson in the presence of Judas among the Twelve: *the difficulty of discerning God's elect.* We who stand in the Reformed tradition and make a great deal of God's election sometimes have errors of our own. And one of the errors is to imagine that we can determine those who are elect and those who are not. That is false. We cannot. Scripture tells us that people look on the outward appearance but that God (and only God) looks on the heart. Moreover, because the outward appearance of an unbeliever can be much like that of a believer, we are forever mixing up the two. We tend to see someone who does something that we do not like and that we think is unspiritual, and we say to ourselves, "Well, that one is certainly not saved." On the other hand, we see someone who measures up to our particular standards of morality, and we say, "He is a Christian." That is not necessarily so. Appearances are important, but they are not incontestable evidence of the presence or absence of the divine life. If we need an illustration by which we can measure the difficulty of discerning the elect, we need only turn to Judas and recognize that here in the Twelve was one who had lived with the other disciples for three years and yet was totally unknown to them in his true character.

I suppose that this says something about Judas too. Judas, I am convinced, was not just a mistaken individual. He was a deceiver, a devil, a hypocrite *par excellence.* Judas lived with the others and pretended that he was one with them, while deep in his heart he was rebelling against everything that Jesus Christ taught; and in the end he would betray him. Judas was certainly a hypocrite. But the point is that the disciples were unaware of this. Moreover, even when the Lord pointed out that one of their number would betray him, not one of them understood who this one was until Jesus revealed the matter to John.

Once Jesus told the story of a farmer who planted a field of wheat and of an enemy who sowed weeds among the wheat. After the enemy had sowed his weeds, the servants, who knew about it, came to their master to ask what to do. "Shall we root up the weeds and get rid of the enemy's work?" they asked. The master replied, "No, because in doing that you tear up the wheat also. Let them grow up together. In the end we will harvest the entire field, collect the wheat, and then cast the weeds into the fire where they will be burned."

As we apply that story to the church in our age, we recognize at once that it teaches that since (1) some of God's people are so much like weeds and (2) some of the devil's people are so much like wheat, we cannot tell the difference between them. So in essence Jesus says, "Do not worry too much about having a pure church. Be as pure in doctrine as you can, but do not worry too much about weeding out all unbelievers. "Because," he says, "if you do, I am afraid you are going to lose some of my people doing it." We cannot discern the elect, and it is good that we cannot. We must leave that in the hands of the Lord.

There is a third lesson here also. It is the *patience of the Lord Jesus Christ.* Have you ever thought what marvelous patience the Lord had in order to tolerate Judas? He knew that the Scriptures said that one of the Twelve would betray him. He knew that Judas was that one. Yet throughout the years of his ministry, so far as we can tell, not only was Jesus patient with Judas, he was so patient that not one of the disciples ever detected any telltale differences in Jesus' dealings with him that might cause them to be suspicious of him. That is the marvelous grace, the patience of our Lord. You say, "But that is beyond anything we see on earth." That is true; it is. Yet that same patience of the Lord Jesus Christ extends to all who are truly his, as he sees us disobey him, persist in our own way, and offend him constantly in thought, word, and deed.

John and Judas

The second part of the story has to do with the contrast between John and Judas. "One of them, the disciple whom Jesus loved, was reclining next to him. Simon Peter motioned to this disciple and said, 'Ask him which one he meant.' Leaning back against Jesus, he asked him, 'Lord, who is it?' Jesus answered, 'It is the one to whom I will give this bread when I have dipped it in the dish.' Then dipping the piece of bread, he gave it to Judas Iscariot, son of Simon."

As I reconstruct the seating arrangement in the upper room, it seems to me (indeed, it has seemed this way to most commentators) that John must have been on Jesus' right side and that Judas must have been on Jesus' left. They did not sit around a table the way we do today, the way Leonardo da Vinci showed it in that great painting of the Last Supper that hangs in Milan, Italy. They reclined, usually on their left side so that their right arm would be free to feed themselves. This meant that each man would have his head against the chest of the man to his left. John, on the right side of Christ, simply leaned back to ask his question. Jesus reached around to his left to give the bread to Judas.

So Judas was on one side of Jesus. John was on the other. Both were near Jesus, but John was close to his heart.

Who would you rather be? Notice that John was in a good place to ask questions. When you are close to the heart of the Lord you can always ask questions. In fact, that is the best place in the world to ask questions. We are not always so close to the Lord, however. Sometimes we are farther away. Sometimes we are very far away. Moreover, the thing that keeps us away is our sin, because sin is an offense to the Lord, and we sense it, even in our sinful state. So we turn our backs to him; we move away; we try to get out of his visual range. Then either we catch the gaze of Christ, confess our sin, and return to the place of blessing, or we go determinedly on in our sin and suffer the inevitable results.

To be near the heart of the Lord is the best place in the world to ask questions. But notice also that it is the best place to get answers. Some answers we always have. The Bible gives them. But there are other answers that are not given publicly, some that the Lord will not shout. For these we must be close to him. Such answers are heard only as we look up into his face, as we see it reflected in his Word, and hear the still, small voice of the Holy Spirit as he whispers to us.

And It Was Night

We miss the importance of this event unless we recognize that Jesus was honoring Judas until the end. The seat at the Lord's left was the place of honor, and this was where Judas was. As the disciples went into the upper room, we know that they were disputing about who should have the highest place (Luke 22:24). In those circumstances the Lord must have said, "Judas, I would like you to sit next to me this evening. I would like you to be here where you and I can converse." We are not told what the Lord said to Judas, but I cannot imagine that they went through the entire meal without the

Lord speaking graciously to him, showing his love in every gesture and in every inflection of his voice. Furthermore, the giving of the bread was an honor, and to receive it was to make a pledge of loyalty. So at this point in the meal, in spite of the fact that Jesus had both loved and honored him, Judas hardened his heart and received the bread, saying in effect, "Thank you, Master. I am yours." He lied. He played a role.

Jesus, who knew it, said to him, "What you are about to do, do quickly." At this, Judas understood, I suppose, that he was found out. He left immediately, and, John concludes by noting, "It was night."

Light and darkness are important symbols in this narrative. In the earliest verses of the Gospel, John, speaking of the coming of the Lord Jesus Christ, says, "In him was life, and that life was the light of men." Then, in the eighth and ninth chapters, Jesus is quoted as saying, "I am the light of the world." We know, as we turn to the other Gospel accounts of the crucifixion, that during the time Jesus was on the cross, darkness came over the land from noontime to about three in the afternoon. Each reference makes the point obvious: Jesus is the light. So the converse is that to leave Christ's presence is to go into darkness; and not just the darkness of a physical night either but spiritual darkness, which means death and damnation.

There were times when the disciples were to go through dark hours. The Lord was going to be crucified. When that occurred, they were going to feel forsaken and would begin to scatter. He who had been the center of their life was to be taken from them. But their darkness, however deep, was not to be compared with the darkness that engulfed Judas Iscariot. They knew darkness; yet he lived who was their light. The resurrection was coming, and in his presence they were once more to see light. But Judas? Judas went his own way. He turned from Christ and so found that darkness that endures forever.

Jesus is lovely. Jesus is holiness, love, truth, grace, patience, mercy, peace, and everything else good that we could ever imagine. Indeed, not only is he all of these qualities in himself; he is the source of them for all believers. How foolish it is, then, to turn from him to that which is the absence of these good things! God grant that our hearts may be made right before him and that the Holy Spirit, who applies these truths, may make the Lord Jesus Christ central in all that we do and say.

170

Christ Glorified Now

John 13:31–32

When he was gone, Jesus said, "Now is the Son of Man glorified and God is glorified in him. If God is glorified in him, God will glorify the Son in himself, and will glorify him at once."[1]

Have you ever been in a place where a number of friends were gathered, all of whom wanted to discuss something that was important to them but who were unable to because someone who was not really with them in spirit was present? If you have, it may also be that you have noticed what happened when the unsympathetic person finally left the group. At once the conversation brightened up, and comments that had been bottled up came flowing forth naturally.

That was the situation in the upper room on the last night Jesus spent with his disciples before his crucifixion. Here were friends, all of them quite close. They had spent the last three years in one another's company. But in their midst was one who was not really with them in spirit: Judas. True, Judas was not known in his true character to the apostles. But Jesus knew his nature and understood clearly what it was that he was about to do. Judas was about to betray Jesus to his enemies. So, as long as Judas was there, Jesus was somewhat constrained in what he could say to the gathering. He acted in order to get their attention, once in the foot washing and once more in the giving of the bread to Judas, but he seems to have held back in his teaching until the traitor's departure. Suddenly Judas is gone, however, and at once the atmosphere is cleared. Now Jesus is perfectly free to speak and the disciples to listen. At this point, then, Jesus begins to speak of his coming glory, the new commandment, heaven, and the future outpouring of the Holy Spirit on his followers.

The text says, "When he was gone, Jesus said, 'Now is the Son of Man glorified and God is glorified in him. If God is glorified in him, God will glorify him in himself, and will glorify him at once'" (vv. 31–32).

Layers of Glory

It is interesting that the theme of the glorification of Christ (and therefore also of God the Father) comes first in this series of heart revelations. And it is interesting, too, with what intensity Jesus speaks of such glorification. The word itself (either "glorified" or "glorify") occurs five times in just these two verses, and a careful analysis will show that it has three distinct references and two meanings.

The two meanings correspond to the two major uses of the important Greek word *doxa*. *Doxa* (meaning "glory") is related to the ancient verb *dokeo*, which in the early days of the Greek language meant "to seem" or "to appear," and then later "to hold an opinion of" someone or something. In time the sense of the word changed to that of holding only a *good* opinion about someone, and at that point, the noun, which originally meant only "an opinion," came to mean "a good opinion" and consequently either "praise" or "honor." All these ideas are important in the biblical vocabulary. For to have a right opinion of God is to be "orthodox" (orthodox means "a right opinion"), and to ascribe right opinions to God is to praise or worship him. This can be put in a slightly different form by saying that God's glory consists of his intrinsic worth embodied in his character, and that the acknowledgment of this worth by those who are his people is worship.

There is also a meaning of the word "glory" which is largely external. This is the sense of glory which is associated with light. We have it, for instance, in every Old Testament reference in which God is described as dwelling in glory unapproachable. Such glory was veiled by the cloud that covered Mount Sinai, where God came down to talk to Moses and, as the result of which, Moses' face glowed with a transferred brilliance. The same idea is present at the transfiguration of Christ on the mountain in Palestine. In each of these events, glory is the outward brilliance appropriate to, and normally accompanying, a revelation of God.

These distinctions are necessary for understanding the verses before us, for wherever the present tense is used we must understand Jesus to be using the word in the first sense; that is, as a revelation of his own (or the Father's) true worth or character. In this case the reference is to the revelation of God's character through the crucifixion. Whenever the future tense is used, we must understand Jesus to be using the word in the second sense; that is, as a reference to that future glory that Christ received as a result of his resurrection and subsequent ascension into heaven.

Glory in Christ's Passion

The first reference to glory in these verses is in the present tense: "Now is the Son of Man glorified." When did the Lord say, "Now is the Son of Man glorified"? The answer is that he said it in the upper room while looking forward to his crucifixion, immediately after that event was set in motion by the departure of Judas. Jesus had said to Judas, "What you are about to do, do quickly." Judas left to arrange for the betrayal of his Lord. Jesus, knowing that the final act of the drama was now underway, turned to his disciples, and said, "Now is the Son of Man glorified."

How is this so? How can the crucifixion be glorification? The answer is in what the crucifixion means.

First, although we may not think so and the world as a whole cannot understand so at all, the crucifixion is undoubtedly *the central and most significant point of world history*. Nothing that has happened in the world's history from the beginning of creation until now, or will ever happen before that day when all things will be wrapped up in Christ, is as significant as the crucifixion. Here that great drama, which God had planned from before the foundation of the world, was brought to its focal point and acted out. Men of all races, social status, and levels of understanding have been saved by it.

There is another way in which the cross is Christ's glory. At the cross, he *reversed the conduct of the first Adam* and thus turned the history of our race around. Paul works this out in detail in the fifth chapter of Romans, pointing out that "as the result of one [Adam's] trespass was condemnation to all men, even so also the result of one act of righteousness [Jesus'] was justification that brings life for all men" (Rom. 5:18). When Adam decided to disobey God, it was as if he fell over a cliff carrying the whole string of his descendants with him. Imagine a group of mountain climbers working their way up the side of a mountain. They are all roped together, and Adam is in the lead. Adam loses his footing and falls. Because of the rope, every one of the climbers is pulled over the edge of the cliff after Adam. The whole race follows him. But there, at the end of the line, is the Lord Jesus Christ; and he stands fast. Because the Lord Jesus Christ does not succumb to temptation, because the Lord does not sin, because he is therefore able to offer himself up as the perfect sacrifice for human sin, and does so, he becomes the only stable and safe point of humanity. Consequently, those who are united to him by faith are saved by him. The fall of Adam, which led to destruction, is reversed in Jesus Christ. By his atonement, Jesus leads those who are his own to safety.

Finally, we find in Hebrews 2:14 that the death of the Lord Jesus Christ also *reversed the power of Satan* and so brought to an end the power of that wicked one. In this, Christ is glorified. "Since the children have flesh and blood, he shared in their humanity so that by his death he might destroy him who holds the power of death—that is, the devil." The "sting of death is sin, and the power of sin is the law," Paul tells us in 1 Corinthians 15:56. But the Lord Jesus Christ provided an atonement for sin and thus broke the power of sin over those who are his own people.

God Glorified

The second reference to glory in this verse is also in the present tense, for the verse goes on to say that *God* is glorified in Jesus Christ. This is also significant, because once again Jesus is talking of the crucifixion. How is God glorified in Christ's crucifixion?

First, the *justice* of God is revealed. Paul works this out in Romans 3:26, where he says that through the death of the Lord Jesus Christ God proved himself to be "just, and the one who justifies those who have faith in Jesus." The argument goes something like this. Paul is acknowledging that throughout the entire Old Testament period those who looked forward to the coming of a redeemer were saved by God. That is, Abraham was a saved man; Isaac was a saved man; Jacob was a saved man. But the question could have been raised at that period, "How is God just in saving them?" He offers them forgiveness, that is true. He saves them from the penalty of their sin. But what of the sin? Where is it punished? God justified these men, but he does not seem to have been just in doing so. "But he was," says Paul. "He justified them on the basis of the death of Christ, which was still future." Consequently, when Christ died on the cross, sin was punished in him and God was seen to be just in his previous acts of forgiveness. At the Cross the justice of God in forgiving sinners was revealed, as it were, for the first time. Now people can look to the cross and say, "God is not only the One who justifies the ungodly; God is also the One who is just in so doing." So God is glorified in his justice through what Christ has done.

Second, God's *holiness* is revealed. On this point Arthur W. Pink writes wisely. "He is 'of purer eyes than to behold evil, and canst not look on iniquity' (Hab. 1:13), and when Christ was 'made a curse for us' (Gal. 3:13) the thrice Holy One turned away from Him. It was this which caused the agonizing Saviour to cry, 'My God, My God, why hast thou *forsaken* me?' Never did God so manifest His hatred of sin as in the sufferings and death of His Only-begotten. There He showed it was impossible for Him to be at peace with that which had raised its defiant head against Him. All the honour due to the holiness of God by all the holy angels, and all the cheerful obedience and patient suffering of all the holy men who have ever existed, or ever will exist, are nothing in comparison with the offering of Christ Himself in order that every demand of God's holiness, which sin had outraged, might be fully met."[2]

There is a third way in which God is glorified at Calvary. *The faithfulness* of God is revealed there. In the Old Testament period we find God promising a deliverer. Adam and Eve are in the Garden. They have sinned. They have eaten of the fruit of the forbidden tree. When God comes to them in the Garden they hide from his presence. They are sinful; God is holy; and they cannot stand the sight of his holiness. The Lord asks, "What have you done?" and the whole story comes out. But God provides for them. He kills animals, clothing them with their skins. Then, in promised blessing, he points to the future and says, "The day is coming when the seed of the woman will rise and crush the head of the serpent." Genesis 3:15 contains this promise of a redeemer. But Adam and Eve died, and the Savior had not yet come.

Farther on in the Old Testament we find God appearing to Abraham. God says, "Abraham, I am going to bless you and all the nations through you. I am going to do it through your seed." Abraham believes that. He believes that at one particular time an individual will come who would be the world's Savior. Yet Abraham lived to an old age and died, and Jesus had not come.

We turn to the prophets and we find God speaking through them. We find him telling Isaiah that One is coming who would be "pierced for our transgressions" and "crushed for our iniquities." The "punishment that brought us peace" would be on him (Isa. 53:5). We find God telling Micah that the Messiah would be born in Bethlehem of Judah (Mic. 5:2). He declares through Malachi that the Savior will come as "the sun of righteousness" risen with "healing in his wings" (Mal. 4:2). He says that this One will be preceded by a forerunner, who will appear like the prophet Elijah (Mal. 3:1–3; 4:5–6). God gave the prophets these and many other promises. Yet they all died, and the Savior had not come.

Had God forgotten his promises? Are God's people destitute of hope? Is God unfaithful? One day an angel appears to a virgin in Nazareth and announces that the Messiah is to be born at last. To Joseph he says, "You are to give him the name Jesus; because he will save his people from their sins" (Matt. 1:21). Thus the Lord Jesus Christ enters the world, goes through his ministry, proceeds to the cross, and there dies to accomplish the defeat of Satan that was promised back in the earliest pages of the Old Testament and reiterated many times thereafter. God is shown to be faithful, and he is glorified in that.

Finally, God's *love* is also revealed at Calvary. Nothing in all history reveals God's love as does the cross of Jesus Christ. In fact, so great is this revelation of his love that God appeals to it as proof of his love. Romans 5:8 says, "But God demonstrates his love for us in this: While we were still sinners, Christ died for us." How do we know that God loves us? We know that God loves us because the Lord Jesus Christ gave his life to redeem us from sin. In this is God glorified.

> O when we view God's grand design,
>   To save rebellious worms,
> How vengeance and compassion join
>   In their sublimest forms.

Our thoughts are lost in rev'rent awe—
    We love and we adore;
The first archangel never saw
    So much of God before!

Here each Divine perfection joins,
    And thought can never trace,
Which of the glories brightest shines—
    The justice or the grace.

The Coming Glory

At this point of our study we might well wish to stop. But we cannot stop quite yet, for Christ's words go on to speak of glory one last time, on this occasion in the future tense. He says, "If God is glorified in him [at the cross], God will glorify him in himself, and will glorify him at once." This means that if God is glorified by the special nature of Christ's death, as he is, then he will immediately proceed to place a new and special glory upon Christ through his resurrection, exaltation, and ascension to power at the Father's right hand.

I think the Lord must have yearned for it all to be completed at this point. He was willing to go to the cross. He embraced it gladly because it meant our salvation. But he looked beyond the cross to that day when the Resurrection would take place and the power of the cross would be evident, to that moment when he would ascend once again to his Father and would there minister for us as our great high priest, having presented the blood of his sacrifice as the atonement for our sin (see Heb. 9:11–14).

If Christ is glorified now, as he is, and if he is going to return one day in glory, I wonder how you will respond to him when you see him in his splendor. Will you look upon him as One whom you have spurned? Will you see him as One whom you said had no bearing upon your life, no word for your situation, One whose death means absolutely nothing and whose glorification is meaningless? Or will you receive him as One whose death means everything to you and whom you have sought to glorify by your obedience? I trust that it will be the latter—it should be—and that you will indeed serve him until your life's end.

171

The New Commandment

John 13:33–34

"My children, I will be with you only a little longer. You will look for me, and just as I told the Jews, so I tell you now: Where I am going, you cannot come.

"A new command I give you: Love one another. As I have loved you, so you must love one another.

The Gospel of John has been given many fine titles in the long history of its exposition, but none are more fitting than those that identify it as the Gospel of God's love. It has been called "God's love letter to the world." But if this is so, then it is probably also true that either John 3:16 or the verses to which we come now are its heart. They are those in which the Lord Jesus Christ speaks to his disciples out of his great love for them, reminding them of that love and encouraging them to love one another.

The Preface

Verse 34 is the key verse of this section, but it is nevertheless significant that it is preceded by another that is, in some sense, its preface. The preface says, "My children, I will be with you only a little longer. You will look for me, and just as I told the Jews, so I tell you now: Where I am going, you cannot come" (v. 33). As I read the various commentators on this Gospel I find a discussion of why the disciples could not follow Christ and of the difference between their inability and the inability of the Jews.

(The same words were spoken to the Jewish leaders earlier.) But I do not find an explanation of the connection between this verse and the great verse following. Yet it is in this connection that the importance of the verse lies.

What is its significance? It is along two lines. First, it is evident that since the Lord Jesus Christ was about to depart from the world, the only example of true love that the world had ever known was about to be taken from it. Jesus was himself love, for he was God and "God is love" (1 John 4:8). He was about to prove that love by dying on the cross. Yet in the very act of dying, which was to be followed by his resurrection and ascension into heaven, he was to be taken from humanity. How, then, were men and women to know what true divine love is? How were they to see love demonstrated when he was about to be taken from them? The answer is that they were to see it in those who are Christ's disciples. Jesus is being taken, but now the disciples are to love as he loved. It is as if Jesus had said, "I am going; therefore you must be as I have been in this world."

The second way in which the preface is important is in its transference of the love the disciples felt for him to one another. There is no doubt that each of the disciples (Judas excluded, who by now, however, had left the upper room) loved Jesus. Whatever he said they would do. Several had just prepared the upper room for this last dinner. Peter is about to say that he will die for Jesus if necessary. It is true, of course, that their love was not as strong as they thought it was. Peter would not die; in fact, he would deny his Master. The others would scatter at the moment of the arrest in Gethsemane. Nevertheless, they did truly love him. And yet, just as certainly as they loved him, so is it certain that they did not really love one another with anything even approaching that intensity. On the contrary, they were actually jealous of one another. They were disputing over who should be greatest. They would not wash the others' feet. In this situation Jesus, who is about to be taken from them, points out that now it is precisely one another whom they must love.

The vertical love of disciples for the exalted Christ must be expressed horizontally in their love for all other Christians. Moreover, the horizontal love, which can be seen by everyone, is proof of the vertical dimension.

Things New and Old

In the thirteenth chapter of Matthew, in a section of Christ's teachings dealing with the kingdom of God, Jesus speaks of a teacher of the law being like an "owner of a house, who brings out of his storeroom new treasures as well as old" (v. 52). At this point he is himself like that teacher, for he follows his preface by the giving of a command that is at once both new and ancient.

The command to love is old in that it existed before Christ's coming. In its simplest and best-known form it is found in Leviticus 19:18, which says, "Do not seek revenge or bear a grudge against one of your people, but love your neighbor as yourself. I am the LORD." This is the verse to which Jesus referred when he was asked his opinion concerning the first and greatest commandment. He said that the greatest commandment was that recorded in Deuteronomy 6:5—"Love the LORD your God with all your heart and with all your soul and with all your strength." The second was Leviticus 19:18.

But if the commandment was an old commandment, as it must have been if it is recorded in one of the first five books of the Old Testament, in what sense is it new? Indeed, how can Christ call it "a new command"? The answer is that it was raised to an entirely new level and given an entirely new significance by Jesus. We can say that it is given a *new object;* it is to be exercised according to a *new measure;* it is to be made possible by a *new power.* Each of these is involved in Christ's saying.

In the first place, the command to love received a *new object.* It is true that the verse from Leviticus declares that the Jew is to love his neighbor as himself. But the neighbor involved is a Jewish neighbor only. The first half of the verse makes this plain, for in a parallel sentence the reader is told that he is not to hold a grudge against any of "your [also his] people." This is a physical, family relationship. In Christ's command, by contrast, the relationship is spiritual, for the neighbor is any believer in Jesus.

Something else about this new object is very important. Jesus says that the disciples are to love one another and that this is to be a witness to the unbelieving world. However, it is obvious from Christ's own example and from his teaching elsewhere that this is not to be a love that is held back from unbelievers. Even the very nature of the relationship makes this clear, for if the relationship involved is spiritual, then obviously there is no way of knowing who might be included in the company of believers should God so move. When the relationship was physical, the limits were obvious. One was supposed to love other Jews. Gentiles were not to be loved. They were sinners, those whom God obviously wished to destroy. But when the relationship became spiritual, the whole matter was broadened. This spiritual, Christian brotherhood is created by God's drawing together those of all races and languages. Consequently, the Christian is to love every individual—everyone; for anyone can be a special one for whom Christ died.

Alexander Maclaren, that great preacher of another generation, speaks of the newness of such love as it battered the ancient world's societies. "When the words were spoken, the then-known civilized Western world was cleft by great, deep gulfs of separation, like the crevasses in a glacier. . . . Language, religion, national animosities, differences of condition, and saddest of all, differences of sex, split the world up into alien fragments. A 'stranger' and an 'enemy' were expressed in one language by the same word. The learned and the unlearned, the slave and his master, the barbarian and the Greek, the man and the woman, stood on opposite sides of the gulfs, flinging hostility across. A Jewish peasant wandered up and down for three years in His own little country, which was the very focus of narrowness and separation and hostility, as the Roman historian felt when He called the Jews the 'haters of the human race'; He gathered a few disciples, and He was crucified by a contemptuous Roman governor, who thought that the life of one fanatical Jew was a small price to pay for popularity with his troublesome subjects, and in a generation after, the clefts were being bridged and all over the Empire a strange new sense of unity was bearing breathed, and 'Barbarian, Scythian, bond and free,' male and female, Jew and Greek, learned and ignorant, clasped hands and sat down at one table, and felt themselves 'all one in Christ Jesus.'"[1]

The commandment of Christ does not only have a new object. It also is to be exercised according to a *new measure*. What was love before this, after all? A vague feeling of good will? A sense of pride in one's race? A need to defend a neighbor or to free a family member who had become a slave? Yes, this and perhaps a bit more. But it was not that measure of love seen in the fact that the God of the universe would take human form, suffer, and die for those who were ungodly in order that, almost in spite of themselves those who hated God and had tried to turn from him might be redeemed from the chains of sin and brought into glory. "This is love," writes John in the fourth chapter of his magnificent first letter, "not that we loved God [because we did not], but that he loved us and sent his Son as an atoning sacrifice for our sins" (v. 10).

The measure of this love is the standard found in 1 Corinthians 13. "Love is patient, love is kind. It does not envy, it does not boast, it is not proud. It is not rude, it is not self-seeking, it is not easily angered, it keeps no record of wrongs. Love does not delight in evil, but rejoices with the truth. It always protects, always trusts, always perseveres. Love never fails" (vv. 4–8). This is the love Jesus brought, and it was a new thing in this world.

Third, the command to love is also new in that it is made possible by a *new power*. The power is the power of the Holy Spirit, the very life of the Lord Jesus Christ in each believer. How much we need this! Without it we cannot love as Christ loved; for such love cannot be achieved by human energy.

Our Great Example

There is one more point to be seen in these two verses: Jesus is himself our example as we obey his command. He indicates this in the second half of verse 34, in which he says, "As I have loved you, so you must love one another." It is not just that we are to love. It is that we are to love *as he loved us*. His love is to be the full measure of our love for one another.

How can we speak about this practically? One way is to return to the verses from 1 Corinthians cited earlier. When they were quoted before they were quoted exactly as they are printed in our Bibles. This time read them with the word "Jesus" substituted for the word "love." "Jesus is patient, Jesus is kind. He does not envy, he does not boast, he is not proud. He is not rude, he is not self-seeking, he is not easily angered, he keeps no record of wrongs. Jesus does not delight in evil, but rejoices with the truth. He always protects, always trusts, always perseveres. Jesus never fails." Clearly, the substitution of "Jesus" for "love" is quite proper, for Jesus is obviously the embodiment of such love. Our hearts acknowledge it to be so, and we rejoice in the fact.

Now make another substitution. We are told in our text that we are to love as Christ loves. But since 1 Corinthians 13 reveals the way that Christ did love, we (if we love in that way) should be able to substitute our name for his. We should be able to put "I" where "love" is printed. "I am patient, I am kind. I do not envy, I do not boast, I am not proud. I am not rude, I am not self-seeking, I am not easily angered, I keep no record of wrongs. I do not delight in evil, but rejoice with the truth. I always protect, always trust, always persevere. I never fail." When we read it this way the result is humbling, for we recognize that we do not love as Jesus loves. We do not even understand such love. And we find ourselves praying, "Oh, Lord Jesus, teach me to love others as you love."

When we pray this way God will help us, and we will begin to grow in the love and knowledge of the Lord Jesus Christ.

Let Us Love

We should get more out of this command than the disciples did on the first occasion on which it was spoken. We think that they must have been struck by these great words and have remembered them vividly, but this was not the case. On the contrary, not one of them really heard the command or understood what it meant.

We know this because of the course of the discussion that follows verse 35. We remember that Jesus had begun his discussion of the new command by informing the disciples that he was going to leave them and that they would not be able to follow him in his departure. They heard this, and it filled them with dismay. It crowded all other thoughts from their minds. Next, Jesus talked about his new command, but they did not hear him, for he had barely finished talking about it when Peter broke in to ask, "But, Lord, where are you going?" Peter had been thinking about Christ's earlier announcement and was returning to it. Jesus stopped to deal with Peter's questions, and before he could get back to the subject of the new commandment Thomas responded, "Lord, we don't know where you are going, so how can we know the way?" Jesus answered Thomas, and he never did get back to the great command.

Jesus is not frustrated by human preoccupation, however. So, after many years had passed, the Holy Spirit spoke to John the evangelist, who was present on the earlier occasion, and caused him to write a book which is in one sense an exposition of the new commandment. The book is 1 John, and it expounds the new commandment completely.

In all, the new command is talked about in four separate passages: 1 John 2:7–11; 3:11–18; 4:7–21; and 5:1–5. But the key passage is 4:7–21, in which the words "love one another" occur three times. In each case a different reason is given why this exhortation must be heeded.

The first reason why we should love one another is that love is *God's nature.* John says, "Dear friends, let us love one another, for love comes from God. Everyone who loves is born of God and knows God. Whoever does not love does not know God; for God is love" (1 John 4:7–8). John's argument is that, if we truly are God's children, we will bear the characteristics of our Father.

Second, John tells us that we should love because love led to *God's gift.* In these verses John reminds us that we were spiritually dead men and women before God the Father sent his Son to die for us. Being dead we were not able even to understand what he had done. But when Christ died for us, and when by the work of the Holy Spirit we were made alive spiritually, we were able to believe on Christ and recognize the love of God in Christ, which stood behind the sacrifice. Consequently, having thus come to know love and take the measure of love, we are to love. John's way of putting it is: "This is how God showed his love among us: he sent his one and only Son into the world that we might live through him. . . . Dear friends, since God so loved us, we also ought to love one another" (vv. 9, 11).

Finally, we are told that we should love one another in that love is *God's present and continuing activity.* God is not creating the world today; he has already done that. He is not sending Jesus to die; Jesus has already died. What God is doing is working in Christians through love in order that others who do not yet know him might see him through such divine activity. John writes: "No one has ever seen God; but if we love one another, God lives in us, and his love is made complete in us [and, thus, men see him]" (v. 12).

Do those who are not yet Christians see God in you? It is a breathtaking thought. But this verse teaches that they can and will, if you will love others. Will you? Remember, this is not a divine invitation, as if Jesus had said, "Won't you please love others?" It is not even one of a series of steps to successful living, as if he had said, "You will be happier if you love one another." It is Christ's new command. Love one another! God grant that we shall and that, in doing so, we may truly be his disciples.

172

Marks of a True Disciple

John 13:35

"By this all men will know that you are my disciples, if you love one another."

Once when I was working for the evangelical thought journal *Christianity Today,* I heard Carl F. H. Henry, then the editor, say that he wished Christians in our day could have an easily identifiable mark that would at once distinguish them as Christians. "Something like an armband," he said. That was some time ago. Since then, the Jesus Movement gave us the sign of an upraised index finger, meaning "One Way." I have noticed that now even evangelicals are often wearing crosses and other religious symbols. But for some reason, Henry's remark has stuck with me through the years, and it has made me notice "signs" or writings about signs that I might not have noticed otherwise.

One important essay was entitled "The Mark of the Christian" by Francis Schaeffer. It appeared first as a small booklet and then as a final postscript in the volume *The Church at the End of the 20th Century.* That study was based on John 13:35, "By this all men will know that you are my disciples, if you love one another." According to Schaeffer, love is "the mark that Jesus gives to label a Christian not just in one era or in one locality but at all times and all places until Jesus returns."[1]

Another piece along the same lines is a chapter in the book *The Love Life* by Donald Grey Barnhouse. It is entitled "Art Not Thou Also One of His Disciples?" and is based on the text I have already mentioned, John 13:35, plus two others: John 8:31 and John 15:8. In this study I want to take these three texts and, using what has been written about them, explore the essential features of one who would be Christ's true disciple.

There is a popular use of the word "Christian" by which many would claim to be Christians who are, nevertheless, not disciples of the Lord Jesus Christ at all. Barnhouse points out that the word "Christian" originally came about because those who believed in Christ at Antioch followed him so closely that those who observed them wanted to identify them by the name of their Master. The people of Antioch said, "These are followers of Christ. They are Christ-ones, Christians. They follow him. They are his." Today, by contrast everyone calls himself a Christian. By some, America is called a Christian nation. Anything that has even the vague flavor of Western religion or culture about it gets the name. But few who call themselves Christians actually follow Jesus.

Obviously, there is a kind of Christianity that is like this, but it is not discipleship. True discipleship is far different. What is it? It is expressed well in 2 Corinthians 8:5, "They gave themselves first to the Lord and to us in keeping with God's will." Discipleship is giving oneself wholeheartedly to Jesus.

Continuing in Christ's Word

The three texts in John's Gospel I have just mentioned show the marks of a true disciple. The first of these is John 8:31. "To the Jews who believed him Jesus said, 'If you hold to my teaching, you are really my disciples.'" The first mark of a disciple is continuation in the word that Christ has spoken.

Two things are necessary if we are truly to do this. First, we must *hear* that Word; this means that we must read it, study it, memorize it, and continually put ourselves in a place where it is faithfully taught. The trouble with the discipleship of many begins right here. The Word is taught, but they do not want to hear it. The Word is available, but they do not like what it says. So they hide from it. What are such Christians like? They are like the man Harry Ironside tells about in one of his writings. The man had come to church occasionally with his wife, but he was very irregular in his attendance. So Ironside asked the wife about it. "Doesn't your husband like coming to church?" he asked.

"I think he does," she said. "But he has difficulty with your sermons. He hears the teachings, but he doesn't like them. So he stays home. He says that if he comes one Sunday, it takes him weeks to get over it."

That is true for many. And that is one reason why people who used to be seen around your church are not seen there so often. They know what the Word of God says, but they do not want to heed it. So they refuse to listen, and eventually they reject even their Christian friends. It is interesting that in this same chapter of John there is a verse in which Christ speaks to his enemies, saying, "Why is my language not clear to you? Because you are unable to hear what I say" (v. 43). Here were unbelievers who, lacking the Holy Spirit, were unable even to hear Christ's speech. No wonder they misunderstood him. But what are we to think of those who claim to possess the

Holy Spirit, who should be able to understand Christ's words, but who refuse to hear them?

The second thing that is necessary, after we have heard Christ's word, is to *continue* in it. This means to continue to hold to it by faith, even though we may not understand it fully. The disciples were doing this. We remember as we read this chapter that Jesus had been preaching some startling truths to those who would listen to him, and as a result people were overflowing with questions. "How can a man be born again when he is old?" "How can this man give us his flesh to eat?" "What does he mean, 'You will look for me and not find me and where I go you cannot come?'" These were the questions that were raised by his teachings. But we notice that they were raised by the people at large and not by the disciples. The disciples followed him and, therefore, although they certainly did not know all the answers, they believed what they understood and continued in it faithfully.

Barnhouse, from whom I am borrowing much of this material, tells the story of an eight-year-old girl who was joining a church. One of the elders asked her, "Have you read the Bible?"

"Yes, I have."

"Do you understand it?"

"Yes," she said, "all of it!"[2]

Well, that is very nice. For her age and mentality, she had understood what she had read. Moreover, it had spoken to her heart, and she had heeded it. This is what the disciples were doing. It is what each of us should do. We may not understand all that is in the Bible. Indeed, we do not. But we can understand what we know and follow in it. Barnhouse writes: "Obviously the disciples did not understand everything, but they believed what they knew and they continued in His doctrine. As soon as they learned more, they believed that also; for that's the method in Christian life. We are not born again with the full content of doctrine neatly stored in categories in our brain cells, but we go on as babes. We walk as children, desiring the sincere milk of the Word that we may grow thereby."[3] Unquestioning faith is the first mark of a true disciple.

Love One Another

The second mark of a disciple is found in the verse to which we have come in our study of John 13, verse 35. "By this all men will know that you are my disciples, if you love one another." It is this verse that is the basis of Schaeffer's study.

There is a unique quality in this verse that sets it off from the others we are considering. It is Christ's reference to the world. In the first verse (John 8:31), Jesus says that continuing in his word will make those listening to his word be his disciples indeed. But there is no reference to how this will affect the world. In the verse to which we come next (John 15:8), Jesus says that a disciple is one who bears "much fruit." But the content refers to the fact that the bearing of fruit will glorify God, not that it will affect humanity, although, of course, it does. It is only in this second verse (John 13:35), with its emphasis upon observable love, that the world is taken into serious consideration. Why is this so? It is so because of what Jesus says about love. Jesus says that it is the mark by which his disciples are to be known as Christians, not only to him or to one another, but to everyone.

Schaeffer says that this is frightening, and he is right. For it is as if "Jesus turns to the world and says, 'I've something to say to you. On the basis of my authority, I give you a right: You may judge whether or not an individual is a Christian on the basis of the love he shows to all Christians.' In other words, if people come up to us and cast in our teeth the judgment that we are not Christians because we have not shown love toward other Christians, we must understand that they are only exercising a prerogative that Jesus gave them.

"And we must not get angry. If people say, 'You don't love other Christians,' we must go home, get down on our knees, and ask God whether or not they are right. And if they are, then they have a right to have said what they said."[4]

What kind of love must we show if the world is to look at it and conclude that it is explainable only by the fact that we are Christians? Obviously it must be a special kind of love. What are its characteristics? How does such a special love operate? Fortunately, the answer to these questions is given to us in 1 John, a book that, as suggested in the last study, was written in some measure as a commentary on the new commandment.

In one sense, nearly everything in 1 John deals with the new command, for even its other two great themes (righteousness and sound doctrine) relate to it. But to be concise, it is possible to find a rich and fully rewarding answer in just three verses, 3:16–18. These verses say, "This is how we know what love is: Jesus Christ laid down his life for us. And we ought to lay down our lives for our brothers. If anyone has material possessions and sees his brother in need but has no pity on him, how can the love of God be in him? Dear children, let us not love with words or tongue but with actions and in truth." These verses teach that one aspect of Christian love is its action. Moreover, they show that such love is to be exercised at personal cost, if need be, and that it is to be shown to anyone who is needy.

One thing John says is that "we ought to lay down our lives" for one another. Obviously, it is not often the case, at least today, that Christians are called upon to lay down their lives in the literal sense. But just because this is so, we should not pass over the idea too quickly. True, we do not often have opportunities to literally die for someone else. But we do have opportunities to "die to self" or, as we could also say, to "sacrifice our own interests" continually.

The gospel of God's love in Jesus Christ has never been taken to anyone but that some Christian has sacrificed for it to happen. Even if it only means crossing the street to bear a simple witness, some Christian has thought about it, prayed about it, and then ventured to do it (sometimes with great fear and trembling), risking the loss of the friendship or even ridicule. Farther afield the sacrifices are greater. Parents sacrifice their children to allow them to go to distant lands where they may even die in God's service. Individuals send money to support these children and to underwrite other works. Some give their time to Christian social service projects, all at some (and sometimes even great) personal sacrifice.

Another place for sacrifice is the home. Today's culture glories in self-satisfaction, teaching that if one is not personally and fully satisfied, he or she therefore has a right to break off the marriage relationship. But this is not God's teaching. God's teaching is that we are to die to self in order that the other person might be fulfilled and that it is only as this begins to happen that we ourselves find satisfaction. Do you show observable Christian love in your home? Can unbelievers tell that you are a Christian by the way you treat your wife or your husband?

John's words in verse 18 are a true conclusion. "Let us not love with words or tongue but with actions and in truth." It is when we love sacrificially and by deeds that we show ourselves truly to be Christ's disciples.

Fruit-bearing

The third mark of a true disciple is found in John 15:8. "This is to my Father's glory, that you bear much fruit, showing yourselves to be my disciples." Fruit-bearing is the third mark of being a disciple.

The context of John 15 gives the steps for successful fruit-bearing, and the first is to recognize *our own inability* to produce it. Three verses before this, in verse 5, Jesus says, "Apart from me you can do nothing." Does it say, "Apart from me you cannot do the *big things*. Apart from me you cannot do *much*"? No, that is not it at all. It says, "Apart from me you can do *nothing*." So the first step toward successful fruit-bearing is to recognize our own nothingness and so start with Christ. Activity is no substitute.

Barnhouse tells a story in which he discusses this problem. A man came to him once, after he had given a portion of his life to Christian work, and said, "It's all been fruitless."

"How did it begin?" Barnhouse asked.

The man sadly told the following story. "I remember so well," he said. "I was in my room studying, and as I was looking at the Bible, the Holy Spirit started to speak to me. He was putting His finger on things in my life that shouldn't have been there. It made me restless and I closed the Bible, got up, and went out into the other room and picked up the telephone. I called another Christian and said, 'You know, I am greatly moved at the need for such and such a thing; couldn't we start a Christian work for them?' Well, we got together and we started a Christian work, and we gave ourselves to that great activity—work, work, work—and nothing ever came of it."[5]

The reason why there was no fruit-bearing was that there was no true discipleship.

Then there is the second step for successful fruit-bearing, and this is to *remain* in Jesus. To recognize that we can do nothing is connected with remaining, of course; for when we know our need we are encouraged by that very knowledge to abide in Jesus. Nevertheless, the two are not the same. To recognize our nothingness is negative. To remain is a positive thing. It is to draw near when the Spirit begins to speak through the Word (as he did in Barnhouse's story), and to change our way of living accordingly (as the man did not). "Remain in me, and I in you," said Jesus. For "no branch can bear fruit by itself; it must remain in the vine. Neither can you bear fruit unless you remain in me" (John 15:4). To remain in Christ is to allow him to work through us for Christ's glory.

Are You a Disciple?

John 13:35 is followed by three verses in which Jesus foretells his denial by Peter. When Jesus was arrested Peter was unwilling to go home without knowing the full outcome. So he followed afar off and eventually saw Jesus taken into the courtyard of the high priest. The soldiers undoubtedly shut the large door after them. But there was a smaller door, kept by a maid; and John, who knew the house and had access, went to this door and called Peter. As Peter passed through the entrance, the maid who kept the door asked, "Are you not one of this man's disciples?"

Unfortunately, Peter forgot the protestations he had made earlier and, so, denied his Master. "I am not," he said. Then, while warming himself by the fire that warmed Jesus' enemies, he denied him twice more. The incident shows that even one of the inner band of the apostles may yet fail in discipleship.

Are we Jesus' disciples? Are you? Am I?

No doubt most of us will answer gladly, "Yes, I am his disciple." But as we think about it, let us think about discipleship according to the definition Jesus himself gave to it. Jesus defined a disciple as one who continues in his Word, loves the brethren, and bears much fruit. Do we do each of these? Jesus said, "If you hold to my teaching, then you are really my disciples." He said, "By this all men will know that you are my disciples, if you love one another." He said, "This is to my Father's glory, that you bear much fruit, showing yourselves to be my disciples." God grant that we may do each of these things as we drop all lesser loyalties and draw ever closer to him.

173

Darkness before the Dawn

John 13:36–38

Simon Peter asked him, "Lord, where are you going?"
Jesus replied, "Where I am going, you cannot follow now, but you will follow later."
Peter asked, "Lord, why can't I follow you now? I will lay down my life for you."
Then Jesus answered, "Will you really lay down your life for me? I tell you the truth,
before the rooster crows, you will disown me three times!"

John 13, which concludes with Jesus' warning to Peter that he would deny him, has two main characters other than the Lord himself: Judas and Peter. Judas betrayed his Lord. Peter denied him. Looking at the matter from the outside, as we sometimes do, there seems to be little difference between the two acts; each was a failure to stand by Christ in his hour of apparent need. Yet, by looking more closely we see there is a world of difference. One act was that of an antagonist. The other was a momentary failure by one who at heart was still a great friend and disciple of the Lord.

William Barclay puts the contrast like this: "Judas' betrayal of Jesus was absolutely deliberate; it was carried out in cold blood; it must have been the result of careful thought and careful planning; and in the end it deliberately and callously refused the most poignant appeal. But there was never anything in this world less deliberate than Peter's denial of Jesus. Peter never meant to do it. He was swept away by a moment of weakness."[1]

We would add to Barclay's analysis that the reason for the difference is that Judas, unlike Peter, was not a true believer in Christ. Consequently, when John gets to the end of Judas's story, telling how he left the company of the Twelve to conspire to give his master over into the hands of his enemies, he concludes, "and it was night." This is the night of eternal darkness brought about by a separation from God. By contrast, the prophecy of Peter's denial is at once followed by Christ's words of reassurance, "Do not let your heart be troubled" (John 14:1).

The story of Peter's denial is not as depressing as that of Judas' betrayal. Yet it is hardly encouraging either. For if Peter, the acknowledged leader of the Twelve, fell, so can any of us.

Anyone Can Fall

This is really the first lesson of these verses, and it should not be passed over quickly. It needs to be made often. Paul makes the point in the first half of 1 Corinthians 10:13, a verse about temptation. "No temptation has seized you except what is common to man. God is faithful; he will not let you be tempted beyond what you can bear. But when you are tempted, he will also provide a way out so that you can stand up under it."

As we read that verse we notice that the first half indicates that temptation will come to everyone, for this is "common to man." This is not Paul's main point. It is only a secondary one. Paul's main point is that God has provided a way for his children to escape temptations. When temptations come, they are not to think that they are experiencing something extraordinary and therefore despair, but rather they are to know that they are only experiencing what others have experienced before them and so turn to God, who has delivered others and can deliver them. This is Paul's main point. But basic to it is the truth that temptations do come to everyone and that anyone can fall into them.

One of the devil's tricks in temptation is to get us to think that the temptation is somehow extraordinary and, thus, that we cannot possibly be expected to resist it. But if that fails, he would like us to think instead that we are beyond temptation.

Sometimes we get to thinking that we are too old, that the battle has passed us by, that we are on vacation (or some such thing), and that we therefore do not need to be on guard against sinning. If that is the case, we need to learn from David in regard to his great sin with Bathsheba. How old do you suppose David was when he sinned with Bathsheba? We tend to think of sexual sins as being sins of youth, of the time when a young man is supposed to sow his wild oats. But this was not the case with David. David must have been at least fifty years old. He had served for some time under Saul, followed by years in hiding, followed by a reign of seven and a half years at Hebron (beginning when he was thirty years old), followed by a reign in Jerusalem during which time he subdued most of Israel's enemies. It was only at the end of this period, when he had made the mistake of staying home from one of the battles, that he saw Bathsheba bathing on a roof near the palace, invited her over, and committed adultery with her.

On the other hand, we look at Peter and find him to be in the prime of life. Moreover, we find him well aware of the dangers that faced both himself and the others at this time in Christ's ministry. He is as prepared to face them as anyone could be. Peter had heard Thomas say, as the little company was about to go up to Jerusalem for the last time, "Let us also go, that we may die with him" (John 11:16). He knew that danger threatened. Besides, he had bought a sword. We know this because, when the enemies of Christ came to arrest him in the Garden of Gethsemane, Peter drew the sword and went after the man who appeared to be leading the column.

Finally, we notice that Peter (unlike David) had even been warned of what was coming. This is what our text is about. Jesus had foretold his own departure, and Peter had objected, saying, "Lord, why can't I follow you now? I will lay down my life for you."

Jesus replied, "Will you lay down your life for me? I tell you the truth, before the rooster crows, you will disown me three times" (vv. 37–38). This is ironic, of course, for it was actually the Lord who was about to lay down his life for Peter. Nevertheless, in these words Peter had a prophecy of the danger that awaited him. He had only to remain faithful until morning, until the cock should crow. Yet in spite of the fact that he understood the danger, was prepared to meet it, and was forewarned by the Lord's own solemn prophecy, he fell.

David was *not* prepared for temptation, so he fell. Peter *was* prepared, yet he also fell. The point is that anyone can fall. Temptations come to anyone, at any age, at any time, and anyone can fall into sin as a result of them.

Steps of Peter's Fall

The second truth we should notice as we study these verses is that there were steps to Peter's fall. When a fall comes, it seems to come suddenly, without warning. But it is seldom the case that a fall is without some sad preparation.

A number of years ago, Philadelphia television stations showed a film recording the spectacular demolition of the Hotel Traymore in Atlantic City. The Traymore was one of the grand old resort hotels, constructed of great blocks of stone, to which generations of Philadelphians had gone for vacation during the hot summer months. It was an Atlantic coast landmark. Yet it had become obsolete and was sold to make way for newer construction. Many people knew of the sale, but few were prepared for the suddenness with which the old hotel would come down. One minute it was there on the television screens; the next, there was a blast and the old hotel simply gave way and settled into the rising clouds of dust. The whole demolition took only one or two minutes. Someone looking at this might be amazed at how this could happen. "How could the hotel be destroyed so suddenly?" he might ask. But a person who knew what was involved could explain that for months the demolition experts had been working within the hotel to place explosives within the main support columns and to wire the charges so that they would detonate together. It seemed the work of a moment. It was actually the result of a long process of careful preparation. It is the same with temptation. The fall seems sudden; but it is prepared by numerous steps, as the fall of Peter indicates.

The first step in Peter's fall was *overconfidence*. This is evident in every part of the story, but particularly from the questions Peter asked. The Lord had told Peter that he was going away and that Peter could not follow him, and Peter had asked, "Lord, where are you going?" In this context, the question is not as straightforward as it seems to be. It is actually a protest against Jesus' having told him that he, Peter, could not come after him. It really means, "I will follow you wherever you go. Tell me where you are going, so I may prove it." Then, when Jesus had replied by repeating that Peter could not follow him now but that he would hereafter, Peter had protested, "Lord, why can't I follow you now? I will lay down my life for you." This was little short of a direct contradiction of the Lord's words, for Peter was implying that he could follow Christ, in proof of which he was prepared to lay down his life for him.

What are we to think of Peter's audacity? We cannot condemn it completely, for it obviously flowed from love for Christ and from a desire to abide with him always. But it was also ignorant, and it flowed from overconfidence. What did "following" Jesus mean? Peter did not really know what was involved. Moreover, he had not yet learned the truth of Christ's statement recorded just a chapter later: "Apart from me you can do nothing" (John 15:5).

In his overconfidence Peter failed, not at his weakest point, but at his strongest. He was no coward. He was ready to die for Jesus; yet, he trembled at the innocent question of a serving maid. How is this to be explained? Pink answers, "Only on the ground that [God permitted it] in order to teach him and us the all-important lesson, that if left to ourselves, the strongest is as weak as water. It is in conscious weakness that our strength lies (II Cor. 12:10)."[2] Pink adds correctly that we often look down on others in their sin and imagine that what they are doing we could not possibly do. But we are wrong in thinking that way. For the "seeds of *every* sin are latent in our hearts, even when renewed, and they only need occasion, or carelessness, or the withdrawal of God's grace for a season, to put forth an abundant crop."[3]

We need to know this, for if we would conquer temptation, we must begin with the knowledge that, unless Christ holds us, we are bound to fall. Elsewhere I have told the story of a friend of mine who once had a job of stringing wires at a summer camp. To do this he had to climb a telephone pole. I was there as he was taught. "In order to climb the pole you have to lean back," he was told. "Lean back on the broad leather belt that surrounds you and the pole. It will hold you. You need to lean back or else your spikes will not press into the wood and hold, and you will slip." My friend listened and then tried it. But he was afraid to lean back. So his spikes would not enter the wood, and he got nowhere at all. At last he got the idea. He leaned back, the spikes took hold, and he began to climb. Unfortunately, when he was about three feet off the ground he got worried about falling and thought that he could improve things somewhat if he just pulled himself closer to the pole. But when he did that the spikes came out, and he slipped back down, getting covered with splinters in the process.

It is the same spiritually. God has ordered life in such a way that we cannot climb spiritually without leaning on him, trusting him to hold us. If we do not lean on Jesus, God will allow us to slip (as Peter did) and get covered with splinters. He will allow this so that we will come to trust him and not ourselves.

A Downward Path

The next step in Peter's fall was a *failure to pray*. This is a connecting failure, of course; for being confident of his own ability, Peter did not feel his need of God and so failed to ask him for help.

Again, this should never have happened. For if we read the parallel accounts of this evening's activities, we find that Jesus had explicitly warned the disciples to pray. "Pray that you will not fall into temptation" were his words. In all, he said this three times. He said it when he and the disciples had first entered the Garden of Gethsemane and he was about to withdraw to pray privately (Luke 22:40). He said it a second time to Peter after he had returned and found the disciples sleeping (Matt. 26:40–41; Mark 14:37–38). He said it a third time just before the multitude arrived to arrest him and Judas kissed him as the mark of identification (Luke 22:46). Peter was told to pray three times. Yet so great was his confidence, or drowsiness, which is much the same thing, that he let his opportunity pass by and was unprepared when the temptation to deny Jesus eventually overtook him.

Do you pray lest temptation overtake you? Do you "pray without ceasing," as Paul admonished those at Thessalonica to do (1 Thess. 5:17)? I know that it is hard work. At times it is terribly difficult. But there is no time when we need more to pray than when we feel too tired to do it or when the cares of the world press in upon us, depress us, or dull our thinking.

There was a third step to Peter's fall. Luke tells us about it, saying that, when they had arrested Jesus and were leading him to the house of the high priest, "Peter *followed at a distance*" (Luke 22:54). Under the circumstances, we can understand how it happened. At the moment of the arrest the disciples scattered in panic, most of them apparently making their way back over the Mount of Olives in the darkness to Bethany where they had been spending each evening of the Passover week. The psychology of the narrative indicates that they would flee away from Jerusalem, where the danger lay, to Bethany, rather than in the direction in which the Lord was taken. But Peter apparently did not run, or else hid for a time or stopped running, with the result that he saw Jesus being led away and followed after him, while being hidden by the darkness. It is understandable. It is what I would have done. But where is the bravery of that one who said he would die with Jesus if that should be necessary? Where is Peter's courage now? Peter was caught off guard; he was not praying as Jesus was. So fear had suddenly conquered his heart, and he was hiding lest he be detected.

What Peter did on this occasion is characteristic of too many Christians. They want to be followers of Jesus, but they follow afar off for fear of the consequences. They know rightly that the focus of the warfare is where Jesus stands. So they think they will be safer if they are not so close to him. Are they safer? Of course not. The only safety for any disciple is to follow closely behind Jesus.

Then, finally, toward the end of the story, we find Peter warming himself at the fire in the courtyard of the high priest. He is *in the company of Christ's enemies and is benefiting from them.* This is not to be taken as meaning that we should forego all contact with the world, for we should not. Jesus himself said that he was leaving us in the world rather than taking us from the world so that we might be a witness to the world. But it does mean that we must not profit from the activities of those who would do Christ harm. Moreover, we must avoid becoming too chummy with them, for we lose our integrity in that way and then cannot stand for Jesus. Peter failed to guard himself at this point. Consequently he fell into an incognito role and soon denied his Lord—at the last, we are told, even with oaths and cursings (Matt. 26:74; Mark 14:71).

Is this to be our path? Temptations will come, and we can succumb to them. We can be like Peter in his downward path. Or we can resist. To resist we must do the opposite of what Peter did on this occasion. First, rather than being overly confident, we must be underconfident. Or, to speak more correctly, we must refuse to have confidence in ourselves at all. Second, we must pray regularly and earnestly. Third, we must follow closely behind Jesus, not afar off as Peter did. Finally, we must be careful not to profit from the activities of those who are really Christ's enemies.

Not Cast Off

At this point our study of Peter's denial could properly stop, for we have learned enough to profit immensely. But we should not only see that anyone can fall and the steps that led to Peter's fall, which we have seen. We should also see the activity of Jesus on Peter's behalf, knowing that he was about to fall. What did Jesus do? He warned Peter, that is true. But that is not all he did. We are also told: (1) that Jesus prayed for Peter, and (2) that he later came to Peter in order to recommission him to service.

First, Jesus prayed for Peter. And, as we might expect, his prayers were answered. Luke tells us about it in his Gospel. In this account Jesus is speaking to Peter and says the following: "Simon, Simon, Satan has asked to sift you as wheat. But I have prayed for you, that your faith will not fail. And when you have turned back, strengthen your brothers" (Luke 22:31, 32). Put in language that we can better understand, this means that Satan had come to Jesus boasting that Peter was nothing but a bag of hot air and that if he, Satan, were allowed to blow on him, Peter would sail away like chaff when the wind separates it from the grain at threshing time. Jesus answered that there was indeed a great deal of chaff in Peter but that Satan was wrong in thinking that Peter was nothing but chaff. "My grain is in Peter," he said. "Consequently, I will let you blow on him; but when you are done all you will have succeeded in doing is blowing away some of the chaff. Peter will be stronger than before." Here Jesus announced Peter's victory even before it happened. But he added that he would pray for Peter that his faith would not fail. Peter would fail to pray, but the Lord would pray for him.

Second, the Lord appeared to Peter after Peter's fall and after his own resurrection to recommission him. The story is found in the postscript to John's Gospel. Peter had denied three times. The Lord asked three times, "Simon, son of John, do you truly love me?"

Three times Peter answered, "Yes, Lord, you know that I love you."

Jesus replied, "Feed my sheep."

Did Jesus cast off Peter? He had every reason to do so. Peter had denied him. He might have judged Peter unfit for further service or even for salvation. But this is not the Lord's way. He came again to recommission Peter to service. Did God cast off Abraham after he had left Ur of the Chaldees for the Promised Land but had stopped at Haran? No. God came to Abraham a second time with the identical promise of great spiritual blessing. Did God cast off Moses after Moses had decided that he could free his people by his own strength, killed an Egyptian, and then had to flee from Egypt to Midian? No. God came to Moses with a new revelation of himself, one that contained a promise to do what Moses had attempted but had found himself unable to do. Did God cast off Jonah after Jonah had fled from him, falling so deeply into sin that he declared he would rather die than go to Nineveh? No. God came to Jonah a second time also.

So God comes to us a second, third, fourth, even a hundredth or thousandth time, if necessary, that we might fellowship with him. Moreover, none of us would be where we are at this moment if God had not so operated with us. We are unfaithful; yet he abides faithful. He loves each of his own "to the end" (John 13:1). Do we deserve it? No. But we can respond to it, saying, as did Isaac Watts,

> When I survey the wondrous cross
> On which the Prince of glory died,

My richest gain I count but loss,
   And pour contempt on all my pride.

Were the whole realm of nature mine,
   That were a present far too small:
Love so amazing, so divine,
   Demands my soul, my life, my all.

When we think that we are standing, we are about to fall. But when we conquer our pride and lean upon Jesus, we find him to be all we need. We love him, and we find his love sufficient for each emergency.

174

Calm Words for Troubled Hearts

John 14:1–3

"Do not let your hearts be troubled. Trust in God; trust also in me. In my Father's house are many rooms; if it were not so, I would have told you. I am going there to prepare a place for you. And if I go and prepare a place for you, I will come back and take you to be with me that you also may be where I am."

What is a Christian to do when the world he knows falls in? What is he to do in the day of great trouble?

This is not an idle question because, although we do not always like to think about it, life *is* filled with troubles. Disappointment is a trouble, and there are many disappointments. We are disappointed with ourselves, for we are not always what we want to be. We want to be strong, but we are weak. We want to be successful, but we experience many failures. We want to be liked, but often people are at best indifferent to us. We are also often disappointed with other people, with a husband, wife, son, daughter, friend, employer, partner, employee, or whatever the case may be.

Circumstances, too, are a source of troubles. In some cases we can do something about the circumstances, and we try to; but this is not always so. Poverty cannot always be changed, and poverty is troubling. The loss of a loved one is also beyond our control, and this is devastating. So is loss of a job, sickness, or even uncertainty about the future, the last of which is particularly unsettling in these times.

And what about spiritual troubles, when it seems as though the Lord's presence is withdrawn and we are plunged alone into what has well been described as the "dark night" of the soul? What are we to do in such circumstances? What are we to do with despair? The answer is that we are to take ourselves in hand and by a deliberate exercise of mind strengthen our faith in God. We are to think of him and so overcome trouble by reminding ourselves of the power and promises of God and by trusting in him.

Our text is a call to us to become strong Christians, not the kind who weep and wail and expect everyone to pity them, but rather the kind who are of great stature in faith and who are a source of strength to others. The text says, "*Do not let* your hearts be troubled" (John 14:1).

Cause to Be Troubled

There are two important things about this text, and the first, quite paradoxical in view of what I have just said, is that frequently we have cause to be troubled.

It would not be necessary to make so much of this point if it were not that there is a kind of Pollyanna Christianity in our day that seeks to deny it. It is the kind of Christianity that pretends that there are no troubles for any truly surrendered child of God. This view of life takes Romans 8:28 to mean that only good things come into the life of one who truly loves God ("And we know that in all things God works for the good of those who love him"), rather than seeing that the verse actually says that evil will indeed come but that God will nevertheless accomplish his own good purposes in spite of it. This view is unrealistic and uninformed, for evil does exist. Troubles do come. Death is an enemy. So, rather than denying these things, we must begin by a realistic recognition of them.

Obviously, it was this that prompted Christ's saying, for it was clear to him that from a human viewpoint the disciples, to whom he was speaking, had cause for deep agitation.

For one thing, he himself had been troubled. We know this because we are told about it in the previous chapter: "After he had said this, Jesus was troubled in spirit" (v. 21). Was this not unusual and troubling in itself? Was it not a cause for dismay that he who had been their stay in every troubled sea, their refuge in every hostile crowd, should be troubled? Moreover, he had also indicated that he was about to be taken from them. He had said it before, but they had not fully understood him. Now the message got through, and they were in turmoil. He was their life. For him they had left family, home, and occupation. What would they do once he was gone from them? What could fill the void left in their aching and anxious hearts?

Nor is this all. If there were nothing more, the disciples might have comforted themselves with the thought that, regardless of what might happen, still they loved him and would be faithful to him or to his memory forever. But they were really not free to think this, for he had told them that one of their number, Judas, should betray him, and that another, Peter, should deny him three times before morning.

Did the disciples have cause to be troubled? Certainly they did! From this we learn that it is not wrong to honestly recognize and even analyze our problems.

We may add another point also. It is also not wrong to recognize and openly acknowledge things that trouble others. Here is a useful principle in counseling. Sometimes when a person comes to us with a problem, as people do to me constantly, we want to minimize their problem. We want to say, "But that is not so bad. Think how things could be worse." We may even want to tell stories of those we know who were in even worse circumstances. But we must not do this. Nothing is gained by minimizing the problems. Instead, we must hear the troubled soul out, and we must acknowledge that in many, if not all, cases there is that which rightly troubles him. Indeed, we must even "mourn with those who mourn," as Paul says in the great ethical section of the letter to the Romans (12:15).

More Cause Not to Be

So Christians are realists. They are realists about all life's problems. At the same time, however, we must add that they are realists about the power of God and his promises. And this means that although there is cause to be troubled, nevertheless, there is even greater cause not to be. This is the second important point. Regardless of what there may be to cause us to be troubled as Christians, there is more cause not to be troubled.

What are the reasons why we should not be troubled? In these verses there are five of them. First, we know Jesus. He is God. He knows about us and our circumstances. He is able to deal with them. Therefore, there is every reason to trust him. Jesus indicates this when he issues the challenge, "Trust in God, trust also in me."

Frankly, there are a number of ways in which these lines may be taken, due to the fact that in both parts of the sentence the verb "trust" may be in either the indicative ("You trust") or the imperative mood ("Trust!"). In Greek the two forms are identical. Thus, there are four ways to translate the sentence: (1) "You trust in God; you also trust in me"; (2) "Trust in God! Trust in me!" (3) "You trust in God; trust in me also"; and (4) "Trust in God, as you trust in me." Of these four, the first may be rejected because it is nothing more than a statement, and an exhortation of some kind is demanded by the context. The last may also be rejected because it suggests a backward relationship. The disciples were obviously not to begin with their faith in Jesus and then work up to faith in God, for it is a need for faith in Christ that is indicated. So possibilities two and three are left: "You trust in God; trust also in me" and "Trust in God; trust in me!"

To be sure, there is not a great deal of difference in these two translations, and both make good theology. Still, in spite of the great weight of many recent versions, it seems to the writer that the translation of the older, Authorized Version is preferable. Why should the disciples be urged to believe in God in this situation? True, it is always good to be urged to believe in God, but in this situation the problem is that Jesus was about to be taken from the disciples and that they were troubled by thoughts of this parting. They did not really doubt that God would take care of them in some far off, general sense. But they did not understand how Jesus could go, how he could apparently be abandoning them. So what does Christ say? In these circumstances it is as though he turns to the disciples and says, "Look, I know that you trust God; trust me also, precisely in these circumstances. Believe that I know what I am doing, that I am going away for a purpose, that the purpose will be accomplished, and that I will again return to you so that we can be together." This he said in the face of his own execution.

Here was the first reason why the disciples were not to be troubled. They knew Jesus, and they had every reason to trust him.

So do we. In fact, we have even more cause than those first disciples, for they stood on the far side of the resurrection and did not know, as we do, that the cross of Christ was our salvation or that the resurrection was to follow it. Did Jesus know what he was doing? Of course he did! Could he be trusted? Certainly! Then let us also trust him. Whatever the circumstances, whatever the hardship, let us believe that he has a purpose in those circumstances and is most certainly working them out for our own spiritual good.

A Home in Heaven

The second reason Jesus gives why we should not be troubled is that there is a place prepared for us in heaven. "In my Father's house are many rooms," he said; "if it were not so, I would have told you. I am going there to prepare a place for you" (v. 2).

For many people, talk of a home in heaven smacks of escapism, as if in the face of trials the Christian is to turn his back upon life and live only for glory. It is the "pie-in-the-sky" philosophy. This has been true in some cases. Some have indeed turned from life when they should have been living it victoriously. Some have been escapists. But there are also circumstances where those who are not escapists have nevertheless gained great comfort and strength from these promises.

I think of one example. Not long ago I visited a member of my congregation who had been confined to a home for incurables because of crippling arthritis. She was always in constant pain and had wasted away in this home for many years. At this time this poor woman, who never complained and who never talked about herself or her condition unless someone asked about it, was near death. As we talked, I asked her, "Ida, do you still love Jesus?"

Her eyes glowed through her suffering as she replied, "Yes; oh yes! And I do long to be with him. I am so anxious for him to take me home." The death of a Christian is not like the death of an unbeliever, for the Christian knows where he or she is going. He is sure of his heavenly home.

Moreover, the *life* of a Christian is not (in most cases) like the life of an unbeliever. For, knowing his destiny, knowing that he will again see Jesus in that heavenly home, the faithful Christian follows him now and lives for him. Paul indicated this when he wrote: "Join with others in following my example, brothers, and take note of those who live according to the pattern we gave you. . . . But our citizenship is in heaven. And we eagerly await a Savior from there, the Lord Jesus Christ" (Phil. 3:17, 20). John also speaks of this when he writes, "Dear friends, now we are children of God, and what we will be has not yet been made known. But we know that when he appears, we shall be like him, for we shall see him as he is. Everyone who has this hope in him purifies himself, just as he is pure" (1 John 3:2–3). To know our destiny is a great incentive, not only for the enjoyment of peace in the midst of turmoil but for godly living as well.

Our Personal Dwelling

The third reason Jesus gave the disciples why they should not be troubled is that he was going to prepare a place for them. On the surface this seems to be much the same point as before; that is, that there is a heavenly home and that there are many abiding places in it. But it is not really a repetition. It is something more. There is a place called heaven. Jesus was going there. But in addition to this he tells them that there is work that he is going to do for them once he gets there.

What did Jesus refer to when he said that he was going to prepare a place for his disciples? I am not sure that there is a full answer to that question, because I do not know of any passage of the Bible that bears directly upon it. As I think about it, I wonder if the fact that we ask that question does not hide the verse's true meaning. We read the verse "I am going there to prepare a place for you" and focus on the word "prepare." What if we were to focus on the words "for you" instead? In that case, the emphasis would not be upon whatever architectural alterations the Lord may be making in heaven, but rather upon the fact that it is for us as individuals that he is altering it. In other words, it would be the promise that in that great home of the Father's there is a place being prepared particularly for us.

Have you ever decorated a room for someone special? If you have, you know what it is to make a room suit one particular personality. If it is a daughter, you make the room pretty. You hang up her pictures. You make a place for her hobbies. If it is a son, the room might have airplanes or model cars. If it is for Grandma, the room might have her favorite books; and it might be far from the playroom or the children's bedrooms. We take care in such preparation. Are we to think that Jesus will take less care for those whom he loves, who are to spend eternity with him?

With Jesus

The fourth and fifth points may be taken together. They are: first, that Jesus is returning again for those whom he has left behind and, second, that from that point on they will be with him forever. He said, "And if I go and prepare a place for you, I will come back and take you to be with me that you also may be where I am" (v. 3).

There have been those who have identified this coming of the Lord Jesus with the coming of the Holy Spirit at Pentecost spoken of later. But this is not right. In the case of the Spirit, Jesus comes to the believer and the believer receives him. In this verse, Jesus receives the believer so that the believer may be with him in heaven. Clearly, this is what Paul describes so vividly when he says, "For the Lord himself will come down from heaven, with a loud command, with the voice of the archangel and with the trumpet call of God, and the dead in Christ will rise first. After that, we who are still alive and are left will be caught up together with them in the clouds to meet the Lord in the air. And so we will be with the Lord forever" (1 Thess. 4:16–17).

There is comfort in that. Indeed, there must be; for Paul immediately follows this with the admonition; "Therefore encourage each other with these words" (v. 18).

We Can Do Something

At this point we return to the question asked at the beginning of this study: "What is a Christian to do when the world he knows falls in? What is he to do in the day of great trouble?" The answer once again is that he is to take himself in hand and by a deliberate exercise of mind, in which he brings such great truths as these to remembrance, increase his faith in God. He is to remind himself of and then meditate upon God's great strength and promises.

There are those for whom this does not sound spiritual at all and who, therefore, prefer to grope around in the dark, waiting for some great shaft of light to break through. But this was not Christ's teaching. He did not say, "Mull over your problems." He did not even say, "Tell me about them," though, of course, we are free to do that. He said, "*Do not* be troubled; *do not let* your present troubled state continue." So if Jesus says, "Do not let your heart be troubled," then our hearts *need* not be troubled. We can be victorious if we will remind ourselves of what we know of him and trust him.

175

A Place for You

John 14:2–3

"In my Father's house are many rooms; if it were not so, I would have told you. I am going there to prepare a place for you. And if I go and prepare a place for you, I will come back and take you to be with me that you also may be where I am."

One reason why those who believe in Jesus Christ should not be troubled by adverse circumstances is that they have a home in heaven. However, as soon as we begin to talk about heaven we create a problem, for in the thinking of most people heaven is not an interesting subject. This was not always so. There was a time in the history of the western world when thoughts about the life to come were popular. But ours is a secular and scientific age. Thus, in today's world, thoughts about heaven seem to be either a form of escapism or mere speculation.

Thoughts of Heaven

We suffer from this purely secular outlook, as will be shown. But as we begin to study about heaven, let us take note that heaven should be far more interesting to us than we naturally imagine. For one thing, we should recognize that heaven is likely to become increasingly interesting to us as we grow older. D. L. Moody tells of a man who testified that in his youth he thought of heaven largely as a great shining city, filled with vast walls, domes and towers, and populated by millions of angels, all of whom were strangers to him. But then his little brother died. After that he thought of heaven as a great shining city, filled with vast walls and towers and unknown angels, but now also with one little fellow he knew. When a second brother died there were two he knew. Acquaintances died. In time one of his children went to be with Jesus; this one was followed by another and then still another. By this time the man seldom thought of walls and towers. He thought of those residents of the Celestial City whom he knew, and his interest in heaven intensified. Toward the end of his life so many of his acquaintances had gone to heaven that it sometimes seemed to him that he knew more persons in heaven than he did on earth. And, of course, his thoughts fixed increasingly on that distant place.

Moreover, it is not only as we grow older that we should find heaven interesting. To be sure, when we are younger the emotional ties that bind an older person to those who have gone ahead are lacking. But we are going there some day, if we are Christians. Should we not be interested in the place where we will spend eternity?

I remember the great interest my wife and I had when, in the early days of our married life together, we determined to go to Europe where I was to pursue my graduate studies. Our destination was Basel, Switzerland, about which we knew virtually nothing. Were we disinterested? Not at all! I remember how we poured over maps and books containing geographical and other information, for we wanted to know what Basel was like. How big was Basel? What was the climate? Was it an old city or a new one? What was its history? What belongings should we take with us? Most people will recognize our interest in Basel to have been a proper one. How much greater should a Christian's interest be in that place to which Jesus has gone, which he is preparing for us.

Should we not have a great interest in these verses in which the Lord himself talks about heaven? Do we not want to ponder the words: "In my Father's house are many rooms; if it were not so, I would have told you. I am going there to prepare a place for you. And if I go and prepare a place for you, I will come back and take you to be with me that you also may be where I am" (vv. 2–3)? I think we do. Therefore, although we have studied these verses once, we are going to deal with them again in this and the following study.

A Real Place

As we look closely at these words, the first thing we notice is that, according to Jesus, heaven is a genuine place. When we say this, we do not mean that we are therefore able to visualize it adequately, even with the help of biblical symbols. For example, we read in the Bible of a city whose streets are paved with gold. But we are not necessarily to think that these streets are like our streets or that the gold is what we identify as the seventy-ninth element on the atomic charts. Streets speak of permanence, gold of something precious and valuable that does not rust or deteriorate. In the same way, we do not think that there are necessarily literal crowns in heaven, although there may be. There may not be harps as we conceive of them. These things are symbols; so, while they point to reality, nevertheless they may not themselves be reality.

Yet none of this is to be taken as meaning that heaven is therefore anything less than a real place, as real, perhaps even as localized, as New York or San Francisco. On the occasion of his address in the upper room Jesus did not describe heaven, but he did call it a place to which he was going, from which he would return, and to which he would one day take all whom the Father had given him.

The word "heaven" is used in three different ways in the Bible. It is used of what we would call the atmosphere, the heaven of birds and clouds. It is used of those great spaces in which the planets and stars are found. This is sometimes also called "the firmament." Finally, it is used of the heaven of heavens, which is the home of God. It is this—a place just like the other places—about which these verses are speaking.

All this presents difficulties for some persons, and for two reasons. First, there are those who observe that God is described as being pure spirit—that is, as having no bodily form—and who therefore conclude that heaven is the abode or state of pure spirits. But the idea that heaven is merely a state and therefore everywhere and nowhere is not according to Scripture. True, God is a spirit; he does not have a concrete, visible form. But Jesus does. He has become man for all eternity. The angels also have bodies. So do we, not only in this life but also in the life to come. If this were not so, the teaching about the resurrection of the body would be meaningless. These bodies must be somewhere. As I read the accounts of Christ's postresurrection appearances, I recognize that the heavenly body of Christ (after which our heavenly bodies are patterned) possesses qualities that we do not yet have. His body could move through closed doors, for instance. It could vanish and then reappear. Still, it is a true body and must be localized. Heaven is the place where our bodies shall be, though we will presumably be able, like Jesus, to move freely.

The second reason why some people have difficulty thinking of heaven as a genuine place is linked to scientific considerations. These people are aware of the vast distances of our universe as well as the fact that no one using any of the gigantic telescopes of our time has ever seen anything like heaven. They say, "If Jesus had ascended into heaven beginning in A.D. 30 and if he had accelerated until at last he was traveling at the speed of light, he would not yet have reached the farthest star, let alone heaven, wherever that may be located. How then are we to imagine that heaven is a real place, that Jesus went there, and that he is coming again to take us to be with him?"

This is an important problem. For if there is no material, spatial heaven, then the Lord Jesus Christ did not ascend into it in his body. And if this is so, then we must abandon the idea of a bodily resurrection of the Savior and all that goes with it, which is most of Christianity. Indeed, we will find ourselves in the position described by Paul when he declared that "if Christ has not been raised, your faith is futile; you are still in your sins" (1 Cor. 15:17). But why, on the other hand, must we thus limit the Creator? On one occasion, when Donald Grey Barnhouse was asked a question about ascending at the speed of light, he replied, "Why do you wish to slow the Creator to the speed of light? He who created the universe is able to move with the speed of thought, and it is possible to think from here to the remotest point of the universe as quickly as it is to think down to the corner drugstore."[1] We readily admit that we do not understand how this operates; we cannot think clearly beyond known physical laws. But God is not bound by the laws he has created. Consequently, all things—literally, *all things*—are possible to him.

Our Heavenly Home

There is a second thought in the phrase we have been considering, "a place for you." For it tells us that heaven is not only a place; it is a home. This is the import of the last two words, "for you."

As I have thought about this phrase I have been helped by the Swiss doctor Paul Tournier, who has taken the words as the title of one of his books on counseling. In that book, *A Place for You,* he deals with the idea of a place and of the need we all have for it. For instance, at the beginning of the book he tells of a young man whom he had once counseled. The young man had been born into an unhappy home, had developed a sense of failure—first failing to reconcile his parents and then in an inability to settle down into any one area of life—and at last had come to see Tournier. Together they explored the young man's problems. On one occasion, as he was trying to look at himself objectively and put what he saw into words, the student looked up at his counselor and said, "Basically, I'm always looking for a place—for somewhere to be."[2]

This, says Tournier as the book unfolds, is a basic desire of the human heart. It is the desire to have a genuine place of our own, a home, a place where we belong and know ourselves to belong. The problem, says the counselor, is that many people apparently never find this place and so spend much of life wandering.

Tournier is not insensitive to the need that we have to find a home spiritually. Here we think of Adam and Eve and of their expulsion from their garden home in Eden because of their sin. We think of Cain, who, because he killed his brother, was condemned to a life of wandering. He had no home. In Genesis 11 we find men trying to create a city in which homes will be established. But the men of Babel are in opposition to God, and so God scatters them. Again they are made homeless. Here, then, is a great motif of Genesis. Sin brings alienation, and one aspect of alienation is that men lose their home.

With the coming of Abraham we find a new and heartening element. To be sure, God's first dealings with Abraham are to take him from his home, for it is a sinful place filled with idols and idol worshipers. But in return for the place he has lost God promises him a new home—"a land I will show you" (Gen. 12:1). What is more, God gives the boundaries and indicates the specific territory involved. It is "from the river of Egypt to the great river, the Euphrates—the land of the Kenites, Kenizzites, Kadmonites, Hittites, Perizzites, Rephaites, Amorites, Canaanites, Girgashites and Jebusites" (Gen. 15:18–21). The names are concrete. These are real names. They occur in real history. Thus they show God's awareness of the fact that the men and women he has created need a real place to be.

When we turn to the New Testament, we find Abraham praised, not because he fixed his hope on an earthly home (important as that is), but because he looked for a heavenly home. The Bible says, "For he was looking forward to the city with foundations, whose architect and builder is God" (Heb. 11:10). This means that although earthly homes are necessary and valuable, they are nevertheless and at best not permanent and that, consequently, the basic need for a home (going back to Eden) is fully met only when the Lord Jesus Christ himself prepares a home for us in heaven. Now we are in a strange land, even in an enemy's country. But in that day we shall be in the Father's house and shall be home. This is our destiny.

Can anyone still feel that thoughts about heaven are otherworldly and therefore improper for Christians? Does anyone think that thoughts like these are escapism? This reality is anything but escapism.

Here again let me illustrate from Tournier's psychology. Take a child. Who is the child who spends a lifetime wandering about, always unable to find a place where he can belong and can make a sure contribution? Is it the child who has a home or the child who does not? Obviously, it is the child who does not have a home. Writes Tournier, "When the family is such that the child cannot fit himself into it properly, he looks everywhere for some other place, leading a wandering existence, incapable of settling down anywhere. His tragedy is that he carries about within himself this fundamental incapacity for any real attachment." On the other hand, "The child who has been able to grow up harmoniously in a healthy home finds a welcome everywhere. In infancy all he needs is a stick placed across two chairs to make himself a house, in which he feels quite at home. Later on, wherever he goes, he will be able to make any place his own, without any effort on his part. For him it will not be a matter of seeking, but of choosing."[3]

It is the same spiritually. Who are those who seek to escape from this world? It is not those who are certain of a home in heaven. The ones who try to escape from this world are those who have no sure, spiritual mooring and who are therefore still searching. They may study theology and even write books about it, but they are lost. They have no sure foundation, and their views and interests shift constantly. Those who do not try to escape are those who have their home. They may not be in it as yet. They may not even understand what it is like precisely, for they look through a glass darkly. Still, it is a home for them; and, therefore, because they have this home, they are at home anywhere. They can form friendships. They marry for life. They can commit themselves to a Christian work or even a secular work and labor for years without being restless and unfulfilled.

The world needs such satisfied men and women. It needs people who can be at home here—in spite of the world's evil—precisely because they have a home in heaven.

Do You Have a Home?

The final point is in the form of a question. Do you have a home? Are you one for whom Jesus has gone to prepare a place in heaven?

At the beginning of this chapter you read a story that was often related by that great evangelist D. L. Moody. Here is another. There was a man who had great wealth. He was dying. When the doctor told him he could not live, the lawyer was sent for to make out his will. The dying man had a little girl who was about four years old. She did not understand what death meant. But when her mother told her that her father was going away, the little child went to the bedside and looked into her father's eyes and asked, "Papa, have you got a home in that land you are going to?" The question sunk deep into the man's soul, for he had spent his time and energy accumulating great wealth. In this life he enjoyed a grand home, but now he had to leave it.

I would ask that of you. It is certain that you are going away, for it is appointed unto man once to die. Have you a home where you are going? Has the Lord Jesus Christ, your Savior, gone to prepare it for you?

If you want to be able to say yes to that question, all that is necessary is for Jesus to become your Savior, for he says that he has gone to prepare a place for all who trust him. Apart from his work no one can enter heaven. Heaven is a place of holiness, and none but holy ones can dwell there. On the other hand, for all who trust his work, who believe that he is indeed the Savior from sin, that he died for them particularly, and who receive him as that Savior and promise to follow him as his faithful disciples until their life's end—for these heaven is that certain and blessed home that we have even now but that, nevertheless, still awaits us at our journey's end. If you have never believed in the Lord Jesus Christ, do so now. Receive him as your Savior, and know the joy of possessing a place prepared for you by his own skilled hands.

176

Heaven

John 14:3–4

"And if I go and prepare a place for you, I will come back and take you to be with me that you also may be where I am. You know the way to the place where I am going."

Many human beings are anxious about whether or not they will recognize their friends in heaven. They are Christian people. Often they have no doubt that they will *be* in heaven; for, as they point out, "to be away from the body [is to be] at home with the Lord" (2 Cor. 5:8). Still they are confused about what is to happen in the life to come and wonder whether or not they will recognize those who have gone on before them. "Do you think I will know my Bill?" "Will I recognize Sally?" These are the questions they ask me, and I think that I understand them. For obviously, if we will not recognize our friends and family, then heaven inevitably loses much of its attractiveness for us. And—let us put it frankly—it is hard to see how we can really be happy there, regardless of how dazzling the streets or how beautiful the music of the angels.

On the other hand, there is also a sense in which I do not understand these questions. The reason I do not understand them is simply that the Word of God is so explicit about our mutual recognition. We *will* know each other. Bill will know Sally. Sally will know Bill. We will know parents and children, friends, and those who have died in the Lord before us. This truth is suggested in our text. Therefore, I want to look at it again before we move on to other subjects.

We Will See Jesus

The place to begin in this discussion, however, is not with our recognition of each other and enjoyment of each other but with the fact that we will see Jesus and enjoy him. We begin here as a simple matter of priority, for we will want to see him even more than a departed husband, wife, parent, child, or grandparent. But we begin here for another reason also. We begin here because, if we begin with Jesus, then our reunion in heaven becomes (as it will be) a truly spiritual and godly reunion. If we forget this priority, then in our minds our reunion with loved ones becomes something only a little removed from a family get-together with all the failures of such a human affair.

This is what will make heaven a real home to us. True, having our loved ones there will be a part of it. But the thing that will make heaven a true home is being with Jesus. On this point D. L. Moody used to tell of a child whose mother became very sick. While the mother was sick one of the neighbors took the child away to stay with her until the mother should get well again. But instead of getting well, the mother grew worse and died. The neighbors thought that they would not take the child home until after the funeral was over, and that they would not tell her about her mother being dead. So after a while they simply brought the little girl home. At once she went to find her mother. First she went into the sitting room to find her mother; then she went into the parlor to find her mother. She went from one end of the house to the other, but she could not find her. At last she asked, "Where is my mama?" When they told her that her mama was gone, the child wanted to go back to the neighbor's house again. Home had lost its attraction for her since her mother was not there any longer. Moody writes, "It is not the jasper walls and the pearly gates that are going to make heaven attractive. It is being with God."[1]

To know that we are going to heaven is a wonderful thing. But more wonderful still is the fact that we shall see Jesus and shall be able to express to him that praise and love he deserves for having left heaven to come to earth and here die for us sinners. Of this truth Fanny Crosby once wrote:

> Some day the silver cord will break,
>   And I no more as now shall sing;
> But O, the joy when I shall wake
>   Within the palace of the King!
>
> And I shall see him face-to-face,
>   And tell the story—Saved by grace;
> And I shall see him face-to-face,
>   And tell the story—Saved by grace;

> Some day my earthly house will fall—
> I cannot tell how soon 'twill be;
> But this I know—my All in All
> Has now a place in heav'n for me.

This expectation of the redeemed child of God is a glorious theme, the reality of which makes heaven a true home for us. Indeed, heaven becomes a proper home only when we have the first priority.

A Reunion

But the point at which we began is not whether or not we will see and recognize Jesus but whether or not we will see and recognize each other. Will we recognize each other? Of course, we will. What is more, there are many indications in Scripture that this will be so.

One very encouraging indication comes from the Old Testament in a phrase often used in connection with the death of the patriarchs. It is the phrase "and he was gathered to his people." It occurs in texts like these: "Then Abraham breathed his last and died at a good old age, an old man and full of years; and he *was gathered to his people*" (Gen. 25:8); "Altogether Ishmael lived a hundred and thirty-seven years. He breathed his last and died, and he *was gathered to his people*" (Gen. 25:17); "Then he [Isaac] breathed his last and died and *was gathered to his people,* old and full of years. And his sons Esau and Jacob buried him" (Gen. 35:29); "When Jacob had finished giving instructions to his sons, he drew his feet up into the bed, breathed his last and *was gathered to his people*" (Gen. 49:33); "Aaron *will be gathered to his people.* He will not enter the land I give the Israelites" (Num. 20:24); and "Then the LORD said to Moses, 'Go up this mountain in the Abarim range and see the land I have given the Israelites. After you have seen it, you too *will be gathered to your people,* as your brother Aaron was" (Num. 27:12–13).

Many Old Testament scholars regard the phrase "and he was gathered to his people" as being nothing more than a conventional way of saying that he died. It is to be explained, so they say, by the thought that the individual was being placed in the same graveyard as those who had died before him. But this is hardly satisfactory in the case of the Bible stories involved. When Abraham died he was buried in a cave at Machpelah in the land that was to become Israel, but it was not the burial place of his ancestors. They had been buried back in Ur of the Chaldees, and his father had been buried at Haran. Moreover, in reading the account of his death, it is hard to overlook the fact that Abraham is said to have been gathered to his ancestors in verse 8 of Genesis 25, but to have been buried only in verse 9. Consequently, the phrase "gathered to his people" cannot refer to the burial but must refer to the death itself as a result of which Abraham joined those who had gone before him.

The same thing is true of Moses, who died by himself in the mountain. The Book of Deuteronomy even tells us that "no one knows where his grave is" (Deut. 34:6).

The comment of David upon being told of the death of Bathsheba's child is also important, for it shows that David believed in a personal reunion with departed loved ones in the life to come. God struck the child so that it became sick and died. While it lay languishing David, who understood that he was to blame, prayed for the child and fasted, lying all night upon the earth. So great was his grief and concern that when the child died, those who were close to David were afraid to tell him lest his grief should know no bounds. David detected the change in their attitude, however. He asked, "Is the child dead?" When they told him that the child had died, David surprised them by rising from his place of mourning, washing himself, dressing, and resuming his duties as leader of the nation.

The servants asked about his change of attitude, since they could not understand it. David explained, "While the child was still alive, I fasted and wept. I thought, 'Who knows? The LORD may be gracious to me and let the child live.' But now that he is dead, why should I fast? Can I bring him back again? I will go to him, but he will not return to me" (2 Sam. 12:22–23). This last comment does not mean merely that David would eventually die himself. For the point of the story is that David comforted himself (and Bathsheba) after the child's death, and there would be no comfort unless David believed that, although he could not bring the child back, nevertheless, one day he would see the child again in heaven.

If we turn to the New Testament, we find an additional indication of these same truths in the events that took place on the Mount of Transfiguration. On this occasion the Lord Jesus Christ took three of his disciples, Peter, James, and John, with him into the mountain and was transformed into a form showing his celestial glory. Moreover, Moses and Elijah, two other glorified saints, appeared beside him. Luke calls them "men"; that is, not disembodied spirits, and he reports that Peter and presumably also the others recognized them. Peter said, "Master, it is good for us to be here. Let us put up three shelters—one for you, one for Moses and one for Elijah" (Luke 9:33). Here both Moses and Elijah had retained their identities and were recognized by the three disciples.

Christ's story about the rich man and Lazarus makes a similar point, for the Lord told how the rich man went to hell and, being in torment, lifted up his eyes and saw "Abraham far away, with Lazarus by his side" (Luke 16:23). Here is a case that involves recognition of the departed, not only as they appear in this life, but as they appear to each other in the life to come.

Finally, there is a fine text from the lips of Jesus in which he speaks of many Gentiles joining with believing Jews in a great reunion in heaven. We read, "I say to you that many will come from the east and the west, and will take their places at the feast with Abraham, Isaac and Jacob in the kingdom of heaven" (Matt. 8:11). This is a great promise, but it is not possible unless there is to be a full recognition of all who have died. Clearly the patriarchs are to know each other at this holy reunion, and so will all those who have died in Christ and who will be gathered to the reunion from the far corners of the earth. In that day we may well be surprised to see many in heaven whom we do not expect to be there. And we will be just as surprised not to find many there whom we thought would be present.

Many of us have lost believing loved ones. Or, if we have not lost them and yet live long enough, we will lose them. But we have not lost them ultimately, for they are with Jesus, and we will yet be reunited with them.

All We Are Meant to Be

It has been pointed out, first, that we shall see Jesus and, second, that we shall see and recognize each other. The third point is that we shall see each other, not as we are now or have been but as we are meant to be. This truth is conveyed in the text mentioned earlier, which says that we shall see Christ face to face. It says, "Dear friends, now we are children of God, and what we will be has not yet been made known. But we know that when he appears, we shall be like him, for we shall see him as he is" (1 John 3:2).

Until recently, every time I read that verse I focused on the word "we" and read it as if it said "I." I read that "I will be like him" and took comfort in that. But now I am impressed with something else that is also true. It is not only that I shall be made like Jesus. It is that we *all* shall be like him. As a result, the sin, ignorance, anger, hate, weariness, and perversity that so often mar our relationships now will be eliminated. In that day we will have a fresh view of each other, for we will see each other, not as we have come to know each other here below, in our sin, but rather as we were meant to be.

Moreover, we will see each other rewarded for faithful service in this life, for the Bible speaks of crowns that will be given to those who are faithful. The Lord himself has said, "Behold, I am coming soon! My reward is with me, and I will give to everyone according to what he has done" (Rev. 22:12). I am sure that there is a wrong way of thinking of rewards. If we are serving only for what we can get out of the arrangement, we are no more than hirelings. Again, if we are working for rewards in this life—for money or the praise others may (or may not) give us—we are not fit to be Christ's servants. On the other hand, there is a right way to think about rewards, for the prospect of rewards is set before us as one reason why the patriarchs and other biblical characters were faithful. They had much to discourage them. Often there were severe trials, hardships, beatings, pain, and ridicule. But they endured because they were "looking ahead to [their] reward" (Heb. 11:26).

One of our great hymns, written by Heinrich Schenk early in the eighteenth century and translated into English by Francis Cox, speaks of these rewards:

Who are these like stars appearing,
    These before God's throne who stand?
Each a golden crown is wearing;
    Who are all this glorious band?
Alleluia! Hark, they sing,
Praising loud their heavenly King.

Who are these of dazzling brightness,
    These in God's own truth arrayed,
Clad in robes of purest whiteness,
    Robes whose lustre ne'er shall fade,
Ne'er be touched by time's rude hand?
Whence come all this glorious band?

These are they who have contended
    For their Savior's honor long,
Wrestling on till life was ended,
    Following not the sinful throng;
These, who well the fight sustained,
Triumph through the Lamb have gained.

In the day of our heavenly reunion we shall have those rewards, if we are faithful. And we shall rejoice in the triumphs of other Christians. Do you not think, since this will be true, that you could rejoice with them now? We tend to be critical of one another; and, of course, sometimes there are grounds for it. We do sin; we are unfaithful. But by God's grace we are also, at times, faithful, for which we shall be rewarded. If only we could see this, we would regard one another differently. We would rejoice in the triumphs, rather than bemoan the faults. We would pray for one another fervently.

So let us pray and work. Let us do so until the day when the entire ransomed church of God is raised to be with Jesus and is made like him.

177

"I Am the Way and the Truth and the Life"

John 14:5–6

Thomas said to him, "Lord, we don't know where you are going, so how can we know the way?"

Jesus answered, "I am the way and the truth and the life. No one comes to the Father except through me."

There are many offensive things about Christianity, at least for some people, but the chief offense of Christianity is its founder and his extraordinary claims. It is true that the claims of Jesus of Nazareth often are not spoken of or taken at face value; when that happens it is possible to present Jesus as the lovely, indulgent rabbi who was everyone's friend. But sooner or later his claims about himself become known, and the offense emerges.

Not long ago I was talking with a Hebrew Christian whose work is in Jewish evangelism. He talked about the various approaches being made to Jewish people today, some of which go to great lengths to avoid the offense I have been talking about. He pointed out that in some Hebrew-Christian organizations the word "Jesus" is not used. Instead, members of the group speak of *Yeshua* or *ha Mashiach* ("the Messiah"). Moreover, he explained that he had done this recently himself, to a great degree. But then he added, "I have found out that in the end this does not always accomplish a great deal. For whether you speak of *Yeshua* or *ha Mashiach* or the Messiah, eventually, if you are giving a true Christian witness, it is still Jesus you are talking about, and the offense remains."

I found my friend's words interesting, for they expressed in one area what I had already found to be true in others. Eliminate the true Jesus of Nazareth with his exclusive claims, substitute another Jesus, and Christianity will be popular. But preach the true Jesus, and some will inevitably be offended.

A Threefold Solution

Our expository study of John's Gospel has brought us to what is probably the most exclusive (and offensive) of all Christ's sayings. Indeed, it is probably the most exclusive statement ever made by anyone.

This is not to say that Jesus' other sayings, if properly understood, are not also exclusive; for in all his teaching he spoke with a sense of supreme authority and not as the other teachers before him (Matt. 7:29). Still, this saying is one of a number of exclusive claims given special prominence in John's Gospel, and even within this unique body of material it is exceptional. The sayings I am referring to are the "I am" statements of the Gospel, five of which have already been studied in our verse-by-verse exposition. The first was John 6:35—"I am the bread of life. He who comes to me will never be hungry, and he who believes in me will never be thirsty." This is a claim to be able to fulfill the deepest spiritual hungers of our race. The next four "I am" sayings were: "I am the light of the world" (8:12; 9:5); "I am the gate" (10:7, 9); "I am the good shepherd" (10:11, 14); "I am the resurrection and the life" (11:25). Each of these is a categorical and exclusive saying, as is the one yet to come—"I am the true vine" (15:1, 5). But none is as comprehensive and therefore also as objectionable as the one to which we come now.

In this verse Jesus says categorically, "I am the way and the truth and the life." Then he adds, lest anyone should misunderstand him, "No one comes to the Father except through me" (14:6).

At the same time, we must acknowledge that if these words are true, as Christians believe they are, then, although they are indeed exclusive, they ought not to be offensive, for they are actually what we most need as human beings. They should be received with joy and thanksgiving. Before sin entered the world, Adam and Eve, the first people, enjoyed a threefold privilege in their relation to God. First, they were in communion with God. Second, they knew God and the truth that flowed from him. Third, they possessed spiritual life. However, when they disobeyed God and fell into sin, they lost this privilege. Instead of enjoying communion with God, they experienced alienation from him. Instead of knowing the truth, they fell into falsehood and error. Instead of possessing life, they began to know death. For God had promised, "When you eat of it [that is, of the tree of the knowledge of good and evil] you will surely die" (Gen. 2:17).

This is our human condition. We are alienated from God, ignorant of the truth, and condemned to spiritual and eventually physical death. The glory of Christ's claim is in its being a divine answer to our problem on each of these three levels. Instead of alienation, there is "the way" to God. Instead of ignorance and error, there is "the truth." Instead of death, there is "the life." So this text is actually the gospel, the good news of God.

All in Jesus

And it is all in Jesus; for the point of the verse—indeed, we can hardly miss it—is that Jesus is the answer on each of these three levels. This point is also reinforced by the context. As he spoke these words, Jesus was about to be crucified, and his disciples were aware, at least in part, that his soul was troubled about it. They realized that the approximately three-year relationship between them and him was coming to an end.

In their confusion the disciples began to ask questions, four of which occur in the immediate context of Jesus' claim to be the way, the truth, and the life. Peter asked the first one. Jesus had said that he was going away from the disciples; so Peter asked, "Lord, where are you going?" (13:36). A few moments later Thomas asked the question in a slightly different way. "Lord, we don't know where you are going, so how can we know the way?" (14:5). Philip asked, "Lord, show us the Father" (14:8), that is "Won't you give us a theophany?" Finally, the Judas who is usually called Jude demanded, "Lord, why do you intend to show yourself to us and not to the world?" (14:22). These four questions from four different men all arise out of the same situation and betray the same interests. Moreover, in each case Jesus answers them in virtually the same way. In one sense, he seems not to answer them directly at all. Yet, in another sense, he answers them on a most profound level; in each case he directs the thoughts of the disciples toward himself.

Jesus tells Peter that, although he cannot understand where Jesus is going now, one day he will follow him there. He answers Thomas's question about the way by saying, "I am the way." He tells Philip, "He who has seen me has seen the Father." To Jude's question about how Jesus will show himself to his own disciples, he replies by teaching about the future indwelling of his Spirit within every believer. In each case, Jesus is the answer to the problems involved. Is it alienation from God? He is the way. Is it a need for illumination? He is the truth. Is it death? He is the life.

The Way: Reconciliation

Each of these is important, of course; so each must be taken in its turn. The first to be considered is "the way." A way supposes two points, for it is the path from one point to another. In this case it is the way from man's total ruin in sin to the Father.

What do we mean by man's total ruin in sin, from which we need to be led by Christ to the Father? First, we mean the *guilt of sin*. The problem we deal with is how such sin can be put away. We are sinners in God's sight. God declares it, and our consciences concur with God's judgment. But what shall be done? Reformation will not do; for payment of a future debt can never discharge a past debt, and it is our past especially that haunts us. Some hope simply for God's mercy. But an act of mercy that does not also satisfy the claims of justice is unworthy of the great God of the universe. Besides this, God's mercy is already freely offered in Christ.

What shall be done? How shall sin be removed? The only way is that which God has already revealed in Jesus. God has sent his own Son, made a man, to enter into a covenant union with his people so that he becomes one with them and eligible to bear their sin upon himself. He undertakes to be their substitute, dying in their place, bearing in his own body God's just wrath against sin, and then by his death removing the guilt and punishment of that sin forever. As a result of Christ's death in place of his people, sin has been blotted out as by a thick cloud (Isa. 43:25; 44:22), removed "as far as the east is from the west" (Ps. 103:12), placed behind God's back (Isa. 38:17), cast "into the depths of the sea" (Micah 7:19). Our sins are forgiven (Col. 2:13) and forgotten (Heb. 10:17). They are gone.

Would you escape from your sin and the guilt that goes with it? Jesus is the way. He is the perfect and only way.

Besides this, Jesus is also the way from *the power of sin* to the Father. This too is our concern; for we do not wish only to be justified, we wish to live a life pleasing to the Father. How is this done? It is done through Jesus and the knowledge of our position in him. Charles Haddon Spurgeon once spoke of this in these words: "Whenever I feel that I have sinned, and desire to overcome that sin for the future, the devil at the same time comes to me and whispers, 'How can you be a pardoned person and accepted with God while you sin in this way?' If I listen to this I drop into despondency, and if I continued in that state I should fall into despair, and should commit sin more frequently than before; but God's grace comes in and says to my soul, 'Thou hast sinned; but did not Jesus come to save sinners? Thou art not saved because thou art righteous; for Christ died for the ungodly.' And my faith says, 'Though I have sinned, I have an advocate with the Father, Jesus Christ the righteous, and though I am guilty, yet by grace I am saved and I am a child of God still.' And what then? Why, then the tears begin to flow, and I say, 'How could I ever sin against my God who is so good to me? Now I will overcome that sin,' and I get strong to fight with sin through the conviction that I am God's child."[1]

Doubts and fears drive the Christian farther into sin, for they obscure God. Faith in God leads to holiness; for this causes us to stand against sin and go on knowing that the way is forever open for us into God's presence.

The Truth: Illumination

The second of Christ's claims is to be "the truth," especially the truth about the Father, which includes all other truth. He did not say, "I have come to *tell* you the truth about the Father." Nor did he say, "I have come to point to the truth about the Father." He said, "I *am* the truth." "I and the Father are one," said Jesus (John 10:30). "He who has seen me has seen the Father" (John 14:9).

What do we see in Jesus about God the Father? What do we learn about reality? First, that God is *personal*. He is a person. He is not an impersonal force in the universe, a force that has merely set the world in motion or governs it impartially through the abstract laws of matter and motion. The existence of a god like that might explain some scientific phenomena, but it would not explain self-conscious life, such as that possessed by animals or man. God is not impersonal. God is one who, with the full traits of personality, desires to communicate with persons and wants them to know him. Through Jesus, we know that he wants that.

In him we also see that God is *holy*. We cannot learn that God is holy from looking in any other direction. In the world we see both good and evil, order and disorder, and often the two are mingled. In the heavens we see impartiality at best, if not rather cold indifference or hostility. If we were to judge from what we see in the world or in the heavens, we could only conclude that God is amoral or that he does not care about evil. But Jesus is holy. He is without sin. He has declared that God is like himself in his holiness.

Jesus also reveals that God is a God of *mercy*. He is a God of love. So we are told, and indeed we see it demonstrated, that God is not deaf to the cries of mankind. Even while requiring justice, God came to people, willing to die for them, in their place, and thus provide peace, joy, goodness, self-control, and all other blessings of the Christian life. A personal, holy, loving God—that is what Jesus has to tell you about him.

The Life: Regeneration

The third part of Christ's claim is to be "the life"—for all who believe on him, the emancipator from death. On this point, Arthur W. Pink writes: "The whole Bible bears solemn witness to the fact that the natural man is spiritually lifeless. He walks according to the course of this world; he has no love for the things of God. The fear of God is not upon him, nor has he any concern for His glory. *Self* is the center and circumference of his existence. He is alive to the things of the world, but is *dead* to heavenly things. The one who is out of Christ exists, but he has no spiritual life. When the prodigal son returned from the *far* country the father said, 'This, my son, was *dead*, and is alive again; he was lost, and is found' (Luke 15:24)."[2] Christ can make such persons alive. Indeed, he promises to give life to all who will come to him.

This makes for great encouragement in the living of the Christian life, for if the life Christ gives is God's life, then that life is eternal life. And the Christian can no more perish than can God the Father. This is what is taught in John 3:16, that verse that so many know. "For God so loved the world that he gave his one and only Son, that whoever believes in him should not perish but have eternal life."

Does it really mean everlasting life? Yes, it does. And in case we are still inclined to doubt it, Jesus adds just a few chapters later, "My sheep listen to my voice; I know them, and they follow me. I give them eternal life, and they shall never perish; no one can snatch them out of my hand" (John 10:27–28).

Will You Come?

Christ came that you might have life. Will you come to him right where you are? You *can* come. You can come *now.* Jesus does not require you to do anything. What could you do, even if you wished to do something? Would you seek to find the way to God and then walk in it? How can you? He is the Way, and he has come to you rather than making you come to him. Would you study to find out the truth before you believe in God? How can you do that? He is the truth; Scripture presents him fully to your eyes. Would you attempt to awaken yourself out of your spiritual lethargy by self-effort? How can you do even that? He is the life you need; he offers himself to you freely.

There is nothing to do, except to receive him by faith. There is nothing to achieve, no improvements to be made, no lessons to learn. Just believe on Jesus. Accept him for what he claims to be—the way to God, the truth about God, the life of God. Jesus did not say, "I am one of an indefinite number of equally valid ways to God, an aspect of truth, or a phase of life." He said, "I am *the* way and *the* truth and *the* life; no one comes to the Father except through me."

178

The Only Way Home

John 14:6

Jesus answered, "I am the way and the truth and the life. No one comes to the Father except through me."

The exclusive claim of the Lord Jesus Christ to be "the way and the truth and the life" is wrapped up in three phrases. He claims to be the way to God, indeed, the only way; he claims to be the truth about God, himself the truth; and he claims to be spiritual life, not merely the way to life. We would think, as we read that phrase, that it has said all that needs to be said. Yet, as we read the Lord's own words, we find that immediately after saying, "I am the way and the truth and the life," he says the whole thing over again in different words, lest we misunderstand it. He says, "No one comes to the Father except through me." If the Lord stated this a second time, lest we misunderstand it, then we should look at it a second time also.

Only through Jesus

Taken together, these phrases mean that Christianity makes an exclusive claim. People sometimes suggest that we are narrow-minded as Christians when we say that Christ is the only way to God, and we have to confess that this is precisely what we are at this point. We are as narrow as the Lord Jesus Christ. The Lord said—this is the emphasis of the verse—that he is the only way to God. There is no other way. So while it would be nice for us to equivocate on this point and say, in order to win friends and influence people, that other ways have some value—though we would like to say this, we are nevertheless unable to do so. Rather, we find ourselves affirming with the Lord Jesus Christ and with all the biblical writers that there is no salvation apart from Jesus.

Many verses teach it: 1 Corinthians 3:11—"No one can lay any foundation other than the one already laid, which is Jesus Christ"; Acts 4:12—"Salvation is found in no one else, for there is no other name under heaven given to men, by which we must be saved"; 1 Timothy 2:5—"For there is one God and one mediator between God and men, the man Christ Jesus."

If you are one who is rejecting all this, if you are one who perhaps is interested in Christianity but not exclusively, if you think that perhaps Jesus Christ is *a* way to God but not *the* way to God, I want to stress that, according to his teaching, he is the only way and that any attempt to find another way is folly, is bound to produce despair, and is perverse. The tragedy is that apart from the grace of God folly, despair, and perversity characterize each one of us. We are fools because we seek another way. We despair because there is no other way to be found. We are perverse because God has told us that there is only one way. Therefore, in turning from him to try to find another way we dishonor him.

The Fool Has Said

First, there is the folly of trying to find another way. Why is it folly? It is folly because, if a way to God has been provided, it is nonsense to look for another. Who would seek for a second cure for cancer if a perfect cure had been found?

Yet this is the folly of the human heart in spiritual things. Jesus told about it in a parable that concerned a rich man. This man thought the way to life was through material possessions, so he spent a lifetime accumulating worldly goods. He was a farmer. He had produce. His wealth was in the storage of his barn. When the barn became too small for what he was accumulating, he said, "I'll tear down my old barn and build a bigger one that can hold my possessions." The Lord's comment on that man's life was: "You fool! This very night your life will be demanded from you. Then who will get what you have prepared for yourself?" (Luke 12:20).

It is not the preacher who calls the unbeliever a fool. If that were the case, it would mean little indeed. The unbeliever could simply say to the preacher, "You are the fool for believing as you do." No, God is the one who calls men fools, fools for refusing to come to him in the way he has provided.

If we explore a bit deeper to find out why this is so, we find that it is because we are determined to provide for ourselves. During World War II, my father served as a doctor in the air force in the southern part of the United States. When he was released from military service he and the family began to drive northward to the family home in western Pennsylvania. It was only a few days before Christmas. So it was no surprise that on the way we ran into an early blizzard in the mountains of Tennessee. The storm got worse and worse and eventually halted our progress. At one point, however, before we had stopped for the night and as we were going uphill in a little mountain area with a dangerous precipice at our right, a car up ahead stopped. My father realized that, if the car ahead stopped, he would have to stop and, if he stopped, he would immediately begin to slide over the precipice. So he grabbed a blanket, jumped out of the car, ran around to the back wheels and stuck the blanket under one of them to stop our descent. We were stopped. But there we were, stranded in the blizzard on the mountainside.

My father was an Irishman, and at this point two things characterized him: first, pride in his achievement and, second, determination to bring off another. He had saved us from going over the precipice. Now he was going to get us up the mountain. So he began to work, shoveling snow and placing boards and blankets under the tires. He worked for about an hour, but without much success. All the time my two sisters and I, my mother, and my aunt were in the car, getting colder and colder. We were very depressed. Suddenly a truck with wonderful traction came by. This truck moved ahead of us and stopped. It was obvious that the driver knew he could get going again. He got out, came back to my father and said, "I have a chain. Would you like me to hitch onto your car and take you up the mountain?"

Do you know what my father said? He said, "No, thanks. We're doing fine." And he did do fine! But it was about sixty cold and gloomy minutes later!

God says that we are exactly like this spiritually, except for the fact that it does not matter whether we spend an hour, two hours, a year, or a lifetime. We are never going to get ourselves going up the road to salvation. So Jesus says, "Look, I've come to provide the way to salvation. I am the way. Don't be so foolish that you turn your back on me out of pride."

No Exit

Second, you are not only foolish, you are also on a trip to despair. If Jesus is right when he says, "I am the way . . . no one comes to the Father except through me," then no other way can be found. The Father is the source of all spiritual blessings. The way to the Father is through Jesus. If you are trying to find another way, you are never going to get those spiritual blessings. To go in any other way is to embark upon a road that has no exits and no destination.

Paul spells it out in the Book of Romans, pointing to the different ways men and women try to reach God. There are three categories. First, there is the way of *natural theology*. This is the way of the man who goes out into the field at night and says, "I am going to commune with God in nature." It is the man who says, "I worship God on Sunday afternoon in my golf cart." Paul says that this is a dead end, because you cannot find God in nature. No man has ever found God in nature. You can find things about God in nature, but these condemn you.

Romans says that nature reveals two things about God. It reveals the "Godhead" of God, that is, his existence, and it reveals his "power," because obviously something or someone of considerable power stands behind what we observe. That is all that can be known of God in nature. So if you think you are going to find God in nature, you are destined to emptiness in your search. You cannot worship an eternal power; you cannot worship a supreme being; you cannot worship a law of nature. Moreover, says Paul, "You don't even try!" Because when you say to yourself, "I'm going to worship God in nature," what you are really doing is using nature as an excuse to avoid God. Actually you do not want to be with Christian people, nor do you wish to be under the preaching of the Word. You find it disturbing. What you are really trying to do is to escape from God into nature. If you worship anything at all, it is nature you worship; and the worship of nature is idolatry.

Some years ago, after I had given a message along these lines, a woman said, "I found that to be true in my work with the beach crowd in California."

I asked, "What do you mean?"

"Well," she said, "we used to have meetings on the beach, and I used to witness to the surfers. When I would speak to them about God, they would reply that they worshiped God in nature. At first I didn't know what to say, but after a while I caught on. I learned to ask, 'And what is God?' They would reply, 'My surfboard is my god.'" At least that is honest, but it is paganism and idolatry.

Second, there are people who try to find God in the way of human *morality*. They say, "God certainly likes good men and women; therefore, I'll be good, and I'll get to him that way." Paul says that this line will lead you to despair also. Why? We see the answer when we reason as follows. If God loves good people—and it is true that he does—how good do they have to be? The answer is that they have to be absolutely good, perfect, because God can settle for nothing less. But no one is perfect. So Paul says, "When you start like that, when you start thinking that you are going to please God by getting better and better, you fail to see that even if you could achieve the maximum goodness possible to anyone in this world, you would never get to God in that way because it would not be good enough.

We have a strange situation in the church today. The church has a message to proclaim; it begins with the total depravity of man. But this is offensive to most people. So the church gets cold feet at this point—ministers do, of course—and it backs off from preaching these things. Ministers say, "We admit that the Bible does say that all are sinners; it does say that all are dead in trespasses and sins; but it does not really mean that. It is hyperbole. What it really means is that we just need a little help. People are really pretty good underneath. So if we just appeal to their natural goodness, they'll come and be Christians. Besides, they'll join our churches and give us money."

Does the world congratulate the church for congratulating the world? Not at all! The world knows that this is not true. So you have people like Jean Paul Sartre and other existentialists leaping to their feet to say, "If the church is not going to tell the truth, we are going to tell the truth! We know that when you scratch beneath the veneer of mankind, when you get rid of the social conventions, when you get rid of the desire to be acceptable with other people by matching up to certain preestablished patterns of behavior, what you find beneath the surface is garbage. You find a sewer of corruption." The existentialist does not have the answer. The despair of the existentialist is proof of what lies at the end of his road. But at least he speaks out; he is not silent.

Then, in Romans 2:17–29, Paul says that there is a third way that people try; it is the way of *religion*, a sort of formalism. This person says, "If I cannot be righteous, at least I can do things that God likes. I'll be baptized. I'll be confirmed. I'll go to communion." Paul says that this leads to despair also. Why? Because it is based on a false conception of God. It suggests that God will settle for externals. Does he? No! People may settle for externals, but not God; he looks on the heart. God sees that although you can go through the rite of baptism, it does not mean a thing if your heart is not cleansed. He sees that although you may come to communion, it does not mean a thing unless you have first fed on Jesus Christ by faith and have drunk at that stream that he provides.

An Insult to God

To say that one is a fool for looking in another direction than Christ sounds insulting. To say that it leads to despair sounds grim. But there is worse to come. For seeking a way other than Jesus is not only foolish and leads to despair, it is perverse. It is insulting to God. How is it insulting? It is insulting because Jesus *said,* "I am the way and the truth and the life; no one comes to the Father except through me." So if you go another way, it is not merely that you are doing something for yourself, and it is certainly not the case that you are doing something praiseworthy. What you are really doing is saying to the Lord Jesus Christ, "Lord Jesus Christ, you are a liar!"

Do you think that God is going to be proud of you for trying to find your own way? Do you think that God is going to admire you for that, love you for that, praise you for that? God is going to regard this for what it is, an insult to the Lord Jesus Christ his Son, because that is the equivalent of saying, "You, Lord Jesus Christ, you in whom the Father is well pleased, cannot be trusted."

Furthermore, to seek another way is not only an insult to Christ, it is an insult to the love of God who planned the way of salvation out of his great love for the sinner. What the Lord Jesus Christ did was in fulfillment of the desires of his Father. He said, "I come (in the volume of the book it is written of me) to do your will, O God" (Heb. 10:7). It was God's will that Jesus Christ, his Son, should die in your place. So it is an insult to God to ignore it. Do you think that it was easy for God to send Jesus Christ to die for you? I am asking you fathers: Would it be easy for you to give up your son or your daughter, to see that son or daughter killed, in order that someone else might be saved? I ask you mothers: Would it be easy for you to have a son or daughter killed in your sight, to turn your back when you could save that son or daughter, in order to have someone else saved? Of course not! You who are brothers: Would you give up a sister? You who are sisters: Would you give up a brother? If it is not easy for you, why should you think that it would be easy for God? Yet that is what God did for you.

Do you think it was easy for the Lord Jesus Christ to stand with his disciples on the verge of his crucifixion and say, "I am the way"? He knew what it meant to be the way. It meant that he had to go to the cross; he had to die; he had to suffer; he had to have the Father turn his back on him while he was made sin for us; he had to have the wrath of God poured out upon him. That is what it meant when the Lord Jesus Christ said, "I am the way . . . no one comes to the Father except through me." Yet he said it.

Come . . . Come

So I ask: Is it anything but sinful, obstinate perversity for someone to say, "That is all very nice, but I am going to go another way"? To go another way is to condemn yourself to hell! For there is no other way. "There is one God and *one* mediator between God and men, the man Christ Jesus" (1 Tim. 2:5).

How foolish it would be, how much despair is involved, how perverse on your part to go away, saying, "Well, that is all very interesting, of course; but I'm going to look a bit farther." *Today* is the day of salvation! This may be the last opportunity you will ever have! I cannot promise that you will ever hear the gospel again. I cannot promise that the Holy Spirit will ever speak to your heart again, if he is speaking at this moment. Heed the invitation and come! The Bible says, "The Spirit and the bride say, 'Come!' And let him who hears say, 'Come' Whoever is thirsty, let him come; and whoever wishes, let him take the free gift of the water of life" (Rev. 22:17).

179

How to See God

John 14:7-11

"If you really knew me, you would know my Father as well. From now on, you do know him and have seen him."

Philip said, "Lord, show us the Father and that will be enough for us."

Jesus answered: "Don't you know me, Philip, even after I have been among you such a long time? Anyone who has seen me has seen the Father. How can you say, 'Show us the Father'? Don't you believe that I am in the Father, and that the Father is in me? The words I say to you are not just my own. Rather, it is the Father, living in me, who is doing his work. Believe me when I say that I am in the Father and the Father is in me; or at least believe on the evidence of the miracles themselves."

In the fourteenth chapter of John's Gospel, in the midst of the last discourses, one of Christ's disciples makes a request with which most Christian people can identify. The disciple was Philip. The request he made was, "Lord, show us the Father." It was the request to see God.

There are times when each of us earnestly wishes that the experience Philip asked of the Lord Jesus Christ could be possible. We know, of course, that God does not possess a tangible form. We even know that this is only what we ought to expect and that it is desirable. But still there are times when God seems so remote, so untouchable, that we earnestly wish we could see him. We would like to gaze upon God and hear his voice in words that actually strike our eardrums. In such moments we believe that if we could have this experience, then we should find it easier to live for God in the midst of this world. And—we must be honest here—we sometimes imagine that God is holding out on us, making it more difficult for us by denying this experience. Have you ever had these thoughts? If you have, then the words of the Lord Jesus Christ to Philip in the upper room should be of great interest to you.

Knowing God

We must notice, however, before we begin to look at Christ's answer, that Philip's question arose in the context of Christ's teaching about knowing God, so that in this case Jesus actually provoked his disciple's question. A moment before Jesus had taught that he was the sole way to God. "No one comes to the Father except through me," he said. Then he went on, "If you really knew me, you would know my Father as well. From now on, you do know him and have seen him" (v. 7). What do you think of that statement? Do you think that it is easily comprehensible? Do you grasp its meaning at once? This statement makes one stop and ponder. However, if it does that for us now, at this point in history, I am convinced that it most certainly had that effect upon the disciples and was therefore spoken by Jesus precisely for that purpose.

In other words, it is apparent from the nature of the statement, and the context, that Jesus spoke as he did in order to provoke a discussion on this subject. He was about to leave his disciples. He knew that when he should be taken from them they would be plunged into a dark and melancholy despair. In their despair God would seem extremely remote. Consequently, he introduced the subject in order to teach them that they had already seen God and were therefore to know him from this time forward, whether they realized it or not.

"From now on, you do know him and have seen him," he said. Philip fixed his thoughts upon the idea of seeing, as we often do, and demanded, "Lord, show us the Father and that will be enough for us" (v. 8).

Limitations of Seeing

As Philip asked this question he was probably thinking of those Old Testament examples in which a person or group of persons is said to have seen God. Moses was one. He had asked to see God's glory, and God had replied, "I will cause all my goodness to pass in front of you, and I will proclaim my name, the LORD, in your presence" (Exod. 33:19). Then the Lord placed Moses within a cleft of rock, covered the space with his hand, and passed by. Elijah had a similar experience when the Lord caused a great wind, an earthquake, and a fire to pass before his prophet, though the Lord was not in the wind, the earthquake, or the fire. He was in the still small voice that Elijah heard afterward (1 Kings 19:11–12). There is also a verse that tells us that Moses and Aaron, Nadab and Abihu, and seventy of the elders of Israel "saw the God of Israel. Under his feet was something like a pavement of sapphire, clear as the sky itself " (Exod. 24:10).

None of these passages mean that the persons involved actually saw God as he is in himself. God had told Moses, "You cannot see my face, for no one may see me and live" (Exod. 33:20). Still, the experience of the others was something great, and this was good enough for Philip, whatever it was. He therefore asked Jesus, whom he believed could do anything, for a theophany.

But how did the Lord reply? Instead of granting the request or even attempting to explain why Philip's desire was unwise or impossible, Jesus began to teach what it really means to see God, and how to see him. The point with which he began was the limitation of the kind of seeing Philip had in mind.

To understand this point we need to see the contrast implied in Christ's next statement. Philip had said, "Lord, we would *know* God if we could just *see* him." But Jesus says, making the contrast, "It is strange that you say that, Philip. For I have been with you three years. You have seen me throughout that period, and yet you do not know me. Why then do you think that seeing would help you know God?" This is the meaning of the statement, "Don't you know me, Philip, even after I have been among you such a long time?" (v. 9). Obviously, the kind of seeing that Philip had in mind does not lead to a true knowledge of anyone.

A Right Kind of Seeing

The Lord Jesus Christ did not stress merely the limitations of the kind of seeing Philip envisioned, however. He also talked about the right kind of seeing, a seeing centered entirely in himself. He is the object of it. Jesus continued, "Anyone who has seen me has seen the Father. How can you say, 'Show us the Father'? (v. 9). True, there is a seeing that is inadequate. But, on the other hand, there is a seeing that is altogether right. In this seeing, the sequence is obviously: (1) seeing the Lord Jesus Christ with understanding, (2) coming to know Jesus as a result of that seeing, and (3) coming to know God through knowing Jesus.

But what kind of seeing is this? The seeing involved is illustrated by the story of Peter and John's trip to the tomb of Jesus, recorded just six chapters farther on in John's Gospel. In that story three different words are used for "seeing," though each is translated by the identical word "see" in our Bibles. The first is *blepō*. It is used of John who, having outdistanced Peter in the race to the tomb, stooped down "and looking in, *saw* the linen clothes lying." This is the simplest word for "see." It merely means that the image of the graveclothes within the tomb had impressed itself upon the retina of John's eyes. In a few moments Peter arrived. Since he was not one to stand around doing nothing, Peter pushed John aside and actually entered the tomb. Here he had opportunity to observe the graveclothes; so, in this case, a different word for "see" is used. The word is *theōreō*. It means to "puzzle over" or "scrutinize." In this case, Peter needed to puzzle over the fact that the clothes were there but the body was gone. If the body had been taken away, why were the graveclothes not taken away with it? Or, on the other hand, if the bands had been removed, why were they not scattered about the tomb and the spices spilled? Instead of this, the bands were exactly as they had been when they were wound around the body, and the head cloth was set off by itself just as it had been when it was around the head of the Master. At this point John tells us that he entered, saw what Peter saw, and believed. Only now the word is not *theōreō* or *blepō*. It is *oraō*, which means "to see with understanding." That is why John says that he "saw and believed." He saw that the only thing that would account for the arrangement of the graveclothes was a resurrection.

That is precisely the word used in John 14, where Jesus says that the one who has "seen" him has "seen" the Father. He means that the one who perceives who he is perceives God.

The point can be made in another way also. Notice that Philip had asked to be "shown" the Father. This is the verb *deiknumi*, which, in effect, calls for a demonstration. Jesus replied that what was needed was not so much a demonstration as an apprehension. It is not a seeing but a perceiving that is important.

This has great bearing for us, of course, for if seeing physically is the important thing, we are deprived. Not only can we not see God; we cannot even see Jesus, which was at least Philip's privilege. Jesus is simply not here. We cannot observe him. On the other hand, if perceiving is the true seeing, then we are not deprived at all, for we can perceive Jesus and, perceiving him, can perceive and know God. Indeed, we can know him as well and in exactly the same way as he was known by these believing contemporaries of the Lord Jesus.

Believing Is Seeing

To speak of the Lord's "believing contemporaries" leads us to the final section of these verses, for it can hardly escape the notice of any careful reader that the discussion of knowing and seeing, which fills the first half of the paragraph, gives way to a discussion of belief (or faith) in the second. In the first half, the word "know" occurs four times and the words "seen" or "show" five times. In the second half (including verse 12), not one of these three words can be found. But the word "believe," "believed," or "believes" is repeated four times over.

Why? It is no great mystery. It is merely another example of the New Testament teaching that in spiritual things belief must come first, after which true seeing will follow. Earlier in the Gospel, Jesus had said of the people of his day, "Unless you people see miraculous signs and wonders, you will never believe" (4:48). This was a true description of the thinking of vast numbers of men and women in his time, as we pointed out when we studied that verse. It is the old philosophy, "Seeing is believing," upon which the world operates. But Jesus inverts it. On the occasion on which the words I have just quoted were spoken, Jesus instructed a nobleman, who had come to him for the healing of his child, "You may go. Your son will live" (v. 50), as a result of which the nobleman believed and then saw the thing he had requested. In the same way, in chapter 11, just before he is to raise Lazarus from the dead, Jesus turns to unbelieving Martha and asks, "Did I not tell you that if you believed you would see the glory of God?" (v. 40).

If this is only a human matter, the suggestion that we should believe without sight is absurd. Who wants to believe without sight? No one. And no one does. On the other hand, in spiritual matters it is entirely reasonable to do this, because in this case we are dealing not with a mere man but with God. Jesus is God. To believe him is the most logical act in the universe.

Faith's Object

The matter of seeing God stops with believing on Jesus, but we are not to suppose by this that belief is therefore some subjective, intangible thing, as if we are to work ourselves up to faith by wishful thinking. This is not the biblical idea at all. Consequently, Jesus goes on to talk about belief in two things or, as we might also say, on two levels. The first level is belief in his words; the second is belief in his works. In other words, belief is as objective and tangible as the words and works of Jesus. Jesus does not call for blind faith. He calls for a thinking faith. He here challenges faith by asking us to test his claims on the basis of the things said and the deeds done.

Have you tested Christ's words? In one of his writings Charles Haddon Spurgeon tells of an old unbeliever who was dying. A great Scotch preacher by the name of Innis, came to see him. He inquired of his faith in Christ and was told, "Mr. Innis, I am relying solely on the mercy of God; God is merciful, and he will never condemn a man forever." When he became worse and was nearer death, Mr. Innis went to him again. This time the man said, "Oh, Mr. Innis, my hope is gone; for I have been thinking that if God is merciful, God is just too; and what if, instead of being merciful to me, he should be just to me? What would then become of me? I must give up my hope in the mere mercy of God; tell me how to be saved." The minister then told him of Christ's words and deeds. He told him how Christ had come into the world to save sinners. He told him how he had promised to do this by going to the cross to die in their place, how this had been done, and how Jesus had promised that none of those who had been given to him by the Father should ever be lost. "Ah," said the infidel, "Mr. Innis, there is something solid in that; I can rest on that. I have found that I cannot rest on anything else."[1] There is nothing else. Belief is meaningless unless it rests on the words and works of Jesus.

Little Faith

But perhaps even now you feel that your faith is too small and that you will therefore never come to see God. If this is the case, notice that before he moves on to other subjects Jesus stops to say a word just to you. You may not be able to believe on the basis of his teaching alone, he argues. But you can surely believe on the basis of what he has done. "Believe me when I say that I am in the Father and the Father is in me; or at least believe on the evidence of the miracles themselves" (v. 11). To believe on the basis of the miracles is not the best kind of faith, but it is true faith regardless. It is better than no faith at all.

Better than thinking about faith itself is to think on faith's object.

Some time ago I came upon this illustration from the works of Donald Barnhouse. Barnhouse had been in Palestine and had been taken to the great hall of the Sanhedrin. In that hall there is a window which looks out over the wailing wall, at the base of which stand groups of rabbis, slowly beating their breasts in sorrow for sin while repeating phrases from the Book of Lamentations. As Barnhouse looked he saw that above their heads, along the high expanse of the wall, grew the long trailing plant identified as the hyssop of the Bible.

Barnhouse asked about the plant and learned that it has a remarkably shallow root. Often it is not over a half-inch long. But with this root the hyssop clings to the surface of the rock, drawing its sustenance from the air, wind, rain (when there is any), and small particles of nourishment in the rock itself. From that tiny root the plant flourishes, sometimes growing to a length of twelve or fourteen feet. "What a great plant to grow from such a slender root," thought Barnhouse. What a symbol of the faith God calls for![2]

In itself faith is worthless, just as worthless as the root if it should become unattached. If one grasps the branch and pulls the root away from the rock, the branch will soon die. To be of value the root must cling to the rock. Thus, faith, which is nothing in itself, becomes the key to life when it clings to the Lord Jesus Christ, the Rock of Ages. It is through faith in him that we see God.

180

Greater Things Than Jesus' Things

John 14:12

"I tell you the truth, anyone who has faith in me will do what I have been doing. He will do even greater things than these, because I am going to the Father."

$\mathbf{I}$t is unlikely that any of us has ever been offered a million dollars. But if we can imagine how breathlessly overwhelmed we would be by such an offer, we can begin to appreciate what our reaction should be to the promise of Jesus in John 14:12.

Jesus has been attempting to comfort his disciples, for they were distressed and dispirited at the announcement that he was going away from them. He had promised that he was going to prepare a home for them in heaven and that he was going to return for them so that they could be with him. Then, after dealing with a question raised by Philip, he added solemnly, but obviously also to provide comfort, "I tell you the truth, anyone who has faith in me will do what I have been doing. He will do even greater things than these, because I am going to the Father."

Greater works than Jesus' works! That is the promise. But when we think of it the promise seems unrealistic, if not totally incredible. Jesus had healed the sick, calmed the troubled sea of Galilee, fed thousands with a few small loaves of bread and several fishes, raised the dead. These were great works, probably the greatest miracles we can imagine! We cannot do them. But if that is the case, how could Jesus have said what he did say?

What Kind of Works?

There are only two approaches to this verse other than saying that Jesus was simply mistaken. The first takes it as referring to miracles but then either limits the reference or seeks to explain why such miracles are not done today. The second refers it to a different work entirely.

Some who take the verse as referring to miracles find a supposed qualification in the word "faith." The promise is only for those who have faith in Jesus, such interpreters say. Consequently, since no one does such works today (at least no one we know), we clearly do not believe enough. Our faith is lacking. It is enough to reply to this viewpoint that since we are to do greater works than Jesus' works, it would be necessary for us, according to this interpretation, to have greater faith than his, which is clearly impossible. Besides, Jesus does not say, "Anyone who has faith in me with a sufficient degree of faith" or even "Anyone who has intense faith." He merely says, "Anyone who has faith in me," and that would include not just the strong in faith, but any Christian.

Others recognize these truths but seek to limit the verse by applying it to the apostles only. They did miracles. Consequently, this was a fulfillment. Arther W. Pink is one who apparently holds this view, at least as regards the first half of the verse. He writes, "Some have understood this to refer to *all* the genuine followers of Christ. But this is manifestly wrong, for there is *no* Christian on earth today who can do the miracles which Christ did—cleanse the leper, give sight to the blind, raise the dead. . . . We submit that 'He that believeth on me,' like the expression 'them that believe' in Mark 16:17, of whom it was said certain miraculous signs should follow them, refers to a *particular* class of persons, and that these expressions must be modified by their reference and setting." Pink shows that the verse was fulfilled in the early miracles performed by the apostles, as Hebrews 2:4 seems to indicate—"God also testified to it by signs, wonders and various miracles, and gifts of the Holy Spirit distributed according to his will."[1]

This may be part of the story. But one may wonder, even then, if the disciples for all their miracles may be said to have matched, let alone exceeded, Jesus' miracles. If this is a valid objection, the answer should be sought in a different direction entirely.

Spiritual Works

Here we are helped by the knowledge that God does not look at things as we do and, therefore, certainly does not share our view of what constitutes greatness. Why, for instance, should the physical miracles be considered "great" at all? Why should this be the thing Jesus refers to? One clue that it is not comes from Luke 10, in a passage that gives Christ's response to the disciples after they had returned from their first successful preaching mission. They had returned, we are told, "with joy and said, 'Lord, even the demons submit to us in your name'" (v. 17). In other words, they were thrilled that they had been able to cast out devils. But Jesus replied, "I have given you authority to trample on snakes and scorpions and to oversome all the power of the enemy; nothing will harm you. However, do not rejoice that the spirits submit to you, but rejoice that your names are written in heaven" (vv. 19–20).

Here Jesus explicitly weighed the value of physical miracles over against the value of having passed out of spiritual death into salvation and chose the spiritual miracle without hesitation. If that is so in Luke 10, why should it not be so also in our text from the last discourses?

Leon Morris is one who sees the verse in this light: "What Jesus means we may see in the narratives of the Acts. There are a few miracles of healing, but the emphasis is on the mighty works of conversion."[2] H. A. Ironside concurs: "He was not speaking of miracles. His chief work was not performing miracles but revealing the Father, bringing knowledge of the Father. It was that of which He was speaking. As a result of His three-and-a-half years of ministry, when He left this scene He said good-bye to a group of about five hundred disciples. There were, doubtless, a few more scattered about but not very many. Very few saw in Him the revelation of the Father. But go on a few days—fifty days later. Ah, then Peter and the rest of the eleven stand up on the day of Pentecost and the third Person of the Trinity comes upon them in power and they are prepared to witness for Him. They preached a crucified and risen Christ, and what happened? Three thousand believed! Probably more in that one day than in all the three-and-a-half years of our Lord's ministry. . . . When you realize that when Jesus left this scene, committing His gospel to a little group of eleven men in order that they might carry it to the ends of the earth, at that time the whole world, with the exception of a few in Israel, was lost in the darkness of heathenism. But in three hundred years Christianity closed nearly all the temples of the heathen Roman Empire, and numbered its converts by millions. These were the greater works, and down through the centuries He still carries on this ministry."[3]

Let us summarize what this verse means:

1. The works Christ refers to are spiritual works, primarily the work of regeneration that takes place when the gospel is proclaimed through the power of God's Holy Spirit. This is suggested by two characteristics: first, that the word "things" rather than "signs" or "miracles" is used, and second, that in the phrase "and greater things than these shall he do" the word "things" does not actually occur. There is no word at that point, so the literal translation would simply be "and greater." The point is that Christians will do something greater even than the works of Jesus.

2. The reference in the verse is to every Christian, for this is the only possible meaning of the phrase "Anyone who has faith in me." This does not

mean that every Christian will have the ability to be a great evangelist. There is a diversity of gifts. But it does mean that a testimony that leads to the conversion of any individual is greater, in the Lord's sight, than any physical miracle and that the combined efforts of all God's people, leading to the conversion of millions, is tremendous.

3. Finally, there may also be a sense in which the verse applies to all works of compassion, healing, and progress, which, although not miraculous in a supernatural sense, nevertheless in a nearly miraculous way have followed almost inevitably upon the preaching of the gospel.

The Conditions

The promise of Jesus in John 14:12 is a great promise. It is a thrilling promise, if only because it applies to each one of us personally. Great works! Greater works than Jesus' works! We shall do these, if we are Christ's disciples. And yet, we must not get carried away, for as we look at the text more closely we discover that there are four conditions to actually enjoying Christ's promise.

First, we must *have faith in Jesus*. This is found in John 14:12 itself, for Jesus begins the sentence by saying, "Anyone who has faith in me." That is as much as to say, "If anyone will believe in me" or "What I have to say now is for my followers." Do you believe on Jesus? I do not mean, "Do you believe that he existed?" I do not even mean, "Do you believe that he is who he claimed to be; namely, the Son of God and the world's Savior?" I mean, Is he *your* Savior? Have *you* trusted him as such? Have you let go trusting in your own strength, particularly in spiritual things, and have you allowed him to be your Savior from sin and your Lord? Without the fulfillment of this previous condition, none of the promises mentioned are for anyone.

Second, we must *pray*. This is the first of three additional themes discussed in the next verses (vv. 13–18), all of which are important. The verses on prayer are themselves a great promise: "And I will do whatever you ask in my name, so that the Son may bring glory to the Father. You may ask me for anything in my name, and I will do it" (vv. 13–14). Obviously, praying is itself a condition for doing the mighty works that Jesus talks about earlier. Unfortunately, many of us are like those spoken of in James, who, we are told, "do not have, because they do not ask" (4:2).

Do you ask God specifically to see those you know and for whom you are concerned converted? I do not mean, Do you pray generally? I mean, Do you pray specifically and expect God to answer you? R. A. Torrey tells of one case that could be repeated a thousand times over. One Sunday the mother of the most difficult boy he had ever known came up to him after the service and said, "Do you know _____ (calling her boy by name)?"

Torrey replied, "Yes, I know him." Indeed, everyone knew him.

"You know he is not a very good boy," said the mother.

"Yes," Torrey answered, "I know he is not a very good boy." That, of course, was a decidely euphemistic way of putting it; in point of fact, he was the terror of the neighborhood.

This heavyhearted mother then said, "What shall I do?"

Torrey replied, "Have you ever tried prayer?"

"Why," she said, "of course I pray."

"No," said Torrey, "I don't mean that. I mean have you ever asked God definitely to regenerate your boy and have you expected him to do it?"

"I do not think I have ever been as definite as that."

"Well," said the preacher, "you go right home and be just as definite as that." Torrey then reports that she did go home and was just as definite as that, and that it was probably from that very day, certainly from that week, that the boy was transformed and began to grow up into a fine young man.[4]

We need not believe—we must be honest here—that in every case the prayers we make will have such immediate and striking results. Obviously many do not. On the other hand, we can believe that any prayer that is truly inspired by Christ and in the name of Christ will be answered. The point, however, is not in the time God chooses to take in answering our prayers, but simply that we are to pray. The "greater things" are for those who, first, have believed on Christ, and second, pray.

Third, they are for those whose lives are marked by *a love for Christ expressed in obedience*. This can be seen in the verse that says, "If you love me, you will obey my commands" (v. 15). It is interesting that these two things go together—love for Christ and keeping his commands—and it is clear why this is so. If we do not keep Christ's commands, we cannot really say that we love him; for what we call love is mere sentimentality and affection.

Some time ago I heard a missionary to Nepal talk about spiritual motivation. His name was Thomas Hale, and he and his wife were serving in the remote village of Amp Pipal, about one hundred miles from Kathmandu. He had shown slides of his work, including beautiful panoramas of the surrounding mountains, the fabled Hindu Kush. There were spectacular shots of Mt. Everest. But then the slides were turned off, and he turned to the group and said quietly, "Those are beautiful views, but you must remember that they are taken during the mere ten percent of the time when the mountains are not covered by clouds. Nor do they show the cold, poverty, dirt or disease. Beauty like that will take you to Nepal. But only love for Christ and obedience to his command to evangelize the world will keep you there." He was right. If we are to do great works for Christ, we must have a fervent love for Christ; and we must determine to keep his commandments.

Finally, we must be *empowered by Christ's own Spirit*, the Holy Spirit. This is spoken of in verses 16 and 17, in which Christ says, "And I will ask the Father, and he will give you another Counselor to be with you forever—the Spirit of truth. The world cannot accept him, because it neither sees him nor knows him. But you know him, for he lives with you and will be in you."

In one sense, the presence of Christ's Spirit is involved in all we have been speaking of previously, for we cannot believe without the Spirit. We cannot pray without the Spirit. We cannot love or obey without the Spirit. In another sense, however, this is also a separate point, for in mentioning it, Jesus reminds us that we can do nothing without him. Earlier he had said, "The words I say to you are not just my own. Rather, it is the Father, living in me, who is doing his work" (v. 10). Now it is as if we should say, echoing his teaching, "The words that we speak to you, we do not speak on our own; but the Spirit who dwells in us does the work." Can we say that? It is certain that we will never do the works that Jesus has for us to do until we can.

Words of Jesus

Do you hear Jesus speaking? Do you hear him calling you? He is saying, "I know that you are often discouraged. I know that the world seems harsh and unresponsive to the gospel. But remember this: I have ascended to the right hand of my Father in heaven, from which place I now rule. All authority in heaven and earth has been given to me; and it is on this basis, the basis of my authority, and in my strength that I send you forth to be my disciples. I am Lord over sin, death, hell, and the devil. You shall be lords over these forces also.

"When I was here on earth, I was in weakness. I performed only a few and very small works: I healed the sick, fed the hungry, raised the dead. Finally I let myself be crucified and put to death. Now I am the risen Lord, and it is my pleasure to do greater works than those I have mentioned. I want to do them through you. I have promised to draw people to myself as the gospel is preached. I call you to preach it. I commission you to go into all the world and teach people all that I have commanded you. I promise to go with you, to bless the message, and to overthrow strongholds of wickedness through your proclamation. You, Peter; you, James; John (George, Mary, Susan, Robert—whoever you may be), I promise to bless your witness to the extent that those who hear your message will either have to accept it or else, by rejecting it, complete their own spiritual destruction."

What do you say to that commission? Do not say, "Well, that is nice; but, of course, the Lord doesn't really mean it. There is nothing I can do." Rather say, "Then so be it; I am nothing, but by the grace of God I will do all things, through the strength of my Lord."

181

Praying in Jesus' Name

John 14:13–14

"And I will do whatever you ask in my name, so that the Son may bring glory to the Father. You may ask me for anything in my name, and I will do it."

It is probably impossible to have a greater promise by the Lord Jesus Christ than that recorded in John 14:12, the verse we looked at in our last study: "I tell you the truth, anyone who has faith in me will do what I have been doing. He will do even greater things than these, because I am going to the Father." But if there was a promise that could be considered greater, it would probably be the one that follows immediately afterward: "And I will do whatever you ask in my name, so that the Son may bring glory to the Father. You may ask me for anything in my name and I will do it" (vv. 13–14).

This promise was given to the disciples as one part of Jesus' attempt to comfort them in view of his pending departure. He was going to be taken from them. So he promises, first, that his going will not mean the end of his work on earth—they will continue it (v. 12)—and, second, that it will not mean the end of the communion they have enjoyed with him (vv. 13–14). He will be in heaven and they on earth. But prayer will remove all sense of distance and, indeed, be the key for their doing the "greater things" he promised.

There is comfort in this verse then, but it is not really comfort that makes the verse so striking or, as in the preceding promise, that so nearly takes our breath away. What is most striking is the scope of the promise, for it is not merely that those to whom he was speaking should have the privilege of prayer, nor even that he would hear their prayers and from time to time grant what they should ask. It is that Jesus would hear their prayers and grant their requests always.

There is an idea in vogue today, as Torrey points out in his book entitled *The Power of Prayer and the Prayer of Power,* that prayer does not mean that we are to get what we ask but that it is nevertheless good somehow. That is, we may not get our requests, but we will get something—something just as good as that for which we ask, and perhaps even better. It is no doubt true that many of us do not get what we pray for; for we pray foolishly and self-ishly, and God often does not grant what we ask. It is good that he does not, for we would bring many troubles on ourselves if all our requests were granted. At the same time, however, we have to say that this view is not the doctrine of prayer taught in the Bible, nor, to be specific, is it the doctrine of prayer taught here. The doctrine of prayer, according to the Bible, is that "there are certain people who can pray in a certain way and who will get not merely some good thing, or something just as good as what they ask, or something even better than what they ask, but *they will get the very thing that they ask for.*"[1] It is the promise that if these will ask *anything* in the name of Jesus, they will have it.

"In My Name"

We realize as we say this that there are certain conditions to be met, and the first of these is obviously contained in the words "in my name" or, as we must understand it, "in the name of Jesus." What does this mean? What does it mean to ask something of God in Jesus' name?

It means several things. The first thing it means is that we come to God as those who are identified with Jesus by faith, that is, as Christians. This is very important, for we must begin any teaching about prayer or any study of prayer by realizing that prayer is for Christians only. This is clear from these verses in two ways: (1) the word "you," which refers, not to the world gener-ally, but to the disciples and to those who should follow them in faith; and (2) the phrase "anyone who has faith in me," found just one verse earlier. These phrases limit the verses to Christians. Besides, as we must note, the Bible never promises that God will hear and answer a non-Christian's prayer.

We should add at this point, however, that God sometimes does answer the prayer of a non-Christian. This is what the old Puritan theologians called God's "uncovenanted blessings." But God does not promise to do so. He may hear an unbelieving prayer and answer it, particularly if it is by one in whom he is beginning to work and whom he intends to lead to full faith in Jesus Christ. But for Christians this otherwise fortuitous event is not just a possibility; it is a promise. It is the promise that the one who meets the con-dition of having believed on Jesus Christ (and the other conditions that will come in a moment) will have his prayers answered.

No Other Name

The second thing meant by the phrase "in my name" is that the one approaching God is approaching him on no other basis than on what the Lord Jesus Christ has done. Right here, of course, we have trouble, even as Christians, for often when we pray and do not get what we ask, it is because we have prayed, not in Jesus' name (though we may have said those words), but rather in our name imagining that we have some claim upon God.

R. A. Torrey, whom I mentioned earlier, tells a story that illustrates this point. He had been in Melbourne, Australia, for a series of meetings. One day as he went up onto the platform to speak, a note was thrust into his hands, which read, "Dear Dr. Torrey: I am in great perplexity. I have been praying for a long time for something that I am confident is according to God's will, but I do not get it. I have been a member of the Presbyterian Church for thirty years, and have tried to be a consistent one all the time. I have been superintendent in the Sunday school for twenty-five years, and an elder in the church for twenty years; and yet God does not answer my prayer and I cannot understand it. Can you explain it to me?"

Torrey took the note to the platform with him and read it. Then, because he had rightly detected something in the letter's tone, he answered like this: "It is perfectly easy to explain it. This man thinks that because he has been a consistent church member for thirty years, a faithful Sunday school superintendent for twenty-five years, and an elder in the church for twenty years, that God is under obligation to answer his prayer. He is really praying in his own name, and God will not hear our prayers when we approach Him in that way. We must, if we would have God answer our prayers, give up any thought that we have any claims upon God. There is not one of us who deserves anything from God. If we got what we deserved, every one of us would spend eternity in hell. But Jesus Christ has great claims on God, and we should go to God in our prayers not on the ground of any goodness in ourselves, but on the ground of Jesus Christ's claims."

At the close of the meeting a gentleman came up to Torrey and said, "I am the man who wrote that note. You have hit the nail square on the head. I did think that because I had been a consistent church member for thirty years, a Sunday school superintendent for twenty-five years, and an elder in the church for twenty years, that God was under obligation to answer my prayers. I see my mistake."[2]

Many people make the same mistake. They imagine that because they have done certain things for God they therefore have a claim upon God. But no sinful human being has any claim upon him. Only the Lord Jesus Christ has a claim. To pray in the name of Jesus is, therefore, first, to come to God as a Christian, having believed on Jesus, and, second, to come humbly, recognizing that we have no claims upon him but that Jesus himself does and that we can approach God solely on that basis.

In Raws's Name

Even at this point I suppose there are some who still think that praying in the name of Jesus is like waving a magic wand over our own desires in order to cause them to be granted. Such persons may admit that one must certainly be a Christian in order to pray effectively. They will even admit that we cannot come on the basis of our own merit. Indeed, that was the great Reformation principle! Every Christian knows that! Still, they persist in regarding the name of Christ as an incantation to get their desires. We need to add a third point, therefore. To pray in Jesus' name is to pray as one who lives the life of Christ. Consequently, it is to pray as he would pray and for what he desires.

Ralph L. Keiper had an excellent illustration of this point. He used to point out that at the Keswick Bible Conference grounds at Keswick, New Jersey, there is a work for alcoholics known as the Colony of Mercy. Through this colony, under the direction of its founder William Raws, son Addison C. Raws, and a grandson William A. Raws, men who have been ruined by drink are introduced to the Savior and are restored to society as they allow the Lord to be the remedy for their ruin.

Let us suppose, as Keiper suggests, that one of the men becomes tired of the rules of the colony and so leaves it for the nearby town, where he heads for the nearest bar. He enters and says to the bartender, "Give me a shot of gin in Raws's name."

The bartender is about to fill the order when the owner steps around the corner and asks, "What did you say you wanted?"

"I want a shot of gin in Raws's name!" answers the man as he places his right foot on the bar rail.

The owner of the saloon begins to question the customer. "Do you mean Addison Raws of the Colony of Mercy, the man whose father founded the Colony, and whose work it is to take a bum like you and make a man of him? Is this the Raws you mean?"

"You're right as a rabbit, Mister," says the derelict. "He's the very man."

The face of the owner clouds over with sternness. "You are a liar!" he says. "How dare you charge this drink to Raws? If you were really coming in his name, you would have passed this place by, or, if you had come in, you would be looking for someone like yourself to take back to the Colony. Dr. Raws is not a drinking man, and those who name his name are not customers of mine."

Keiper wrote, "To pray in the name of Christ is a serious matter, not to be taken lightly. We ask for many things without regard for our Lord, because we would please ourselves instead of Him. Wives would have husbands saved for the sake of having an inexpensive chauffeur to drive them to 'meetings,' or so they no longer would need to be embarrassed by the ladies of the church who find drinking, unsaved men wretched. Husbands, too, find their prayers unanswered because they continually criticize their wives in private, as well as public, forgetting that Christ never criticized His wife—the Church (1 Peter 3:7). A consistent, Christ-like conduct convinces us that God can trust us with His blessings. God will never waste a blessing or a kindness on a careless, selfish saint."[3]

God Glorified

There is one more requirement. Thus far we have looked at the phrase "in *my* name" and have found that it means the following three things: (1) that we must be Christians, (2) that we must approach God on the basis of Christ's merit and not on the basis of any supposed merit of our own, and (3) that we must pray as Christ would pray while at the same time living a life consistent with his desires. But there is also a second phrase in our text, and that is "that the Son may bring glory to the Father." This is very important, for having said that our prayers must be consistent with the desires of our Lord, we immediately go on to ask, "And what is it that the Lord Jesus Christ desires?" The answer, in its shortest form, is in this phrase. It is that God may be glorified. The application is that, if this was Jesus' desire, then it should obviously be our desire too.

This is a new thought for many people, for we are so filled with the idea that prayer is getting something from God, that we rarely consider that prayer is actually a means by which God gets something from us. What he wants from us is glory, a glory that will lead others to trust him.

Here I wish to draw upon another illustration by Ralph Keiper. Ralph, as those who knew him are aware, suffered from limited vision. What we can see at 100 feet he could see at 10. So obviously there were many times in his early life when he complained to God of his affliction. "Why should I suffer from this limitation? God could do something about it if he wanted to," he reasoned. He prayed about his problem and got nowhere. Moreover, he could not even see the reason for God's delay. He had tried to please the Lord as best he knew how. Why was God silent?

Then one Saturday afternoon, when as a young theological student he was idling over his books, the Holy Spirit began to speak to him and ask several questions: "What is the chief end of man?"

"To glorify God, and to enjoy him forever!" Ralph replied.

"Do you wish to glorify God?" the Holy Spirit countered.

"Of course!" the young student hastened to assure him.

"If you had the choice, what would you rather do, glorify God or have perfect vision?"

Ralph paused for a long while. His "of course" began to weaken. For, as he points out, sight is a very precious commodity, especially to those who do not have it. He had to be honest because the Holy Spirit was watching and knew his heart. He knew that sight was far more precious to Ralph than God's glory. The struggle within was bitter, but Ralph was a victim of grace.

"There is only one answer," he said finally, "and that choice is to glorify God."

The Holy Spirit insisted on continuing his probe. "Do you really believe that God's glory is more important than your vision?" He did not push for an answer, but waited quietly.

At last Ralph surrendered. "My vision, or lack of it, is not worthy to be compared to the glory of God!"

"Do you really wish to glorify God?" the Holy Spirit asked again.

"Yes, I do!"

"If you do, why worry about the method which God chooses for you to glorify him?"[4]

The goal of prayer is not the fulfilling of our own requests; it is the glorification of God. But do we really know that? Remember that while he was here on earth the Lord Jesus Christ glorified the Father. He said in his great priestly prayer of John 17, "I have brought you glory on earth by completing the work you gave me to do" (v. 4). But the way Jesus did this was not by any way that we would call glorious. Jesus was a wandering preacher who, as he himself said, had nowhere to lay his head. He was misunderstood. He was ridiculed. His own disciples did not understand him. Eventually one betrayed him while still another denied him. All deserted him. Then he was arrested, tried, cruelly beaten, and executed. This was not what we would desire, either for Jesus or for ourselves. Yet this was God's will for Jesus, and it was precisely in these things that God was glorified.

Do we really know what that means? If we do, it will not be a matter of indifference; rather it will transform our lives. As life goes on we will undoubtedly suffer many of the things that are common to the life of mankind. We will get sick. Friends will get sick and pass away. Many disappointments will come in our homes, work, and other areas. Eventually we will die. How will you and I react in these circumstances? Will we complain and blame God? Or will we receive these circumstances from his hand and seek to glorify him in them? If we choose the latter, we will be able to demonstrate the reality of God's great grace and peace, produced by God's sovereign choice in suffering Christians.

When sorrows come the world panics. It has no answer in the face of disappointments, no hope in death. We have hope. Moreover, we have the privilege of coming to God in prayer in order that our will might be made increasingly conformable to his will and that others might therefore be led to glorify him through our testimony.

182

"Keep My Commands"

John 14:15

"If you love me, you will obey what I command."

It is hard to imagine a more wonderful series of promises than those from the middle of John 14. One promise is that those who are Christ's shall do even greater works than Jesus' works. Another is that whatever we shall ask by prayer in Jesus' name he will do. In all honesty, however, we must admit (as we have done in our earlier studies of these two promises) that they do have qualifications and that we are often unable to enjoy the full scope of the promises simply because we are unwilling to meet the conditions.

The condition that we now look at is the third in a series of four, as a result of which Jesus will do even greater works in us than he himself did while on earth. It is the condition of obedience flowing from love. But we want to note, as we begin this study, that obedience and love are not only conditions for our doing "greater works" than Jesus' works, though that is true. They are also conditions for the exercise of effectual prayer, mentioned just a verse or two earlier. In these verses Jesus had expressed the conditions of effectual prayer as being prayer "in his name" and "that the Son may bring glory to the Father." Now it is as though he elaborates upon those thoughts, adding that it will also mean love for himself and obedience to his commands. If we do not desire these two things above all, all other petitions will remain unanswered. If we do desire them, they will be answered. As John later says in his first letter to the churches of Asia: "[We]

1105

receive from him anything we ask, because we obey his commands and do what pleases him" (1 John 3:22).

Having said this, however, we may also note that this verse rightly stands alone and therefore conveys lessons of itself. In particular, it teaches us about the proper relationship between love for Christ and Christ's commandments, and what the possession of both of them proves.

If We Love Jesus

The first lesson is the obvious lesson of the verse. It is that *if we love Jesus, we must (and indeed will) keep his commandments.* This truth is important, for it strikes at once at any perversion of the Christian faith by antinomianism.

Antinomianism is an unfamiliar word to most people, but it is not hard to understand. It is the view that the commandments of the Word of God have no proper place in Christianity. Usually the expressions of this view contrast law with grace in a way that eliminates the value of law entirely. Thus, in the name of grace the God of grace, who is also a God of holiness and justice, is eliminated. People are told that law is an enemy of grace, that the God of Sinai is a stern and unlovable deity who is rightly banished from the pages of the New Testament and that today the only possible guide for any ethical system is love. As might be expected, in this system outright disobedience to the commands of God is countenanced. Thus, marriages may be broken up, adultery sanctioned, contracts broken, parents rejected, worldly goods coveted, and countless other things eagerly embraced—so long as the actions do not "hurt" anyone and "love" remains the underlying motivation.

But this is a travesty. We admit, of course—indeed, we must proclaim it widely—that salvation is never by works, that it is always by grace. At this point law and grace *are* opposites. The Book of Galatians stands as a commanding witness to that fact. We will even admit that the proper way to live the Christian life is not by imposing a list of rules (even God-given rules) either upon ourselves or others. To do this may assure an outward conformity to a certain external expression of Christian character. But it does not change the heart. That is why love, not law, must lie at the heart of Christian ethics. In this, the exponents of situation ethics, or the new morality, are right. But having said this, we must immediately go on to add that any love that does not express itself in conformity with the commands of Christ is not the kind of love about which Christ was speaking. Indeed, it is a pseudo-love, a love that is false in itself and that deals falsely with the one espousing it.

A number of years ago, when the so-called "new morality" was at the crest of its popularity, a number of theologians met at one of our prestigious eastern seminaries to discuss it. Most were in favor of the new morality. So the discussion centered on the value of being free from rules and regulations, including those found in the Bible. "But there must be some guidelines," someone said. This was discussed, and at length it was decided that the only acceptable guideline was love. Anything that flowed from love was permissible. Anything was allowed so long as it did not hurt anyone.

While the discussion was progressing along these lines, a Roman Catholic priest, who had been invited to the discussion and who was in the room, became very quiet. At length his silence was noticeable. So the others turned to him and asked, "What do you think? Don't you agree that the only limiting factor in any ethical decision is love?"

The priest replied, "If you love me, keep my commandments." He was right. Love may be a valuable guideline, but only if it is love in conformity with the love of God and therefore also in conformity with the commandments he has given.

This does not devalue love, however, for the two go together. In fact, only love will succeed in moving us to keep the commandments. Here Maclaren has written wisely, "The principle that underlies these words, then, is this, that love is the foundation of obedience, and obedience is the sure outcome and result of love. . . . That is exactly what distinguishes and lifts the morality of the gospel above all other systems. The worst man in the world knows a great deal more of his duty than the best man does. It is not for want of knowledge that men go to the devil, but it is for want of power or will to live their knowledge. And what morality fails to do, with its clearest utterances of human duty, Christ comes and does. The one law is like the useless proclamations posted up in some rebellious district, where there is no army to back them, and the king's authority from whom they come is flouted. The other law gets itself obeyed. Such is the difference between the powerless morality of the world and the commandment of Jesus Christ. Here is the road plain and straight. What matters that, if there is no force to draw the cart along it? There might as well be no road at all. Here stand all your looms, polished and in perfect order, but there is no steam in the boilers; and so there is no motion, and nothing is woven. What we want is not law, but power, and what the gospel gives us, and stands alone in giving us, is not merely the knowledge of the will of God, and the clear revelation of what we ought to be, but the power to become it.

"Love does that, and love alone. That strong force brought into action in our hearts will drive out from thence all rivals, all false and low things. The true way to cleanse the Augean stables, as the old myth has it, was to turn the river into them. It would have been endless work to wheel out the filth in wheelbarrows loaded by spades: turn the stream in, and it will sweep away all the foulness. When the Ark comes into the Temple, Dagon lies, a mutilated stump, upon the threshold. When Christ comes into my heart, then all the obscene and twilight-loving shapes that lurked there and defiled it, will vanish like ghosts at cock-crowing before His calm and pure Presence. He, and He alone, entering my heart by the portals of my love, will coerce my evil and stimulate my good. And if I love Him, I shall keep His commandments."[1]

By This We Know

There is a second lesson in this verse. It comes from the reverse of what we have been saying. Thus far we have said that if we truly love Christ, that is, if we love him with the kind of love about which he is speaking and with which he loves us, we will keep his commandments. But we may also say (for the proposition is reversible) that *if we keep his commandments, we will love (and can know that we love) Jesus.* This reversal is valid, for Jesus makes it himself just a few verses later: "Whoever has my commands and obeys them, he is the one who loves me. He who loves me will be loved by my Father, and I too will love him and show myself to him" (v. 21). John also makes this point in his first letter: "We know that we have come to know him if we obey his commands. . . . But if anyone obeys his word, God's love is truly made complete in him. This is how we know we are in him" (1 John 2:3, 5).

But how does this happen? How can we be assured by obedience that we really are Christ's own? The answer is in the nature of man. In their natural state, men and women are in rebellion against God. Consequently, it is not within them to want to obey God. This is precisely the point Maclaren was developing in the quotation that was given earlier. When a man or woman begins to obey God, first in responding to his offer of salvation in the Lord Jesus Christ and then in a growing desire to live a Christlike life, this is evidence of a divine and supernatural working in his or her life. It is proof that God is present and that he has already begun a regenerative work within the individual.

So take heart, Christian, and be assured of God's saving work in your life. None of this means that we therefore obey God completely, just because we are his. We still sin. That is why John writes, "If we claim to be without sin, we deceive ourselves and the truth is not in us" (1 John 1:8). But it does mean that if you detect within yourself a new yearning to please God, if sin begins to disturb you, if you increasingly long to be like Jesus, then God is at work; and you should rejoice in the truth that "he who began a good work in you will [keep on performing] it until the day of Jesus Christ" (Phil. 1:6).

Love One Another

There is a third truth in this verse, and it is also evident. If we read these words—"If you love me, you will obey what I command"—and then ask, as we must, "But what are Christ's commandments?" we are immediately led back to that greatest of all commandments, found in John 13: "A new command I give you: Love one another. As I have loved you, so you must love one another" (v. 34). In other words, *if we love Jesus, we must (and will) love other Christians.* Do you love others? You must not be too quick to answer, for in the New Testament the love about which Jesus is speaking is very practical. It means at least three things.

First, it means *service.* This is evident from the context in which the new commandment was given. Jesus had just divested himself of his clothing, girded himself with a towel, and then had washed the disciples' feet. The disciples undoubtedly thought this was improper. Peter actually objected, saying, "You shall never wash my feet" (13:8). But Jesus corrected Peter and then taught them all: "You call me 'Teacher' and 'Lord,' and rightly so, for that is what I am. Now that I, your Lord and Teacher, have washed your feet, you also should wash one another's feet. I have set you an example that you should do as I have done for you" (vv. 13–15). That is the picture Jesus gave of true Christianity. It is the attitude that divests itself of its own prerogatives in order to serve others.

Second, the practice of love means *sacrifice.* This means that we are not called to serve only when we can do so conveniently and at no cost to ourselves. It means that we are called to serve at our cost when we would much rather do something else. Jesus did this obviously; for his parable of service, washing the disciples' feet, was completed only when he had gone to the cross and there made the atonement by which alone they could be washed from the contamination of sin.

Finally, the practice of love also means *sharing,* sharing of ourselves, on the one hand, and sharing the gospel of God's grace in Jesus Christ, on the other. Jesus said, "Go into all the world and preach the good news to all creation" (Mark 16:15). He said, "Go and make disciples of all nations, baptizing them in the name of the Father and of the Son and of the Holy Spirit, and teaching them to obey everything I have commanded you. And surely I am with you always, to the very end of the age" (Matt. 28:19–20). How can we claim to love Christ if we disregard this great commandment?

If We Love Others

The final point is a reversal of the third, just as the second point was a reversal of the first. It is this: *if we love others, then we can know that we truly love Jesus and are one of his own.* John says it clearly, "Do not be surprised, my brothers, if the world hates you. We know that we have passed from death to life, because we love our brothers. Anyone who does not love remains in death" (1 John 3:13–14). According to these words, we can be assured that we are truly born again if, in obedience to Christ's commands, we find ourselves beginning to love and actually loving others for whom he also died.

Jesus Loves Me

At this point we must return to the phrase with which our text began: "If you love me." Once again it raises the question: Do we? Do we really love Jesus? Some will hear this question and reply, humbly but nevertheless honestly, "Yes, I do; I really do love him." If that is the case, here is the way to show it—by loving others (as well as himself) and by doing what he desires.

Some will not be able to say this, though they may actually love Jesus more than they are aware they do. If you are one who would like to love him but who has not been able to do it, at least to your satisfaction, let me assure you that you will never learn to love by imposing it upon yourself as a duty. You will never love by saying, "I will love, I will love, I will love," any more than you can stop coughing by saying, "I will not cough." There is only one way in which you will come to love God, and that is by coming to know and believe in his love for you. Love provokes love. His love calls forth yours. Consequently, the way to love God is to learn that he loved you so much that he gave his only begotten Son for your salvation.

Torrey tells of a little girl who came to the great English preacher Mark Guy Pearse one day and, looking up into his face quite wistfully, said, "Mr. Pearse, I don't love Jesus. I wish I did love Jesus, but I don't love Jesus. Won't you please tell me how to love Jesus?"

The preacher looked down into those eager eyes and said to her, "Little girl, as you go home today keep saying to yourself, 'Jesus loves me. Jesus loves me. Jesus loves me.' And when you come back next Sunday I think you will be able to say, 'I love Jesus.'"

The next Sunday the little girl came up to him again, this time with happy eyes and a radiant face, and exclaimed, "Oh, Mr. Pearse, I do love Jesus, I do love Jesus. Last Sunday as I went home I kept saying to myself, 'Jesus loves me. Jesus loves me. Jesus loves me.' And I began to think about his love and I began to think how he died on the cross in my place, and I found my cold heart growing warm, and the first I knew it was full of love to Jesus."[2]

That is the only way any of us ever learn to love Jesus. We begin by learning to believe what the Bible says when it tells us that we are the vilest of sinners but how, nevertheless, Jesus died in our place, the just for the unjust. It tells us that he has "borne our griefs, and carried our sorrows." It shows how he was "pierced for our transgressions" and "bruised for our iniquities," how "the punishment that brought us peace was upon him," how "with his stripes we are healed." We begin by believing on him as the Bible portrays him. Next we see his love and come to love him. Then, because we love him, we keep his commands.

183

That Other Comforter

John 14:16–18

"And I will ask the Father, and he will give you another Counselor to be with you forever—the Spirit of truth. The world cannot accept him, because it neither sees him nor knows him. But you know him, for he lives with you and will be in you. I will not leave you as orphans; I will come to you."

The Christian church reaffirms its faith in the Holy Spirit every time it recites the Apostles' Creed: "I believe in the Holy Ghost." But beyond this rather formal acknowledgment, in large sectors of the church one would be hard pressed to find a reference to the Third Person of the Trinity at all.

J. I. Packer has written of this ignorance: "Christian people are not in doubt as to the work that Christ did; they know that He redeemed men by His atoning death, even if they differ among themselves as to what exactly this involved. But the average Christian is in a complete fog as to what work the Holy Spirit does. Some talk of the Spirit of Christ in the way that one would talk of the Spirit of Christmas—as a vague cultural pressure making for bonhomie and religiosity. Some think of the Spirit as inspiring the moral convictions of unbelievers like Gandhi, or the theosophical mysticism of a Rudolf Steiner. But most, perhaps, do not think of the Holy Spirit at all, and have no positive ideas of any sort about what He does. They are for practical purposes in the same position as the disciples whom Paul met at Ephesus—'We have not so much as heard whether there be any Holy Ghost' (Acts 9:2)."[1]

Why is this? It is hard to say why. But one thing is certain: It is an abnormal situation. It is abnormal from the viewpoint of Christ's teachings, for Christ clearly taught about the Holy Spirit. He did so in the verses we are studying in order to provide comfort to his disciples and to all who should follow them throughout the church age. Knowledge of the Holy Spirit and dependence upon the Holy Spirit are necessary conditions of doing those "greater things" that he mentions in verse 12. Ignorance of the Holy Spirit's work is also abnormal from the viewpoint of the author of the fourth Gospel, for he has shown his interest by including many verses about the Holy Spirit in the last discourses.

Personality or Power?

The first point we must settle in our minds in regard to the Holy Spirit is whether the Holy Spirit is a real person, whose work it is to get hold of us and use us, or whether the Holy Spirit is merely some vague power we are to get hold of and use to our benefit. This is important as a mere matter of truth; for either the Holy Spirit is a real person, or he is not. But it is also important on a practical level. If we think of the Holy Spirit as a mysterious power, our thought will continually be, "How can I get more of the Holy Spirit?" If we think of the Holy Spirit as a person, our thought will be, "How can the Holy Spirit have more of me?" The first thought is entirely pagan. The second is New Testament Christianity.

Reuben A. Torrey, who has written an excellent book on the Holy Spirit, carefully spells this out: "The conception of the Holy Spirit as a Divine influence or power that we are somehow to get hold of and use, leads to self-exaltation and self-sufficiency. One who so thinks of the Holy Spirit and who at the same time imagines that he has received the Holy Spirit will almost inevitably be full of spiritual pride and strut about as if he belonged to some superior order of Christians. One frequently hears such persons say, 'I am a Holy Ghost man,' or 'I am a Holy Ghost woman.' But if we once grasp the thought that the Holy Spirit is a Divine Person of infinite majesty, glory and holiness and power, who in marvelous condescension has come into our hearts to make His abode there and take possession of our lives and make use of them, it will put us in the dust and keep us in the dust. I can think of no thought more humbling or more overwhelming than the thought that a person of Divine majesty and glory dwells in my heart and is ready to use even me."[2]

We see this difference illustrated in the pages of the New Testament, as we might expect. On the one hand, there is the case of Simon the magician, whose story is told in Acts 8:9–24. He apparently believed in Christ through the preaching of Philip at Samaria, for we are told that he "believed . . . and . . . was baptized" (v. 13). But he knew little about Christianity and therefore fell into the mistake of thinking that the Holy Spirit was a power to be purchased. He actually offered the disciples money in order to receive "it." To this, Peter, who was also in Samaria at the time, responded, "May your money perish with you, because you thought you could buy the gift of God with money! You have no part or share in this ministry, because your heart is not right before God. Repent of this wickedness and pray to the Lord. Perhaps he will forgive you for having such a thought in your heart" (vv. 20–22).

The other example is from the beginning of the missionary movement involving Paul and Barnabas. Of this we are told that "while they were worshiping the Lord and fasting, the Holy Spirit said, 'Set apart for me Barnabas and Saul for the work to which I have called them'" (Acts 13:2). In the one case, an individual wanted to get and use God, whom he imagined to be merely a power. In the second case, God got and used two individuals.

Words or Reality?

We must admit that when we begin to talk about the Holy Spirit as a person, we are attempting to put into words something that is actually larger than words. What we are saying is that the Holy Spirit is one member of the Trinity, equal in all ways to both the Father and the Son. But we are not saying that there are three gods, which the term "member" or even "person" seems to imply. There are three persons; but in a way which is beyond our understanding these three are also one. We also confess as the Old Testament does, "Hear, O Israel: The LORD our God, the LORD is one" (Deut. 6:4).

In these verses Jesus speaks of the Holy Spirit saying, "And I will ask the Father, and he will give you another Counselor to be with you forever—the Spirit of truth. The world cannot accept him, because it neither sees him nor knows him. But you know him, for he lives with you and will be in you." This is a great promise, but it is great precisely because of the personality of the Spirit. If the Spirit were only a power, the promise would be in the nature of a compensation—"I am going to be taken from you, but I will give you some*thing* to make up for my departure." This is not what this verse is talking about. It is not a thing that is being given, but rather another divine personality that is being sent. This one must have knowledge, for he will know of the disciples' distress. He must have feelings, for he will identify with them in their distress and comfort them. He must have will, for he will determine to carry out this commission.

The personality of the Holy Spirit is evident from the Scriptures in other ways also. One commentator has summed up the evidence in the following six propositions:

1. The personal actions ascribed to the Holy Spirit prove his personality. An example is John 14:16–18, for there he is promised as a Counselor for Christians. One other example is 1 Corinthians 12:11, in which he is said to be at work in Christians, imparting those spiritual gifts necessary for the well-being of the church.

2. His distinction from the Father and Son and his mission from both prove his personality. Jesus indicates this relationship by saying, "When the Counselor comes, whom I will send to you from the Father, the Spirit of truth who goes out from the Father, he will testify about me" (John 15:26).

3. The coordinate rank and power that belong to the Holy Spirit equally with the Father and the Son prove it. All trinitarian benedictions make this point clearly. Thus, "Go and make disciples of all nations, baptizing them in the name of the Father and of the Son and of the Holy Spirit" (Matt. 28:19). Or again, "The grace of the Lord Jesus Christ, and the love of God, and the fellowship of the Holy Spirit be with you all." (2 Cor. 13:14).

4. The appearance of the Holy Spirit under a visible form at the baptism of the Lord Jesus Christ and on the day of Pentecost proves it. Of the former event it is written, "And the Holy Spirit descended on him in bodily form like a dove. And a voice came from heaven: 'You are my Son, whom I love; with you I am well pleased'" (Luke 3:22). Of the second instance it is written, "They saw what seemed to be tongues of fire that separated and came to rest on each of them" (Acts 2:3).

5. The sin against the Holy Spirit proves it, for this implies offense against a personality. It is mentioned in Matthew 12:31–32.

6. The way in which the Holy Spirit is distinguished from his gifts also proves that he is a person and not merely a spiritual force or power. Thus, in 1 Corinthians 12, after having enumerated the gifts of wisdom, knowledge, faith, healing, miracles, prophecy, the discerning of spirits, tongues, and the interpretation of tongues, Paul writes, "But all these are the work of one and the same Spirit, and he gives them to each one, just as he determines."[3]

Here are six separate and conclusive lines of argument showing that the Holy Spirit is a person. But the problem we have is still probably not so much the doctrine itself as our attitude toward him. Theoretically we probably do believe that the Holy Spirit is a person, the third person of the Godhead. But do we actually think about him in this way? Perhaps we do what a woman did who had attended a series of messages on the Holy Spirit at a Bible conference years ago. She listened carefully and then came up to the speaker to thank him for his teaching. She said, "Before your messages I never thought of *it* as a person." Apparently she was not thinking of him as a person even then.

Is He God?

The first point that the Lord Jesus makes in his teaching about the Holy Spirit is that he is a person, as we have seen. But what sort of a person is he? Is he an angel? Is he a being superior to an angel but inferior to both the Father and the Son? Or is he equal to the Father and the Son? Is he God? Actually, we have already begun to answer these questions in talking about the personality of the Spirit, but the answer is also taught in the verses that constitute our text.

Here the Lord speaks of the Holy Spirit as "another Counselor." It is important in understanding Christ's words to notice that there are two different words for "another" in the Greek New Testament. One word is *allos*, the word we have here; it means "another just like the first one." The second word, *heteros*, means "totally different." Since there are these two words with two meanings it is always important to know which one is used whenever the word "another" occurs in the English text. It is the first word, the word meaning "another exactly like the first one," that is used when Jesus speaks of sending the disciples "another Counselor."

Who is the first Counselor? It is obviously Jesus himself. Therefore, the second Counselor is to be just like him. That is, he is to be another divine being living with them and in them.

Once again, as in the matter of the personality of the Holy Spirit, other parts of Scripture reinforce this teaching. We may summarize the points thus:

1. Divine attributes are ascribed to the Spirit. The word "holy" is itself a divine attribute, at least in its most exalted sense. So also are the attributes of omniscience (1 Cor. 2:10–11; John 16:12–13), omnipotence (Luke 1:35), and omnipresence (Ps. 139:7–10).

2. Works that are exclusively the works of God are attributed to the Holy Spirit. Creation is one example. In the Book of Job we read, "By his breath the skies became fair" (26:13) and "The Spirit of God has made me" (33:4). The Holy Spirit is described as the One who imparts life, another divine work (John 3:6; Rom 8:11). He is the One responsible for the giving forth of the Word of God, the Bible. "For prophecy never had its origin in the will of man, but men spoke from God as they were carried along by the Holy Spirit" (2 Peter 1:21).

3. The Holy Spirit is ranked coordinate with God the Father and God the Son. The benedictions cited earlier are examples of this.

4. The name of God is indirectly given to him. The clearest example of this is in Acts 5:3–4, where Peter says to Ananias, "Ananias, how is it that Satan has so filled your heart that you have lied to the Holy Spirit? . . . Thou hast not lied unto men, but unto God."

Practical Theology

Does it really matter that we know and constantly recognize that the Holy Spirit is divine? Yes, it does, for if we know and constantly recognize his deity, we will recognize and rely on his work. If we do not, then we will foolishly rely on our own limited wisdom, love, strength and other resources, and forfeit that which he alone can provide.

In his writings on the Holy Spirit to which I referred at the start of this study, J. I. Packer asks these pertinent questions: "Do we honour the Holy

Spirit by recognising and relying on His work? Or do we slight Him by ignoring it, and thereby dishonour, not merely the Spirit, but the Lord who sent Him? In our faith: do we acknowledge the authority of the Bible, the prophetic Old Testament and the apostolic New Testament which He inspired? Do we read and hear it with the reverence and receptiveness that are due to the Word of God? If not, we dishonour the Holy Spirit. In our life: do we apply the authority of the Bible, and live by the Bible, whatever men may say against it, recognising that God's word cannot but be true, and that what God has said He certainly means, and will stand to? If not, we dishonour the Holy Spirit, who gave us the Bible. In our witness: do we remember that the Holy Spirit alone, by His witness, can authenticate our witness, and look to Him to do so, and trust Him to do so, and show the reality of our trust, as Paul did, by eschewing the gimmicks of human cleverness? If not, we dishonour the Holy Spirit."[4]

The personality and deity of the Holy Spirit, as well as other truths about him, are practical teachings. What remains is that we take them down off the shelf of high theology and put them to work in our lives.

184

The Role of the Holy Spirit

John 14:16–18

"And I will ask the Father, and he will give you another Counselor to be with you forever—the Spirit of truth. The world cannot accept him, because it neither sees him nor knows him. But you know him, for he lives with you and will be in you. I will not leave you as orphans; I will come to you."

There are many things we may want to learn about a person when we are first getting to know him or her. But in most cases our first questions are two: first, Who are you? and, second, What do you do? The first can be answered by a name, followed by a brief description of where the person comes from and to whom he is related. The second generally deals with the person's occupation. We may follow a similar procedure in these introductory studies to the doctrine of the Holy Spirit. In the last study we asked: "Who are you?" We saw that the Holy Spirit is a divine being, equal to God the Father and God the Son in all respects. Now we want to ask what the Holy Spirit does.

Christ Glorified

In one sense the question is nearly unanswerable, for if the Holy Spirit is God, as he is, then all that God the Father does and God the Son does, the Holy Spirit also does. Thus, it is proper to say that the Holy Spirit created the universe, planned the great work of redemption, was active in the entire ministry of the Lord Jesus Christ, raised him from the dead, called forth and is directing the church, and will one day bring all things together in subjection to him who is the Father of all. Indeed, there are verses in the Bible that make these points, as we have seen.

On the other hand, we must also recognize that the Bible emphasizes different activities for each of the three members of the Godhead, according to which it is possible to say, for example, that the Father is principally active in the work of creation and that the Son is principally active in the redemption of our race. Therefore, although it is almost impossible to say all that the Spirit does in the first sense, it is possible to speak of the primary emphasis of his ministry in the second.

So what does the Holy Spirit primarily do? Some would answer by saying that the Holy Spirit is active most of all in the sanctification of Christians or in the inspiration of the Bible or in giving specific gifts to individuals within the church. These things are true, but they are not the best answers. The best answer is found in John 16:13–14, in which the Lord Himself says of the Spirit's work, "But when he, the Spirit of truth, comes, he will guide you into all truth. He will not speak on his own; he will speak only what he hears, and he will tell you what is yet to come. He will bring glory to me by taking from what is mine and making it known to you." These verses tell us that the role of the Holy Spirit is primarily to glorify Christ. Indeed, when they are correctly understood, all the other activities that might be mentioned—sanctification, inspiration, the imparting of gifts, even the work of creation—are included within this one great and overriding purpose.

So we can learn a lesson from this, right at the beginning. We are told that the Holy Spirit will not speak of himself, but of Jesus. Therefore, we may conclude that any emphasis upon the person and work of the Spirit that detracts from the person and work of the Lord Jesus Christ is not the Spirit's doing. It is the work of another spirit, the spirit of antichrist, whose work it is to detract from Jesus (cf. 1 John 4:2–3). Important as he is, the Holy Spirit is never to preempt the place of Jesus in our thinking. On the other hand, wherever Jesus is exalted—in whatever way—there the Third Person of the Trinity is at work.

Spirit of Truth

How specifically does the Holy Spirit glorify the Lord Jesus Christ? He does so in four areas.

First, the Holy Spirit has glorified Jesus (past tense) by teaching about the Lord Jesus Christ in the Scriptures. This is deeply involved in the teaching of these last discourses, for one of the points Jesus makes is that after he would be gone, the Holy Spirit would lead the disciples into all the truth concerning Jesus, and as a result of this they would be able to preach the true gospel and record infallibly, in the pages of the New Testament, the teachings of Jesus and the meaning of his teachings and ministry. This is what he is talking about when he says, "When the Counselor comes . . . he will testify about me" (John 15:26). Or again, "I have much more to say to you, more than you can now bear. But when he, the Spirit of truth, comes, he will guide you into all [the] truth" (16:12–13).

This is a tremendous word for the disciples. They knew, no doubt, that in the Old Testament period the Holy Spirit had come upon certain prophets, kings, and other leaders in order to speak through them in what eventually came to be the Old Testament. They might even have known—though they undoubtedly came to know it more fully after the resurrection—that the central message of the Old Testament was the promise of God to send a Redeemer, who was the Lord Jesus Christ. Now they are told that the same Holy Spirit, who inspired the Old Testament so that those living in the Old Testament period might anticipate the Messiah and look to him for salvation, is going to come upon them—indeed, be in them—so that nothing about Christ's work or teachings necessary for our salvation and the growth and ordering of the church might be lost.

That is precisely what happened. Some of the events and teachings they recorded were things they had heard and seen and that they remembered. Other points were revealed to them later for the first time. In both cases these men were led by the Holy Spirit. In fact, it was as true of them as Peter said it was of the Old Testament authors: "For prophecy never had its origin in the will of man, but men spoke from God as they were carried along by the Holy Spirit" (2 Peter 1:21).

In this work the Holy Spirit amply glorified the Lord Jesus Christ, for he prepared for his coming through the inspiration of the Old Testament that told men what to expect and when to expect him. Then he preserved the story of his coming and gave the only true interpretation of it through the inspiration of the New Testament books.

Born of God

Second, the Holy Spirit glorifies the Lord Jesus Christ by drawing men and women to him. This has been discussed so often in our exposition of John's Gospel that it does not need to be presented fully now. We need only to point out that apart from this activity of the Holy Spirit, irrespective of the inspiration of the Bible, no one would ever have come to Jesus.

The verses about the Holy Spirit that we are studying make this plain. Apart from the work of the Holy Spirit in leading men and women to Christ, no one can either see, know, or receive spiritual things. They cannot *see* because they are spiritually blind. As Jesus said, "Unless a man is born again, he cannot see the kingdom of God" (John 3:3). They cannot *know* because the things of the Spirit "are spiritually discerned" (1 Cor. 2:14). They cannot *receive* either the Holy Spirit or the Lord Jesus Christ because, as Jesus said, "No one can come to me unless the Father who sent me draws him" (John 6:44).

The Holy Spirit opens blind eyes so that the unregenerate may see the truth. He unfogs their minds so that they may understand what they see, and then gently woos their wills until they come to place their faith in the Savior. Without this work there would not be a single Christian in the world. By means of it the Holy Spirit saves us and glorifies the Lord Jesus.

Reproducing Christ

Third, the Holy Spirit glorifies the Lord Jesus Christ by reproducing him in believers. He does this in three ways: (1) by leading the Christian to greater victory over sin, (2) by praying for him and by teaching him to pray, and (3) by showing him God's will for his life and enabling him to walk in it.

Here the meaning of the word "counselor" or "comforter" is of great importance. It is unfortunate from the point of view of our trying to understand this term that in the English language "comfort" has been watered down so that it now means little more than a half-hearted attempt to console someone, or that which consoles. It can, for example, be a Linus blanket. In fact, that is not far off linguistically, for one use of the word "comforter" is to describe a certain kind of quilt. That is often what we have in mind when we think of comfort. Comfortable! We think of rolling up in our blanket and consoling ourselves from the hard knocks of this world.

That is not what the word means in the Bible, though a certain measure of consolation is involved in it. To understand the biblical word, we need to go back to the Latin words that lie behind our word "comfort." There are two of them. The first is *cum* (which has had its vowel changed in the process of taking it over into English). It is a preposition meaning "with." The second is *fortis*, from which we get our words fortification, fortify, fortissimo (Italian), fortitude, and fortress. It means "strong" or "strengthen." Put them together, and you have the true meaning of "comforter." A comforter is one who is with you to strengthen you. He is, as one commentator writes, "a ramrod down your backbone to make you stand for the truth; to make you take the right side, even though it's the minority side. The Comforter gives you strength to stand up in face of something that is vile and evil."[1]

This is what the Holy Spirit did with Peter. Peter had denied the Lord on the night of his arrest because he was afraid of a little girl who was only a doorkeeper. But on the day of Pentecost, after the Holy Spirit had come, Peter stood up to preach the gospel before the men who had crucified Jesus, saying, "Men of Israel, listen to this: Jesus of Nazareth was a man accredited by God to you by miracles, wonders and signs, which God did among you through him, as you yourselves know. This man was handed over to you by God's set purpose and foreknowledge; and you, with the help of wicked men, put him to death by nailing him to the cross. But God raised him from the dead, freeing him from the agony of death, because it was impossible for death to keep its hold on him. . . . Therefore let all Israel be assured of this: God has made this Jesus, whom you crucified, both Lord and Christ" (Acts 2:22–24, 36). The Holy Spirit gave Peter a backbone, making him like Jesus, and through him brought glory to the Lord.

Thus far, in trying to understand the word "Comforter" we have only dealt with the meaning of the English word, which comes from the Latin. When we go beyond the English word to the Greek word we find an entirely new, though related, area of meaning, which in turn teaches us more about the Spirit's ministry. The Greek word in this text is *paraklētos*. The first two syllables, *para*, are the Greek word meaning "alongside of." We have it in English words such as parable, paradox, parallax, and parallel. The second two syllables, *klētos*, means "called," as in the Greek word for "church" (*ekklēsia*) meaning the ones who are "called out." *Paraklētos* therefore means "one who is called alongside of" another person as that person's helper.

Incidentally, in the Latin Vulgate the word is translated, not by any variation on our word "comforter" but by the word *advocatus*, which gives us the word "advocate." *Ad* means "alongside of." *Vocatus* is from *vocare*, meaning "to call." So *advocatus* also means "one who is called alongside of" another person as that person's helper. *Advocate* is Latin. *Paraclete* is Greek. But the meaning of the two words is identical.

This idea is further substantiated in 1 John 2:1, although in this case the word *paraklētos* is actually translated "advocate." There we read, "My dear children, I write this to you so that you will not sin. But if anybody does sin, we have one who speaks to the Father, in our defense—Jesus Christ, the Righteous One."

These two are working together for us. Moreover, they are praying for us. We know that the Lord Jesus Christ is praying for us, because in Hebrews 7:25 it says, "Therefore, he [that is, Christ] is able to save completely those who come to God through him, because he always lives to intercede for them." He is praying for us in heaven. We know that the Holy Spirit is praying for us and helping us to pray, because in Romans 8:26 we are told, "In the same way, the Spirit helps in our weakness. We do not know what we ought to pray for, but the Spirit himself intercedes for us with groans that words cannot express."

What should trouble us then? Nothing! We cannot be troubled about our salvation; Christ has purchased it for us, and the Holy Spirit has sealed it to our hearts. Moreover, they are both free to plead our case before the Father. "Who will bring any charge against those whom God has chosen? It is God who justifies. Who is he that condemns? Christ Jesus, who died—more than that, who was raised to life—is at the right hand of God and is also interceding for us" (Rom. 8:33–34). We cannot be troubled about our growth into the image of the Lord Jesus Christ either, for this is the goal of the Spirit's work within us. Paul says: "through Christ Jesus the law of the Spirit of life set me free from the law of sin and death. For what the law was powerless to do in that it was weakened by the sinful nature, God did by sending his own Son in the likeness of sinful man to be a sin offering. And so he condemned sin in sinful man, in order that the righteous requirements of the law might be fully met in us, who do not live according to the sinful nature but according to the Spirit" (Rom. 8:2–4).

Christian Service

The fourth way in which the Holy Spirit glorifies the Lord Jesus Christ is by directing Christ's followers into Christian service and sustaining them in it. This was to be true of the disciples, as most of the verses about the Holy Spirit in the last discourses indicate; he was to direct them in the future in precisely the way Jesus had directed them in the past. This is also true for those who have come after these early followers of our Lord.

One example is in the passage I mentioned briefly, and for another reason, in the last study: Acts 13:2 and the verses that follow. We read in those verses, "While they were worshiping the Lord and fasting, the Holy Spirit said, 'Set apart for me Barnabas and Saul for the work to which I have called them.' So after they had fasted and prayed, they placed their hands on them and sent them off. The two of them, sent on their way by the Holy Spirit, went down to Seleucia and sailed from there to Cyprus" (vv. 2–4). It is clear from these verses that the Holy Spirit calls men and women into definite lines of Christian work and goes with them as they go forth into this work. That is, he not only calls them into Christian work in a general way; he calls in a specific way, pointing to a definite field of endeavor.

Has he led you in such service? Is he leading? If not, you need to begin by wanting that leading and then by seeking it, expecting the Holy Spirit to give guidance.

185

The Fullness of the Holy Spirit

John 14:16–18

"And I will ask the Father, and he will give you another Counselor to be with you forever—the Spirit of truth. The world cannot accept him, because it neither sees him nor knows him. But you know him, for he lives with you and will be in you. I will not leave you as orphans; I will come to you."

In our last study of the Holy Spirit we saw that one of the reasons why the Spirit is given to Christians is to reproduce the character of Christ within them. That is the idea behind the word "Counselor" or "Comforter," for the Comforter is one who is called alongside the Christian to strengthen him or help him in his Christian walk. But this does not always happen, as we know.

What is wrong when Christians fail to live as Christ in this world? The answer given in Scripture is that they have not allowed the Holy Spirit to have his way in their lives. They have "quenched" the Spirit or "grieved" him (1 Thess. 5:19; Eph. 4:30). Consequently, these are urged to "walk" in the Spirit or "be filled" with him (Gal. 5:16; Eph. 5:18). This use of language suggests that, while in the matter of redemption the Holy Spirit works in utter sovereignty, choosing whom he will and rejecting whom he will, in the matter of Christian growth there is by contrast a large measure of human responsibility. True, we can no more sanctify ourselves than we can redeem ourselves. God must do both. But having been made alive by God first, we can nevertheless cooperate in or resist the Holy Spirit's subsequent prodding.

To understand these truths and profit by them it is important that we understand what the Bible is talking about when it speaks of the "filling" of the Holy Spirit and why this is a necessary and continuous experience for every growing Christian.

The Baptism of the Spirit

We must begin with a negative consideration, however; and the negative consideration is that the "filling" of the Holy Spirit is not the same thing as the "baptism" of the Holy Spirit. What is the baptism of the Holy Spirit? The only answer that can honestly be given to that question is the answer that the Bible itself gives, and for that we must look at passages where the term "baptism of the Holy Spirit" occurs. There are seven of them in the New Testament.

Five of these are prophetic in nature; that is, they look forward to the pouring out of God's Spirit upon his people in accordance with Old Testament prophecies such as Isaiah 32:15; 44:3 and Joel 2:28. The distinctive feature about them is that they are related to the ministry of Jesus Christ. Thus, on four occasions John the Baptist is quoted as saying, "I baptize you with water for repentance. But after me will come one who is more powerful than I, whose sandals I am not fit to carry. He will baptize you with the Holy Spirit and with fire" (Matt. 3:11; parallels in Mark 1:7–8; Luke 3:16; and John 1:33). In the fifth instance Jesus is himself quoted as telling the disciples to wait in Jerusalem for the coming of the Holy Spirit at Pentecost: "For John baptized with water, but in a few days you will be baptized with the Holy Spirit" (Acts 1:5). In the Greek of these verses Jesus is called "the Baptist" or "the Baptizer" because it is a characteristic of his ministry to baptize with the Holy Spirit, just as John is called "the Baptist" because it was a characteristic of his ministry to baptize with water.

The sixth of the seven references to the baptism of the Holy Spirit is historic (Acts 11:16). It refers to the gift of the Holy Spirit to the household of Cornelius simultaneously with the belief of these people in Jesus as a result of Peter's preaching. The reference is significant because it shows that the Holy Spirit was to be given to Gentiles just as it had previously been given to Jews; in other words, there were not to be two levels or ranks of Christians within the church.

The seventh reference is the most important because it is didactic; that is, it is a teaching passage rather than just a descriptive one and, therefore, gives us the doctrine upon which the other passages are to be interpreted. This passage is 1 Corinthians 12:13, in which Paul writes, "For we were all baptized by one Spirit into one body—whether Jews or Greeks, slave or free—and we were all given the one Spirit to drink." Two things immediately strike us about this verse. First, the emphasis is upon the *unity of Christians.* The Christians at Corinth had allowed their emphasis upon spiritual gifts to divide them, but Paul writes to stress that they are actually one.

His key argument is that they have been baptized by one Spirit into the one body of Christ. This is an immediate and obvious rebuke to anyone who would allow an emphasis upon a so-called "baptism of the Holy Spirit," defined as a second work of grace, to divide Christians and destroy fellowship.

The second and related emphasis of this verse is upon the *universality of this experience for all believers.* Here the word "all" is decisive, for Paul writes that "we were *all* baptized" and "were *all* given the one Spirit to drink." In other words, the baptism of the Holy Spirit, rather than being something that is a secondary and special experience for some Christians, is actually the initial experience of all by which, indeed, they have become Christians in the first place.

John R. W. Stott, in a valuable study of these verses, summarizes the evidence like this: "The 'gift' or 'baptism' of the Spirit, one of the *distinctive* blessings of the new covenant, is a *universal* blessing for members of the covenant, because it is an *initial* blessing. It is part and parcel of belonging to the new age. The Lord Jesus, the mediator of the new covenant and the bestower of its blessings, gives both the forgiveness of sins and the gift of the Spirit to all who enter his covenant. Further, baptism with water is the sign and seal of baptism with the Spirit, as much as it is of the forgiveness of sins. Water-baptism is the initiatory Christian rite, because Spirit-baptism is the initiatory Christian experience."[1]

The baptism of the Holy Spirit is for all Christians. In fact, if a person has not received it, he is not a Christian; for the baptism of the Holy Spirit is the same as being identified with Christ through saving faith. Moreover, in case we doubt this, we need to note that there is not a single instance in the New Testament in which any believer is urged or commanded to be baptized with the Holy Spirit for the simple reason that he cannot be urged to seek something that has already taken place in his life.

Filled with the Spirit

Having made this point, however, we must immediately go on to say that, although there is no command to be *baptized* with the Holy Spirit, there is, nevertheless, a clear command to be *"filled* with the Spirit," as I pointed out at the beginning of this study (Eph. 5:18).

At this point some will be saying that the distinction just made between being baptized with the Spirit and being filled with the Spirit is a meaningless one. "For what is the point of denying that we are to seek to be baptized with the Holy Spirit," someone might argue, "if in the next breath we admit that we are to be filled with the Holy Spirit, which is the same thing?" But are they the same thing? The point is that they are not and, moreover, that much of the false teaching we have concerning the Holy Spirit comes from failing to see this. For example, the baptism of the Holy Spirit has been closely linked to the experience of speaking in tongues, because the phrase is so often used of Pentecost where that took place. But this took place at Pentecost primarily to indicate that the new age had begun. By contrast, the filling with the Holy Spirit is associated with a wide variety of experiences (tongues being only one among many) and has a different emphasis entirely.

Here again we must go to the texts in which the words "fullness" or "filled with the Holy Spirit" occur. There are fourteen of them—four of them being descriptions of events or circumstances that took place before Pentecost and that are therefore more in line with Old Testament references and experiences, and ten, of events or circumstances after Pentecost. The first four are all in Luke. They refer to Christ (4:1), John the Baptist (1:15), Elizabeth, the mother of John (1:41), and Zacharias, John's father (1:67). Nine of the remaining ten are in the Book of Acts and are descriptive. The last is Ephesians 5:18, in which the command to be "filled with the Holy Spirit" is given.

In the nine verses from Acts, we notice that the company waiting in the upper room on the day of Pentecost was filled with the Spirit (2:4); that Peter received a special filling before speaking to the Sanhedrin (4:8); that the early Christians were filled with the Spirit on one occasion following prayer, as a result of which they began to speak "the word of God with boldness" (4:31); that the first deacons were chosen as being men "full of the Spirit" (6:3); that Stephen, the first martyr, being "full of the Holy Spirit," saw Jesus standing at the right hand of the Father and testified of this fact (7:55); that Paul was filled with the Spirit when Ananias placed his hands upon him, Ananias having been sent to Paul following his experience on the road to Damascus (9:17); that Paul was "filled with the Holy Spirit" on another occasion as a result of which he confronted Elymas, the sorcerer, on Paphos (13:6); and that Barnabas (11:24) and the disciples at Antioch (13:52) were also each filled with the Spirit in other instances.

What is characteristic of these nine descriptions? It is not any external or supernatural manifestation of the Spirit such as a speaking in tongues, for that is associated only with the one reference to the filling with the Spirit at Pentecost. The only thing that is characteristic of all nine passages is that in every instance the person or group of persons who received the filling immediately began to testify to the Christian gospel. That is, they began to bear witness to Christ. The 120 did so at Pentecost. Peter did so before the Sanhedrin. So did the early disciples mentioned in Acts 4. Stephen, Paul, Barnabas, and the disciples at Antioch are other examples. In fact, the only apparent exception is the reference to the first deacons. But, on closer examination, even this is seen to be not a true exception, for we are not told of a filling of the deacons by the Spirit. We are only told that they were men who gave evidence that their lives had already been filled by the Spirit. This was known, no doubt, by the fact that they already were active as witnesses. Moreover, the account of the choice of these deacons is immediately followed by the account of the death of one of them (Stephen), which contains a particularly effective witness.

So the first and most distinguishing mark of a filling with the Holy Spirit is that the person thus filled will be speaking of Jesus. He will not speak of his experience. He will not speak of the need for others to have his experience. He will speak of Jesus. At this point we inevitably come back to Jesus' own words in John 16:12–14: "I have much more to say to you, more than you can now bear. But when he, the Spirit of truth, comes, he will guide you into all truth. He will not speak on his own; he will speak only what he hears, and he will tell you what is yet to come. He shall glorify me; for he shall receive of mine, and shall show it unto you."

We may conclude from this that a filling with the Holy Spirit is the secret of any successful witness of the church to Christ in any age.

Fruit of the Spirit

However, we need to correct what may be a misunderstanding. Some may notice the emphasis of these verses upon testimony and immediately come to the conclusion that the Spirit's fullness has to do only with words. That is not correct, for obviously words are ineffective unless there is a godly life behind them to validate them. Here the command to be filled with the Holy Spirit (Eph. 5:18) comes in; for when it is read in context, it has to do with Christian living.

To be sure, it also has to do with speaking. For no sooner has Paul said, "Be filled with the Spirit," than he goes on to add, "speak to one another with psalms, hymns and spiritual songs. Sing and make music in your heart to the Lord, always giving thanks to God the Father for everything, in the name of our Lord Jesus Christ" (vv. 19–20). But it is ethical, too. Being filled with the Spirit is contrasted with being drunk with wine. That kind of filling, along with the debauchery associated with it, was characteristic of the culture in which the Ephesian Christians lived. Besides, the exhortation is immediately followed by much practical instruction, including the way in which husbands and wives are to live together within a Christian marriage, the necessity for children to obey their parents, the duties of servants, Christian warfare with Satan, and the ministry of intercessory prayer. The context leads us to think of the fruit of the Spirit as that is detailed for us in the letter to the Galatians: "But the fruit of the Spirit is love, joy, peace, patience, kindness, goodness, faithfullness, gentleness, self-control" (5:22–23).

We may divide the results of the fullness of the Spirit as portrayed in Ephesians 5 into two parts, as Stott does in his handling of the passage. There is the part directed toward God, which includes both worship and testimony, and there is the part directed toward man expressed in godly living and fellowship. Writes Stott, "It is in these spiritual qualities and activities, not in supernatural phenomena, that we should look for evidence of the Holy Spirit's fullness." He concludes by noting that this is always "the apostle's emphasis when he is dealing with the subject in the Corinthian, Galatian and Ephesian epistles."[2]

How to Be Filled

Having distinguished between the "baptism" of the Spirit and the "filling" or "fullness" of the Spirit, and having described what the fullness of the Holy Spirit means, we come to the practical question: How then may I be filled with the Spirit? What is my responsibility? What are the steps? If we turn to the Bible for the answers, as we are wise to do, we find that there are three conditions for filling. First, we must not "put out the Spirit's fire" (1 Thess. 5:19). Second, we must not "grieve" the Spirit (Eph. 4:30). Third, we must "live by" the Spirit (Gal. 5:16). The first two are important, but negative. The third is the most important of the three.

No one can say how this will work out in every case, for God's people are different and function differently. But it will at least mean that you will want to keep short accounts with God. Perhaps you will begin each day with a brief thanksgiving for a good night's sleep and a request for guidance in the day's activities. Following the rush of breakfast you may review the day with God as you ride to your job or work in your home. As problems come up throughout the day, you will take these to him, sometimes in brief prayers (for we do not always have a great deal of time to pray when we are working), and you will ask for his direction and the ability to live as the Lord Jesus Christ would do in that situation. At night you will read the Bible and pray. If you are part of a family, you will pray together, talking about the events of the day in the light of God's Word. Finally, before you retire for the night, you will commit the day to God and confess known sin or shortcomings to him. Then you will rest, knowing that he will watch over you and your loved ones.

This means that you will walk with God the Holy Spirit as surely as if he were a visible person accompanying you throughout your day, and you will draw on his strength and counsel. If you will do this—yield to him, confess known sin, and obey him moment by moment—then he will fill you and make you a faithful witness to the Lord.

186

Gifts and Fruit

John 14:16–18

"And I will ask the Father, and he will give you another Counselor to be with you forever—the Spirit of truth. The world cannot accept him, because it neither sees him nor knows him. But you know him, for he lives with you and will be in you. I will not leave you as orphans; I will come to you."

A number of years ago, when Christian bumper stickers had just become popular, a Christian drove up behind a car whose bumper had the sign: "Honk if you know Jesus." He had never seen a sign like this before but thought it was a cute idea. So he blew his horn, expecting the driver in front to wave, smile, or show a "one way" sign. Instead, the driver rolled down the window and shouted back. "Stop blowing your blankety-blank horn. Can't you see I'm waiting for a red light?"

The story is funny because we recognize that, if a person claims to be a Christian, then a certain standard of conduct may be expected of him. We do not expect him to be perfect, but we do expect him to show some of the fruit of Christian character exemplified so noticeably by the Lord Jesus Christ. Paul wrote of it in his letter to the Galatians: "But the fruit of the Spirit is love, joy, peace, patience, kindness, goodness, faithfulness, gentleness, self-control" (Gal. 5:22–23). We are right to expect this, for one of the goals of the Holy Spirit of God, by whom one becomes a Christian, is to reproduce this character, the character of the Lord Jesus Christ, within us. We touched on this in our second study of the Holy Spirit, for there we saw that one way in which the Holy Spirit glorifies Christ is by reproducing the character of Christ within the individual believer. The subject is related to our third study also, for if we are filled with the Spirit, then we will not fulfill the lust of the flesh (Gal. 5:16); rather, the fruit of the Spirit will abound.

One Fruit

The most important thing that can be said about the fruit of the Spirit is that it is *one* fruit and that it is therefore to be present in its entirety within each Christian. That is why the word is singular ("fruit") instead of plural ("fruits"). This is not true of the "gifts" of the Spirit to which we come next, for they are given to one or another Christian by the Spirit as the Spirit wills. Thus, one may be a teacher, another a pastor, still another an evangelist, and so on. There are different gifts; no one possesses them all. By contrast, each and every Christian is to possess all the Spirit's fruit. The reason for this is in the nature of the fruit itself, for when we ask, "But what is this fruit?" the fullest answer is that it is simply the likeness of the Lord Jesus Christ in his followers. Christ cannot be divided, nor can the likeness of Christ. So if Christ is present within, the character of Christ will begin to show itself in its fullness.

1. It is appropriate that *love* should lead the list of the Spirit's fruit; for "God is love" (1 John 4:8), and the greatest of all Christian virtues is love (1 Cor. 13:13). Divine love gives this word its character; for God's love is great (Eph. 2:4), unmerited (Rom. 5:8), transforming (Rom. 5:5), and unchangeable (Rom. 8:35–39). God's love sent Christ to die for our sin. Now, because the Spirit of Christ, which is characterized by love, is implanted within the Christian, the believer is to show a great, transforming, sacrificial, and unmerited love both to other Christians and to the world. It is by this that the world is to know that Christians are indeed Christ's followers (John 13:35).

2. *Joy* is the virtue that corresponds in the Christian life to mere happiness. On the surface they are related. But happiness is dependent on circumstances—when fortunate circumstances are removed happiness is removed with them—while joy is not thus dependent. A Christian can be joyful, therefore, even in the midst of great suffering.

3. *Peace* is God's gift to mankind, achieved by him at the cross of Christ. Before the cross we were at enmity with God. Now we are at peace, God having made peace with us. We are to show the effects of that peace in all circumstances through what we would call "peace of mind" (Phil. 4:6–7). It is to reign in the home (1 Cor. 7:12–16), between the Jew and the Gentile (Eph. 2:14–17), within the church (Eph. 4:3; Col. 3:15), and in the relationships of the believer with all men (Heb. 12:14).

4. *Patience* is the virtue of putting up with others, even when that virtue is severely tried. It is often used of God who shows great patience in his dealings with fallen and rebellious men and women.

5. *Kindness* is that attitude out of which God acts toward men. If the Christian is to be kind, he must act toward others as God has acted toward him.

6. *Goodness* is similar to kindness, but it is most often reserved for situations in which the recipient does not merit the goodness. It is linked to generosity.

7. *Faithfulness* is trustworthiness or reliability. This virtue involves truth which in turn is part of the character of God. It is the virtue that will make a servant of Christ die rather than renounce his profession or, to put it on a less exalted plane, will make him suffer great inconvenience rather than go back on his word. The one who is faithful will do what he says he will do; and he will not quit when the going gets tough. This word is also descriptive of the character of Christ, the faithful witness (Rev. 1:5), and of God the Father who always acts thus in regard to his people (1 Cor. 1:9; 10:13; 1 Thess. 5:24; 2 Thess. 3:3).

8. *Gentleness* is the virtue of the man who is so much in control of himself that he is always angry at the right time (as against sin) and never angry at the wrong time. It was the preeminent virtue of Moses, who is praised for being the meekest man who ever lived (Num. 12:3).

9. The final manifestation of the Spirit's fruit is *self-control,* the quality that gives victory over fleshly desires and that is therefore closely related to chastity both of mind and conduct. Barclay notes that it "is that great quality which comes to a man when Christ is in his heart, that quality which makes him able to live and to walk in the world, and yet to keep his garments unspotted from the world."[1]

Fruitful Christians

What makes the difference between a fruitful Christian and a nonfruitful one or, as we may also say, between one who produces the fruit of the Spirit and one who exhibits only the works of the flesh? One answer to that question is suggested by the image of fruit bearing. Here we turn to John 15 in which the Lord Jesus Christ says to his disciples, "I am the true vine, and my Father is the gardener. He cuts off every branch in me that bears no fruit, while every branch that does bear fruit he prunes so that it will be even more fruitful. . . . Remain in me, and I will remain in you. No branch can bear fruit by itself; it must remain in the vine. Neither can you bear fruit unless you remain in me. I am the vine; you are the branches. If a man remains in me and I in him, he will bear much fruit; apart from me you can do nothing" (vv. 1–2, 4–5). This answer has three parts.

First, in order to be fruitful, the branch, which bears the fruit, must be attached to the vine. That is, it must be *alive* and not merely a dead piece of wood. In spiritual terms this means that the individual must first of all be a Christian. Without the life of Christ within only the acts of the sinful nature are possible: sexual immorality, impurity and debauchery, idolatry and witchcraft, hatred, discord, jealousy, fits of rage, selfish ambition, dissensions, factions and envy, drunkenness, orgies,, and the like (Gal. 5:19–21). The fruit of the Spirit becomes possible when the life of Christ, conveyed by the Spirit of Christ, flows through the Christian.

Second, there must be *cultivation*. This is the point of the opening statement in which Christ terms the Father "the gardnener." This means that God cares for us, exposing us to the sunshine of his presence, enriching the soil in which we are planted, and seeing to it that we are protected from spiritual drought. If we would be fruitful, we must therefore stay close to God through prayer, feed on his Word, and keep close company with other Christians.

Finally, there must be *pruning*. This can be unpleasant at times, for it means that things we treasure will be removed from our lives. Sometimes it may involve suffering. But there is a purpose in the pruning, and that makes all the difference. The purpose is to bring forth more fruit in our lives. William Fitch has written on this theme, "Pruning is an art which only a great master can really employ; and God is such an artist. He knows the branches in each bush that are not bearing fruit. He cuts them down. We should be grateful for such wonderful care. He never gives up. He is determined that his children should 'grow in grace' and that thereby they should manifest the fruit of Christian grace in all its purity and glory. So the heavenly husbandman works with us, cleanses us, prunes where necessary, and plants a crop. Do we flinch? Perhaps, but we do not lose courage when we know that there is a purpose in our pain."[2]

Gifts of the Spirit

But God does more than simply work from within us as individuals. He also surrounds us with external helps, especially in the form of Christian ministries. These are the gifts of the Spirit. So the gifts of the Spirit (as well as the fruit of the Spirit) must be studied. There are three major New Testament passages in which these gifts are discussed: Romans 12:6–8; 1 Corinthians 12 (the gift of tongues is discussed more fully in chapter 14); and Ephesians 4:7–16.

The first thing we notice as we look at these chapters is that *the gifts mentioned vary* from passage to passage. For example, only two gifts occur in all three chapters: the gift of prophecy (meaning "proclamation") and the gift of teaching. These were obviously of crucial importance in Paul's thinking. The gift of being an apostle is mentioned in two places, in 1 Corinthians 12:28 and Ephesians 4:11. Some of the gifts may be different ways of speaking the same thing, as "contributing to the needs of others" (Rom. 12:8) and "those able to help others" (1 Cor. 12:28). But aside from these few repetitions and possible exceptions, all the gifts—there are at least twenty of them—are different. In other words, the emphasis of the passages is not upon a certain list of gifts that are always to be present within the church at any period of its history or in any given locality, but rather upon the fact that the Holy Spirit will give whatever gifts the church needs at whatever period of its history.

Obviously, some of the gifts will always be present, the gifts of evangelism, teaching, faith, wisdom, and helps, for example. They are involved in the nature of what the church is to be. A second class of gifts, like the gift of apostleship, will cease. Still others, like the gifts of healing or tongues, may or may not be present. The list is not the most important thing. The point rather is that we can be sure that the Holy Spirit will give what the church needs.

The second thing we notice as we read these chapters is that, although not all persons have the same gifts, nevertheless *each believer has at least one.* This is not as clear as the fact that the gifts vary; but it is true nevertheless, as a careful reading shows. Thus, Paul writes to all the believers at Rome, saying, "We have different gifts, according to the grace given us. If a man's gift is prophesying, let him use it in proportion to his faith. If it is serving, let him serve; if it is teaching, let him teach. . ." and so on (12:6–7). The implication is that we each have a gift and are to use it. Similarly, in 1 Corinthians Paul writes, "Now to each one the manifestation of the Spirit is given for the *common good*" (12:7). Again, "All these are the work of one and the same Spirit, and he gives them to *each one,* just as he determines" (v. 11).

This truth is of great importance, for it introduces us to our personal responsibility. If the gifts of the Spirit were not given to every Christian, we might be permitted to take our ease, assuming that we have not been given a gift and thus are not needed. But since this is not true, since God has given each a gift, we obviously are needed; and the work that God intends to be done will suffer if we neglect to use what has been entrusted to us.

The third emphasis of these three chapters dealing with the gifts of the Spirit is upon *the unity of the church.* Gifts that are truly God-given and are being exercised in the service of good will unite rather than divide Christ's body. This emphasis is clear in every passage, but especially in 1 Corinthians 12 where it occurs throughout. It is stressed there because an unspiritual emphasis upon certain gifts was tending to divide the church at Corinth.

The fourth emphasis is upon the major purpose of the gifts, which is *to build up the church* and *to equip it for service.* Here the Ephesians text is most explicit: "It was he who gave some to be apostles, some to be prophets, some to be evangelists, and some to be pastors and teachers, to prepare God's people for words of service, so that the body of Christ may be built up until we all reach unity in the faith and in the knowledge of the Son of God and become mature, attaining to the whole measure of the fullness of Christ" (Eph. 4:11–13). The church is a complex organism. It needs many things to grow and be healthy, just as our bodies need many kinds of food and exercise to grow strong. If a body receives only starches, it will get fat. If it gets only physical exercise, the muscles will grow strong but the mind will be a pygmy by proportion. The body has a variety of needs, and a balance of services is indicated. In the same way, the body of Christ has varied needs. And God, who cares for that body, has seen to it that the necessary variety of gifts is distributed among the Lord's followers.

It is always sad when everyone in a particular church wants to be an evangelist, or a Bible teacher, or an administrator. At times one of these may be more greatly needed than at another, and many may be raised up to meet that need. But in a normal situation many gifts are present and in a balanced proportion. So we must not try to have the other Christian's gift, if we do not have it. We must simply try to be faithful in exercising our own gift and in helping others use what God has given them.

God Pleased

Years ago, when I was just a small boy and there were only two grandchildren in my grandmother's family, this grandmother (who lived in Florida) planted two small orange trees in her front yard. One was for me, and the other was for my cousin. I seldom saw those trees, for my family lived up north. But every year at Christmastime my grandmother would send me a bushel of oranges from my tree to me and another bushel of oranges from the other tree to my cousin. She said it was to show how nice the weather was in Florida and to encourage us to come and visit her. Well, I cannot adequately tell you what an interest I had in my tree. It was mine, and thus I was very interested in the number and the quality of the oranges it produced. I was proud when they were good oranges. I was disappointed when the tree began to produce fewer oranges (as it did in later years) and also when the oranges were stunted by frost or some other hindrance to their proper development.

In the same way, I am convinced that God the Father looks upon us, his children, with special concern, and is particularly pleased when we are really fruitful. God has provided for us amply in all we need. We must determine to yield to him and walk in the Spirit.

187

What about Tongues?

John 14:16-18

"And I will ask the Father, and he will give you another Counselor to be with you forever—the Spirit of truth. The world cannot accept him, because it neither sees him nor knows him. But you know him, for he lives with you and will be in you. I will not leave you as orphans; I will come to you."

The verses from John 14, which have been our jumping-off place for these studies of the Holy Spirit, do not say a word about tongues as one of the Spirit's gifts to the church. This in itself is significant. But it is almost impossible to speak about the Holy Spirit today without giving at least some consideration to the tongues question. What are we to think of the tongues phenomena? Is it of God? Of the devil? Or is it merely self-induced by those who claim to have had the experience? If it is not of God, what shall we do about it? If it is, what should be its place within the life and experience of the Christian and of Christian churches?

Obviously these questions are of great importance if only because of the great increase in the influence of Pentecostalism in twentiety-century Christianity. In some form or other, Pentecostalism has always been with us, but the modern movement arose from an experience with tongues by Charles Parham, dating from a New Year's Eve service in the year 1900. Following his experience, Parham became an evangelist of the Pentecostal message, and the movement spread rapidly, as a result of which the Pentecostal Assemblies, the Assemblies of God, and the Churches of God were founded. These denominations proclaimed a strong dose of biblical theology and grew continually. Today they are rightly recognized as a "third force" in Christendom; in some areas, such as South America, they are dominant. The new element, since 1950, has been the surprising impact of Pentecostalism on mainline churches.

A Sovereign God

What are we to say of this phenomenon? The one thing we must always say is that the sovereign God of the Bible can do anything he chooses and that, if this means "tongues," so be it. We cannot say that (because "the age of tongues has ended," for example) God cannot give the tongues gift today.

Some have tried to say this on the basis of 1 Corinthians 13:8 which reads: "Love never fails. But where there are prophecies, they will cease; where there are tongues, they will be stilled; where there is knowledge, it will pass away." But to do this is to misuse the text. If the verse is to be taken to mean that the gift of tongues must cease in this current church age, then obviously the gift of knowledge must cease too, for the verse says equally emphatically, "Where there is knowledge, it will pass away." Actually, the verses are looking ahead to the time of Christ's return and are warning that all limited experiences of this present day shall pass when, in that day, we are made like Jesus. This is the point of 1 Corinthians 13:10: "But when perfection comes, the imperfect disappears." Nothing in this passage can be taken to say that tongues have been ruled out by God, with the result that anything passing for the gift of tongues today is either a self-induced psychological phenomenon or demonic.

At the same time we must also say that just because God can do anything does not mean that he has therefore done it, at least in every situation. Or, to put it in slightly different terms, it does not mean that everything that claims to be of the Spirit of God is therefore of God.

1 Corinthians 12, 14

Here we must turn to Scripture, for it is the explicit teaching of the Word of God, not experience (however valid or invalid), which must govern our thinking. On this question, the obvious passages are those from 1 Corinthians in which the apostle Paul deals at length with the issue. Significantly, we notice that he does not condemn the phenomenon. He might have, for the practice of speaking in tongues had proved divisive and Paul was obviously trying to overcome this tendency. Yet he does not condemn it. In fact, he acknowledges that he himself had spoken in tongues, adding "more than all of you" (1 Cor. 14:18).

In reading through these important chapters of 1 Corinthians (chapters 12 and 14) we notice six principles.

The first principle can be seen in 1 Corinthians 12:1–3. It is the principle that *the gift of tongues can be counterfeited.* That is, there is a genuine gift; but there is also a duplication of that gift by other spirits, whether the spirit is of Satan or merely the spirit of the individual. This is certainly what Paul is talking about when he reminds the Corinthian Christians that before their conversions they were "led astray to mute idols," and warns them that it is necessary to test the spirits on the basis of their confession or lack of confession of Christ: "No one who is speaking by the Spirit of God says, 'Jesus be cursed,' and no one can say, 'Jesus is Lord,' except by the Holy Spirit" (v. 3). Apparently the Christians at Corinth had been fooled by the ecstatic utterances of pagan priests before their conversion to Christ. Now they were being fooled by some who professed to speak in the power of the Holy Spirit but were not actually empowered by him.

It is worth noting that in many parts of the world, glossolalia (speaking in tongues) is known in non-Christian circles even today. Buddhist and Shintoist priests speak in tongues when in a trance. The phenomenon exists in much of South America, India, and Australia in a variety of non-Christian environments. So the mere speaking in tongues is in itself no proof of the Holy Spirit's presence.

An example may be of help here. In his excellent book on the Holy Spirit, William Fitch reports the experience of Raymond W. Frame, a member of the Overseas Missionary Fellowship in China. A gifted Chinese preacher had come to Shanghai where, because of his gifts, including his fluency in speaking in tongues, he made quite an impression. Some of his utterances, together with an interpretation by another Chinese Christian, had been recorded, however. And it seemed, as Mr. Frame studied the recordings, that some of the statements in the interpretations were contradictory. He decided to "test the spirit" in line with Paul's admonition in 1 Corinthians 12:3. Thus, when the Chinese preacher was again giving his message in an unknown tongue, the missionary asked, "Thou spirit, speaking in an unknown tongue, do you confess that Jesus is the Christ come in the flesh?"

At first the spirit in the preacher seemed to disregard the question completely. But as the question was repeatedly pressed, a note of clear irritation came into the speaker's voice. At last there was an angry outburst in a dialect of Chinese that was understandable: "Why do you not believe? Do you not know that I have come to do a great work?" Then there was a burst of laughing. Not once did the spirit in the preacher confess Christ. As a result of this test, the preacher was branded a false prophet and put out of the church. He was also discredited among the other churches of Shanghai.[1]

The second principle that Paul lays down is that *there are many different and valuable gifts of the Holy Spirit and the gift of tongues is just one.* He says this in verses 4–11 of chapter 12, stressing that there are different needs in the church and that it is the prerogative of the Holy Spirit to meet those needs by giving the necessary gifts to those whom he has called to work in those areas. "To one there is given through the Spirit the message of wisdom, to another the message of knowledge by means of the Spirit, to another faith by the same Spirit, to another gifts of healing by that one Spirit, to another miraculous powers, to another prophecy, to another distinguishing between spirits, to another speaking in different kinds of tongues, and to still another the intertpretation of tongues. All these are the work of one and the same Spirit, and he gives them to each one, just as he determines" (vv. 8–11).

Why does Paul stress that it is by the *one* Spirit of God that the gifts are given? Apparently, to forestall pride. For if it is true that the Holy Spirit gives a gift to each Christian ("each one," v. 7) and that for his own purposes, then obviously we are unable to take pride in our particular gift over that given to another. The fact that Paul later minimizes the gift of tongues indicates that pride was a particular danger for those who possessed this gift at Corinth.

Growth and Unity

The third of Paul's points is that these gifts are for the *edification and unity of the church* (12:12–27). It follows from this that if a particular exercise of the gift of tongues does not promote growth or, worse yet, if it leads to schism, then either the gift is not of God or it is being exercised in a way contrary to God's purposes for it.

A young man came to me with an interesting story. Two summers before, he had been active in a summer music camp sponsored by one of America's large universities. As a Christian he had longed for some effective Christian witness to the music students. So he was glad when, through the help of other Christian students and with the permission of the university officials, he was enabled to begin a Bible study group and a Sunday worship service. In his judgment these were quite effective. At any rate, a few of the students became Christians.

The following summer the work was begun anew and with high expectations, for the students had learned that the new conductor of the student orchestra was also a professing Christian. The young man who was telling me the story indicated that he had invited the conductor to the Bible study and the services and had asked him to take part. Unfortunately, the conductor did more than take part. He took over! Then he turned the meetings into an expression of worship in which many so-called "charismatic gifts" were evident. The effect, far from being good, was divisive. The fellowship of the Christians was destroyed. Many open doors were closed. Eventually, because of the excesses, university officials banned all Christian meetings from the summer campus. The conductor felt that he had been persecuted; and when the young man protested that he had carried on a Christian work for the whole preceding summer without any harassment, he was told that this was because he had not been sufficiently bold or spiritual in his testimony.

I was in no position to say that the efforts of the orchestra conductor were of the devil. They probably were not. But the gift, if it was a genuine gift of the Holy Spirit, was at least not being exercised properly. It was divisive and far from edifying. By contrast, says Paul, the gifts of the Spirit are given to strengthen the church and unify it.

Fourth, Paul indicates (perhaps in this case to humble those who were boasting of their gift of tongues) that if the gifts are to be listed in the order of importance, *tongues will always come relatively low on the list* (12:28–14:12). This is most marked in 12:28, where Paul actually numbers the gifts: "And in the church God has appointed first of all apostles, second prophets, third teachers, then workers of miracles, also those having gifts of healing, those able to help others, those with gifts of administration, and those speaking in different kinds of tongues." In this list the gift of tongues falls in category five, and even in that category it is listed after healings, helps, and governments. A second way in which Paul makes this point is by his extensive emphasis upon the supreme importance of love. So great is his concern for this that he interrupts his discussion of the problems of gifts to give his great hymn on love, which is chapter 13 in our Bibles. Finally, he concludes that if any of the gifts are to be sought after, it is the gift of prophecy (by which he means the ability to preach and teach the word clearly) rather than the gift of tongues that is desirable (1 Cor. 14:1). He declares from his own case that, although he too speaks in tongues, he would rather speak five words in an intelligible language than ten thousand in an unknown tongue (14:19).

In our case, this would mean that it is far better to be able to present the gospel clearly to a person who is inquiring about it than be able to do any number of supposedly miraculous things that are not edifying.

Dangers and Safeguards

Paul's fifth principle is that *the gift of tongues is fraught with particular dangers* and must therefore be exercised with safeguards. He discusses these in verses 13–38 of the fourteenth chapter.

The first danger is the danger of confusion, or disorder. Paul does not want this, for he seems to regard it as a disgrace or at least an unprofitable thing for God's work to be done in a disruptive way. Here he lays down guidelines. First, do not allow everyone to speak in church at the same time; they should speak one at a time. Second, do not allow everyone to speak, but at the most two or three. Third, do not permit even these to speak in tongues unless there is someone present who has the gift of interpretation and interprets them.

The second danger is the danger of a Christianity without content, which Paul counters by insisting on interpretation. Then as now, Christianity was threatened by an outlook that made experience central and content minor. In this approach the emotional "high" was everything. We see this often today in a kind of emotional Christianity in which experience is all that matters. In facing this, we must, as did Paul, emphasize content and then content again. Francis Schaeffer writes, "We must stress that the *basis* for our faith is neither experience nor emotion but the truth as God has given it in verbalized, propositional form in the Scripture and which we first of all apprehend with our minds—though, of course, the whole man must act upon it."[2] John R. W. Stott argues similarly against what he terms "mindless Christianity."[3]

There is one last point in Paul's discussion of tongues; we need to take note of it too. It is simply that, notwithstanding the dangers of this gift, *no Christian should forbid its exercise.* Specifically he says, "Therefore, my brothers, be eager to prophesy, and do not forbid speaking in tongues" (14:39). If tongues is not your gift, you are not to desire it—at least not more than any other gift, particularly the gift of prophecy. But, on the other hand, if another has been given the gift, you are not to forbid its exercise. Who are you to tell him that he cannot use what God has given? On the contrary, if God has truly given it, to forbid it would be to the church's impoverishment and hurt.

To Each a Gift

One final question: Can the exercise of tongues ever be wrong? The answer is yes, in several situations, including whenever Paul's guidelines in 1 Corinthians are disregarded. The practice is wrong when it is said that speaking in tongues is an essential evidence of the Spirit's presence. It is wrong when Christians are told that, after their conversion, a further Spirit baptism is necessary. It is wrong when it is said to be essential to the fullness of God's work within an individual Christian. Above all it is wrong whenever it diverts attention from Jesus Christ, for it is the Spirit's work to point to and exalt him above all (John 16:13–16).

On the other hand, the dangers and errors in the exercise of this gift should not be an excuse for those who possess other gifts to neglect their exercise. That is a smugness and error of its own. What is your gift? Whatever it is, you are to use it. Is it prophecy? "If a man's gift is prophesying, let him use it in proportion to his faith." Is it ministry? "If it is encouraging, let him encourage; if it is contributing to the needs of others, let him give generously; if it is leadership, let him govern diligently; if it is showing mercy, let him do it cheerfully" (Rom. 12:6–8). It is only as we do this that the church is edified, unbelievers won, and Christ fully glorified.

188

Four Promises

John 14:19–24

"Before long, the world will not see me anymore, but you will see me. Because I live, you also will live. On that day you will realize that I am in my Father, and you are in me, and I am in you. Whoever has my commands and obeys them, he is the one who loves me. He who loves me will be loved by my Father, and I too will love him and show myself to him."

Then Judas (not Judas Iscariot) said, "But, Lord, why do you intend to show yourself to us and not to the world?"

Jesus replied, "If anyone loves me, he will obey my teaching. My Father will love him, and we will come to him and make our home with him. He who does not love me will not obey my teaching. These words you hear are not my own; they belong to the Father who sent me."

If you often have opportunity to comfort a child who has hurt himself while playing, you will readily understand the motives of the Lord Jesus Christ in this passage. Imagine that a child has injured himself and that he has come to you for comfort. The fact that he has come to you means much. Your presence is important. But beyond that there are also several practical things you can do. You can show love. That is, you can kiss the child and hold him in your arms. You can provide information, saying, "There, there, now. It is not really too bad. Look, it is not bleeding. It is only bruised." Or if it is serious, you can get him to the hospital. Finally, you can promise that things will be better. You can say, "Let's put some cold water on it. After that it will stop hurting. Tomorrow it will be as good as new." Anyone who has ever comforted a child knows that in its proper place each of these three things is valuable and that, at least in many cases, the promises seem to be the most valuable of all.

In some sense this is what the Lord has been doing with his disciples in the chapter we have been studying. He had announced that he was departing from them in order to return to the Father, and this had upset them greatly, for he was everything to them. They were downcast, troubled, yes, even afraid. So he began to comfort them—by reassuring them of his love, by providing information, and by giving them some blessed promises. Probably it is the promises more than anything else that make this chapter such a favorite with Christian people.

What are these promises? There has been the promise that Jesus would prepare a place for his own in heaven and that, having prepared it, he would return again for them. He promised that his departure from them would not mean an end to Christian work. For if they truly believe on him, they will be able to carry on his works and, in fact, do even greater works than Jesus has done. He promised that he would answer prayer. And then, perhaps greatest of all, he told of the Holy Spirit whom he would send and who will abide with us forever. In the verses that follow, the verses that are our text, Jesus gives four more promises, all of which relate to his future relationship to the disciples.

The first is a fact: the resurrection. The second is a consequence of that fact: sure knowledge of him and of who he is. The third is a promise of a further revelation: he will manifest himself to them. Finally, there is an explanation of how that further revelation will be possible: by a mutual indwelling.

A Double Resurrection

The first of these promises is a promise of the coming resurrection, but it is cast in such language that it suggests a resurrection on several very important levels. For one thing, it obviously speaks of the resurrection of Jesus himself, for the promise is set in the context of the world no longer seeing him (that is, because he will die) but of the disciples continuing to see him (that is, not only at the present moment but also after the resurrection). Jesus says, "Before long, the world will not see me anymore, but you will see me. Because I live, you also will live" (v. 19).

It is not only the resurrection of Jesus that is spoken of, however, for the last phrase, "you also will live," clearly speaks of their resurrection too. Moreover, since the verses go on to speak of the knowledge that they will have of him following the resurrection and that he will come to dwell within them, it is probably also true that Jesus is suggesting, not merely that they will be raised from the dead physically in some future day, but that they will also enter into the experience of resurrection life now. In other words, the promise is that they are to "come alive" in a new sense following Christ's resurrection.

This was a great promise, particularly to these who were so soon to be confronted with the cruel horror of Christ's death. What were they to think in that hour? They had placed their faith in Christ as the One who was indeed God's Messiah, the salvation of his people. But they had never understood the nature of the cross. With Jesus gone their hopes would be dashed. We would be right to think of them as disappointed, disillusioned, even cynical men. I catch a glimpse of that spirit in the reply of the Emmaus disciples—"We had *hoped* that he was the one who was going to redeem Israel" (Luke 24:21)—and in the vigorous disbelief of Thomas—"Unless I see the nail marks in his hands and put my finger where the nails were, and put my hand into his side, *I will not believe it*" (John 20:25).

Each of these statements arises out of cruel disillusionment, but it was to these men, soon to be struck by death's horror, that Christ makes this promise. "Death is not the end," he says, "not for me, not for you. Moreover, you do not even have to wait until the next life for the promise, for you will begin to enter into the reality of that life now."

Sure Knowledge

The second promise is the promise of certain knowledge of Christ based upon that double resurrection. It is because Jesus has been raised and because we have been given new life that we know him as being who he is. This is what he means when he says, "On that day you will realize that I am in my Father" (v. 20).

The content of this knowledge is that Jesus of Nazareth was God incarnate, that is, that he was fully divine. All else flows from this. And the basis of this knowledge, without which we do not and cannot know, is this double resurrection. On the one hand, it is based upon Christ's own resurrection. Without this there would have been no faith and no knowledge that he was indeed who he claimed to be. He claimed to be God. But if he had died only, no matter how selflessly or courageously, without the resurrection he would rightly be regarded as no more than a selfless and sincere man. He would have been a good teacher, a friend. But faith and knowledge would have stopped at that point. It was only when Christ was raised from the dead that his life was seen to be fully extraordinary and his daring claims vindicated. This is why Paul can refer to the resurrection as the greatest of all Christian evidences in the opening chapter of the Book of Romans, noting that Christ "was a descendent of David, and who through the Spirit of holiness was declared with power to be the Son of God by his resurrection from the dead" (1:3–4).

On the other hand, apart from a corresponding resurrection of spiritually dead men to spiritual life, even this great miracle is insufficient for bringing us to know who Christ is. It is only when God plants his own life within us, thereby enabling us to understand his truth and respond to Christ, that we truly know Christ and embrace him joyfully as the ground of our salvation.

Further Revelation

The third promise is a particularly important one, for it concerns Christ's continuing revelation of himself to those who have believed on him. He says, "Whoever has my commands and obeys them, he is the one who loves me. He who loves me will be loved by my Father, and I too will love him and show myself to him" (v. 21).

This is a step beyond the promise of sure knowledge of who he is, as a careful reading will show. The fact of his historical resurrection and of his gift of the Holy Spirit to us so that we can understand the gospel and believe on him is first in order and is important. But, having come to know who Jesus is and having believed on him, the Christian will then want to know him more fully. In this case, the knowledge will be not so much a knowledge *about* him, leading to faith, but rather a deep knowledge *of* him in which the disciple comes to experience the Lord in the fullest and most personal way. How would this be possible if it were not that Christ himself provides it? There would be no way in which we could know him fully as a living person and close friend. He is not here for us thus to know him. We cannot know him unless he reveals himself. But reveal himself is precisely what he does. The verses that come at the end of this section even go on to say that in the future period of the Spirit's full activity the disciples would come to know Jesus better even than in the days of his physical presence among them.

In what way does the Lord promise to manifest himself to the disciples and to those who follow them? Not bodily, obviously, for the entire point of the discourse is to prepare them for his physical departure. He is not going to manifest himself to them through visions either, for nothing in the Gospel would suggest this. How, then, would he be seen? The answer is that he would be seen in a spiritual sense, as through the revelation of himself in the Bible and through the Holy Spirit's witness to that revelation within the hearts of the disciples and of those who follow them, he is made vividly real. This sounds like fantasy to those who are not born again. But to those who have been made alive by God's Spirit the presence of Christ is more real than anything they can see physically, more real even than their own hands or feet.

"But I am a Christian, and yet Jesus is not that real to me," someone says. Yes, that may be true. But notice that, in the same verse in which Jesus gives the promise of a further revelation of himself, the Lord also gives the conditions upon which that continuing revelation will be given. The conditions are (1) the keeping of his commandments and (2) love.

Have we met those conditions? We suppose, quite often I imagine, that it is possible to enjoy the fullness of the Christian life without a fervent love for Christ, or that it is possible to love without obeying him. We imagine that having been "justified by faith" we thereafter have no need for an obedient walk. But this is not true, and this verse alone should refute it. True, we are saved by faith, and we are to walk in the Christian life by love. But true love as well as true faith will inevitably express themselves in obedience. If they do not, they are not the love or faith about which we read in the Bible. What does it say in James? "Faith without works is dead" (James 2:17). What does 1 John say about this? "This is love for God: to obey his commands" (1 John 5:3). Only when these elements are fully present does Christ fully reveal himself to his disciple.

Here Arthur W. Pink writes wisely, "This manifestation of Christ is made only to the one who really loves Him, and the proof of love to Him is not by emotional displays but by submission to His will. There is a vast difference between sentiment and practical reality. The Lord will give no direct and special revelation of Himself to those who are in the path of *disobedience*. 'He that *hath* my commandments,' means, hath them at heart. 'And *keepeth* them,' that is the real test. We *hear*, but do we *heed?* We *know*, but are we *doing* His will?"[1]

Many Christians would be willing to do spectacular things if by that means they could come to know Christ better. But they are unwilling to do the commonplace things that are involved in simple obedience. Will you do them? If you will, you will most certainly grow in God's grace. If you obey, Christ will increasingly unveil his heart to you. You will come to know him and not just about him. On the other hand, if you fail to obey, he will cease to reveal himself to you, and your own love for him will weaken.

Christ Within

Christ's final promise is found in verse 23. It is the promise of his own personal presence in the Christian through the Holy Spirit. He says, "If anyone loves me, he will obey my teaching. My Father will love him, and we will come to him and make our home with him" (v. 23). The meaning of this is found in his earlier reference to the ministry of the Holy Spirit in which he promised that the Spirit would come to live within each Christian (v. 17).

This was something entirely new at the time Christ promised it. The idea that the Spirit of God would be *with* God's people was not new, for that had been true through all the centuries of the Old Testament dispensation. The Holy Spirit was with Noah in his day, because Peter tells us that the Spirit enabled him to preach while the ark was being prepared (1 Peter 3:18–20). The Spirit was with each of the Hebrew patriarchs. He was with the people of Israel during the days of their wandering in the wilderness. David prayed, "Take not your Holy Spirit from me"—a prayer that was proper for his time but that is not appropriate for a child of God during the church age. In each of these cases the Spirit of God was *with* his people. But now Jesus declares that the One who had been with them in the past was, in a much better way, to be *in* them in the future. Moreover, since he would be in them it is proper to say that the Father and Son would be in them also.

The presence of the Lord within his people is the glorious distinctive of the present time. Therefore, in this age we do not need to go to God and ask that the Spirit be given. He has been given to each of Christ's followers. Rather, it is for us to recognize his indwelling and then allow him to have his way with our lives.

Judge or Savior

Here are four great promises: that we will be made alive spiritually and will be raised as Jesus was raised, that we will know him as God, that we will receive an increasingly full revelation of him (if we continue to obey him and grow in his love), and that he will come to dwell within us by his Holy Spirit. Some of these promises are more or less automatic; that is, they are the product of pure grace and are fulfilled in us regardless of our response or obedience. One promise, the promise of a fuller revelation of Christ, is contingent; it depends upon our obedience and growth in love. What then? Shall we accept the three promises and neglect the one? Shall we neglect the one that is costly? Or shall we rather determine to pursue that promise at all costs, knowing that as we do we will be coming to know that One who is altogether lovely and who out of his great love gave himself for us? To do anything less would be ingratitude and folly. It would be to exchange our spiritual birthright for a mess of worldly pottage.

To those who are not yet Christians, it must be said that although Jesus speaks of an age, this age, when the world will no longer see him, it is nevertheless true that the world will yet see him one day when he is exalted on his throne to render judgment on all because of their misdeeds. You will see him as judge, if you will not see him now. If you see him as judge, it will be to receive his just punishment upon you for your sins. Why wait for his judgment? How much wiser to run to him now, while he is still offered to you as the ground of salvation, and say, "Lord Jesus Christ, I confess my sin; I want you to be my Savior."

189

The Holy Spirit As Teacher

John 14:25–26

"All this I have spoken while still with you. But the Counselor, the Holy Spirit, whom the Father will send in my name, will teach you all things and will remind you of everything I have said to you."

John 14:26 is the shortest of those sections of the final discourses dealing with the Holy Spirit, yet it is probably true that it gives us the fullest definition. The Holy Spirit is described as the "Counselor." We have already seen what this means in our discussion of verses 16–18. He is described as being "holy"—the *Holy* Spirit. Finally, he is described as being a "teacher." Here are three definitions: the Counselor, Holy One, and Teacher. Yet when the verse is looked at closely, it is undoubtedly the last of these, the fact that the Holy Spirit is a teacher, that is emphasized. The role of the Holy Spirit as Counselor is emphasized in the earlier verses. The matter of holiness is emphasized in 16:7–11. But here (as also at 15:26–27 and 16:12–15) the special ministry of the Spirit as teacher is brought forward.

When the Lord says that the Holy Spirit is to "teach *you* all things," the reference is primarily to the apostles. These were those whom Jesus had chosen to be authoritative spokesmen for the truth he had revealed. They were to remember it and then record it in the pages of what has become the New Testament. Moreover, this teaching was to become normative for the church. This same idea is clear in that verse in which the Lord says, "When he, the Spirit of truth, comes, he will guide you into all [the] truth."

Jesus did not mean that all that could possibly be known would be revealed to them. All things that can possibly be known are known only to God. But he did mean that the Holy Spirit would reveal to them the full truth of the gospel centered in Jesus' life, death, and resurrection. And this he did. This was a unique ministry of the Holy Spirit to the apostles.

At the same time, however, there is a secondary sense in which these words apply to Christians who are living today. The Holy Spirit teaches us as well, and the Holy Spirit is the One who brings these things to our remembrance.

Need for Teaching

We need to look at the disciples first, however. Clearly, here were men who needed to be taught. They had been with the Lord Jesus Christ for three years. One might think that they would have understood the essence of his ministry and the gospel. He had spoken to them about these things. But the truth is that, although he had spoken to them about this, nevertheless they had not understood him. It is significant that verse 25 says, "All this I have spoken while still with you." He had spoken to them, but that is not quite the same thing as saying that he had taught them. Obviously he had tried to teach the disciples, and had taught them many other things, but they had not yet really learned the great truths of the gospel. Actually, they were confused men who needed the Holy Spirit's teaching.

They also had a particular problem with learning in this instance, for the Lord had announced his departure to them, and this had so seized upon their minds that they were not really hearing what he was saying. He had spoken about another Counselor, but they were not interested enough in the other Counselor even to learn about him. All they could grasp was that Jesus was to be taken from them.

So the Lord tells the disciples, "You need teaching; you really do. You have heard a lot, but you do not understand it. You need to be taught. I am going. Nevertheless, the Holy Spirit is coming, and one of his roles (a very important role) is to teach you."

The second interesting thing about the teaching of the Holy Spirit is that God himself earnestly wanted to teach the disciples. We see this in the fact that the entire Trinity is mentioned in this verse: "But the Counselor, the *Holy Spirit*, whom the *Father* will send in *my* name, will teach you." In other words, the Father in the name of the Lord Jesus Christ is sending the Holy Spirit to teach the disciples, so much is he interested in having them come to the knowledge of the truth concerning Jesus.

I suppose that if we had been the Lord Jesus Christ, we might have said at this point, "Oh, these dull, dull disciples!" We could even have boasted about the quality of our instruction. We could have said, "It is impossible to imagine a better teacher than they have just had. Furthermore, they have gone through an entire seminary course in three years and have combined formal teaching with on-the-field experience. They have had the advantage of a first-class example. So if they still do not get it, I will flunk them." We might have said that. But this is not the attitude of God. The God who recognizes, on the one hand, that the disciples needed teaching, is the same God who, on the other hand, sends the Holy Spirit in order that they might be taught.

If we ask at that point, "Were they taught?" the answer is yes; of course they were. The proof of it is our Bible. Furthermore, once the Holy Spirit had come, they began to get it quickly, because on the day of Pentecost, Peter, who on an earlier occasion had said when the Lord announced his crucifixion, "Far be it, Lord, that such a thing should happen to you," who did not understand Jesus at all, this same Peter stood up and announced with great understanding that what had occurred in Jerusalem six weeks before had been by the foreordination of God. In other words, the crucifixion of Christ had fallen out in accordance with God's perfect plan and was the heart of redemption. Then Peter preached Christ to the very men who had crucified him, and the Holy Spirit blessed the message so that many came to faith on that occasion. The disciples did learn through the Holy Spirit. Moreover, the Holy Spirit guided them to write these things in the books that became our New Testament.

These books record what the Lord Jesus Christ said and did, explain it, and draw conclusions. In this sense the critics are right when they say that these books are not pure biography, that is, objective historical biography. They are biography with an interpretation attached. But the interpretation, as well as the biography, is that which the Holy Spirit gave.

Our Teacher Too

All this applies primarily to the disciples, but it also comes down to us in a much closer way. For we need to be taught also, and the Holy Spirit, who taught the disciples, is our teacher as well.

Paul writes about it to the Corinthians. He talks first of the fact that in ourselves we are unable to understand spiritual truth, even when it is recorded in the pages of Scripture. But he tells us in addition that the Holy Spirit, the Spirit of truth, who inspired the Bible, speaks from its pages to bring us understanding. "As it is written, 'No eye has seen, no ear has heard, no mind has conceived what God has prepared for those who love him'—but God has revealed it to us by his Spirit. The Spirit searches all things, even the deep things of God. For who among men knows the thoughts of a man except the man's spirit within him? In the same way no one knows the thoughts of God except the Spirit of God. We have not received the spirit of the world but the Spirit who is from God, that we many understand what God has freely given us. This is why we speak, not in words taught us by human wisdom but in words taught by the Spirit, expressing spritiual truths in spiritual words" (1 Cor. 2:9–13).

Here the ministry of the Holy Spirit as teacher is explained. It was exercised, in the first instance, when God revealed truth to the apostles and they recorded it in what would later become canonized as the pages of the New Testament. It is then exercised, in the second instance, when this same Holy Spirit teaches us from the truths that they have recorded.

Remembering

The first part of John 14:26 speaks of the teaching ministry of the Holy Spirit, but there is a second part that speaks of remembrance. "But the Counselor, the Holy Spirit, whom the Father will send in my name, will teach you all things and *remind* you of everything I have said to you." Why, if they were taught all things, does anything need to be brought back to mind? As we begin to reflect on this word, we see that a ministry of the Holy Spirit in helping us remember is necessary because of what we are like and because of the inability of our minds to retain important teachings. It is possible to be well taught, even brilliantly taught, and still forget; or, in the disciples' case, to be taught the meaning of Christ's ministry but forget that upon which it is based.

The Lord's emphasis on remembering teaches us two separate truths. First, it teaches us that the wisdom of God is not a new thing. It is that which God has revealed in the past and that is the same because he is the same. We have a tendency, especially in America and in our age, always to be inventing theology. Churchmen speak about "process theology" today. It means "evolving" theology. But this is not the outlook of the Scriptures. Some of our contemporaries seem always to be searching the Bible in the light of newspapers and popular books in order to come up with something that no one has ever heard before. When they do and when they write a book about it, they get a hearing. This is the nature of *The Passover Plot, The Sacred Mushroom and the Cross,* and some other popular religious books. People buy them and say, "We never heard that before! Therefore, it must be true!" But it is not true, nor is it a product of the Holy Spirit's ministry. The Holy Spirit does not give us new doctrines. Rather, he brings old truths to our remembrance.

So what we preach is not new doctrine but the old doctrine once and for all delivered to the saints. It is the doctrine of man's total inability to help himself spiritually, God's grace in Jesus Christ, the ministry of the Holy Spirit who takes these truths and brings them home to our hearts and minds so that we understand them, and God's unfailing perseverance with his people. We preach that God does not abandon us, that God who has begun to save us in such a marvelous way, giving us a new spirit and creating a new soul, will persevere to the end, at which time he will give us a new body and make us like the Lord Jesus Christ forevermore. These are not new doctrines. They are old doctrines. They are the doctrines that the Holy Spirit brings to our remembrance.

The second truth the word "remind" teaches is that we tend to forget these doctrines, even though we have heard them many times. The history of the church is the history of great blessing through the Holy Spirit, a time of reformation and revival, followed by a gradual forgetting of the message. This happens again and again; so one of the jobs of the minister is to remind the congregation of the old truths. One of the jobs of Christian people is to remind each other of them, and one of the jobs of the Christian church is to remind the world of these old doctrines, even though the world may reject them.

He Shall Testify of Me

This verse also says something else, and we do not want to miss that either. It says that the object of the teaching is Christ. This is true in this text: "He will remind you of everything I have said to you." It is also true in the verses about the Holy Spirit in John 15 and 16: "When the Counselor comes, whom I well send to you from the Father, the Spirit of truth who goes out from the Father, he will testify about *me*. And you also must testify, for you have been with me from the beginning" (15:26–27). "I have much more to say to you, more than you can now bear. But when he, the Spirit of truth, comes, he will guide you into all truth. He will not speak on his own; he will speak only what he hears, and he will tell you what is yet to come. He will bring glory to me by taking from what is *mine* and making it known to you" (16:12–14).

We have a danger, even as evangelical people, of making the Scriptures an end in themselves. We study the Bible as we would a textbook. We memorize the data. But we are always in danger of forgetting that the purpose of the Scriptures is not to exist as an end in themselves, though they will endure forever—"heaven and earth will pass away, but my word will not pass away"—but to reveal Christ to the seeking heart and mind.

God's Power

There is a final point that belongs with what we have been saying. The Holy Spirit is also the One who enables us to teach these truths to others. Teaching spiritual truths cannot be done in the power of the flesh. Paul writes about it in 1 Corinthians in the verses that come just before the ones cited earlier. "When I came to you, brothers, I did not come with eloquence or superior wisdom as I proclaimed to you the testimony about God. For I resolved to know nothing while I was with you except Jesus Christ and him crucified. . . . My message and my preaching were not with wise and persuasive words, but with a demonstration of the Spirit's power" (2:1–2, 4).

Three things are necessary if God's truth is to be properly communicated. First, there must be the revelation of the truth to the apostles by the Holy Spirit. This has been done. Second, there must be the teaching of the Holy Spirit to our hearts, so that, as we read their words, we come face-to-face with the Lord Jesus Christ about whom they wrote. Third, there must be the continuing work of the Holy Spirit to take our testimony concerning this Word and carry it home to the hearts of those who have not yet heard or understood it. Three stages!

But there can be error in each. There are some who do not begin with the Scriptures. They consider the Bible to contain the words of men rather than the very words that the Holy Ghost taught to the apostles. Having thrown out the base, they have nothing on which to stand, and their theology becomes mere speculation. There are others who accept the Bible as the Word of God but who do not allow the Holy Spirit to teach them. They study the Bible in an academic way. Although they may have a high doctrine of Scripture, they do not strive to see the Lord Jesus Christ in its pages. Then there are those who accept the Bible as the Word of God and who do meet with Jesus Christ, but they testify in their own power in a way that brings glory to themselves, and few are won.

We do a farmer's work. First, we prepare the soil. Then we take a seed and plant it. We water it, and we wait for it to grow. But we do not give life to the seed. The seed already has life in it. Moreover, we can scratch a furrow and put the seed in it, but the ground must have the nutrients that God has placed there. And even then the work of God is not finished, for the seed will not grow unless the sun shines upon it. The Holy Spirit must be the sun in our witnessing. We must be faithful in scratching the furrows, watering, even pulling out weeds. But we must look to God to give life.

190

Peace Casting Out Fear

John 14:27–31

"Peace I leave with you; my peace I give you. I do not give to you as the world gives. Do not let your hearts be troubled and do not be afraid.

"You heard me say, 'I am going away and I am coming back to you.' If you loved me, you would be glad that I am going to the Father, for the Father is greater than I. I have told you now before it happens, so that when it does happen you will believe. I will not speak with you much longer, for the prince of this world is coming. He has no hold on me, but the world must learn that I love the Father and that I do exactly what my Father has commanded me.

"Come now; let us leave."

In a sense John 14:27–31 introduces us to an entirely new subject, for this is the first mention of peace in Christ's final discourses. Still, it is not totally unexpected. For one thing, peace is a natural result of the coming of the Holy Spirit to Christ's followers, a matter of which he has just spoken. The apostle Paul tells us that one aspect of the fruit of the Spirit is peace (Gal. 5:22). Furthermore, it is—like Christ's promise of a place prepared for his own in heaven, his return, the fact that his work in them and through them would continue, his pledge to answer their prayers, and the sending of the Holy Spirit to be with them forever—a great reason why they should be comforted. These words even pick up the opening theme of the chapter, reading in this case, "Do not let your heart be troubled and do not be afraid" (v. 27).

This final reason why the disciples are not to be troubled is that Jesus is leaving his peace with them. And if this is so, peace is presented somewhat as Christ's dying bequest to his followers. It is his legacy to them. He is not leaving them destitute or without comfort. True, he is leaving, but he is leaving his peace behind.

Peace in Storm

The beautiful nature of the peace that Christ bequeaths becomes apparent only when we notice the troublesome circumstances out of which these words were spoken and the condition of those to whom Christ's peace was given. It was not a situation marked by outward peace. Christ spoke on the verge of his violent execution. Nor did he speak to those who were already at peace or who were untouched by his imminent arrest and crucifixion. On the contrary, they were already deeply distressed and fearful. Troubles without! Troubles within! It was in this situation that the legacy was given.

The story has occasionally been told of a contest in which artists were to submit paintings and sculptures portraying their understanding of peace. Some showed beautiful sunsets, others pastoral scenery. But the prize went to an artist who had painted a bird in its nest, attached to a branch protruding from the edge of a thundering waterfall. This is the idea involved in Christ's legacy. In times of outward peace anyone can be at peace, or at least many can. But it takes an exceptional peace, a supernatural peace, to prevail in the midst of great outward trouble and inner distress. Christ's peace is just that, exceptional and supernatural. As he explains in these verses, it is a peace that is to be present in his own in spite of the vacillating nature of the world around them, his own absence, and the vigorous activity of the devil and evil persons.

A Vacillating World

The peace that Christ gives is peace in spite of the world's vacillation. We see it in the contrast between the way in which the world gives and the way in which Jesus gives. He spoke of it saying, "Peace I leave with you; my peace I give you."

What is it that characterizes the world's gifts, whatever they may be? *Insincerity* characterizes them. People give, but seldom with motives as high as the gift is supposed to represent. Sometimes the gift is presented only because the gift is expected. *Impotence* also characterizes our giving. That is, even when we are sincere about something, we are nevertheless generally unable to do all that we might like to do. If we wish someone peace, our wish is at best still merely a wish; it does not in itself accomplish anything. The world also gives *scantily*. That is, it always gives less than it could give. This is particularly evident in giving to charitable causes. The world gives with a *selfish motive*. Sometimes this is to be well thought of. Sometimes it is to receive a favor back again. Most objectionable of all perhaps is that the world gives, for the most part, *to those who do not need or do not want the gift.* Most giving is to one's friends, who already have what they need, or to those who are imagined to be rich or important. In addition to all these characteristics, it is also often the case that the world gives but then *takes back again.*

This is not like Christ's giving. He gives sincerely out of a genuine love for his own, effectively, bountifully, at great personal cost (for his gift of peace cost him the cross), and above all to those who clearly need his gift. In the Bible peace is a positive blessing, particularly a right relationship with God from which all other good things follow.

Harry Ironside used to tell this story. At the close of the Civil War, a troop of Federal cavalry were riding along a road between Richmond, Virginia, and Washington, D.C. Suddenly they saw a poor wretch of a soldier, clothed in the ragged remnants of a Confederate uniform, coming out of the bush. He called to the captain of the cavalry unit who drew in and waited for him. "Can you help me?" the soldier called out. "I am starving to death. Can you give me some food?"

"Starving to death?" questioned the captain. "Why don't you just go into Richmond and get what you need?"

The soldier explained, "I do not dare go into Richmond because if I did I would be arrested. Three weeks ago I became so discouraged because of our losses that I deserted from the southern army, and I have been hiding in the woods ever since, gradually making my way north, hoping for a chance to break through to Federal lines. If I should be caught by southern soldiers, I would be shot for deserting the army in time of war."

The captain asked, "Haven't you heard the news?"

"What news?"

"Why, the war is over. Peace has been made. General Lee surrendered to General Grant at Appomattox two weeks ago. The Confederacy is ended."

"What!" said the soldier, "Peace has been made for two weeks, and I have been starving in the woods because I didn't know it?"[1]

This is what it means to have peace with God. It means that the Lord Jesus Christ made peace nearly two thousand years ago for those who are given to him by the Father. They do not have to make their peace with God. Indeed, they could not do it even if they tried. They could not atone for their sins. But Jesus has provided the one perfect atonement so that all who will believe on him may come boldly to God knowing that the ground of hostility has been removed and that they may now find all they need in the storehouse of the Father's great bounty.

But that is only one half of the story, for, having found peace *with* God, these may now enter into the peace *of* God in abundance. What is this peace *of* God? It is the personal peace that Jesus had himself enjoyed while here on earth. Two things are characteristic of it. First, it is a peace based upon one's intimate knowledge of God, a God who is in control of all things. Second, this peace is entirely independent of circumstances. Circumstances raged around Jesus, but he was totally unruffled by them. His enemies foamed with rage in their passionate desire to kill him. But still he went his way, knowing that his life and times were in the hands of a loving, wise, and all-powerful heavenly Father.

"My peace I give you." Have you received that peace? If not, you may ask God for it even as you lay your burden at his feet.

An Absent Christ

The peace about which Christ speaks is also to be present in spite of Christ's physical absence. This is the connection of verses 28 and 29 with the verse that precedes them, for Jesus now speaks of the fact that he is being taken from the disciples. "You heard me say, 'I am going away and I am coming back to you.' If you loved me, you would be glad that I am going to the Father, for the Father is greater than I. I have told you now before it happens, so that when it does happen you will believe."

There are two reasons why the disciples should be at peace even though Jesus was himself physically absent from them. First, because it would be better for Jesus. It would be better for him because he would again be with the Father. This, incidentally, is the true meaning of that sentence at the end of verse 28—"For my Father is greater than I." This has become a favorite verse with Unitarians, Jehovah's Witnesses, and other cultists, who deny the deity of Jesus and who would therefore make him to be less than the Father. They use this sentence to teach that Jesus here confessed himself to be a lesser, created being, although an important one. But while this is the apparent meaning if the verse is looked at only on the surface, it is clearly not the meaning if it is looked at in context. The key word is the conjunction "for." Jesus has told the disciples that they should rejoice in view of his departure and in their love for him. He now gives the reason. "For," he says [that is "because"], "my Father is greater than I." In other words, in the days of his incarnation Jesus had been below the Father in terms of his outward glory and official position. But now he was returning to the Father to assume that great glory and position he had possessed originally. The disciples should rejoice in the exaltation of their Lord that was now in view.

This verse is really a parallel statement to that of Paul, recorded in Philippians 2:5–11. These verses speak of an original, fully divine glory and equality with God the Father possessed by Jesus that, however, he laid aside temporarily in order to become man and die for our salvation. "Therefore God exalted him to the highest place and gave him a name that is above every name, that at the name of Jeus every knee should bow, in heaven and on earth and under the earth, and every tongue confess that Jesus Christ is Lord, to the glory of God the Father" (vv. 9–11). The disciples should recognize that it was better for Jesus that he go.

We ought to apply this to all who die in the Lord. It is true that they will not assume the same glory as Jesus—he is God and they are not—nevertheless, their death will mean their exaltation and perfection. For us their passing is loss. We miss them and are poorer for their death. On the other hand, we rejoice that they have completed their race and are now with Jesus, having been made like him.

The second reason why the disciples were to be at peace even though Jesus was to be taken from them is that the arrangement would be better for themselves. They could not really imagine anything better than having him physically with them. But Jesus repeatedly taught that it would be better for them to have him depart and have the Holy Spirit replace him. Why? Because then they would "believe" (v. 29). At the time he spoke these words the disciples undoubtedly thought they believed. At least they believed all they understood. But they did not understand the reason for his death. They did not understand that his death would be followed by his resurrection. They did not understand that the gospel of salvation founded upon these two great truths was to be preached throughout the whole world until Jesus should come again. It was the work of the Holy Spirit to lead them into an understanding of these great truths and cause them to believe them. Only when this had taken place would they become strong in the faith and be able to carry this same gospel to others.

This should be our faith also. Jesus was telling the disciples that whatever was coming, no matter how tragic it appeared, it was for their own good—for their growth in faith and for blessing in their lives and the lives of others. So must it be for us all. Whatever disturbs us is sent by God for our good. So we should have peace, even in the most adverse circumstances.

An Active Devil

The last two verses of chapter 4 also relate to peace, for they indicate that the peace of Christ should be present even in the face of Satan's activities. Neither a vacillating world, an absent Christ, nor an active devil should upset us. Jesus is speaking of the latter when he announces, "I will not speak with you much longer, for the prince of this world is coming. He has no hold on me, but the world must learn that I love the Father and that I do exactly what my Father has commanded me" (vv. 30–31).

What did Jesus mean when he said, "For the prince of this world is coming"? The prince of this world is the devil (John 12:31; 16:11). Since it says he is coming, Jesus is undoubtedly referring to the activity of the devil in moving Judas to betray him to his enemies, which he was probably doing at that very moment (13:27, 30). In the person of Judas, Satan was literally coming to initiate Christ's arrest and crucifixion. But this did not trouble Jesus, for he had peace even when confronted by Satan's activity.

Satan could do nothing to Christ because "he has no hold on me." This is a hard phrase to render idiomatically in English, but we probably catch the sense of it best if we say that there was no sin in Christ for Satan to latch onto like a handle. He would do his best to destroy Christ. But Jesus would slip through Satan's grasp just as he had earlier slipped through the most hostile crowds. So shall we if we are in Christ. We cannot say, as he did, "The prince of this world . . . has no hold on me." He has plenty in us all. But if we are in Christ, then we may stand with him and achieve the victory over the enemy.

Kept in Peace

The Lord has left a great legacy, a legacy of peace. But have we entered into that legacy? In order to do so, we must be those to whom the gift is bequeathed; we must be Christ's own, his followers. But even if we are, it may still sometimes be true that, just as in terms of a material legacy, one thing or another may keep us from a full enjoyment of it.

In earthly terms physical distance, illness, or incapacity of another kind may keep us from the enjoyment of an inheritance. In spiritual terms other things may do it. Temptation and consequent trials may keep us from peace. We can be so wrapped up in the temptation that we forget the gifts of God. Ignorance will keep peace from us. If we do not know that God is sovereign and that he works all things according to his perfect plan, then our God will be too small for us and we will tremble for him and for ourselves. Sin will also destroy our peace, for we cannot have full fellowship with God when we are willfully sinning. Unbelief will destroy it. All these items will keep our legacy from us. But if, on the other hand, we do what Isaiah refers to in the twenty-sixth chapter of his prophecy, we will know that peace fully. Isaiah speaks in perfect confidence when he says, "You will keep in perfect peace him whose mind is steadfast, because he trusts in you" (v. 3). What is the necessary ingredient? Trusting in God! The staying of the mind upon him! If we look at the churning waves around us, like Peter we will begin to sink. If we focus on Jesus, we will find ourselves walking even on the stormiest seas.

191

"I Am the True Vine"

John 15:1-5

"I am the true vine, and my Father is the gardener. He cuts off every branch in me that bears no fruit, while every branch that does bear fruit he prunes so that it will be even more fruitful. You are already clean because of the word I have spoken to you. Remain in me, and I will remain in you. No branch can bear fruit by itself; it must remain in the vine. Neither can you bear fruit unless you remain in me.

"I am the vine; you are the branches. If a man remains in me and I in him, he will bear much fruit; apart from me you can do nothing."

There have been many guesses about what may have occasioned Christ's parable of the vine and its branches, which extends over the first half of John 15, but it is impossible to be certain of the cause. Since the preceding chapter concludes with the words, "Come now; let us leave," it would seem that the Lord and his disciples left the upper room at this point and began that quiet walk across the city of Jerusalem down into the Kidron Valley that brought them to the Garden of Gethsemane on the Mount of Olives. If that is the case, they may have passed the great golden vine that decorated the door to the Holy Place of the temple or else the vines that grew close to the great walls of the city and stretched along it. This is not certain, however, for the party may have lingered in the upper room even after Christ's statement. Some, who have felt this way for other reasons, have suggested that the vine on the temple may have been visible through a window of the room or that a real vine may have been nearby.

As I say, we do not know the occasion for this parable. We only know that vines were visible everywhere in Judea and that the image of the vine had already been widely used in reference to Israel. "I am the true vine," Jesus said. He then went on to teach about the nature of the church and its fruitfulness, which was to be the result, not of any human achievement, but of its spiritual union with himself. "In me . . . in me . . . in me!" That is the theme of this parable and of the great "I am" saying with which it is launched.[1]

The True Vine

The first point of this parable is the "I am" saying itself, and the obvious emphasis is upon the word "true." "I am the *true* vine," says Jesus. This does not mean that he is true as opposed to that which is false but, rather, that he is the one, perfect, essential and enduring vine before which all other vines are but shadows. The word is used in precisely this sense elsewhere where Jesus is declared to be the "true light" (1:9), the "true bread" (6:32), and the "true tabernacle" (Heb. 8:2).

But there is an even more immediate reference, which almost certainly would not have escaped the disciples. The vine is the preeminent symbol of Israel. Thus, over and over again in the Old Testament Israel is portrayed as God's choice vine or God's vineyard. Isaiah had written, "I will sing for the one I love a song about his vineyard: My loved one had a vineyard on a fertile hillside. He dug it up and cleared it of stones and planted it with the choicest vines. He built a watchtower in it and cut out a winepress as well. Then he looked for a crop of good grapes, but it yielded only bad fruit. . . . The vineyard of the LORD Almighty is the house of Israel, and the men of Judah are the garden of his delight. And he looked for justice, but saw bloodshed; for righteousness, but heard cries of distress" (Isa. 5:1–2, 7). In a similar vein, Jeremiah recorded, "I had planted you like a choice vine of sound and reliable stock. How then did you turn against me into a corrupt, wild vine?" (Jer. 2:21). Ezekiel 15 compares Israel to a vine also, as does Ezekiel 19, "Your mother was like a vine . . . : it was fruitful and full of branches" (v. 10). Hosea wrote, "Israel was a spreading vine; he brought forth fruit for himself" (10:1). One of the best-known passages is from the Psalms: "You brought a vine out of Egypt; you drove out the nations and planted it. You cleared the ground for it, and it took root and filled the land. The mountains were covered with its shade, the mighty cedars with its branches" (Ps. 80:8–10).

The vine was well known, then, as a symbol of Israel. Indeed, a bunch of grapes from the vine is a symbol seen in Israel even today. But the truly extraordinary thing about the use of this image in the Old Testament is that it is always brought forward as a symbol of Israel's degeneration, rather than her fruitfulness. The point of Isaiah's reference is that the vine has run wild, producing sour grapes. "What could have been done more to my vineyard, than I have not done in it?" God asks. Yet it brought forth "wild grapes" (v. 4). Jeremiah terms Israel a "degenerate" and "strange" vine. Hosea calls her "empty," that is, run to leaves. The eightieth psalm is set in the context of a plea for God's renewed favor after the vine has been burned and the hedges broken down.

So here is a vine planted by God to be fruitful but which is not fruitful. And here also, by contrast, is the Lord Jesus Christ who is the true vine. He came from dry ground, but still he grew up before the Lord as "a tender plant" (Isa. 53:2). He was despised of men, but he was perfect and beloved of the Father who, indeed, declared him to be his "beloved Son" in whom he was "well pleased" (Matt. 3:17; 17:5; Mark 9:7; Luke 9:35). Jesus is the One who, by his very nature as the true vine, brings forth fruit unto the Father.

The Gardener

There are two things that the Father is said to do in his care of the vine. First, he is said to "cut off" every branch that does not bear fruit. Generally this has been understood to be a purging away of dead branches in precisely the same sense that branches are said to be "thrown into the fire" and "burned" in verse 6, but I am convinced that most translators have missed the true meaning of the term "cut off" in this instance. Undoubtedly, their translation has been made to conform to what they know or believe is coming in verse 6, but the translation is not the best or even the most general meaning of the Greek word *airo* which lies behind it. The word *airo* has four basic meanings, which are, proceeding from the most fundamental to the most figurative: (1) to lift up or pick up, (2) to lift up figuratively, as in lifting up one's eyes or voice, (3) to lift up with the added thought of lifting up in order to carry away, and (4) to remove. In translating this word by the verb "cut off" the majority of translators have obviously chosen the fourth of these meanings, for the reason suggested above. But the verse makes better sense and the sequence of verbs is better if the first and primary meaning of the word is taken. In that case the sentence would read, "Every branch in me that does not bear fruit he lifts up," that is, to keep it from trailing on the ground.

This translation makes better sense of the passage in every way, and in addition it is much better theology. First, the emphasis of this opening section of the parable is, quite rightly, upon the care of the vine by the Father. It would be strange, granting this emphasis, if the first thing mentioned is the carrying away of unproductive branches. But it is not at all strange to emphasize that the gardener first lifts the branches up so that they may be better exposed to the sun and so the fruit will develop properly.

Second, this lifting up is precisely what is first done with vines, as any one who has watched them being cared for knows. Grapes are not like squash or pumpkins that develop quite well while lying on the ground. They must hang free. Consequently, any branch that trails on the ground is unproductive. It would be a strange gardener who immediately cuts off such a branch without even giving it a chance to develop properly. But it would be wise and customary for him to stretch the vine on an arbor or use some other means of raising it to the air and sun. This is, of course, precisely what vineyards look like, for the vines are always strung from pole to pole on wires.

Third, to translate the word *airo* by "lifts up" gives a proper sequence to the Father's care of the vineyard, indicated by the verb that follows. Thus, he first of all lifts the vines up. Then he cuts off the unproductive elements, carefully cleansing the vine of insects, moss, or parasites that otherwise would hinder the growth of the plant. This last item would have been the ancient equivalent of using insecticides, as is done today.

For these reasons the translation "lifts up" should be preferred. And if this is the case, then the first thing the Father is said to do is to lift the Christian closer to himself. To translate that into spiritual terms, it means that the Father first creates a sense of true devotion in the Christian.

Pruning

The second thing the Father is said to do in his care of the vine is to purge it or prune it. In Greek this word is *katharizo,* which means to cleanse, make clean, or purify. It has given us our English word catharsis. Normally this word would indicate the act of cleansing the vine of anything harmful to it—insects, moss, and so on. But since it is being used of a vine and its branches, it is hard to escape the feeling that pruning is probably also in view. At all events, here the Father is said to be doing a work of removal, removing everything that would prove detrimental to the most fruitful harvest.

In spiritual terms this obviously refers to God's work in removing that which is spiritually detrimental from a given Christian's life. It means to have our bad habits stripped away. It means to have our priorities reordered, our values changed. At times it may mean the removal of friends who are hindering rather than advancing our spiritual growth.

The order of these two activities of the Father are most important, because the reverse only produces hypocrisy. What happens when we go about lopping off so-called unspiritual practices without first being drawn closer to God in true devotion is that we imagine ourselves to be quite saintly, when actually we are not. We begin to look down on others who have not made the same denials. We consider them to be worldly and ourselves spiritual. Moreover, having eliminated these elements ourselves without first having our lives filled with Christ, we discover that we have a vacuum within and that it is easy for something else not at all Christian to fill it. We are like the man in Christ's story who threw one demon out of his house but then suffered greater loss when that demon and seven of his friends returned to repossess him.

What should happen is that we first of all draw near to God and become productive. After that, as the harmful things begin to be cut away, we hardly feel their going. It is a case of maturing, similar to a girl's giving up dolls. No one ever asks a girl to give up playing with dolls. When she is young she plays with them. But as she grows older she becomes interested in a young man, and after this the dolls are just "kid's stuff." The girl does not "give up" dolls. The dolls give her up, because she has grown into a higher sphere of experience. In the same way, as we grow close to the Lord Jesus Christ the dead wood and parasites fall away.

There is one more point connected with the matter of cleansing. It concerns the means by which we are cleansed—the Word of God. Unless we see that the Word must cleanse us, our ideas of purity are man-made and not of God's origin at all. What is more, they are ineffective. David asked the question, "How can a young man keep his way pure?" He answered, "By living according to your word" (Ps. 119:9). Similarly, Jesus says to his disciples, "You are already clean because of the word I have spoken to you" (John 15:3). Nothing will keep sin from us but a careful attention to and application of God's Word. Nothing else will cleanse us.

Remain in Me

The third point in Christ's parable of the vine and the branches is the secret of fruitfulness, which is abiding in Christ. Here Jesus says, "Remain in me, and I will remain in you. No branch can bear fruit by itself; it must remain in the vine. Neither can you bear fruit unless you remain in me. I am the vine; you are the branches. If a man remains in me and I in him, he will bear much fruit; apart from me you can do nothing" (vv. 4–5).

The key sentence in these two verses can mean one of three things. It can be a simple declarative, with the sense, "You *must* remain in me, and I *must* remain in you." It can be a promise: "Remain in me, and I *will* remain in you." Or it can be a command meaning, " *Remain* in me and, thus, see to it that I for my part also remain in you." Probably, as Leon Morris points out, it is the third of these that should be preferred. "Jesus means that the disciples should live such lives that He will continue to abide in them. The two 'abidings' cannot be separated, and 'abiding' is the necessary prerequisite of fruitfulness. No branch bears fruit in isolation. It must have vital connection with the vine. So to abide in Christ is the necessary prerequisite of fruitfulness for the Christian."[2]

I am not a horticulturist, but I am told by those who know such things that a vine needs to be cultivated at least three years before being allowed to produce fruit at all. That is, it must be trimmed and allowed to grow, then be trimmed and allowed to grow again, and so on for a considerable length of time. Only after this does it become useful for bearing fruit. Similarly, there are times in our lives when we seem to go on for considerable periods, undergoing rather radical treatment at the hands of the Father and seeing little fruit come from it. In such times we doubt if there will ever be fruit. But that is only because we cannot see as God sees. We do not have his perspective. Do not get discouraged if that has happened to you. Instead, remember that Jesus promises fruit in due time if we truly remain in him in a close way. We can give our witness, live the Christian life, and, in a sense, refuse to be concerned about the outcome; for, ultimately, God is the One responsible for the vineyard.

You Can Do Nothing

The last sentence of this section introduces a warning, lest in our budding enthusiasm for bearing fruit for God we forget that it cannot be done without him. "Apart from me you can do nothing," says Jesus.

This statement may be applied in two ways. On the one hand, it may be applied to Christians; and if that is done, we have the following: (1) great work to be done, (2) the possibility of attempting to do it, but without Christ, and (3) the inevitable failure that must result from such effort. Spurgeon, who preached a marvelous sermon on just these words, observed, "Without Jesus you can talk any quantity; but without him you can do nothing. The most eloquent discourse without him will be all a bottle of smoke. You shall lay your plans, and arrange your machinery, and start your schemes; but without the Lord you will do nothing. Immeasurable cloud-land of proposals and not a spot of solid doing large enough for a dove's foot to rest on—such shall be the end of all!"[3] It is good that it is so, for if it were not so, I am afraid that we would try to do it all without him. Nothing is what shall come of our efforts, if it is not Christ working.

On the other hand, there is also encouragement in this verse when we realize that it may be applied to those who are yet Christ's enemies. "Without Christ we can do nothing." That is humbling. But if that is true for those who are united to Christ by faith, in whom he nevertheless dwells, how much truer it is of those who are not at all united to him. They may try to do something against the gospel. They may try to destroy Christ's work. But all their efforts will come to nothing, for only the hand of man (and not that of God) is in them.

192

Remaining and Not Remaining

John 15:6–7

"I am the vine; you are the branches. If a man remains in me and I in him, he will bear much fruit; apart from me you can do nothing. If anyone does not remain in me, he is like a branch that is thrown away and withers; such branches are picked up, thrown into the fire and burned. If you remain in me and my words remain in you, ask whatever you wish, and it will be given you."

When the Lord Jesus Christ unfolded his parable of the vine and the branches he knew what he was talking about, for he wished to stress that his disciples must be fruitful, and it is a characteristic of the vine that it is good for nothing except fruit-bearing. If it does not produce grapes, it is worthless.

The reason for this is that the wood of the vine is too soft for any other purpose. A tree might be cut down, sawed into planks, and then used to construct furniture or build a house. But the vine is always gnarled and twisted and cannot yield planks. Besides, it is brittle. Anything built of it would soon break in the user's hands and be worthless. It is not even good for burning. William Barclay points out, in his commentary, that at certain times of the year it was stipulated by law that the people were to bring wood offerings to the temple to supply the fires for the sacrifices. But it was also laid down that the wood of the vine must not be brought, because it was useless for that purpose. It burned too quickly. The only thing that could be done with it, save letting it lie around, was to make a bonfire and destroy it quickly.

This, incidentally, is the basis of the fifteenth chapter of Ezekiel, for in that chapter the prophet is emphasizing the uselessness of Israel in her then-quite-unproductive state. He writes, "How is the wood of a vine better than that of a branch on any of the trees in the forest? Is wood ever taken from it to make anything useful? Do they make pegs from it to hang things on? And after it is thrown on the fire as fuel and the fire burns both ends and chars the middle [that is, it is burned up instantly], is it then useful for anything?" (vv. 2–4).

This is the image that Jesus uses of those who are joined to him in saving faith. So the question immediately arises: Are we who are joined to Christ fruitful? Are we useful to him? Or are we merely a lot of leaves and dead wood, fit for nothing but to be gathered up and burned.

Remaining in Christ

The verse we come to first contains the phrase, *"He cuts off."* But the place to begin is not with the negative. It is with the positive idea: with re-maining. This is true because remaining in Christ is the major idea of this section of John's Gospel. The word "remain" occurs eight times in just seven verses (vv. 4–10), and the thought is alluded to even more often. It is also true because the negative—"does not remain" is bracketed between two positive statements. Verse 5 reads, "If a man remains in me," and verse 7 concludes, "If you remain in me . . ." Besides, we will hardly understand a failure to remain in Christ until we know what remaining means.

In the first place, then, remaining in Christ is for those who are *in Christ already*. That is, Christ's challenge is for those who are already Christians, who have believed on him as the Son of God and Savior and have commit-ted themselves to him as Savior and Lord of their lives. Does this describe you? If so, you can go on to what Jesus is talking about in terms of a full and fruitful life. If not, you must stop at this point or else first come to him. Do not think that Jesus is giving a formula for a full and fruitful life to all men, regardless of their relationship to him. He is speaking to Christians, and he is giving this promise only to them. So come to him if you have not already done so. Say, "Lord Jesus Christ, I admit that my life is unfruitful and that I can never make it fruitful by myself. I need you. Accept me now, not on the basis of my own merit (for I have none), but on the basis of your death on my behalf. Accept me as one of your followers." If you can pray that prayer and mean it, you can be certain that he has already joined you to himself.

The second point is *the remaining*. It refers to conscious decisions or choices in living the Christian life. Ray Stedman writes of this passage, "When our Lord says: *Abide in me* he is talking about the will, about the choices, the decisions we make. We must decide to do things which expose ourselves to him and keep ourselves in contact with him. This is what it means to abide in him. We have been placed into Christ by the Holy Spirit. Now we must choose to maintain that relationship by the decisions we make—decisions to expose ourselves to his Word in order to learn about him, and to relate to him in prayer wherein we converse with him. Decisions to relate to other believers in Body Life experiences; that is, bearing one another's burdens and confessing our faults and sharing in fellowship with one another, wherein we learn about and see Christ in one another. All of this is designed to relate to him—*Abide in me*. If we do that, we are fulfilling this active, necessary decision of the will to obey his Word, to do what he says, and to stay in touch with him."[1]

There is also a third point, found in verse 7. There Jesus says, "If you remain in me and *my words remain in you*, ask whatever you wish, and it will be given to you." This is a point that we have seen earlier in other contexts. It is in chapter 14, for instance. There Christ speaks of love and the expression of love through obedience to his commandments. He says, "If anyone loves me *he will obey my teaching*. My Father will love him, and we will come to him and make our home with him" (v. 23). Or again, even in this present chapter Jesus says, "You are already clean *because of the word* I have spoken to you" (v. 3).

Some people imagine that they can have the person of Christ without the doctrine of Christ. They like the idea of Jesus, but they shy away from his teaching. Some even revolt against it. But their goal is impossible, for he has declared that he will come to none and make his abode with none except those who keep his commandments. Spurgeon once wrote on this theme, "We cannot separate Christ from the Word; for, in the first place, he is the Word; and, in the next place, how dare we call him Master and Lord and do not the things which he says, and reject the truth which he teaches? We must obey his precepts or he will not accept us as disciples. Especially that precept of love which is the essence of all his words. . . . If thou wilt not have Christ and his words, neither will he have thee nor thy words."[2]

Not Remaining

In the midst of these encouraging instructions, there is a frightening note, for Jesus speaks of the opposite possibility, the possibility of *not* remaining in him. In this case, he says, "If anyone doe not remain in me, he is like a branch that is thrown away and withers; such branches are picked up, thrown into the fire and burned" (v. 6).

Here is a problem, a problem for all Christians (I am convinced) and not just Calvinistic ones. What is the problem? It is the language of the verse. Jesus does not say, notice, that if we fail to abide in him we will simply be unfruitful, though that is true. Nor does he say we will suffer the loss of all things and yet be saved, as Paul so clearly does in 1 Corinthians 3:15. Rather, he seems to say that if a man does not remain in him, he shall be cut off from the vine and shall wither and be gathered together with others who have also been cut off and shall be burned. The last verb makes one think of being burned in hell. So the text seems to teach the possibility, if not the fact, that some who were once saved will eventually be lost and be consigned to eternal suffering. Does it teach that? If not, how should verse 5 be taken?

Study of the interpretation of this verse shows that there are three basic views taken of it. The first—the one generally assumed by non-Calvinistic theologians and thinkers—is that its meaning is exactly as I have outlined it and that the doctrine of eternal security or perseverance must therefore be rejected as nonbiblical.

But is this valid? To answer that we must see all that is involved. Assuming that this is the meaning of this text (and perhaps of a few other texts), we are then immediately confronted with many other texts, by far the greater weight of biblical revelation, that contradict it. If we hold to this interpretation of John 15:6, we must reject Philippians 1:6, for instance, for how could Paul be confident that he who had begun a good work in the Philippians would continue it until the day of Christ, if they at any time might be cut off for failing to be fruitful? We must reject Romans 8, for in this case there would be something able "to separate us from the love of God, which is in Christ Jesus, our Lord." We must even, let us note, reject verses in the Gospel of John itself, for some of the clearest statements of the believer's security are found in this book. One example is John 10:27–29. "My sheep listen to my voice; I know them, and they follow me. I give them eternal life, and they shall never perish; no one can snatch them out of my hand. My Father, who has given them to me, is greater than all; no one can snatch them out of my Father's hand." We must reject all these verses if John 15:6 refutes the believer's security.

Moreover, I do not believe that the Christian can really accept this interpretation, at least after it has been carefully thought through. In response to John 10:27–29, Arminians usually say that although God will not allow anyone to pluck us out of his hand, he will, nevertheless, not prohibit us, of our own will, from jumping out, if that is truly our desire. But notice that this is not what John 15:6 is saying. John 15:6 is not saying that we can jump out of God's hand, if we choose to do so, but that God will himself thrust us out—more than that, cut us off from a living union with his own Son—not, we must note, because of some grave sin (blasphemy, murder, adultery, or something worse) but simply because we have ceased to be fruitful, and this by the same God who has pledged himself to defend us against all enemies.

I ask: Can any Christian really believe that? I do not believe he can, at least after he has thought it through clearly. If that were the nature of our God, then we would have been cast off long ago; and we would all be in hell. Instead of this, our experience teaches that God has actually born with our fruitlessness, yes, even with our sin and unbelief, and has out of his great love continuously worked to bring us on in the Christian life. Therefore, to adopt this first view is to slander the character of our God and to set the lie to our own experience.

The second interpretation of this verse is that it applies to those who are nominal Christians only. This, for the most part, is the view of Calvinistic writers—Matthew Henry, Charles Spurgeon, the Puritans, and others. These find support in the immediate context: first, in reference to Israel, the old branch, which, according to Paul's teaching in Romans 11 was cut off in order that the wild olive branches (symbolizing the Gentiles) might be grafted in; and then, second, in reference to Judas, who had apparently been cut off that very evening and was soon to be "burned." These interpreters point out that it is not the word "branch" that is used in verse 5, but rather "anyone"—"If *anyone* does not remain in me . . ."

The difficulty with this approach is that it is hard to believe that it is not true branches, believers in Christ, that are spoken of. For one thing, the argument regarding "man" versus "branch" does not hold up; for neither word is in the Greek of this verse. The Greek word is *tis*, an indefinite pronoun. The meaning, then, is "If anyone [that is, any of the preceding, the branches or true believers] does not remain in me, he is like a branch that is thrown away." Besides, there is nothing in the context to indicate that suddenly a new class of persons, those who have claimed to be Christians but who are not actually regenerate, is being introduced. We may point out that the situation noted by the Calvinistic expositors is a real one—there are those who profess to be Christians but who are not and who will eventually be separated from the true church and be lost—but that is not the point here.

According to the third view, it is the believer's works that are burned, if these works are not of Christ, and it is the Christian's role as a fruit-bearer and not his salvation that is discussed in the passage.

Several observations support this. First, it is fruitfulness rather than salvation that is in view throughout this section of the chapter. True, the matter of burning is often associated with hell and therefore the loss or nonpossession of salvation. But that does not mean that it is always associated with it or that it is associated with it here. On the contrary, burning is not always used of hell, as the passage in 1 Corinthians about works proves. And it is its association with the destruction of useless works rather than with the loss of salvation that is most appropriate in this passage. It is always dangerous to try to interpret a parable on any level other than that involved at its most basic point.

Another observation concerns the actual wording of the verse. It is, for example, "like a branch" that the one who is thrown away is thrown away. Therefore, it is not as a "son" that he is thrown away, but as a fruit-bearer. So far as that is concerned, he may indeed be useless to Christ and the Christian ministry though a Christian. Finally, we note that there is even a change of number between the first part of the sentence and the second. In the first part the important term is singular: "If any*one* does not remain. . . ." In the second part the key term is plural: "such *branches* are picked up, thrown into the fire and burned." The "them" and "they" may well be what issues from the "one" who is thrown away in terms of his usefulness. And if this is the case, then it is the Christian's works rather than the Christian himself that are destroyed.

Lot would be an example here, as Arthur W. Pink points out in his presentation of this evidence. "He was out of fellowship with the Lord, he ceased to bear fruit to His glory, and his dead works were all burned up in Sodom; yet he himself was saved!"[3]

Fruitless Christians?

But shall we rejoice just because we are able to accept the third interpretation and therefore consider ourselves to be safe once again? Shall we relax just because we will not be condemned to hell for our fruitlessness? That would be horrible. Our reaction should be one of horror, rather, to think that it is possible to be saved by Christ, to be cultivated and cared for and coddled by the heavenly husbandman, to be preserved for heaven, and yet not to be fruitful in a proper heart response to the One who has done all this for us. Saved and yet fruitless? Far be it from any Christian to be content with that. It is our shame if we are.

And it is folly too, for if we fail to abide in Christ, we forfeit the two great blessings that are promised to us. The first is fruitfulness. Is it really wise to be fruitless? Does it make sense to be unproductive in the Christian life when we could actually be highly productive to the blessing both of ourselves and those around us? No true Christian can ever agree that this is a wise course of action. The second great blessing is the privilege of answered prayer. It is interesting that Jesus speaks of that explicitly in verse 7, saying, "If you remain in me and my words remain in you, ask whatever you wish, and it will be given you." These are the two great spheres of blessing for those who abide in Christ—fruitfulness and the privilege of answered prayer. It is toward that divinely appointed sphere of operations that each who belongs to Christ should aspire.

193

God Glorified . . . in You

John 15:8-11

"This is to my Father's glory, that you bear much fruit, showing yourselves to be my disciples.

"As the Father has loved me, so have I loved you. Now remain in my love. If you obey my commands, you will remain in my love, just as I have obeyed my Father's commands and remain in his love. I have told you this so that my joy may be in you and that your joy may be complete."

The connection between John 15:7 and John 15:8 is the connection that the glory of God has with prayer according to the will of God, a connection that we have already seen in John 14:13–14 ("And I will do whatever you ask in my name, so that the Son may bring glory to the Father."). But here the emphasis is different. In John 14 the emphasis was upon prayer itself. That it was to be answered was to be a comfort to the disciples. In John 15 the emphasis is upon the glory of God.

In this text the glorification of God is linked to four elements, each of which should be abundantly visible in the life of each Christian. The elements are: fruitfulness, love, obedience, and joy. Each one is linked to the central theme of the chapter, the need for Christians consciously to remain in Christ, and should receive careful attention.

Fruitfulness

The first of these ideas is fruitfulness, which Jesus highlights by saying, "This is to my Father's glory, that you bear much fruit, showing yourselves to be my disciples" (v. 8). The flow of thought is that if we are Christ's and remain in him, then we will be fruitful in the Christian life and God will be glorified in our fruitfulness. Moreover, the fact that we are fruitful will be a proof that we are indeed Christ's disciples.

At this point we should probably talk about the real meaning of fruitfulness, for if we fail to do that or if we define fruit wrongly, we are inevitably going to discourage some Christians, which we should not do. Let me explain what I mean. If we begin with a phrase like Paul's words of expectation in writing to the Romans—"that I might have a harvest among you, just as I have had among the other Gentiles" (Rom. 1:13)—and if we therefore identify the fruit of the Christian life with converts to Christ, then we will discourage any who, for whatever reason, do not see many come to the Lord. And we will discourage those who, because of sickness or old age or whatever unfavorable circumstances, are unable to do much and who are therefore made to feel they are useless.

It is true, of course, that these other items may be looked at as fruit in a certain sense. The Bible does so itself. But the real fruit is that listed in Galatians 5:22–23: "The fruit of the Spirit is love, joy, peace, patience, kindness, goodness, faithfulness, gentleness, self-control." This fruit is the fruit of Christ's own character within us. It is his love, joy, peace, and so on, within the Christian. Once we see this, we see that a fruitful life can belong to any child of God regardless of his age or circumstances. He or she need not be disheartened by advancing years or by suffering. In fact, the person may even be encouraged by them, for it is in such circumstances that the character of the Lord can shine brightest and others can best see that he is truly his Lord's disciple.

Do not think that in taking this approach I am denying the need for fruit in the sense of conversions. We obviously need these too. But the starting point, indeed the indispensible heart of the Christian's witness, is this divine character. Apart from it, the effort to save others is like an apple tree trying to produce other apple trees. It cannot be done in that fashion. First, the apple tree must produce apples. After that the apples, which contain apple seeds, will produce other apple trees.

Love

The second of Christ's emphases is love. This follows naturally since love is a fruit of the Spirit. In fact, it is the chief fruit, for "the greatest of these is love" (1 Cor. 13:13). Jesus speaks of it saying, "As the Father has loved me, so have I loved you" (v. 9).

As I look at that verse I see three parts to it. The first part is a *declaration of love:* "I have loved you." We know that these are wonderful words to hear at any time, if they are true. "I love you." "I have loved you from the moment I first set eyes upon you." "I will always love you." This is the basis of any good marriage, when the love expressed is the fullest measure of love. It is the basis of a Christian home in the love between parents and children. In a different sense it is the basis of friendship and certainly of fellowship within the church. But if this is true when the words are spoken by mere men and women, how much more wonderful they are when spoken by the Lord Jesus Christ, as here, and when we are the ones loved. This is an astonishing love, for there is nothing in us that could give cause for it. We are sinners. Jesus is holy. We have rebelled against God. Nevertheless, Jesus loves us.

The steps of the expression of his love are these. To begin with, he loved us with an electing love. This is the stage of love revealed in Deuteronomy 7 in relation to Israel: "For you are a people holy to the LORD your God. The LORD your God has chosen you out of all the peoples on the face of the earth to be his people, his treasured possession. The LORD did not set his affection on you and choose you because you were more numerous than other peoples, for you were the fewest of all peoples. But it was because the LORD loved you . . ." (vv. 6–8). He loved you because he loved you. That is the heart and full substance of it. As Spurgeon has written, "Election is based upon affection, and that affection is its own fountain."[1]

Next, the Lord became a man like us, so great was his love for us. It is written of love in marriage, "For this reason a man will leave his father and mother and be united to his wife, and they will become one flesh" (Gen. 2:24). Thus did the eternal Son. He left his Father's home in heaven to come to earth to woo and wed his bride, the church. He redeemed her. The incarnation is Jesus becoming like us so that we might become like him.

Finally, having elected us in love and become like us in a human form, Jesus died for us. Jesus said, "Greater love has no one than this, that he lay down his life for his friends" (John 15:13). That is true, and the greatest example of it is the death of Jesus himself. Said Spurgeon, "That laying down of life in our Lord's case was specially a proof of love, for he died voluntarily; there was no necessity upon him, as upon us, to die. Other men, if they died for us, would but pay the debt of nature a little before its time; but Jesus died who needed not to die, so far as he himself was concerned. He died also amid circumstances of pain, and shame, and desertion, which made that death peculiarly bitter. The death of the cross is to us the highest proof of our Savior's infinite love of us. He must die the death of a felon, between two thieves, utterly friendless, the object of general ridicule; and this he must do as bearing our sins in his own body. All this makes us say, 'Behold how he loved us!' O beloved! can we doubt Christ's love, since he laid down his life . . . ?"[2]

It is not only a sublime declaration of love that we have in this verse. We also have *the measure of that love;* for Jesus says, "*As the Father has loved me, so have I loved you.*" I suppose that we would rejoice in the love of Christ for us even if his love were but a part-time or half-hearted thing. For him to love us at all would be remarkable. But this is not what he says; nor is it the case. Jesus says that he has loved us, not with an imperfect or even a "perfect" human love, but rather with the greatest love there is; namely, the love which has existed within the being of the Godhead from all eternity and which will exist to all eternity, the love of the Father for him and (we must obviously add) his love for the Father. Is there a greater love than that? It is impossible that there could be. This love is without beginning or end. It is without measure. It is without change. It is according to the measure of this great love, and consequently with that love itself, that Christ loves us.

One thing more. First, we saw Jesus' declaration of his love for us. Second, we saw the measure of that love. Third, we have *the challenge of love,* which is, in this case, to "continue" it. If we continue in his love, then we will be remaining in him and prove fruitful.

Obedience

The third word in this catalog of elements contributing to God's glory is obedience, though it is expressed in a challenge to keep Christ's commands, as has been done elsewhere. "If you obey my commands, you will remain in my love, just as I have obeyed my Father's commands and remain in his love" (v. 10).

Are we tired of this emphasis by now, this emphasis upon Christ's commands? I suspect that we are; but if we are, the fault is in us and not the commands. For, as John says in his first epistle, "His commands are not burdensome" (1 John 5:3). Jesus said, "My yoke is easy and my burden is light" (Matt. 11:30). Then what is wrong? I suspect that what is wrong with us is that we are not really as anxious to do Christ's commands as we would like to think we are; thus, the emphasis upon obedience (we have had it several times already in the last discourses, and we will have it several times more) exposes our halfhearted commitment to the will of Christ and so gives birth to feelings of true guilt.

What happens to us is precisely what happened to Peter when, following the resurrection, the Lord was recommissioning him to service. Peter had denied the Lord three times in the presence of the servants and soldiers in the courtyard of the high priest. So Christ recommissioned him with a threefold pattern. He asked him, "Simon, son of John, do you love me more than these?"

Peter was aware of his recent failure, but he did love Jesus. So he replied in what I believe to be an air of genuine humility, "Yes, Lord; you know that I love you."

Jesus said, "Feed my lambs."

After a short time Jesus asked Peter again, "Simon, son of John, do you love me?" Peter replied that he did.

Again Christ gave the commission, "Feed my sheep."

Finally the Lord asked Peter the third time, "Simon, son of John, do you love me?" This time we are told, "Peter was grieved because he asked him a third time, 'Do you love me?' And he said to him, 'Lord, you know all things; you know that I love you.'"

Jesus said, "Feed my sheep" (John 21:15–17).

Why was Peter grieved? He was grieved because the third repetition reminded him of his threefold denial and hence awakened grief and true guilt for what he had done. Moreover, the questioning had suggested that perhaps, just perhaps, Peter's first effusive answer, "Yes, Lord, you know that I love you," could not be taken at quite its face value. Peter was always prone to blurt something out, but did he really mean it? Did he mean it enough to take a servant's role in caring for Christ's sheep? Did he mean it enough to continue to fulfill this or any other command of Christ until his life's end? Ah, that was quite a different matter. And Peter, like us, did not enjoy being reminded of his weakness.

We need to be reminded anyway. That is the point of the repetition. "If you love me, obey my commands" (14:15). "Whoever has my commands and obeys them, he is the one who loves me" (14:21). "If anyone loves me, he will obey my teachings" (14:23). "If you obey my commands, you will remain in my love" (15:10). "You are my friends if you do what I command you" (15:14). The point is obvious. We must keep Christ's commands if we are to be Christ's disciples and grow in his love.

Let us note one thing further. It is true that we are reminded to obey all that Jesus has given us by way of instruction. But even as he tells us this, Jesus points out that he is asking of us no more than he has already asked and given of himself. "Just as I have obeyed my Father's commands and remain in his love" is his comparison. We can be encouraged by this, knowing that the One who instructs us has himself set the pattern and will give us strength to do as he requires.

Joy

In the last verse, Jesus introduces the fourth and final element that is to be in us and by which the Father shall be glorified. It is joy. Christ adds it, I am sure, to indicate that his commands actually lead in precisely the opposite direction from being grievous. They lead to the fullness of that joy that is of God and that is rightly listed as the second virtue in the list of the Spirit's fruit in Galatians. Jesus says of this virtue, "I have told you this so that my joy may be in you and that your joy may be complete" (v. 11).

This sentence speaks of the Christian's joy in three senses: joy attained, joy abiding, and joy abounding. Joy is to be *attained* as a result of the things Jesus had been teaching. This is the reason why the Christian must abide in him, so that the views, outlook, and aspirations of the Master will be those of the disciples as well. This is the reason for the twofold repetition of the word "joy"—"my joy" and "your joy." The joy of Jesus is to be the joy of the disciple. His joy was a wonderful thing, for it was not deterred by suffering or any other circumstance. In fact, it rejoiced in hardship; for we read that

Jesus "for the joy that was set before him endured the cross" (Heb. 12:2). Where did he find that joy? The answer is in his intense desire to do the will of his Father: "I have set the LORD always before me. Because he is at my right hand, I will not be shaken. Therefore my heart is glad and my tongue rejoices" (Ps. 16:8–9).

Second, the verse speaks of joy *abiding*—that "my joy may *be* [remain] in you." The point of this phrase is that joy does not necessarily remain. Many things can destroy it. Sin can destroy it. So can disobedience or unbelief. David confessed this in the great fifty-first psalm, crying out to God, "Restore to me the joy of your salvation" (v. 12). It was not that his salvation was lost, only that the joy had evaporated. This always happens when we become separated from Christ in the sense of having the fellowship that once was ours broken. In contrast to this, we must abide in him; for when we abide in him the joy abides also.

Finally, the verse speaks of *abounding* joy. This is the meaning of the clause "and that your joy might be complete." I wish that all Christians were more joyful, and, as I read this verse, I sense that the Lord desires this too. Unfortunately, there are many long faces and dour looks. There is too much defeat, too much unhappiness. It does not need to be that way. Rather we should be able to rejoice in Christ, even in the face of arrest, beatings, crucifixion, and death, as he did.

When joy, linked to fruitfulness, love, and obedience, is found in the life of a Christian, all can see it and know that the source is divine. We can never produce these things. We cannot produce the Spirit's fruit. We cannot produce love. We cannot produce joy. But Jesus can do it as we abide in him.

194

No Greater Love

John 15:12–14

"My command is this: Love each other as I have loved you. Greater love has no one than this, that he lay down his life for his friends. You are my friends if you do what I command."

There is something charming about the word "friend" or "friendship." It is due partly to our desire for a close friend or friends and partly, too, to our remembrance of them. We look to our past and can almost mark the major periods of our lives by friends we have had. We think of the friends who went to grade school with us and of the things we did with them. Perhaps at the point of going into high school we made different friends, and we think sometimes, not only of the friends, but of the adventures we had—sometimes adventures that the teachers or other authorities did not entirely appreciate. We have had college friends and those we have acquired later in life. We value friendship and know that we would be much impoverished if we had no friends at all.

It is this awareness that probably gives the verses to which we now come their special appeal, for in them the Lord Jesus Christ, the great incarnate God of the universe, speaks of friendship in terms of our relationships to him. He calls us friends, saying, "Greater love has no man than this, that he lay down his life for his friends. You are my friends if you do what I command you."

Human Friendship

When Jesus says, "You are my friends," it is evident that he is speaking to us on the human level in terms we can clearly understand. And he is doing so—we cannot fail to see it—so that we might contrast his friendship, which is great and perfect, to even the best of the other friendships we have known.

The best known of the biblical examples is the friendship between Jonathan, the son of King Saul, and David, the young hero of Israel. Jonathan was in line for the throne. But David was so evidently blessed of God that the people were saying that he should be the next king. Here was cause for great antagonism, antagonism between the apparent rights of the one and the supposed aspirations of the other. But there was no antagonism. Instead there was a great and beautiful friendship. It was a case in which each sacrificed in order to put the other's interests ahead of his own.

Sometimes the love that exists between one friend and another leads to the ultimate sacrifice, to death. A friend of mine tells that as he was growing up he knew a man who in a sublime moment of self-sacrifice gave his life to try to save his grandson. The two were out in a boat on the Monongahela River in West Virgina, and neither of them could swim. The child, for one reason or another, fell overboard and was drowning. So the man jumped in after the child. Both drowned. But afterward when they found the bodies, the grandfather still had the young child clutched in his arms. He had been so anxious to save his grandson that he had not even opened up his arms to attempt to swim to save himself.

When we hear a story like that we tend to become silent, for we know that we stand before something sublime. It is the ultimate sacrifice, the sacrifice of one's life. Because of such sacrifices we understand what the Lord is saying when he declares in clear reference to his own self-sacrifice: "Greater love has no man than this, that he lay down his life for his friends."

Friend of Sinners

On the other hand, it is not really fair to talk about Jesus' sacrifice in merely human terms, for his death surpasses anything we can imagine. It may not happen often, but sometimes one human being will voluntarily die for another; still, this gift never equals or even parallels Jesus' sacrifice. We see this when we reflect on Jesus' death.

First, when we begin to reflect on Jesus' death we recognize that his death was exceptional if only because *Jesus did not have to die*. That is not true of us. We are mortal. We must die. But Jesus was immortal and therefore did not have to die. Indeed, he was life itself; for he said, "I am the way and the truth and the life" (John 14:6). He could have come into this world, performed a full and varied ministry, and then have returned to heaven without ever having experienced death. On the other hand, of us it is said, "Man is destined to die once, and after that to face judgment" (Heb. 9:27). What does this mean in terms of self-sacrifice? Merely this. If you or I were to give our lives for someone else, while that would undoubtedly be a great and heroic sacrifice, it would nevertheless at best be merely an anticipation of what must eventually come anyway. We would simply be dying a bit sooner than normally. The Lord did not need to die under any circumstances.

Second, the death of the Lord Jesus Christ is exceptional in that *he knew he would die*. Again, this is not usually the case when a mere man or woman gives his or her life for another. Few who die in this way do so knowing in advance that they will die. Rather, it is usually the case that although the act is a risk and death is possible, they nevertheless think they may escape death while yet saving their friend. People take calculated risks and sometimes die, but they do not often die deliberately. Jesus by his own testimony deliberately went to the cross to die for our salvation.

There is another area in which the love of the Lord Jesus Christ for his friends shines brighter than any love of which we are capable. The text says that we are Christ's friends and that he was going to give his life for his friends. But if we think of this closely and honestly, we must recognize that, when the Lord Jesus gave his life for us, strictly speaking *we were not exactly his friends*. True, he calls us friends. It is also true that we become his friends. But we become friends because of his act, because of his electing grace toward us manifesting itself in the atonement and in the ministry of his Spirit by which our natural rebellion against God is overcome and our hearts are drawn to love and serve Jesus. When he died for us, or (if we may push that even farther back) when in eternity past he determined to die for us, he did so while we were yet enemies or were forseen to be enemies. It was "while we were still sinners, [that] Christ died for us" (Rom. 5:8).

Here especially do we see the wonderful love of the Lord Jesus Christ. So long as we think of ourselves as being somewhat good in God's sight we do not see it. But when we see ourselves as God sees us, then the surpassing worth of the love of Christ becomes evident.

It is this that leads up to the verse I have just quoted from Paul's treatment of the human condition in Romans. The opening chapter of that book deals with man's sin, showing how all men and women have possessed a certain knowledge of God but have turned from that knowledge in order to worship a god of their own devising. Paul says that a certain knowledge of the existence and power of God is disclosed in nature and in the consciences of all men and women. But we have rejected that knowledge. Paul says, "For although they knew God, they neither glorified him as God nor gave thanks to him, but their thinking became futile and their foolish hearts were darkened. Although they claimed to be wise, they became fools and exchanged the glory of the immortal God for images made to look like mortal man and birds and animals and reptiles " (Rom. 1:21–23).

There are certain consequences of this, as the chapter goes on to show. We have given up God. So, says Paul, in a certain sense God has given us up. He has given us up to certain consequences. Three times in this chapter we read that "God gave them over." In every case, however, we are told what God gave them over to. This is important, for it is not as if God were holding the human race in his hand and then let go with the result that the human race simply drifted off into nowhere. If I let go of an object, the object falls. I have not given it up to nothing. I have given it up to the law of gravity, and the law of gravity draws it downward. In the same way, God gives us over to the sad consequences of our rebellion.

First of all, God has given us over to "sexual impurity" (v. 24). That is, when we turn our backs upon God, who is perfect in his purity, we inevitably become dirty spiritually.

Second, God has given us over to "shameful lusts" (v. 26). That is, the good affections we have and that we rightly cherish become warped because they are severed from their source. Love becomes lust. A proper sense of responsibility becomes the driving pride of personal ambition. Self-sacrifice becomes selfishness, and so on.

Third, God says that he has given us over to a "depraved mind" (v. 28). This means that we have developed a way of thinking that is antagonistic toward God so that we are constantly devising philosophies and actions that try to eliminate his presence from our lives.

These important verses from Romans give God's assessment of the human race. He made us. More than this, he made us in his own image. But we have rebelled against him and defaced that image. Instead of God's glory, we have advanced man's depravity. Instead of his sovereignty, we have sought human autonomy. Instead of holiness, we have sin. Instead of love, hate. Yet, in spite of our depravity, Christ came to be our friend and prove his friendship by dying for us. As Paul states, "At just the right time, when we were still powerless, Christ died for the ungodly. Very rarely will anyone die for a righteous man, though for a good man someone might possibly dare to die. But God demonstrates his own love for us in this: While we were still sinners, Christ died for us" (Rom. 5:6–8).

Spiritual Death

There is one more reason why the love of the Lord Jesus Christ for his friends, seen in his death for us, is superior to all human loves. *The death of the Lord was a spiritual death,* whereas ours, if we are Christians, is only physical.

If we were to give our life for someone else, the death we would endure would be only physical. We cannot die spiritually in the place of another person. But that is precisely what Jesus Christ did. Death is separation. Physical death is the separation of the soul and spirit from the body.

Spiritual death is the separation of the soul and spirit from God. This is what makes hell such a terrible place; those in hell are separated from God. And because God is the source of all good—all joy, peace, love, and other blessings—hell is the opposite. It is misery, unrest, hate, and so on. This is the separation that Jesus endured for us. He died physically also; that is true. His death was particularly painful and degrading. But the truly horrible aspect of his death was his separation from the Father when he was made sin for us and bore sin's punishment.

This is the meaning of the cry wrung from his lips in that moment: "My God, my God, why have you forsaken me?" I do not know how to explain that. I do not know how it is possible for the second person of the Godhead to be separated from the first person of the Godhead, even for a brief time, as this was. But this is what happened as Jesus experienced ultimate spiritual death in order that we might never have to experience it. Love like that goes beyond our best understanding.

These truths and more are involved in Christ's statement: "Greater love has no man than this, that he lay down his life for his friends." We read that and acknowledge its truth. But then we go on to say, "Yes, and greater love has no one at all—either man, devil, or angel—than that the Lord Jesus Christ, the Lord of glory, should die a spiritual death for us sinners."

Do you know him as the One who demonstrated his love and friendship for you by thus dying? Is he your friend in that sense? If not, you are not yet truly a Christian. But you can be. You can find him to be your friend, indeed, a superlative friend. As the hymn says:

> There's not a friend like the lowly Jesus,
> No not one! No not one!

You need only come to him, confessing your sin and acknowledging your need of him to be your Savior.

Friends of Jesus

There is one other question that arises from our text. I have asked, "Is Jesus your friend?" This is the question that emerges from verse 13 in which Jesus speaks of his love and, therefore, of his friendship for us. But in the next verse we have what might be called the other side of that question. It is, "Are you Christ's friend?" Jesus suggests this when he declares, "you are my friends if you do what I command you" (v. 14).

I am glad the Lord put it as he did, for I suppose that if we had come to him and had asked, "Lord, you have shown yourself to be a friend to us; what must we do to be your friends?" Jesus could have answered, "You have my example of what a true friend is; do that." But if he had said that, we would have been discouraged. How could you or I do that—love as he loves, give ourselves as he gave himself? It is impossible for us to die spiritually for someone else. If Jesus had required us to do all he did, it would be impossible to become his friend. But he did not say that. Instead, he put the requirements in our terms and on our level, saying, "You can be my friends if you will only do what I command you." This means that we are to show our friendship to him by simple obedience.

Did I say "simple"? Yes, it is simple; but it is simple *obedience,* and this means that it must be active, continuous, and in all things. We see that our obedience must be *active,* for Jesus said, "You are my friends if ye *do. . . ."* Unfortunately some Christians talk about the Christian life as though it consisted largely in refusing to do certain things. If we fall into that way of thinking, we imagine after we have refused to drink alcohol, refused to play cards, refused to have extramarital sex, refused to cheat in business, and so on, that we have done a great deal. But we have not. We have obeyed negatively but not positively. Christ calls upon us to love one another, and that cannot be done except in very practical ways. We are also to pray. We are to worship with other Christians. Our lives are to be marked by good deeds. It would make a great difference in the lives of many Christians if, as they read their Bibles and pray each day, they would pause as part of their devotions to ask what practical things the Lord would have them do.

Second, our obedience should also be *continuous.* Jesus did not say, "If you do what I command and then quit" or "If you do it on Sundays" or "If you do it when you feel like it." The verb is a present subjunctive meaning "If you are doing." The idea is of continuous action, day after day, year after year. There is no vacation from being a disciple of the Lord.

Finally, our obedience is to be *in all things,* for he says, "If you do *whatever* I command you." It means coming to him in love to do whatever he asks of us, not picking and choosing as some do, not exalting those aspects of the Christian faith we like and neglecting those we dislike. Rather it means coming with that yielded humility of mind and body that places us prostrate at his feet and asks from that position, "Lord, what will you have me do?" It is only when we ask that question and mean it that we find ourselves being lifted up to do the great errands of our king, and not as slave either, but rather as a friend of Jesus.

I asked earlier, "Is Jesus your friend?" Now I must ask, "Are you Christ's friend by this definition?" God grant that you might be, to your own great joy and to the praise of his glory.

195

Fruit, More Fruit

John 15:15–17

"I no longer call you servants, because a servant does not know his master's business. Instead, I have called you friends, for everything that I learned from my Father I have made known to you. You did not choose me, but I chose you and appointed you to go and bear fruit—fruit that will last. Then the Father will give you whatever you ask in my name. This is my command: Love each other."

Apart from the fifteenth chapter of John's Gospel, in which the Lord Jesus Christ calls his disciples friends, I do not know of any other characters in the Bible who are called friends of God except Abraham. But this one case is significant, because the nature of the relationship of God to Abraham is an illustration of the main point of Christ's teaching here. Abraham is called "the friend of God" in James 2:23, and the reference in James is either to 2 Chronicles 20:7 (in which Abraham is called "your friend," "your" being God) or Isaiah 41:8 (in which Abraham is called "my friend") or both. The significance of the term is in the fact that God spoke freely to Abraham and thus repeatedly opened his mind to him. The classic example is God's conversation with Abraham just before the destruction of Sodom and Gomorrah. In this conversation God said, "Shall I hide from Abraham what I am about to do?" (Gen. 18:17). The answer was no, for the story goes on to record how God revealed the coming destruction to Abraham and how Abraham, knowing that Lot was in Sodom, interceded for the righteous who lived in those cities.

Communication is essential to friendship. Friends speak to one another. They bare their souls and tell their troubles. They share their aspirations. It is no surprise then that in the upper room, in the midst of those conversations in which Jesus calls his disciples friends, the Lord of glory shares his thoughts with them. Already he has done this in reference to his death and resurrection, heaven, the coming of the Holy Spirit after his ascension, and other doctrines. Now he does so in reference to his special calling of them to fruitful service.

He declares that they are his friends because "everything that I learned from my Father I have made known to you" (v. 15).

Friends, Not Servants

One thing that characterizes our friendships is autonomy in the area of choosing whom we will befriend and whom we will not befriend. Generally speaking, that exercise of autonomy is mutual for the persons involved. For example, when we meet another, three reactions are possible so far as friendship is concerned. First, we may not like him or her, and he or she may not like us. In that case we try to be polite to the other person, but no friendship develops. Second, we may like the other person, but he or she may not like us, or vice versa. In that case also no friendship develops unless, of course, the one who dislikes the other changes his or her mind. Third, there may be a mutual attraction. It is only in this latter situation that the people involved become friends. This means that we have a choice in the matter, and so does the other person. We consider this essential to friendship. Yet, in striking contrast to our understanding of the matter, in these verses Jesus stresses that we have become his friends, not because we chose him (because we did not), but because he in his great mercy chose us.

Do we think that we have chosen him? If we do, we have not sufficiently recognized the depth of our own depravity or the unmerited nature of God's grace. The true situation is that we had not only failed to be his friends; we had actually become his enemies, having rejected his rightful rule over us and having spurned his love. The friendship is established only when God acts in Christ to remove the barrier. It is only after he has spoken of laying down his life for us that the Lord Jesus speaks of his disciples as friends.

There is a second difference. It is seen in the purpose clause of verse 16 ("I chose you and appointed you to *go* and bear fruit") and in the command that follows ("This is *my command:* Love each other"). Does it not seem strange from our conception of friendship that Jesus should speak of choosing his friends in order that they might do something and, which is perhaps even worse, immediately follow his declaration of friendship with a command? We would not think of choosing a friend for what he or she could do. That sounds calculating and ignoble. It is not worthy of friendship. Moreover, we would not think of commanding our friend to do something, at least not if we wished to retain him as our friend.

How can Jesus do this? Is his friendship less than human friendships? Or is he teasing, that is, pretending to be our friend when actually he is not? The answer is in the nature of the friendship involved. For this, while true friendship, is nevertheless not a friendship between two equals but between sinful and limited human beings and God. Consequently, the full dimensions of that relationship (which always involve our sin, ignorance, and finitude as well as God's holiness, omniscience, and total sovereignty) are involved. We are God's friends—by grace. But that does not mean that we can approach God as his equal or dictate the terms of the friendship. It means that we must approach him in gratitude always bearing in mind that the friendship exists because he has stooped to our estate.

Fruitful Christians

Having placed the matter of friendship in its proper perspective the Lord goes on to disclose the privileges of that friendship in terms of a life of fruitful Christian service. Here, therefore, the purpose clause emerges, not as a qualification upon the nature of the friendship (though in one sense it is that) but rather as the glorious privilege and destiny of all whom the Lord Jesus Christ calls friends. "You did not choose me, but I chose you and appointed you to go and bear fruit—fruit that will last. Then the Father will give you whatever you ask in my name" (v. 16). This statement of purpose has two parts, each of which is introduced by the important Greek word *hina* ("in order that"): first, that they might be fruitful and, second, that their prayers might be answered.

This is not the first time the word "fruit" has occurred in this chapter, but it carries the understanding of fruitfulness a step farther than any of the previous occurrences. In these verses there is a fourfold progression.

1. In the first part of verse 2 the Lord speaks merely of "fruit." There are no qualifying adjectives. His teaching is that it is the purpose of the vine's branches to bear *fruit* and that he is concerned that they do so. In studying this verse and (in chapter 14) the fruit of the Spirit, we saw that the fruit is primarily those aspects of character that it is the Spirit's work to produce in the life of believers. The fifth chapter of Galatians describes it as "love, joy, peace, patience, kindness, goodness, faithfulness, gentleness, self-control" (vv. 22–23). In a secondary sense, the word "fruit" may also refer to good works, which flow from these characteristics, and to converts to Christianity.

2. In the second half of verse 2 the Lord adds a modifier to the word "fruit," saying, "Every branch that does bear fruit he prunes so that it will bear even *more fruit*." "More" is a searching word, as Andrew Murray has noted in his valuable devotional study *The True Vine*. The reason it is searching is that "as churches and individuals we are in danger of nothing so much as self-contentment. The secret spirit of Laodicea—we are rich

and increased in goods, and have need of nothing—may prevail where it is not suspected. The divine warning—poor and wretched and miserable—finds little response just where it is most needed."[1] So let us not be content with little fruit. Regardless of past blessings, there is always more that God has for us in growth of Christian character, service, evangelism, and other blessings.

3. Seven verses farther, in verse 8, we have another modifier. This time the Lord says, "This is to my Father's glory, that you bear *much fruit*, showing yourselves to be my disciples." Christians often seem to want little to happen—perhaps because they consider "much" of anything to be worldly, including spiritual growth and successes. But whatever the reason, it is certain that Christ is thinking in different terms here, for here he speaks of "much fruit" and of the fact that "much fruit," rather than merely "fruit" or "more fruit," is to the glory of God. Do we believe him? Then we must strive to achieve much, knowing that little fruit brings but little glory either to the Father or the Son.

4. Finally, in the verse we are studying, we come to the last stage in this progression. It is "fruit that will last" (v. 16). Not all fruit does last. In fact, in purely agricultural terms no fruit really lasts. Pears perish. Apples become rotten. Berries, oranges, and grapefruit spoil. In human terms much that we do also belongs in this category. We work, but much of our work and the fruits of that work pass away. In time we will ourselves pass away. Does nothing remain? Does all pass? One thing remains, and that is the fruit produced in the life of the Christian by the Lord Jesus Christ. He is eternal. Therefore, his work is also eternal and will never perish. We come close to this in a bit of doggerel that says:

> Only one life! 'T'will soon be past.
> Only what's done for Christ will last.

Is Christ at work in you? Or is it just you working? Here every Christian worker should pause and ask what he or she is accomplishing in the light of eternity. We should remember that it is possible to build great monuments out of wood, hay, and stubble. A haystack can be quite a large thing. But these will not last. Rather, we are to build with the gold, silver, and precious stones provided by God and assembled by the Lord Jesus Christ according to his blueprint.

Intercession

The second purpose of Christ's calling of us to be friends is that "the Father will give you whatever you shall ask in my name." I must admit that when I first looked at that clause, I found myself wondering why it is introduced here in what is apparently a repetitive way. The inducement to pray is not new. We have had it several times already (14:13–14; 15:7).

It would be a sufficient answer to say that the promise is repeated simply because we need to hear it and because we are so lax in our life of prayer. But as I think about the context in which Jesus speaks of this new friendship and of his command that we love one another, it seems to me that he is probably thinking here of that particular type of prayer known as intercession. Intercession is prayer for others. What should be more natural for the one who along with others has been brought into this great brotherhood and sisterhood of Christianity than that he or she should pray earnestly for those others who are also Christ's friends? If they are Christ's friends, then they are our friends too. And we must pray for them, as indeed they also must pray for us. In this respect we must be like a towering vine, anchored upon earth but reaching up to that rarified and invigorating atmosphere of heaven in which we meet the Lord and have our requests met by him.

Love One Another

The last verse of this section returns to the theme with which verses 12–17 began, to "love one another." It is not the first time that this command has been given, and if we are sensitive at this point, it is possible that we are just a bit irritated at Christ's repetition. In John 13:34–35, Jesus said, "A new command I give you: Love one another. As I have loved you, so you must love one another. By this all men will know that you are my disciples, if you love one another." In the next chapter Christ speaks frequently of our need to love him. Then, in chapter 15, we read, "My command is this: Love each other as I have loved you" (v. 12). Why this constant repetition? And why are we irritated? The answer to both questions is the same: we do not love one another. Therefore, we feel guilty about it and know that we need to be reminded.

John himself learned this, for, in imitation of Jesus, he repeats the command in his first letter to the churches of Asia. "Love one another," he says in 4:7. "Love one another," he repeats just four verses later (v. 11). Then a third time, "Love one another" (v. 12). We are to love one another because of God's great love toward us and because of Christ's command.

Do we? Do we love one another within that bond of friendship created by the Lord Jesus Christ and according to his own love and standards? Let me list some things that love within friendship does.

1. *Love prays for the other.* Job is a significant example. Job had lost all that he valued, including his family, health, and property. In his misery his "friends" had turned against him though pretending to give comfort. Truly, if anyone ever had a right to spurn friendship, it was Job. Yet at the end of the story, after God had intervened to disclose his true purposes and reveal his anger at the counsel of Job's friends, we read that Job prayed and that God blessed Job greatly. For whom did Job pray? "After Job had prayed *for his friends,* the LORD made him prosperous again and gave him twice as much as he had before" (Job 42:10).

2. *Love sticks close to the friend when the friend is in trouble.* Solomon knew what it is to have a friend who sticks close, for he wrote: "A man of many companions may come to ruin, but there is a friend who sticks closer than a brother" (Prov. 18:24). He indicates the same thing a chapter earlier saying, "A friend loves at all times, and a brother is born for adversity" (Prov. 17:17).

3. Finally, *love also gives and gets.* This double activity is seen in Christ's parable of the two friends, one of whom visited the other in the night to say, "Friend, lend me three loaves of bread, because a friend of mine on a journey has come to me, and I have nothing to set before him" (Luke 11:5–6). In the context of Christ's parable the friend who is in bed is reluctant to get up to give to the one asking, yet eventually does, the point being the superior worth of the friendship of God, who gives to all men liberally and is not hard to be entreated. The parable ends, "Ask and it will be given to you; seek and you will find; knock and the door will be opened to you" (v. 9). I tell the story, however, not to stress the willingness of God to give (though that is a valuable lesson) but rather to show the nature of that friendship that goes out of its way to supply what another needs.

We would not want to imply that we should spend time in prayer meetings when it is within our power to give to those who are in need. That is like dedicating a gift to God *(corban)* when parents are destitute. On the other hand, if we are thinking spiritually, we know that we have nothing to give of ourselves. We cannot meet the other's spiritual need. Yet, by God's grace, we have a friend who can meet those needs, even the Lord Jesus. "Friend, . . . a friend of mine on a journey has come to me, and I have nothing to set before him." Can we think that if we pray that way, recognizing our own need, Jesus will not provide all that the friend of ours (who is, therefore, also a friend of his) lacks? Of course not. Therefore, we must love and give and pray. And we must be friends of Christ, as well as of one another.

196

Hated for No Cause

John 15:18–25

"If the world hates you, keep in mind that it hated me first. If you belonged to the world, it would love you as its own. As it is, you do not belong to the world, but I have chosen you out of the world. That is why the world hates you. Remember the words I spoke to you: 'No servant is greater than his master.' If they persecuted me, they will persecute you also. If they obeyed my teaching, they will obey yours also. They will treat you this way because of my name, for they do not know the One who sent me. If I had not come and spoken to them, they would not be guilty of sin. Now, however, they have no excuse for their sin. He who hates me hates my Father as well. If I had not done among them what no one else did, they would not be guilty of sin. But now they have seen these miracles, and yet they have hated both me and my Father. But this is to fulfill what is written in their Law: 'They hated me without reason.'"

The complaint is sometimes made against some American evangelists that, while they may faithfully proclaim the advantages of Christianity, they nevertheless do not adequately confess the disadvantages from the human point of view. In particular, they do not stress the cost of discipleship nor that the one who faithfully follows Christ will be persecuted. I cannot say how true this criticism is. It is probably less true today than it was a few years ago. But whatever the case, the failure does not stem from Jesus. He was totally honest about discipleship. True, he taught the many and great advantages of following him—eternal life, access to the Father through prayer, the gift of the Holy Spirit, a home prepared by him in heaven. But at the same time he never glossed over the fact that love for him would mean the world's hatred.

We have a prominent example of this in the verses that form the second half of John 15. Up to this point Jesus has stressed the blessings that naturally come to one who has left all to follow him. He has been doing this in order to comfort the disciples, for they were rightly distressed at thoughts of their Lord's pending departure. But now the emphasis changes, and instead of privileges Christ speaks of persecution. The dominant theme is the hostility of the world to Christ and his followers, the word "hate" or "hatred" being repeated seven times. Earlier he had spoken of "his own," now of "the world." Before, it was "friends," now "enemies." First he declared his "love" for them and exhorted them to love; in these verses he warns of the world's "hatred."

These verses are of great importance, if for no other reason than that we might learn of the great gap between those who are Christ's own and the world. If we understand it, we will not raise so many questions as to whether there is harm in this or that. We will not ask how worldly we can be. Rather, we will seek the will of God in all things and strive for God's glory.

The World's Hatred

Christ begins by talking about the hatred of the world for the disciples. But the thrust of the verses is not only to say that they will be hated; it is also to show why. There are three reasons.

First, the disciples of Christ will be hated because they are not "of the world" (v. 19). When John uses the term "world" (as he does five times in just this one verse), he is using it not of the world globe, the earth, or even of the human race that populates the earth. Rather, he is using it of the world system. It is the world of men in rebellion against God, and consequently, it is inclusive of the world's values, pleasures, pastimes, and aspirations. It is said of the world in this sense that it does not know God (1 John 3:1) and that it rejected Jesus (John 1:10). This is the world that hates Christ's followers, and the reason it hates them is that they are not of it. The world hates them for the difference.

In Barclay's commentary on John there are several illustrations of this principle, all from purely secular sources. The first concerns the man who invented the umbrella. Today umbrellas may be seen everywhere and are not at all unusual. But when Jonas Hanway first tried to introduce the umbrella into England and walked down the street beneath one he was pelted with dirt and stones. He was actually persecuted. Again, there is Aristides of Athens. Aristides lived during Athens' golden era and was an outstanding man. He was called Aristides the Just. Yet he was banished from Athens. Why? When one of the citizens was asked why he had voted for Aristides' banishment, he answered, "Because I am tired of hearing him always called the Just." A third illustration is Socrates. Socrates was known as the human gadfly because he was always calling upon others to examine themselves and think deeply, but for this they hated and killed him. Barclay concludes, "To put it at its widest—the world always suspects nonconformity. The world likes a pattern; it likes to be able to label a person and to classify him and to put him in a pigeon-hole. And anyone who does not conform to the pattern will certainly meet trouble."[1]

If this is true of any difference at all, as it seems to be, how much more true is it of that radical difference caused by the transformation of some individuals by the Spirit and power of Jesus Christ. Here is a difference that makes the unusual qualities of Hanway, Aristides, or Socrates pale by comparison. Christians have been with Jesus and have become like him in part. They are not like the world—at least they had best not be. They have other experiences, loyalties, and goals. So the world hates them.

There is a second reason Jesus gives for the world's hatred of his disciples, and this is that he has "chosen" them out of the world. He says, "You do not belong to the world, but I have chosen you out of the world. That is why the world hates you" (v. 19). What is the meaning of this? It is merely the old subject of election. Christ elected the disciples to salvation. He chose them for a specific work in this world. Therefore, although the world rejects Christ's salvation and despises his work, it also hates those who have been chosen by him for it.

There is probably nothing that the world hates more than the doctrine of election. Certainly it was this more than anything else that caused the world's virulent hatred of Christ during the days of his ministry. In John 6, after Jesus had begun to talk about election, pointing out that no man is able to come to him unless drawn by the Father and that those who do not come to him do not because they cannot, we read that many of his disciples "turned back and no longer followed him" (v. 66). Similarly, in John 8, after he had taught the same thing, we read, "Then took they up stones to throw at him" (v. 59). Nothing so stirs up the hatred of the worldly mind than the teaching that God in sovereign grace elects some and does not elect others.

Third, because it hates Christ, the world hates Christians because of their identification with Christ. This truth is probably present in verse 19 of our text also, as we see when we read the verse with an emphasis upon the word "I." "I have chosen you out of the world. That is why the world hates you." This emphasis is justified because of the drift of the verses that follow. There Christ says, "If they have persecuted me, they will persecute you also. If they have obeyed my teaching, they will obey yours also. They will treat you this way because of my name" (vv. 20–21).

Here is the crux of the matter. Why does the world hate Christians? It hates them because it hates their Master. Hatred does not exist because of what Christians are in themselves; they are nothing. It does not exist because of what they have done; they are harmless (or at least they should be). Hatred exists because the world hates Jesus and because Christians are identified with him by virtue of his call.

Christ Hated

Why?

But in a sense, this only pushes the problem back one step, for having explained the first hatred by the hatred of Jesus, we immediately ask: But why does the world hate Jesus? It is a perfectly valid question. Jesus answers it in verses 22–24.

The first reason is that the world hates Jesus because of his words. Jesus states this by saying, "If I had not come and spoken to them, they would not be guily of sin. Now, however, they have no excuse for their sin. He who hates me hates my Father as well" (vv. 22–23). Why should they hate Jesus for his words? There are people whom we might hate for their words. Some men's words are arrogant, and people are opposed to them for their arrogance. We all hate pride and show it no pity, save in ourselves. But Jesus was not arrogant. Rather, he was entirely humble, the most perfectly humble man who ever lived, who even when he was afflicted "did not open his mouth" (Isa. 53:7). Some men's words are selfish. Everything revolves around themselves, and they are rightly despised for that. But Jesus was not selfish. He actually gave up his divine prerogatives in order that he might become like us and die for our salvation. Some person's words are mean. But can we hate Christ for that? He was not mean. Instead, he was loving and gentle. He said, "Come to me all you who are weary and burdened, and I will give you rest" (Matt. 11:28). In still other cases the words men speak are hypocritical, and they are hated for that. But the Lord was not hypocritical. Instead, he is the only man who ever lived whose word could always be trusted, who never said one thing while meaning another.

Then what does Christ mean when he says that his words are one cause of men's hatred? How can this be if they were not arrogant, selfish, mean, or hypocritical? That is just the problem. Before Christ came and spoke, men and women could get by with relative goodness. They could have a little arrogance, but not too much; a little selfishness, but not too much; a little meanness, a little hypocrisy. Moreover, they could be thought good because of the limitation. After Christ came this was revealed for what it is: sin. People hated the exposure.

Ironside tells a story to illustrate this point. Years ago, at the time of the opening up of inland Africa by missionaries, the wife of an African chief happened to visit a mission station. The missionary had a little mirror hung up on a tree outside his home, and the woman happened to glance into it. She had come straight out of her pagan environment and had never seen the hideous paintings on her face, or her hardened features. Now, gazing at her own face, she was startled. She asked the missionary, "Who is that horrible-looking person inside the tree?"

"It is not the tree," said the missionary. "The glass is reflecting your own face."

She could not believe it until she was holding the mirror in her hand. When she had understood she said to the missionary, "I must have the glass. How much will you sell it for?"

The missionary did not want to sell his mirror. But she insisted so strongly that in the end he thought it would be better to sell it to her and thus avoid trouble. A price was set, and she took the glass. Fiercely she said, "I will never have it making faces at me again." She threw it down and broke it to pieces.[2]

Men and women hated the Lord Jesus Christ for much the same reasons. That is why they hate him today and hate the Bible. Christ and God's Word reveal our true selves, and we do not like the revelation.

There is a second reason why the world hates Christ, and that is his works. He indicates this by saying, "If I had not done among them what no one else did, they would not be guilty of sin. But now they have seen these miracles, and yet they have hated both me and my Father" (v. 24). In this case, as in the previous verses, it is not that men and women actually were sinless before Christ's coming; that is clearly untrue. It is that his works, like his words, brought sin to light.

This word "miracles" is very significant in John's Gospel. Earlier in these studies we looked at the important term "signs," John's characteristic term for a miracle.[3] John uses "signs" seventeen times, but he uses "miracles" (often translated "works" in the NIV) twenty-seven times; and of those twenty-seven times, eighteen apply exclusively to what Jesus has done. On occasion this word refers to what we would term miracles, for example, "I did one miracle, and you are all astonished" (7:21). But it also refers to all that Christ does, as when he prays to the Father, saying, "I have brought you glory on earth by completing the work you gave me to do" (17:4). The distinct characteristic of this term is that the works are God's works. Thus, we find Christ saying, "I tell you the truth, the Son can do nothing by himself; he can do only what he sees his Father doing, because whatever the Father does the Son also does" (5:19). Just before healing the man who had been born blind he said we "must work the work of him who sent me" (9:4). When we put the term in this context, we see that the works of Jesus are the works of God and, therefore, the revelation of God. The works of God and the revelation of God are brought to their proper climax and completion in the ministry of Jesus.

This is precisely why the world hates Jesus. It hates him because he was doing the works of God; and the works of God, like the words of God, reveal our spiritual bankruptcy. Before we had Christ's works for comparison, our works looked pretty good. But next to his deeds, even the best of ours looks shabby.

In the final analysis, then, the hatred of the world for Christ's followers may be reduced to this. The world hates Christ's followers because it hates Christ, and the world hates Christ because it hates God the Father.

Two Judgments

What will our reaction be at that point? If it is the reaction of the world, it might be that we should write off discipleship as a bad bet. Discipleship? That is a fine thought if it leads to glory with Christ. But hatred? Persecution? A cross? Who wants those? Would it not be better to simply walk a bit closer to the world and its ways and so escape the world's judgment?

That reaction seems wise, so long as we give no thought to God's assessment of the situation. Write God off, and the option of a pleasant and favored life seems preferable. But place God in the picture, give attention to his judgment, and the balance changes. For what is God's judgment? It is suggested at the end of this passage by that verse in which Christ quotes from the Old Testament saying, "But this is to fulfill what is written in their Law: 'They hated me without reason'" (v. 25). The quotation here is either from Psalm 35:19 or Psalm 69:4, but the source is not significant. The significant thing is that in these verses God himself expresses a judgment upon the world's hatred of Christ and Christ's followers, saying that it is entirely without cause, groundless, unfair, without any justification. It is therefore blameworthy and culpable.

What will God do in the face of that situation? Will he ignore the injustice? Can he ignore it? He cannot. Rather, he will move against those who have hated or ignored his Son. He will judge them. And he will receive and honor those who have taken their place alongside Jesus and who in quiet faith and determination have borne the world's ridicule with him.

Finally, there is also a word for those who have taken their stand with Jesus and have known the world's hatred. If this has been true of you, you will know that the favor of the world is not worthy to be compared with the favor of Jesus toward his own and that the world's fellowship, for all its joviality, cannot compare with our fellowship with Christ. You would not think of returning to what you were before you met Jesus. But hatred from others can have the effect of making one hard, and out of that hardness there can arise a desire to strike back in fierce retaliation. This is not Christ's way. Therefore, if you are in danger of this, remember that it is said of Christ, "They hated me *without reason.*" Then, in imitation of him, make sure that *you* give no cause to hatred either. Let such enmity as there is be provoked only by your fellowship with your Lord.

197

He Will . . . You Will

John 15:26–27

"When the Counselor comes, whom I will send to you from the Father, the Spirit of truth who goes out from the Father, he will testify about me. And you also must testify, for you have been with me from the beginning."

Could anything be more exciting than being a coworker with God? I hardly think so. Yet this is what is promised to every faithful Christian in the pages of God's Word. If your boss should call you up tomorrow morning and say, "I have been watching your work and have been very satisfied with it; I would like you to become a partner with me in directing the affairs of the company," you would be thrilled. You would be even more thrilled if the call should come from the President of the United States asking you to be a member of his cabinet or a special counsel in the area of your expertise. How much more delighted should we be, then, that the sovereign and eternal God has appointed us coworkers with him in carrying the gospel of salvation to this world!

Where does God say that we are appointed coworkers with him or with Jesus Christ in this ministry? The passage I am thinking of as I use that word is 2 Corinthians 6:1, in which Paul says, "As God's fellow workers we urge you not to receive God's grace in vain."

The idea also occurs in the words of Christ in the midst of the final discourses as he instructs his disciples concerning the coming of the Holy Spirit. Here Christ says, "When the Counselor comes, whom I will send to you . . . he will testify about me. And you also must testify" (John 15:26–27).

He will testify . . . you must testify. It is the combination of these two testimonies, however strange it may seem, that God uses to exalt Christ and draw men and women to him. And yet, lest we get too carried away in thinking about being coworkers with God, we need to note that the Lord mentions the Spirit's witness first and only after this does he mention our own. Our witness is necessary, but it is powerless without the presence and supernatural activity of God's own Spirit. Only he can illuminate the unregenerate mind and move the rebellious will of man to embrace our Savior.

Witness of the Spirit

How does the Holy Spirit bear his witness? Or, to put it in slightly different words, in what does the testimony of the Holy Spirit consist? There are two answers. One is the work of the Holy Spirit in directing the writing of the books of our Bible. The other is the Spirit's work in bringing those objective truths home to the subjective experience of the individual Christian.

The witness of the Spirit in directing the writing of the Bible is clearly involved in this section, for the next chapter goes on to speak of it explicitly. "When he, the Spirit of truth, comes, he will guide you into all truth. He will not speak on his own; he will speak only what he hears, and he will tell you what is yet to come. He will bring glory to me by taking from what is mine and making it known to you" (16:13–14). "The truth" that was to be revealed is the truth of the Christian gospel, centering in Jesus' ministry. It involved the past ("he will remind you," 14:26) and future ("he will tell you what is yet to come," 16:13). In this ministry there is special reference to the official role of the apostles as the recipients of the witness.

This is taught at several other key places in the Bible. Second Timothy 3:16 says: "All Scripture is God-breathed and is useful for teaching, rebuking, correcting and training in righteousness." This verse teaches that the Scriptures of the Old and New Testaments are the result of the direct breathing out of God and that the vehicle of that divine "spiration" was the Holy Spirit.

Similarly, 2 Peter 1:21 teaches that the Holy Spirit directed the human writers of the Bible so that the work they produced, while still in one sense the work of men, was nevertheless precisely what God himself desired. The verse says, "For prophecy never had its origin in the will of man, but men spoke from God as they were carried along by the Holy Spirit."

This puts the Bible in a category of its own, for it is not like other books. It is true, if we speak only on a human level, that from time to time human authors are what we may choose to call inspired. That is, they are wrestling with a problem and then suddenly are confronted with a great solution or with an exceptional way of stating what they desire to say. They write it. Later, when we come to what they have done, we are so impressed that we say, "Well, he must certainly have been inspired when he wrote that." But this is a loose use of language, and it is not what we are speaking about when we say that the Bible is inspired. When we speak of the Bible being inspired we mean that in a unique way the Holy Spirit came upon the human authors so that what they produced was what God desired, both in the whole and in its parts. It is this that makes the Bible distinct.

The Internal Witness

There is also a second way in which the Holy Spirit bears witness to the Lord Jesus Christ. He continues to bear a witness (present tense) by speaking through the Bible to carry the truths of the Bible home to the individual human mind and heart.

The experience of this truth is what lay at the heart of, and was fundamentally new in, the Protestant Reformation. When the Reformers spoke of the unique authority of the Scriptures they spoke of *sola Scriptura* ("Scripture alone"). But this meant more to them than the simple idea that God had revealed himself to men through the Bible. The new element was not that the Bible, being given by God and through the channel of his Holy Spirit, speaks with God's own authority. The Roman Church held to that as well as the Reformers. The new element was the Reformers' belief, substantiated by the explicit teaching of Scripture and by their own personal experience of Bible study, that the Bible interprets itself to God's people from within, due to the fact that the Holy Spirit has not ceased to speak through it to their hearts. It was this discovery that freed them from an improper and debilitating dependence upon traditions and the decrees of church councils. These may have had value, but they were ultimately unnecessary, for God is not only able to teach but also does teach his people without them.

What is this activity of God's Spirit? The Reformers called it "the internal witness of the Holy Spirit," for they wished to stress that it was the subjective or internal counterpart of the objective or external revelation embodied in the pages of the written Word of God.

Their own experience of Bible study taught them this, but they also noticed that this particular function of the Holy Spirit is repeatedly revealed in God's Word. For example, "The wind blows wherever it pleases. You hear its sound, but you cannot tell where it comes from or where it is going. So it is with everyone born of the Spirit" (John 3:8). Or again, from the last discourses, "But the Counselor, the Holy Spirit, whom the Father will send in my name, will teach you all things and will remind you of everything I have said to you" (John 14:26). Similarly, in his first epistle John writes of this, extending the principle from that special ministry of the Spirit toward the apostles to a more general ministry for all believers, "But you have an anointing from the Holy One, and all of you know the truth. . . . As for you, the anointing you received from him remains in you, and you do not need anyone to teach you. But as his anointing teaches you about all things and as that anointing is real, not counterfeit—just as it has taught you, remain in him" (2:20, 27). Later in the same letter John adds, "It is the Spirit who testifies, because the Spirit is the truth" (5:6).

Paul writes of the same reality. "We have not received the spirit of the world but the Spirit who is from God, that we may understand what God has freely given us. This is what we speak, not in words taught us by human wisdom, but in words taught by the Spirit, expressing spiritual truths in words" (1 Cor. 2:12–13).

Comprehension, Conviction, Commitment

We may break this down a bit by asking, "When we say that the Holy Spirit speaks through the Bible to the individual heart, precisely what does the Holy Spirit do? What are the results of his ministry?" There are several answers.

First, the Holy Spirit gives *comprehension*. Apart from the ministry of the Holy Spirit there is no understanding of spiritual things. The Bible is taught, but men and women do not comprehend it. The gospel is proclaimed forcefully, but the unregenerate consider it nonsense. What is wrong? Is it the nature of the Bible or the inability of the preacher? What is wrong is that the Holy Spirit has not yet granted understanding. This is what Paul is speaking about in 1 Corinthians 2 when he says, "The man without the Spirit does not accept the things that come from the Spirit of God, for they are foolishness to him, and he cannot understand them, because they are spiritually discerned" (v. 14). Without the internal witness of the Holy Spirit, the unregenerate comprehend nothing of the gospel. On the other hand, where the Holy Spirit is at work, understanding follows. This is true regardless of the obstacles to comprehension.

In his discussion of this theme, R. A. Torrey refers to it as the explanation of something that every experienced Christian worker has noticed. He speaks of sitting down beside a person who has expressed a desire to know more about salvation through Christ and of trying to explain the gospel. The Bible is opened. Texts that speak of Jesus as the atoning, risen, and returning Savior are shown, but the inquirer does not see it. The truths are those the person needs to see and believe in order to be saved, but he stares blankly. He sees nothing. The worker goes over it again, but still there is no understanding. A third time! Suddenly, with face lighted up, the person exclaims, "Oh, I see it. I see it. Jesus is God, and he died for me. I only have to believe it to be saved." He does believe it, and he is saved. What has happened? Torrey writes, "Simply this, the Holy Spirit has borne his testimony and what was dark as midnight before is as clear as day now. This explains also why it is that one who has been long in darkness concerning Jesus Christ so quickly comes to see the truth when he surrenders his will to God and seeks light from him."[1]

The second thing the Holy Spirit brings is *conviction*. This is necessary too because it is not enough merely to have a comprehension of spiritual things. Comprehension is necessary. But if we have a proper comprehension, this will involve an understanding of our own sin and we will need to be convicted of our sin. The next chapter speaks of this, for Jesus says, speaking of the Spirit, "When he comes, he will convict the world of guilt in regard to sin and righteousness and judgment: in regard to sin, because men do not believe in me; in regard to righteousness, because I am going to the Father, where you can see me no longer; and in regard to judgment, because the prince of this world now stands condemned" (John 16:8–11).

America will never experience a great revival until there is a deep and disturbing recognition and confession of both personal and national sin. It is the Holy Spirit's work to bring such conviction.

Third, the Holy Spirit will also bring *commitment* to the Lord Jesus Christ. Having comprehended the gospel and having been convicted of sin to the point of repentance, the one to whom the Holy Spirit bears his witness then commits himself to Christ as Lord and Savior.

We have an example of this in the story of Philip and the Ethiopian treasurer. The Ethiopian had been to Jerusalem to worship God and while there had apparently bought a scroll of the prophet Isaiah. He was sincere in his search, but he did not understand spiritual things, so he was puzzled by what he read on his way back to Ethiopia. God sent Philip to him. When Philip arrived, the Ethiopian had come to Isaiah 53: "He was led like a sheep to the slaughter, and as a lamb before the shearer is silent, so he did not open his mouth. In his humiliation he was deprived of justice. Who can speak of his descendants? For his life was taken from the earth" (Acts 8:32–33; cf. Isa. 53:7–8). He wanted to know of whom the prophet was speaking.

Philip taught him about Jesus and how he died for our sin, as Isaiah indicates. At this point, having been given understanding and having been convicted of his own sin, the Ethiopian asked to be baptized as a sign of his commitment. He said, "I believe that Jesus Christ is the Son of God" (v. 37). This is what happens when the Holy Spirit is at work.

Is he at work in your heart? Do you know that Jesus Christ is indeed the Son of God, as he claimed to be, and do you understand that he died in your place, the just for the unjust, that he might save you from sin? Are you convicted of sin so that you are sorry for sin and willing to turn from it? Have you reached the point of committing yourself to Jesus? If you have, say, "Lord Jesus Christ, I am a sinner, but I believe that you are the Son of God and that you died for me. Accept me now as one of your children and help me to follow you faithfully until my life's end."

Human Witness

Finally, there is a word here for those who have heard the witness of the Spirit and responded to it. The Holy Spirit is witnessing, but you must also bear witness, and it is only because of his witness that yours has promise of succeeding. This is why Jesus, immediately after he has said, "The Spirit . . . will testify about me," goes on to add, "and you also must testify" (v. 27).

Moreover, there is a reminder of what constitutes an effective human witness. There are three elements. First, there must be *assurance* that the gospel is indeed true. This is suggested in Christ's reference to the Holy Spirit as the Spirit of truth, for if the Spirit of truth has borne his witness to your mind and heart, one of the inevitable results will be your conviction that what he has testified to you concerning Christ is factual. There can be no true witness on your part without that, just as there can be no true conversion without it. John R. W. Stott, Rector Emeritus of All Souls' Church in London, has said correctly, "No man or woman is truly converted who is not intellectually converted."[2] So, too, there is no true witness that is not at its heart a proclamation of facts that the witness knows beyond any doubt to be true.

Second, there must be a *personal experience* of that truth. In other words, it is not enough merely to be intellectually convinced of something, important as that may be. It is also necessary to have entered into the reality of it personally. This, Jesus indicates when he says, referring to the witness of the apostles, "And you also must testify, for you have been with me from the beginning." Today neither you nor I can reenact the experience of the apostles. But it is not altogether different to say that we must experience the Lord Jesus Christ as they did. Certainly we must spend time with him through our periods of personal Bible study and prayer. And we must attempt to put into practice what we learn of him in those sessions.

Finally, there must be a *verbalized testimony*. That is, you must speak about these things to others. It is not enough merely to be convinced of the truth of the Christian faith and have experienced it yourself. You must seek to tell others what you have known and experienced.

198

No Strange Trial

John 16:1–4

"All this I have told you so that you will not go astray. They will put you out of the synagogue; in fact, a time is coming when anyone who kills you will think he is offering a service to God. They will do such things because they have not known the Father or me. I have told you this, so that when the time comes you will remember that I warned you. I did not tell you this at first because I was with you."

Many times in my ministry I have had occasion to speak of the liberal church as "the secular church." But to be perfectly honest, I must point out that there are areas in which the evangelical church is also secular. One of these is in some forms of evangelism. By this I mean that we are inclined to present the gospel in such a favorable light that the disadvantages (from a human point of view) of following Christ are forgotten. Granted that in spiritual terms there are no disadvantages. Spiritually, all we lose is our sin, and in its place we gain the fullness of God's salvation. Nevertheless, from the point of view of the unregenerate person there is a cost to discipleship, for it means leaving anything that might deter us from God's will for our life, taking up our cross, and following Jesus.

Jesus stated the cost clearly, as we know. For example, at the beginning of the Sermon on the Mount, in those verses that delineate the character of those who should be his disciples, Jesus says, "Blessed are those who are persecuted because of righteousness, for theirs is the kingdom of heaven. Blessed are you when people insult you, persecute you and falsely say all kinds of evil against you because of me. Rejoice, and be glad, because great is your reward in heaven" (Matt. 5:10–12). In these verses, Jesus indicates that the normal expectation for one who follows him is persecution.

Moreover, this is what the disciples, who listened to Jesus on that occasion, learned from him and remembered vividly. Thus, we find that the beatitude about persecution is quoted twice in 1 Peter, once in chapter 3 ("But even if you should suffer for what is right, you are blessed," v. 14) and once in chapter 4 ("If you are insulted because of the name of Christ, you are blessed," v. 14). Peter adds, "Dear friends, do not be surprised at the painful trial you, are suffering, as though something strange were happening to you. But rejoice that you partake in the sufferings of Christ, so that you may be overjoyed when his glory is revealed" (4:12–13). Paul, who had himself endured much persecution (2 Cor. 11:22–33), writes to Timothy, "In fact, everyone who wants to live a godly life will be persecuted" (2 Tim. 3:12). To some he says, "For it has been granted to you on the behalf of Christ not only to believe on him, but also to suffer for him" (Phil. 1:29).

Forewarned and Forearmed

It is along precisely these lines that the Lord Jesus Christ speaks of persecution in the verses that open the sixteenth chapter of John. He has already spoken of persecution once (in 15:18–25), but now he returns to the same theme, explaining that he has done so in order to forewarn and thus forearm the disciples. He says, "All this I have told you so that you will not go astray. They will put you out of the synagogue; in fact, a time is coming when anyone who kills you will think he is offering a service to God. They will do such things because they have not known the Father or me. I have told you this, so that when the time comes you will remember that I warned you. I did not tell you this at first becasue I was with you" (16:1–4).

Clearly these verses are a continuation of the disclosure of the coming hatred of the world for Christ's followers, recorded in the previous chapter. But they are not merely a repetition of what was said earlier. They have emphases of their own. One new emphasis is the specifics of the coming persecutions: excommunication and murder. The other, quite startling revelation is that these will be inflicted upon the disciples, not by the secular world but by religious persons.

Excommunication

The first matter, then, is this penalty of excommunication, which Christ indicates by saying, "They will put you out of the synagogue" (v. 2). To gain the full force of this we must understand that exclusion from the synagogue was not at all like a person being denied membership in a local church congregation today. To be denied membership in a contemporary American church, or even to be put out of it for one reason or another, is not serious. There are always other denominations. There are even other churches with different attitudes within the same denomination. And if worse comes to worst and you are unable to gain admission to any church, it is still no big loss, for it is possible to function well in American society without any church membership.

This was not the case in the matter of excommunication from the Jewish synagogue. For one thing, excommunication meant separation from the spiritual life of Israel. For the one who was excommunicated there would be no worship, no sacrifices, not even the reading of the Scripture—for the Bible was not available to normal people. The Scriptures could be found and heard only in places of worship. To be excommunicated meant losing those benefits and more. It meant losing all that Paul talks about in Romans, when he says of the Jewish people, "Theirs is the adoption as sons; theirs the divine glory, the covenants, the receiving of the law, the temple worship and the promises" (Rom. 9:4).

Moreover, the banning of an individual from the synagogue would have a devastating effect upon his social life and his economic well-being. Former friends would shun him, considering him worse than a pagan. He would be exiled from his family, ostracized. He would lose his job or else, if he was self-employed, his customers. He would even be refused the right of honorable burial. So in speaking of excommunication from the synagogue Jesus was warning his disciples against a threat with fearsome consequences.

The unique thing about this (and the following example of murder) is that, according to Christ, the persecution was to come from religious people, in this case from Judaism's spiritual leaders. This is worth noting, for it is the fact that persecution comes from our religious superiors that makes it so emotionally devastating. Persecution can also be bad if it comes from the secular world, but it does not strike us at the same point. It is external. When it comes from the religious authorities, it strikes inwardly, for the argument is always that they, not we, are the true church and have the true religion. It is the persecuted one that is always called a heretic.

And sometimes he is. Consequently, the persecuted one (if he is at all honest and even a bit humble) must find himself asking, "Are the authorities right? Can I actually be on the right track with all this great weight of opinion and tradition against me?"

At this point I have been greatly helped by reading the exposition of John 16 by Martin Luther, for Luther felt the weight of such opinion in his own excommunication by the Roman church of the sixteenth century. We usually think of Luther in his strongest moments, because he is the hero of the Reformation. We think of him as unaffected by the papal decrees. But Luther was not unaffected. Rather, he portrayed himself in the role of

Jeremiah, who was required to stand before the Judaism of his day and declare it bankrupt, adding that God's judgment was quickly coming upon Judah and the city of Jerusalem, but who was shaken by his own stance and preaching. The leaders rebuked him saying that they were God's people. They even quoted Scripture to refute his prophecy, for had not God promised to David that there should never fail a king of Judah to sit upon his throne? Luther found himself asking, as did Jeremiah, "Am I to stand up alone and preach against your people, your kingdom, your priests, and your Word? For that, of course, is where your name is; they have your Law, your temple, and both the spiritual and the worldly government, ordained by you yourself. Who am I to oppose singlehandedly all that is God's? I would rather say that they are right, retract my preaching, or at least keep silence."[1] Luther understood the force of the taunts against him: "You are a heretic and an apostle of the devil. You are preaching against God's people and the Church, yes, against God himself." This must affect every sensitive Christian. Consequently, this is where the pain of this particular persecution comes in.

What does one do in these circumstances? Fortunately for the Reformation, Luther was also sensitive to Scripture, for he replied that the only ground on which a true servant of God can hold his own against such logic is that which Paul sets down in Romans 9:6, 7—"For not all who are descended from Israel are Israel. Nor because they are his descendants are they all Abraham's children." Persecutors always claim to be the true church, the people of God, but the claim alone does not make it so. There is an old German proverb that says, "Not all who carry long knives are cooks." In the same way, not all who lay claim to the title "church" are *the* church. Not all who wear ecclesiastical garb and who preach sermons are God's ministers.

Who are God's ministers? They are those, says Luther, who confess Christ and his work, as the Bible presents them. The true church is composed of those who so believe. The Bible, which is the Word of God, is the standard. On that standard one can correctly ask, not how many persons teach a certain doctrine or even how important are those who teach it, but rather, "What are the doctrines they teach?"

We need people to ask that question today and then to stand by what the Bible teaches. The weakness of the churches in our time is that those within the various denominations will not evaluate the opinions and programs of those denominations by the Word of God and then stand against all that is in opposition to it. So long as this is true the churches will never be strong. Moreover, there will be persecution.

What then? Well, if God in his infinite wisdom permits those who merely profess the name of "church" to excommunicate, persecute, or otherwise relegate to the sidelines those who are determined to live by the Bible's authority, let it happen. Our task is to be forewarned and faithful.

Killed in God's Service

The second specific mentioned by the Lord Jesus Christ is murder. Obviously this is not always the experience of Christ's followers—Jesus speaks only of a "time" when this will happen—but it has been far more common than most people realize. In the early years some of the apostles and many normal believers were killed by the Jewish authorities or by Jewish instigation. Later execution was inflicted by Rome, at first in random fashion and then in a more systematic way as in the cities of Lyon and Vienne in southern France. Under Decius and Diocletian the killing of Christians became the policy of the Empire. Persecutions filled the Middle Ages, climaxing in the Reformation period. In more modern times there have been deaths in pagan lands, in tribal settings, and even in the more sophisticated countries of the modern East and West.

The interesting dimension in all this is that the killing of Christians is almost entirely by religious people and for religious reasons. It is as Christ said: "Anyone who kills you will think they are offering a service to God" (v. 2). Luther in his vigorous manner comments, "It pains one beyond measure that the Christians, who undergo such suffering, must die not only without any sympathy but also amid the greatest ignominy, derision, and mockery, yes, amid all the joy and exultation of the world, which sings nothing but *Deo gratias* and *Te Deum laudamus* when it happens."[2]

Rejoice! Rejoice!

What is it that can allow a Christian to rejoice in persecutions, even such severe persecutions as these Christ mentions? There are several answers. First, persecution demonstrates to the Christian and others that *the Christian is identified with Christ*. This is involved in Christ's explanation of the world's conduct in verse 3: "They will do such things becasue they have not known the Father or me." In other words, here is another statement of that radical distinction between Christ's own and the world that was introduced at the start of chapter 13 and that has characterized most of the teaching in this section of the Gospel. On the one side is the world, which knows itself but which does not know God. On the other side are believers, who are known of God and who know God, but who are not known by the world and are, in fact, even hated by it. To be hated by a world that does not know either the Father or Christ is therefore a mark of being identified with both of them.

Second, the Christian can rejoice in persecutions because he knows that they are not accidents but rather that *God has certain purposes*. This is one whole point of Christ's teaching in this section, for here he is telling of the persecutions to come in order that the disciples "should not be offended" and that, when the time should come, they might "remember that I warned you." This means that through the coming persecutions the disciples' faith would be strengthened.

Another purpose is growth in practical holiness, for persecutions strip away the unnecessary dross in our lives and draw us closer to Jesus. Peter knew this. He had heard Christ teach it. Then he experienced it in his own life and in the lives of those who had come to faith under his ministry. Thus, when some of these people went through persecutions, he wrote to them about it, saying, "In this you greatly rejoice, though now for a little while you may have had to suffer grief in all kinds of trials. These have come so that your faith—of greater worth than gold, which perishes even though refined by fire—may be proved genuine and may result in praise, glory and honor when Jesus Christ is revealed. Though you have not seen him, you love him; and even though you do not see him now, you believe in him and are filled with an inexpressible and glorious joy" (1 Peter 1:6–8). Peter was pointing out that persecution is the crucible in which God purifies the precious part of Christians' lives.

In one of my earlier writings I shared an illustration that Billy Graham has sometimes given of this principle. He tells of a friend who went through the Depression, losing a job, a fortune, a wife, and a home. But he was a believer in Christ and so held tenaciously to his faith, even though he was depressed and cast down by circumstances. One day in the midst of his agony he stopped to watch some men doing stonework for a large church in the city. "What are you going to do with that?" he asked a man who was busy chiseling a piece of triangular stone.

The workman stopped and pointed to a small opening near the top of the spire. "See that little opening up there near the top?" he asked. "Well, I'm shaping this down here so that it will fit in up there." The friend said that tears filled his eyes as he walked away from the workman, for it seemed that God had spoken to him personally to tell him that he was perfecting him for heaven through his earthly ordeal.[3]

The third reason why a Christian can rejoice in persecutions is that they more than anything else allow the believer to show forth the *supernatural radiance of the Christian life.* If all is going well in your life and you rejoice, what is so remarkable about that? But if all goes wrong and you rejoice, that is remarkable and others will notice. Paul and Silas sang praises to God at midnight in the jail at Philippi. The jailer had seen many prisoners. He had seen sullen prisoners, rebellious prisoners, hopeful prisoners, dejected prisoners. But I am sure that he had never seen prisoners who could rejoice in the midst of severe beatings and captivity, as Paul and Silas were doing. Thus, when the Lord subsequently opened the gates of the prison to permit the faithful missionaries to leave it, the jailer fell at their feet demanding, "Sirs, what must I do to be saved?" He had seen Jesus in them.

199

Witness for the Prosecution

John 16:5–11

"Now I am going to him who sent me, yet none of you asks me, 'Where are you going?' Because I have said these things, you are filled with grief. But I tell you the truth: It is for your good that I am going away. Unless I go away, the Counselor will not come to you; but if I go, I will send him to you. When he comes, he will convict the world of guilt in regard to sin and righteousness and judgment: in regard to sin, because men do not believe in me; in regard to righteousness, because I am going to the Father, where you can see me no longer; and in regard to judgment, because the prince of this world now stands condemned."

One great teaching of the Word of God is that believers may always reckon their losses among their greatest gains. This is true in the ultimate sense, for Jesus said, "Whoever loses his life for me and for the gospel will save it" (Mark 8:35). But it is true in regard to lesser things also, things like disappointments, sickness, financial setbacks, persecution. The difficulty is that we often do not believe this and so sorrow at what seems to be a great loss.

This was true for the first disciples, as our text indicates. God was sending the Holy Spirit to them through the departure of Christ, and yet they were sorrowful. He had prepared a great gift for them, but they could think only of their loss. They were despondent. Jesus, who knew their sorrow, began to teach them once more about the Holy Spirit. Previously he had spoken of the time when he had been with them. "Now," he says, "I am going to him who sent me, yet none of you asks me, 'Where are you going?'

Because I have said these things, you are filled with grief. But I tell you the truth: It is for your good that I am going away. Unless I go away, the Counselor will not some to you; but if I go, I will send him to you" (vv. 5–7). These verses lead into the longest discussion of the ministry of the Holy Spirit to be found in John's Gospel, a discussion in which a twofold ministry of the Spirit is unfolded: first, a ministry to the world and, second, a ministry to the apostles. This study deals with the first of these two activities.

The Spirit and the World

The question for us is: What does the Holy Spirit do in relationship to the world? Obviously, the answer is in verse 8 and in those verses that follow—"When he comes, he will convict the world of guilt in regard to sin and righteousness and judgment." But what does this mean? How does the Holy Spirit "convict" the world of anything?

The verb that lies behind our word "convict" has two main meanings: "to reprove" or "to convince." The meaning must be determined from the context. If the translation "to reprove" is chosen, the idea will be that of reproving someone or some group of people for an error previously held or a wrong previously committed. If the translation "to convince" is chosen, the idea will be that of convincing them of some truth previously unknown or unrealized. In this passage the choice would therefore be between a work of the Holy Spirit in rebuking the world for its sin, without any necessary thought of salvation, or a work of conviction concerning the true state of things so that the world might turn from sin to faith in Jesus as the Savior.

Which is to be chosen? The fact that it is the "world" that is spoken of favors the idea of conviction. In John, the word "world" most often denotes non-Christians, that is, the world of people in opposition to God. If that is the case here, then a conviction of the world for its sin seems appropriate. Unfortunately, the matter is not as simple as that. For one thing, nowhere else in the Scriptures is the Holy Spirit pictured as having such a ministry to the unregenerate world. He is said to restrain the world's evil. He is said to convince those whom God has chosen to be his own of their sin and so lead them to repentance and faith. But the work of convicting the world for sin is always associated, not with the ministry of the Holy Spirit in the present day, but with the exposure of sin by God before the judgment seat of Christ. Second, not all items mentioned in the verses that follow this are reprehensible, and therefore the idea of conviction is not applicable. True, the world can be reproved for its failure to believe on Jesus Christ (v. 9), but it can hardly be reproved of righteousness because Christ goes "to [his] Father" (v. 10) or of judgment because "the prince of this world now stands condemned" (v. 11). By contrast, the world can be *convicted* of sin, righteousness, and judgment as they are connected with these items.

For these reasons it seems best to consider this passage as involving a slight departure from John's normal use of the word "world." True, it is still the world of men in opposition to God upon whom the Spirit works. But the work is that divine power of conviction that, in spite of the darkness and resistance of the carnal mind, brings those whom God has given to Christ to repentance. In this light the passage becomes the greatest statement of the Spirit's work of conviction and regeneration in the entire Bible and a ground of great encouragement to us, as it undoubtedly also was to the apostles.

Conviction of Sin

The first reality the Holy Spirit convicts the world of is sin, and Jesus immediately gives the explanation: "because men do not believe in me" (v. 9). This may mean, "He will convict the world of wrong ideas of sin which they have because they do not believe," "He will convict the world of its sin because, without this conviction, they do not believe," or "He will convict the world of the sin of unbelief."[1] Any of these three translations is possible, and John may even be suggesting more than one, as is his manner. But if the idea of conviction with a view to salvation is the major thought of this passage, then the second interpretation is primary, for the root sin is that which puts self at the center of things and therefore spurns belief. It is only as this is brought to light that there is salvation.

The Holy Spirit convicts the world in two senses. First, like a prosecuting attorney he secures a verdict of "guilty" against the world. But then, second, the Holy Spirit also brings this guilt home to the human consciousness so that men and women are disturbed by sin and seek alleviation from it.

An example of this ministry occurs on the occasion of the Holy Spirit's coming in power on the day of Pentecost. The disciples had been gathered together in one place awaiting the coming of the Holy Spirit. He had come upon them visibly, as a result of which they went into the streets of Jerusalem where Peter preached a sermon. Peter told how this coming of the Spirit was the fulfillment of the prophecy of Joel and how the Holy Spirit was given in order that men and women might call on Jesus and be saved. He preached Jesus, concluding his sermon by saying, "Therefore let all Israel be assured of this: God has made this Jesus, whom you crucified, both Lord and Christ." We are then told that "when the people heard this, they were cut to the heart and said to Peter and the other apostles, 'Brothers, what shall we do?'" (Acts 2:36–37). When Peter answered their question, three thousand believed and were saved.

This was a remarkable response, but it was not due to Peter's brilliant analysis of the gospel or to his eloquence. If he had preached this sermon the day before, nothing would have happened. No one would have believed. He and the others would have been laughed at. What made three thousand believe? The answer is that the Holy Spirit had come and had begun to do his work of conviction of sin in the world. This is why they were "cut to the heart" and asked, "What shall we do?"

We cannot convict men and women of sin. Neither can those to whom the gospel is preached convict themselves. It is this that lay at the heart of the controversy between Pelagius and Augustine and later between Arminius and the followers of Calvin. Neither Pelagius nor Arminius denied that salvation was by grace, for they were not ready to assert that Jesus did not have to die, the Bible did not have to be given, the Holy Spirit did not have to be sent, and so on. But they did deny that it was all of grace in the sense that man makes no move toward God unless God first convicts and then draws him. Pelagius put it like this. He said that the will of man is always free and that it can therefore always choose or reject anything offered to it. As to the gospel, grace makes the offer. But the ultimate criterion by which any individual is either saved or lost is his will. Pelagius did not understand that it is impossible for the individual either to become aware of his sin or to understand and respond to the gospel without the Holy Spirit's previous and supernatural activity in his life. He has a will, but without the Spirit's activity the will is always deflected from God to its own destruction.

In one of his books Reuben A. Torrey illustrates this from his own experience. At one point in his ministry a number of officers of the Chicago Avenue Church, where he served, were burdened over the fact that there was so little profound conviction of sin in their meetings. There were conversions, Torrey noted, but few were coming with an apparently overwhelming conviction of sin. One night one of the officers said, "I am greatly troubled by the fact that we have so little conviction of sin in our meetings. While we are having conversions and many additions to our church, there is not that deep conviction of sin that I like to see. So I suggest that we, the officers of the church, meet from night to night to pray that there may be more conviction of sin in our meetings."

The suggestion was taken up, and the meetings began. A few days later on a Sunday evening Torrey noticed a man in the congregation whom he had not seen before. He was showily dressed. He had a large diamond blazing from his shirt front. Torrey rightly guessed that he was a gambler. As the preacher held forth, this man kept his eyes riveted on him. After the service Torrey went to the room where they always dealt with inquirers and there found this gambler. He was terribly agitated. "I don't know what is the matter with me," he groaned. "I never felt this way in my life. I was starting out this afternoon to go to Cottage Grove Avenue to meet some men and spend the afternoon gambling. But as I passed the park some of your young men were holding an open-air meeting, and I stopped to listen. I saw one man testifying whom I had known in a life of sin, and I waited to hear what he had to say. When he finished I went on down the street. I had not gone far when some strange power took hold of me and brought me back and I stayed through the meeting. Then this gentleman spoke to me and brought me over to your church. I heard you preach." Here he stopped and sobbed, crying, "Oh, I don't know what is the matter with me. I feel awful. I never felt this way before in my life."

"I know what is the matter with you," Torrey replied. "You are under conviction of sin, for the Holy Spirit is dealing with you." Torrey then pointed him to Christ, and the man asked Jesus to forgive his sins and was born again. It was the beginning of many striking conversions in the Chicago Avenue Church.[2]

There is one more thing about this convicting work of the Holy Spirit in relation to sin. It is that the sin of which the Holy Spirit convicts men is the sin of unbelief. "In regard to sin, because they do not believe in me," Jesus says. Notice that it is not conviction of the sin of gambling, though that may come in time. It is not the sin of adultery, or drunkenness, or pride, or stealing primarily, but the sin of refusing to believe on Jesus. Why is this? It is not because the other sins are not sin or that they need not be repented of and renounced, for they must be. It is just that belief in Christ, the one thing God requires for salvation, is that which is hardest for the natural man even to acknowledge, let alone attain. Does the average unbeliever look on unbelief as sin? Not at all! If anything is true, it is the opposite. He generally looks upon unbelief as a mark of his supposed intellectual sophistication. "I am glad that you can believe those things," he says with an air of condescending superiority (he really means, "that you can believe that nonsense"), "but I cannot." He thinks it a matter for pride that he is an agnostic or an atheist. Or, if he does not take that tack, he looks to you for pity, saying, "I wish I could believe as you do, but I can't. There must be something wrong with me."

Real conversions take place when both these excuses are withered away by the Spirit's heat. As Torrey says, "When the Holy Spirit touches a man's heart, he no longer looks upon unbelief as a mark of intellectual superiority; he does not look upon it as a mere misfortune; he sees it as the most daring, decisive and damning of all sins and is overwhelmed with a sense of his awful guilt in that he had not believed on the name of the only begotten Son of God."[3]

Christ's Righteousness

Second, the Holy Spirit is said to convict men and women of righteousness. "In regard to righteousness," says Jesus, "because I am going to the Father, where you can see me no longer" (v. 10). There are two ways in which this can be taken.

On the one hand, it can mean that the Holy Spirit will show the world what true righteousness is, an action made necessary by the fact that Christ is no longer here to demonstrate the meaning of righteousness in his own person. Apart from Christ none of us has any understanding of what God's righteousness is. We think of it in terms of human goodness, for we imagine that some people have 10 percent goodness, others have 30 percent, still others have 60 or 70 percent, and then there is Jesus, the best of all, who scores 100. But this is not what God's goodness is. If this were the case, then confrontation with Christ would have the effect of making us want to try harder. We would see that we are not as good as he is but that he represents what is possible. We would try to be better. This, however, is not what happens when men and women meet Jesus. What happens is that they are impressed with the totally different characteristics of his righteousness and with the fact that for them it is totally unattainable. The reaction, rather than being a renewed determination to try harder, is despair: "Depart from me, for I am a sinful man, O Lord." Because the Lord Jesus Christ is no longer with us here on earth, it takes another divine personality, the Holy Spirit to create this awareness in the world.

On the other hand, there is another way in which these words can be taken. They can be taken as showing, not primarily what righteousness is but rather where that righteousness can be found. It cannot be found here. We know only human righteousness. But it can be found in Christ, who was once here but is now at the Father's right hand.

I do not know which of these is to be preferred, and again both may be possible. However, if the second meaning is possible, even in a secondary sense, then it suggests something interesting, something which Spurgeon saw and wrote about in one of his sermons. Spurgeon has pointed out that in human affairs, if a person is convicted of wrongdoing, the next step is judgment. If the jury renders a verdict of guilty, the next words are those of the judge, who says, "The defendent will be remanded to the keeping of the sheriff, and this court will reconvene next Tuesday for sentencing." But notice God's procedure. It is true that the conviction of sin is followed by judgment. Verse 11 does follow verse 9, but God interpolates a process. It is the provision of righteousness in Christ, so that the one who believes on Christ might be saved from judgment. Spurgeon writes, "The Lord takes a man, even when he is sinful and conscious of that sin, and makes him righteous on the spot, by putting away his sin and justifying him by the righteousness of faith, a righteousness which comes to him by the worthiness of another who has wrought out a righteousness for him."[4]

So here is a great promise: not only that the Holy Spirit will convict the world of sin, which neither you nor I can do, but that he also will direct them to Christ where alone that true righteousness, which we are all lacking, can be found.

Satan Judged

The final aspect of the Spirit's work mentioned in these verses is to convict the world "in regard to judgment, because the prince of this world now stands condemned" (v. 11). Once again, there are difficulties of interpretation. But the best view seems to be that the Holy Spirit will convince the world that there is such a thing as judgment, which is proved by the judgment of Satan and the breaking of his power at the cross.

No one wants to believe in judgment. We want to think that we can do what we wish with impunity and that no day of reckoning will come. Sometimes we are even encouraged in this by the thought that God does not seem to judge immediately and that evil often seems to go unpunished. But this is false thinking. It is true that God does not visit his judgments upon the sinner immediately and that evil often seems to go unpunished. God is longsuffering in his judgments. Still, they come eventually and inevitably, and of this, God's judgment upon Satan is proof. In his second epistle, Peter makes the same point concerning false teachers, showing that God judged the fallen angels, the world of Noah's time, and the cities of Sodom and Gomorrah. He then concludes by saying, "The Lord knows how to rescue godly men from trials and to hold the unrighteous for the day of judgment, while continuing their punishment" (2 Peter 2:9).

If the individual will not come to Christ, who has died for him in order that his sin might be punished and that God's own righteousness might be applied to his account, then he will experience such judgment. How much better it is to come to Christ now in this the day of grace.

Human Channels

There is one last point. It is true that this passage is primarily about the work of the Holy Spirit by which he convicts the world of sin and thus points men and women to Jesus Christ as the Savior. But notice that, while it is true that it is the Holy Spirit who convicts men and women of sin, he nevertheless does it through us. Jesus indicates this in these verses, saying, "It is for your good that I am going away. Unless I go away the Counselor will not come to you; but if I go, I will send him to you. When he comes [to you], he will convict the world of guilt in regard to sin and righteousness and judgment" (vv. 7–8). This means that the Lord is sending the Holy Spirit to believers and that it is as he works through them and in them that he convicts the world.

Every conversion recorded in the Book of Acts was through the agency of someone who was already saved. Jesus bore witness to the Twelve. They bore their witness on Pentecost and the days following. Even Paul, that great witness who had such an unusual conversion while on the way to Damascus to persecute Christians, was converted through others. For, in advance of his experience, he had witnessed the stoning of Stephen and had heard his great sermon, recorded in Acts 7. And even after his experience, while he was in Damascus, Ananias was sent to him as the human instrument through whom the Holy Spirit then did his work. Cornelius also fits this pattern. True, he had witnessed an angel. But the angel did not tell him the gospel. Rather, the angel said, "Send to Joppa for Simon who is called Peter. He will bring you a message through which you and all your household will be saved" (Acts 11:13–14).

This is God's way: by the power of his Spirit working through human channels, like you and me. Are you his instrument? You can be. Draw near to him; ask him to cleanse you. Allow him to make of you an unobstructed channel for his grace.

200

More Words to Come

John 16:12–15

"I have much more to say to you, more than you can now bear. But when he, the Spirit of truth, comes, he will guide you into all truth. He will not speak on his own; he will speak only what he hears, and he will tell you what is yet to come. He will bring glory to me by taking from what is mine and making it known to you. All that belongs to the Father is mine. That is why I said the Spirit will take from what is mine and make it known to you."

In the second chapter of John there is a story with an interesting final line. The story is of Jesus changing the water in six stone waterpots to wine at a wedding in Cana of Galilee, and it ends with the remark of the master of ceremonies to the bridegroom after he had drunk the wine Jesus made. He said, "Everyone brings out the choice wine first and then the cheaper wine after the guests have had too much to drink; but you have saved the best till now" (v. 10). The situation is the same as that which we find in John 16:12–15.

We are nearing the end of the final discourses. Only a summary follows. So the startling thing is that Jesus introduces a new and totally unexpected subject. What is more, it is in a sense the best of all he has been saying.

How can it be the best? That is a hard question to answer when we think of what he had been teaching, particularly in these last discourses. He had taught about heaven. He had taught how to get there. Then he had taught about the works that those who were his disciples should do. He had taught about prayer, saying that whatever the disciples should ask in his name he

1215

would do. Best of all, he had taught about the Holy Spirit, how he should come after Christ had himself returned to heaven and how he should comfort the disciples, teach them, cause them to be spiritually fruitful, and finally convict the world of its sin in order that it might find righteousness in Christ and escape God's judgment. It is at this point, after all that teaching, that the words we are studying come in.

How can this last subject be the best of all? The answer is in the nature of the subject itself: Christ's promise of even more teachings to come. Jesus says, "I have much more to say to you, more than you can now bear. But when he, the Spirit of truth, comes, he will guide you into all truth. He will not speak on his own; he will speak only what he hears, and he will tell you what is yet to come" (vv. 12–13). In other words, although Jesus had taught his disciples what seem to us to be many significant doctrines, there were nevertheless many more things still to be taught. Although he was departing, it would be the work of the Holy Spirit to communicate these teachings.

A New Revelation

Even at this point, we have not really captured the full wonder of Christ's promise, however, for by reading these verses closely, particularly in the original language, we find that it is not simply that the Holy Spirit was going to teach the disciples in the same sense, for instance, that the Holy Spirit may be said to teach us. He would presumably do that for the disciples also, as for us, but that is not what the verses mean. The true sense emerges when we learn that an important word has been dropped out of verse 13 in several versions. It is the word "the," and it comes before "truth." When we understand this, we see that it is not just into some general idea of truth that the Holy Spirit is said to be coming to guide the apostles, but rather into all "the truth," that is, into a definite body of material centering on Christ. This, we recognize, is nothing other than the New Testament. So the promise is that the Holy Spirit would be the vehicle of a new revelation through those specifically commissioned to this ministry. The Revised Standard Version and the New English Bible render this verse correctly.

This is startling. If the disciples understood what Jesus was saying, it was startling to them, for they were Jews and were therefore well aware of the unique, divine character of the Old Testament. They knew, as the Book of Hebrews says, that "God spoke to our forefathers through the prophets at many times and in various ways" (1:1). They knew that the law had come "through Moses" (John 1:17). They believed that the law was "holy, righteous and good" (Rom. 7:12). This law was in every Jewish synagogue. It was God's greatest gift to Israel. How, then, could there be a further revelation? It would have seemed unnecessary, unbelievable. Yet this is precisely what Christ was promising.

This is not a promise of inspiration that is made generally to all Christians in all periods of the church. If we think like that, we fall into

William Barclay's error. If you turn to Barclay's discussion of this passage, you find that he says two things. First, he says that these verses teach that "revelation is bound to be a progressive process."[1] Expressed rightly, that is true. God has revealed himself progressively in a certain sense in the writings that compose our Bible, but Barclay takes it to mean, first, that the earlier revelations were imperfect or wrong (at least in part) and, second, that there is no end to God's revelation. In combination, this means that Jesus is still imparting truth today and that this truth can modify, correct, or supercede the truth previously given. This is not Jesus' teaching, nor is it suggested or permitted by this passage. On the contrary, Jesus is teaching that the Holy Spirit would lead the disciples into a supplementary but definitive new revelation that thereafter would be the church's authoritative standard of doctrine.

The second thing Barclay says in his commentary is that the operation of the Holy Spirit to lead us into truth applies in all areas. He gives some examples. First, he notes that when H. F. Lyte wrote the hymn "Abide with Me," he had no feeling of actually composing the verses. Instead, he wrote them—so Barclay says—as if by dictation. Next, Barclay talks about music, noting that Handel said of his writing the Hallelujah Chorus of the *Messiah:* "I saw the heavens opened, and . . . God sitting on the Throne." Finally, Barclay adds that the same is true of the scientist who discovers something that will help the world and make life better for the human race.[2]

We have to make a distinction here, however, for it is not that "Abide with Me" is not a beautiful hymn, or that the Hallelujah Chorus is not truly an inspiring composition, or that a scientist may not be guided by God to discover something that will be beneficial to humanity. Certainly the Holy Spirit works in that way. He works in every area of life. But these things are in a different category from what the Lord is talking about in John 16:12–15. What the Lord is promising to do here is to work by the Holy Spirit in the apostles to give us our New Testament. This revelation is authoritative and inerrant, as the others (even if we refer to them by the terms "revelations" or "inspirations") are not.

This is a point at which we have to allow the whole weight of the Word of God to come to bear. Reuben A. Torrey has a good discussion of this in his book *The Person and Work of the Holy Spirit.* He points out, first, that there is a diversity of gifts according to the Word of God and that this diversity relates to different positions in the church and church history. Torrey turns to 1 Corinthians to show this. Thus, in 12:4–6, Paul says, "There are different kinds of gifts, but the same Spirit. There are different kinds of service, but the same Lord. There are different kinds of working, but the same God works all of them in all men." Later in the chapter, while still thinking about these gifts, he writes of the various people involved. "And in the church God has appointed first of all apostles, second prophets, third teachers, then workers of miracles, also those having gifts of healing, those able to help others, those with gifts of administration, and those speaking in differ-enct kinds of tongues. Are all apostles? Are all prophets? Are all teachers? Do all work miracles? Do all have gifts of healing? Do all speak in tongues? Do all interpret?" (vv. 28–30). Paul here relates the gifts to the various of-fices, saying that some gifts apply to one office and other gifts to another. We therefore rightly expect that God gave the apostles their own particular function and gift.

Second, says Torrey, there are passages that teach that the particular function of the apostles was to receive the new revelation. An example is Ephesians 3:2–5. Again Paul is writing. "Surely you have heard about the ad-ministration of God's grace that was given to me for you, that is, the mystery made known to me by revelation, as I have already written briefly. In read-ing this, then, you will be able to understand my insight into the mystery of Christ, which was not made known to men in other generations as it has now been revealed by the Spirit to God's holy apostles and prophets." Paul's point is that his teaching was profound not because he was a particularly brilliant person but because God had revealed this teaching to him. His unique role (along with the other apostles) was to receive and record this revelation.

Finally, Torrey makes the point that this revelation is embodied in words. Note what Paul says: "This is what we speak, not in words taught us by human wisdom but in words taught by the Spirit, expressing spiritual truths in spiritual words" (1 Cor. 2:13). This is the biblical picture. So we under-stand that in John 16 the Lord Jesus Christ is pointing to that day—it was not far off at that moment—when the Holy Spirit would speak through these apostles as he had spoken in time past unto the fathers by the prophets. In other words, there was to be a New Testament, a new chapter in the history of God's dealings with men.[3]

Diverse Revelation

These verses also say something else. They tell about the nature of this new revelation, giving general categories of its content. These are three. Sometimes, as I read the notes in the Scofield Bible, I am not particularly impressed with what is written. But in this particular case the notes are re-markable. At the bottom of this page in my Bible we are told that Jesus out-lined the general categories of the New Testament revelation in advance and that these are: historical, doctrinal, and prophetic. This is exactly right. The New Testament fulfills this pattern precisely.

First, there is a *historical* element to the New Testament. This is involved in verse 13, in which Jesus says of the Holy Spirit, "He will guide you into all [the] truth." That is, "He will guide you into the truth concerning me." In 14:26 the historical element is made even clearer, for there Christ says, "He will teach you all things and remind you of everything I have said to you." In other words, the disciples were likely to forget certain things that happened, but the Holy Spirit would bring these historical events to their minds. What events are these? Obviously, they are the events connected with Jesus' life, death, and resurrection. Do we have that in the New Testament? Of course. This is the substance of the Gospels—Matthew, Mark, Luke, John—and also Acts.

Christianity begins with a historical revelation. It is this that sets Christianity off from other religions. It sets it off from mythology. It sets it off from philosophy. These systems of thought conceive of religion largely as a pattern of ideas and of salvation as learning certain things. But this is not the essence of Christianity. Christianity has ideas, that is true; but the ideas are based upon fact, and the facts are determinative.

The historical basis also cuts Christianity off from an evolutionary religion. Such a religion says that people thousands of years ago had primitive ideas of God but that, as they grew in knowledge, their ideas of God grew and their writings about God showed progression. This went on and on up to the New Testament period and then beyond it to the point where today we can drop certain things we consider unworthy of a true conception of God and add other things we consider to be valuable. Christianity's historical base undercuts all that; the basis of the revelation is the historical action of God in history. This centers primarily in the cross of Christ. God did something at the cross. He did not just teach an idea. He did not just show himself in some vague way. He atoned for sin at the cross; he also revealed his love and showed his judgment. Any understanding of the faith that departs from that historical basis is heresy.

Doctrine

Second, there was also to be a *doctrinal* element in the New Testament. This is indicated by Jesus when he says, again of the Holy Spirit, "He will take what is mine, and make it known to you" or, as in 14:26, "He will teach you all things." Do we have that in the New Testament? Of course, we do. We have it in the Epistles, beginning with the great letter to the Romans, which unfolds Christian doctrine in its fullest form, continuing through the Epistles that deal with particular problems in theology, and ending with those books that are pastoral in nature—1 and 2 Timothy; Titus; 1, 2, and 3 John; 1 and 2 Peter; and Jude.

This is also important, because, while it is true that we must stress facts, while it is true that we must say that Christianity differs from all other religions because of the fact that God has done something in history, still it is not just the mere fact of God's having done this that is important; it is also what the facts mean. Thus, we say that God came in Jesus. But the significance of that is that God is revealed in certain categories. Because of Jesus, we know God to be love, justice, compassion, mercy, and many other attributes. Or again, we say that Jesus died. True enough! But that in itself is not significant. All men die. Why did he die? At this point we need teaching. So the Epistles are given to show us why Jesus Christ died and what the full implications of this are. He died for sin. He died for our sin, in our place. Moreover, he died in order that he might call out a people destined to be conformed to his own image and to be with him forever. The Epistles teach these as well as other doctrines we need to learn.

Things to Come

Finally, there is the *prophetic* element. Jesus indicates this when he says at the end of verse 13, "And he will tell you what is yet to come." Do we have that in the New Testament? Yes, we have. We have it scattered throughout the New Testament in various references (Matthew 24; 25; Mark 13; Romans 11; 1 Corinthians 15; etc.), but particularly in the Book of Revelation.

What shall come when the Lord returns in power at the end of the age? There can be a preoccupation with prophecy that is debilitating. A person can become so fascinated with what is to come that he does not live for Christ now. Sometimes that happens. But the importance of prophecy is in the indication that God is still at work in history. He does not just deal with us in some static way so that our period of history is absolutely identical with that of those who lived in an earlier period and with that of those who will come later. Rather, God is doing unique things in history—working with people, unfolding a plan—so that what each one does is important. Moreover, these workings are leading up to the day when the Lord will return, at which time God will have gathered his own out of the world and will have demonstrated the reality of the Christian faith in such a way that all will see that the Lord's way is the only way that anyone can be personally fulfilled and find true blessing.

These verses also tell us why this revelation—involving history, doctrine, and prophecy—has been given. The Lord indicates this by saying, "He will bring glory to me by taking from what is mine and making it known to you" (v. 14). It is not just that we are told certain doctrines in order that we might know things. Nor are the end times revealed so that we can simply have a private inside track to the meaning of history. These things are taught to us in order that the Lord Jesus Christ might be glorified. This is the Holy Spirit's ministry. "He will not speak on his own," said Jesus, "he will ... [take] from what is mine and [make] it known to you" (vv. 13–14).

As you study the Bible the Holy Spirit will continue to do the work he began in an authoritative way with the inspiration of the New Testament documents. The Holy Spirit, the true author of these books, will lead you to see the Lord Jesus Christ and bring you to the point of increasing obedience and service to him.

201

Joy in the Morning

John 16:16–22

"In a little while you will see me no more, and then after a little while you will see me."

Some of his disciples said to one another, "What does he mean by saying, 'In a little while you will see me no more, and then after a little while you will see me,' and 'Because I am going to the Father'?" They kept asking, "What does he mean by 'a little while'? We don't understand what he is saying."

Jesus saw that they wanted to ask him about this, so he said to them, "Are you asking one another what I meant when I said, 'In a little while you will see me no more, and then after a little while you will see me'? I tell you the truth, you will weep and mourn while the world rejoices. You will grieve, but your grief will turn to joy. A woman giving birth to a child has pain because her time has come; but when her baby is born she forgets the anguish because of her joy that a child is born into the world. So with you: Now is your time of grief, but I will see you again and you will rejoice, and no one will take away your joy."

Are you one of those people who always wakes up in the morning with a smile on your face and a buoyant spirit in your heart? I am not. So I confess that when I come to a verse like Psalm 30:5—"Weeping may remain for a night, but rejoicing comes in the morning"—I have to understand it in poetical terms. It is worth trying to do this, however, for the idea of joy after a nighttime of sorrow is an important biblical theme. We have it in the passage we come to now: "I tell you the truth, you will weep and mourn while the world rejoices. You will grieve, but your grief will turn to joy."

1221

In general terms, we understand what this means. It means that for a Christian, sorrow endures for just a time and then is replaced by a joy that no one can take from us. Unfortunately, when we study the entire passage more specifically, we soon find that there is some uncertainty as to what Jesus is referring. The first part of this passage speaks about "a little while" when the disciples will not see him and then "a little while" after which they will see him. But because this has several possible applications, it is probable that having read that passage we find ourselves in the position of the disciples, who said, "What does he mean by 'a little while'? We don't understand what he is saying" (v. 18).

As I look at these words I suspect that this ambiguity is intentional. It is not that the Lord is vague in his teaching, of course. He makes things as clear as he can possibly make them. It is rather that by means of such ambiguity he suggests more than one meaning. Here the Lord is talking about a little while when he will not be seen, a time marked by sorrow, and then after that space of time, another time in which he will be seen again and which will therefore be joyful. This apparently deliberate ambiguity suggests three different levels of interpretation. First, it can refer to Jesus' death and the days of his entombment, during which time he was not seen, and then the resurrection that follows with its renewed sight of him. Second, it can indicate the periods before and after Pentecost, for now, because of the ministry of the Holy Spirit, we see him in a spiritual way that was not possible previously. That is suggested by the tie-in of these verses with those preceding. Finally, it may describe the church age, this short time in which we do not see Christ with our physical eyes, but after which, when the Lord will return in glory, we will see him face-to-face and have earth's sorrows transmuted into eternal joy.

I would like to take each of those meanings, show how it is supported by the context, and trace its importance.

Death and Resurrection

First of all, then, these verses refer to the death and resurrection of Jesus. This is the first and most obvious interpretation simply because Christ is here speaking to his disciples, trying to comfort them on the eve of his arrest and separation from them. They are going to sorrow, but he wishes to show them that very soon, following his resurrection, they will again be joyful.

Jesus has already talked along those lines. For example, in John 13 the Lord had been talking about his glorification, saying, "Now is the Son of Man glorified, and God is glorified in him" (v. 31). This refers to his exaltation to heaven by his crucifixion, death, resurrection, and ascension. But it is immediately followed by the words: "I will be with you only a little longer. You will look for me, and just as I told the Jews, so I tell you now: Where I am going, you cannot come" (v. 33). Peter understood this "little while" to be imminent even though he did not comprehend much more than that, for he asked, "Lord, where are you going?" Jesus replied, "Where I am going, you cannot follow now, but you will follow later" (v. 36).

When we take the passage in this sense, we recognize that this was precisely the experience of these early disciples. Jesus was their friend. They loved him with a love that had grown intense because of his love for them and fellowship with them over the three-year period of his ministry. Then, although he had tried to prepare them for it, he was suddenly taken from them and crucified. They were plunged into despondency and near disillusionment.

There were multiple reasons for their great sorrow. First, they sorrowed because of their personal loss. They were warmly attached to him, and he was gone—gone forever, so they thought. Since they had left all to follow him and since he had become their all in place of what they had lost (and much more besides), they were left with a vacuum in their lives. This was comparable to the kind of sorrow we have at the death of one greatly loved. Yet it was far more intense, because in this case it was the Lord of glory, Jesus Christ, who was removed.

Second, they sorrowed additionally because of the world's attitude to Christ's crucifixion. The Lord alludes to this in John 16:20, saying, "You will weep and mourn while the world rejoices." In other words, the sorrow of the disciples would be intensified because the world, far from sorrowing at the loss of Jesus, actually rejoiced that he was now out of their way and would no longer be a bother to them. As the disciples sorrowed during this interim they knew that the scribes and Pharisees, those who represent the spirit of the world, were actually rubbing their hands in glee. They were saying, "At last we've gotten rid of him; we won't have him exposing us anymore. Things will get back to normal." The sorrow of the disciples was intensified because of that.

Third, their sorrow during those days must have been particularly acute because of their disappointments. Every time we catch a glimpse into what they were thinking about during this interim we are impressed with how disappointed they were. There is the story of the Emmaus disciples. They were on their way home. The Lord appeared to them on the way and asked why they were downcast. They told him about Jesus, explaining how he had been crucified by the leaders of the people. Then they uttered what is certainly one of the most poignant lines in Scripture, "But we had hoped he was the one who was going to redeem Israel" (Luke 24:21). They had put so much of their hope in him and he had been taken away from them. Their hopes had been crushed.

Disappointment explains the attitude of Thomas, who said, "Unless I see the nail marks in his hands and put my finger where the nails were, and put my hand into his side, I will not believe it" (John 20:25). It was not that Thomas was particularly disbelieving. None of the other disciples believed either until they had seen Christ. It was only after he appeared that they had come to faith. But Thomas, in a bitterness born of acute disappointment, said, "You're not going to overcome my grief by some mystical story of a resurrection. I'm the one, let's not forget, who said, 'If he goes up to Jerusalem, he will die; if we go with him, we must be prepared to die also.' I warned you about it. He died. So don't try to put me off with fairy tales." It was disappointment that made him speak that way.

The disciples experienced acute sorrow because of their loss, the joy of the world, and disappointments. But then came the resurrection, and their sorrow was changed into joy. It was not that their sorrow was followed by joy, that joy came afterward but what was sorrow still remained. No, the sorrow was itself changed into joy so that what had been the cause of their sorrow before was now in equal measure joyous. Before the resurrection the death of Christ appeared to be a total tragedy. It was meaningless to the disciples because they did not understand that this was God's atonement for the sin of the world. It was only the death of one they deeply loved. But when Jesus rose from the dead they understood that the cross was not a tragedy but a triumph. Did you ever notice as you have read the New Testament that the cross of Christ is never referred to in a tone of sorrow? It is true that when the disciples tell about their own feelings during the three days between the crucifixion and the resurrection, as they do in the Gospels, they reflect in a historical way that they sorrowed then. But afterward whenever they wrote about the cross they spoke of it not as a cause for sorrow but as a cause for joy. Paul even speaks of the cross as his "glory" (Gal. 6:14). If there were nothing but the crucifixion, glorious as that might be, we would not understand it and it would be a cause of sorrow for us. But having had a resurrection, having known that the One who was crucified and buried rose again on the third day according to the Scriptures, as the Bible itself tells us, we rejoice in that the cross is now seen to be a victory.

This incidentally, is why Lent should not have the extraordinary and exaggerated character that it does in some circles. For some it becomes a kind of mock funeral for Christ in which they try to work themselves into a depressed state leading up to Good Friday. That is all artificial. There is nothing genuine about it. For Jesus is living, not dead; and although we must remember the cross and its agony, we remember it as that great act that procured our salvation, and we rejoice in it.

Spiritual Sight

Second, we must refer these verses to Pentecost and the coming of the Holy Spirit for the church age. This is not reading something into the passage, because it is suggested to us by the context. In the first part of this chapter the Lord has been talking about the Holy Spirit. He has talked about the ministry of the Holy Spirit, first, to the world—bringing some to faith in Christ, convicting them of sin and of righteousness and of judgment

(vv. 7–11)—and then, second, also to the apostles in a special sense so that they might become vehicles of the New Testament revelation as they remembered, understood, interpreted, and recorded what Jesus had done (vv. 12–15). The verses end by saying that when the Holy Spirit comes he is not going to speak of himself but rather is going to speak of Jesus and make him known. Then, immediately following that and in the same context, the Lord begins to speak of the little while when we will not see him and then the little while after which we will see him. In this context we, therefore naturally think of the church age in which the Holy Spirit makes the Lord Jesus Christ visible to Christian people, not physically but spiritually, as he reveals the Lord to us in the pages of the Word of God.

Someone will perhaps say at this point, "But I do not see the Lord Jesus Christ even in a spiritual way. There are times when he is far from me. I would like to see him, to feel him close, but I am afraid that the Lord seems far away. He seems to be locked in a previous age of history." If that is the case, then you have to approach the Lord in the only way he can be found in this age, that is, through a study of the Word. This is really the burden of the passage as I understand it.

Moreover, there is a second part to that, for it is not enough that we just come to the Scriptures in a certain academic way and study them, important as that may be. Rather, as we find the Lord presented to us in the Scriptures, there must be that personal interaction with him that brings us face-to-face with his holiness and causes us to turn from sin in order that we might go his way.

I am sure that this is what the author of Hebrews had in mind when, in the twelfth chapter, he talks about our "looking to Jesus, the author and perfecter of our faith." Hebrews 11 is the great chapter on faith. You would think that by the time the author had come to the end of that chapter, having cited the great heroes of faith of the Old Testament, he would have stopped, taken a deep breath, and perhaps gone on to something entirely different. But that is not the way he was thinking. Rather, he thinks of a present application according to which we, like those previous heroes, should turn from sin and pursue that which is set before us by Jesus: "Therefore, since we are surrounded by such a great cloud of witnesses, let us throw off everything that hinders and the sin that so easily entangles, and let us run with perseverance the race marked out for us. Let us fix our eyes on Jesus, the author and perfecter of our faith, who for the joy set before him endured the cross, scorning its shame, and say down at the right hand of the throne of God" (Heb. 12:1–2).

If being aware of Jesus is to turn sorrow into joy in the present age, it must be based, first, upon a study of the Scriptures, and second, upon a deliberate turning from anything that would hinder discipleship. It is turning from sin in order that we might press on to what is ahead.

When we talk along those lines it is almost impossible not to think also of that chapter in Philippians in which the apostle Paul says almost the same thing in giving his testimony. He has already said in the third chapter what it meant for him to become a Christian. It meant to have come to know Christ. Now he expresses his desire to know him even better: "I want to know Christ and the power of his resurrection and the fellowshiip of sharing in his sufferings, becoming like him in his death" (3:10). He concludes that section by saying, "Brothers, I do not consider myself yet to have taken hold of it. But one thing I do: Forgetting what is behind and straining toward what is ahead, I press on toward the goal to win the prize for which God has called me heavenward in Christ Jesus" (3:13–14).

Our Blessed Hope

Third, there is also a sense in which this applies to the Second Coming. Even with the vision of Christ through the Holy Spirit in this age there is still often great cause for sorrow, because we have disappointments, personal loss, and sin; and that keeps us from God. But it is not permanent. Jesus is coming. It is only a little while. Then sorrow will be turned into joy. We tend to think that the return of Jesus Christ is delayed—it is because we are locked in time—but that is why that phrase "a little while" is so important. It seems to us at times, as it always seems to skeptics, that "everything goes on as it has since the beginning of creation" (2 Peter 3:4). But this phrase says that the present state is only temporary. It is short, and after it is over all present sorrows will be turned into joy. The phrase "a little while" is mentioned seven times just in this one passage.

There is an obvious progression here. First, there is the revelation of the Lord at the time of the resurrection, a revelation that went beyond anything that the disciples had previously known. Second, there is the revelation of Jesus to his people during this age. This is even better. Jesus said, "It is for your good that I go away. Unless I go away the Counselor will not come to you; but if I go, I will send him to you" (John 16:7). Finally, there is that perfect revelation of Jesus when he returns in his glory at the end of time. If the progression applies in that historical sense, it should also apply to our own personal relationship to and knowledge of Jesus. We should know him better this year than we did last year, and better next year than this year. That is what we should desire. Let us see that it is fulfilled as, by the grace of God, we study the Bible and seek to enter into a full knowledge of our Lord.

202

Another Prayer Promise

John 16:23-27

"In that day you will no longer ask me anything. I tell you the truth, my Father will give you whatever you ask in my name. Until now you have not asked for anything in my name. Ask and you will receive, and your joy will be complete.

"Though I have been speaking figuratively, a time is coming when I will no longer use this kind of language but will tell you plainly about my Father. In that day you will ask in my name. I am not saying that I will ask the Father on your behalf. No, the Father himself loves you because you have loved me and have believed that I came from God."

The verses that conclude the sixteenth chapter of John and, therefore, also the final discourses of Jesus with his disciples, are in the nature of a summary. That is, they produce no new themes but rather repeat with some variations that which has already been taught. This does not mean that these themes are unimportant, however. On the contrary, it means that they are of the greatest importance. For of all that Jesus has taught in these discourses it is these, rather than the other themes, that he brings forward once again and stresses in his final words prior to the arrest and crucifixion.

One theme is his own origin and destiny, that is, his full divinity both before and after the years of his incarnation. We find this in verses 28–30. A second theme is the assurance that those who follow Christ may have peace even though, as in the case of the disciples, they would all be scattered when he was seized by the temple authorities. This peace is based on his own victory over the world and is discussed in verses 31–33. In the verses we are to study now, Jesus again teaches his disciples about prayer.

Why is prayer important? Reuben A. Torrey answers that question comprehensively and wisely in a little book entitled *How to Pray*, listing eleven reasons: (1) Because there is a devil and because prayer is the God-appointed means of resisting him; (2) Because prayer is God's way for us to obtain what we need from him; (3) Because the apostles, whom God set forth to be a pattern for us, considered prayer to be the most important business of their lives; (4) Because prayer occupied a prominent place and played a very important part in the earthly life of our Lord; (5) Because prayer is the most important part of the present ministry of our Lord, since he is now interceding for us (Heb. 7:25); (6) Because prayer is the means God has appointed for our receiving mercy from him and of obtaining grace to help in time of need; (7) Because prayer is the means of obtaining the fullness of God's joy; (8) Because prayer with thanksgiving is the means of obtaining freedom from anxiety and, in anxiety's place, that peace that passes understanding; (9) Because prayer is the method appointed for our obtaining the fullness of God's Holy Spirit; (10) Because prayer is the means by which we are to keep watchful and be alert at Christ's return; and (11) Because prayer is used by God to promote our spiritual growth, bring power into our work, lead others to faith in Christ, and bring all other blessings to Christ's church.[1]

In these verses we find four teachings: (1) the nature of prayer, (2) the privilege of prayer, (3) the conditions of effective prayer, and (4) a new prayer promise.

The Nature of Prayer

The nature of prayer is indicated by the word "ask," which is repeated five times. Once it refers to asking something of Jesus. The remaining four times it refers to asking something of the Father in Christ's name. The interesting thing is that these two askings are treated as if they were parallel, meaning that Jesus was considering prayer to the Father as identical in its essential nature with the conversation the disciples had been having with him.

If we see this clearly, we see that prayer must be lifted out of some mysterious realm of religious rites or practice, where only special people can go, and instead be brought down to the common experience of normal men and women. It means that prayer is essentially a conversation in which we talk to God. "For," says Jesus, "in precisely the same way in which you have been asking questions of me during our time together, so shall you ask of God the Father after I return to heaven."

We get a feeling for the kind of questions we may ask the Father by seeing what the disciples had to say in the preceding chapters. "Lord, where are you going?" (13:36). "Why can't I follow you now?" (13:37). "Lord, we

don't know where you are going, so how can we know the way?" (14:5).
"Lord, show us the Father" (14:8). "Lord, why do you intend to show yourself to us and not to the world?" (14:22). "What does he mean by saying, 'In
a little while you will see me no more, and then after a little while you will
see me,' and 'Because I am going to the Father'?" (16:17). These questions
were not very perceptive; they reveal much ignorance. But they are natural
and quite unaffected. That is the point. They are an indication of what the
tone of our own prayers should be.

The Privilege of Prayer

Second, these verses indicate something of the privilege of prayer. This is
implied in what we have been saying about prayer's nature, for Christ's
point is that now, as a result of his death and resurrection, those who will
come in his name may come to the Father with the same freedom and boldness that had characterized his disciples' approach to him during the days
of his earthly ministry. What is more, they may come knowing that their requests will be granted.

We must not think that the disciples had not prayed to God before
Christ's resurrection. Undoubtedly, the disciples had often asked the Father
for things directly just as they had asked Jesus for things directly. Jesus had
even given them a prayer pattern that began with the words "Our Father in
heaven" and that included the requests, "Give us today our daily bread, . . .
forgive us our debts, . . . and lead us not into temptation" (Matt. 6:9–13).
But before this the disciples had not asked anything of the Father in
Christ's name. Now they are to do so and are to know that on that basis
whatever they should ask the Father he would give them (v. 23). The next
verse urges, "Until now you have not asked for anything in my name. Ask
and you will receive, and your joy will be complete" (v. 24).

This verse puts the privilege of prayer on the same level as the verses
from the fourteenth chapter which we considered earlier: "And I will do
whatever you ask in my name, so that the Son may bring glory to the Father.
You may ask me for anything in my name, and I will do it" (vv. 13–14).

The Conditions of Effective Prayer

The third teaching in these verses is the conditions of effective prayer,
conditions embodied in the phrase "in my name," which is repeated three
times (vv. 23–24, and 26) and is to be supplied mentally in one additional
instance (after "ask" in v. 24). Jesus says, "I tell you the truth, my Father will
give you whatever you ask in my name. Until now you have not asked for
anything in my name. Ask and you will receive" (vv. 23–24). And again, "In
that day you will ask in my name" (v. 26).

What does it mean to approach the Father in the name of Christ? It
means several things, a number of which were suggested earlier in our study

of John 14:13–14. In the first place, it means *to come to God as one who is identified with Jesus Christ by faith,* that is, to come as a saved person. When we speak of the name of Jesus we do not mean just a mere human name, as if the name "Jesus" is all we are talking about and as if it were no different than any other name. Jesus' full name is "the Lord Jesus Christ." And this means "Jehovah, the Savior, God's Anointed." "Lord" is the English translation of either of two Hebrew words: "Jehovah," the great Old Testament name for God, or "Adonai," which also refers to him. So to speak of "the *Lord* Jesus Christ" is to speak of One who is entirely divine, the incarnate God. We receive an impression of the significance of this title when we remember that the early Christians would not affirm the lordship of Caesar (*Kyrios Kaisar*) because it meant ascribing a divinity to the emperor that belonged to Christ alone.

The next part of the name, "Jesus," is the Greek form of the Hebrew name Jehoshua, meaning "Jehovah is salvation." When the angel announced Christ's name to Joseph before his birth, Joseph was told, "You are to give him the name Jesus, because he will save his people from their sins" (Matt 1:21).

"Christ," the last part of the name, is the Greek equivalent of the Hebrew word *mashiach* ("Messiah"), both of which literally mean "anointed." It refers to One who is anointed by God to perform the work of redemption.

When we put these together we see that to come to the Father in the name of the Lord Jesus Christ is to come to God believing (1) that Jesus is fully divine, the unique Son of God, and (2) that he performed the full work of saving people by his death and resurrection, which he was anointed by God to do. Since this is the minimum definition of what it means to be a Christian, this is the equivalent of saying that prayer is for Christians only. It is a family privilege. God does not promise to hear the prayer of anyone who comes to him in any way but through faith in the person and work of his unique and beloved Son.

Second, praying in the name of the Lord Jesus Christ means *praying on the basis of his merit* and not on the basis of any merit of our own. The illustration of drawing money out of a bank is perfect in this connection because it involves a person's name. If I go to a bank with a check that I have signed and attempt to draw the stipulated amount of money from the bank, I am asking in my own name. If I have an account sufficiently large to cover the amount requested, the check will be cashed. If I do not have an account or if I have insufficient funds, it will not be cashed. But if, on the other hand, I go to a bank with another person's name signed to the check and if he has great resources on deposit, then it does not matter whether I have an account or not. The check is honored because of his name and his deposits.

That is what it means to come to God on the merit of Christ. Torrey, who uses this illustration in the book from which I quoted earlier, concludes, "So it is when I go to the bank of heaven, when I go to God in prayer. I have nothing deposited there, I have absolutely no credit there, and if I go in my own name I will get absolutely nothing; but Jesus Christ has unlimited credit in heaven, and he has granted to me the privilege of going to the bank with his name on my checks, and when I thus go, my prayers will be honored to any extent."[2]

There is one more thing that praying in the name of Christ means. It means *praying in line with Christ's character and objectives,* that is, praying as he would under identical circumstances. Stedman writes on this point, "To ask in anyone's name means to ask as though you were that person. This means we are to ask for what Jesus would want, what he is after, and not for our own desires."[3]

Can we really know what Christ is after? Can we know his will? Yes, we can. First, by means of his Word, and second, by the ministry of the Holy Spirit who interprets that Word to us and correctly guides our petitions.

It is impossible to overestimate the importance of knowing and studying the Bible if we are to know the will of God. Nothing can ever be allowed to replace it. Occasionally, very occasionally, God reveals his will to us by extraordinary means, as he did to Moses at the burning bush or to Gideon by means of his fleece or to David by the voice of a prophet. But these are unusual means. The normal way of knowing the will of God is by what God has revealed of his purposes and character in the Bible and by the work of his Holy Spirit who takes what is written there and brings its meaning and contemporary force home to our hearts and consciences. Paul speaks of this latter part of the Spirit's ministry in prayer in its Godward aspect in Romans 8:26–27, saying, "In the same way, the Spirit helps us in our weakness. We do not know that we ought to pray for, but the Spirit himself intercedes for us with groans that words cannot express. And he who searches our hearts knows the mind of the Spirit, because the Spirit intercedes for the saints in accordance with God's will."

There are times when we do not know the will of God, and when that is the case we must pray cautiously allowing the Holy Spirit to interpret our prayers aright. But when we know God's will, as we do wherever it is revealed in Scripture, then we may pray confidently in the name of the Lord Jesus Christ and know that we shall receive the petitions that we have requested of him.

A New Prayer Promise

The fourth and final element of these verses is the new promise they give regarding prayer. It is in two parts. First, there is the promise that God will give spiritual understanding to those who ask him. This is the point of verse 25, which on the surface seems to break up the main thought of the passage. In verse 25 Jesus says, "Though I have been speaking figuratively, a time is coming when I will no longer use this kind of language but will tell you plainly about my Father." We read that verse, and we think that suddenly the theme of the discourse has shifted; first, Jesus was talking about prayer, now he is talking about the nature of his teaching. But this is not a change. It is rather that Jesus was recognizing as he spoke that the disciples were not really understanding his teaching and that much of what he said was therefore a "dark saying" to them. "But this will not last forever," he says, "for one of the things you may ask for in prayer is understanding. If you ask, you will receive it." Do you and I lack understanding? Does the Bible at times seem a closed book to us? Are certain sayings of Christ or certain doctrines "hard"? If so, we have this promise that, if we ask, we will receive understanding. Jesus has said that he will show us "plainly about [the] Father."

Then, too, the promise of this passage concerns joy, for, says Jesus, "Ask and you will receive, and your joy will be complete" (v. 24). How does prayer promote joy? One way is that when we get what we ask this naturally satisfies us and makes us conscious of the favor of God toward us. But this is only part of the story. The other part is that prayer makes God himself real so that, as we pray and receive what we asked for, God is actually there dispensing the gift and meeting with us on the personal level.

I spoke to a woman who had cancer and knew at the point at which I talked with her that she did not have long to live. We talked about Christ and heaven and about God's purposes in suffering, and after we did we prayed together. I prayed fervently and specifically, but she prayed much better. In her prayer she quietly thanked God for his special and very vivid presence with her in these days, citing several examples, and she expressed her joy in him. It was evident as she prayed that God's presence with her was real and that she rejoiced in him in a way that clearly overshadowed her concern about the cancer.

It is a joy to stand in God's presence in the name of Jesus and make and receive requests of him. Do you know that joy? If not, you must take time actually to come into the presence of God and learn to pray. If you need help, he will help you. He will help you because he loves you and wants to be known by you, as Jesus indicates (v. 27).

203

Great Origin, Great Destiny

John 16:28–30

"I came from the Father and entered the world; now I am leaving the world and going back to the Father."

Then Jesus' disciples said, "Now you are speaking clearly and without figures of speech. Now we can see that you know all things and that you do not even need to have anyone ask you questions. This makes us believe that you came from God."

Some time ago in Toronto, Canada, I was talking with a young man about the various errors in theology, and I pointed out that most often heresy results from emphasizing one part of biblical truth at the expense of other parts, as a result of which even that one part is distorted. "That is true of the Trinity," he said. I agreed, for at this point error consists in emphasizing the unity of God at the expense of the diversity of persons or emphasizing the diversity at the expense of the unity. The first heresy is unitarianism. The second is polytheism or Arianism. As our conversation went on we pointed out that the same thing is true of the doctrine of Christ's person. Some overemphasize the deity, others the humanity. The true position is that Christ is both God and man in one person.

In thinking about the difficulty theologians have in keeping Christian doctrines straight and in balance, it is always somewhat of a surprise and relief to discover that the difficulty is never apparent in the Bible. The doctrines are there. God is both three and one. Christ is both God and man. But these truths are never stated in a labored or highly technical form. Instead, they seem to flow from the narrative or doctrinal sections of the books as easily as any other statement.

We have an example of this in the section of the Gospel of John now before us. It is toward the end of the final discourses, which close with chapter 16. The Lord is speaking, of course; and he says, "I came from the Father and entered the world; now I am leaving the world and going back to the Father" (v. 28). This statement concerning his true nature, his heavenly origin, and his heavenly destiny, is profound but, at the same time, so simple that the disciples listening to him were led to exclaim, "Now you are speaking clearly and without figures of speech. Now we can see that you know all things and that you do not even need to have anyone ask you questions. This makes us believe that you came from God" (vv. 29–30). Beyond doubt, the disciples did not understand all that Christ was saying, but they were impressed that he knew their questions even before they asked them and could answer them simply. We should also be impressed as we begin to see all that is involved in Christ's statement.

I see four parts to verse 28. First, there is the doctrine of his heavenly origin; it involves Christ's preexistence and his full divinity. Second, there is the doctrine of the Incarnation, voluntarily assumed. Third, there is his voluntary return to God by way of crucifixion, burial, resurrection and ascension. Fourth, there is the matter of his heavenly destiny.

A Heavenly Origin

The first part of Christ's statement deals with his heavenly origin, for Jesus said, "I came from the Father." This, interestingly enough, is the main part of what the disciples understood, for their response was, "This makes us believe that you *came from God*" (v. 30).

What did they understand Christ to be saying? They undoubtedly understood Jesus to mean that he was the Messiah, for this was a common way of talking about the Messiah's coming into the world. Nicodemus said, when he encountered Jesus, "Rabbi, we know you are a teacher who has come from God. For no one could perform the miraculous signs you are doing if God were not with him" (John 3:2). The people who witnessed the miracles of the multiplication of the loaves and fish in Galilee exclaimed, "Surely this is the Prophet who is to come into the world" (John 6:14). That they were speaking of the Messiah in this sentence is proved by the fact that they then wanted to make him king, which we read about in the next verse. Similarly, Martha confessed, "Yes, Lord, I believe that you are the Christ, the Son of God, who was to come into the world" (John 11:27). At the least, then, this sentence indicates that Jesus was the one sent into the world by God for the work of redemption.

But it also means more than this, as Martha's additional phrase, "the Son of God," indicates. For it is not just that Jesus was a special servant of God's but rather that in addition to this he was with God from all eternity and was himself God. I do not know if the disciples understood this entirely, but it is certainly Christ's teaching, as other statements show.

For example, in reference to his heavenly existence before the incarnation, Jesus told the Jews, "Before Abraham was born, I am" (John 8:58). His hearers understood this to be blasphemy because they immediately took up stones to kill him. On another occasion Jesus said, "No one has ever gone into heaven except the one who came from heaven—the Son of Man" (John 3:13). He said, "What if you see the Son of Man ascend to where he was before?" (John 6:62). He said, "I have come down from heaven not to do my will but to do the will of him who sent me" (John 6:38). Even more impressive than these statements is that great assertion from the seventeenth chapter: "I have brought you glory on earth by completing the work you gave me to do. And now, Father, glorify me in your presence with the glory I had with you before the world began" (vv. 4–5).

Here are claims to both preexistence and deity, and they are so frequent throughout the public and private teaching of Christ that we can truthfully say that if we do not know this about him, we can in truth know nothing. Jesus claimed to be God and to have come forth from God. Is it true? Or was it false and therefore devilish teaching? Alexander Maclaren saw the issue clearly over a generation ago and expressed it as follows: "The meekest, lowliest, and most sane and wise of religious teachers made deliberately over and over again this claim, which is either absolutely true, and lifts him into the region of the Deity, or else is fatal to his pretensions to be either meek or modest, or wise or sane, or a religious teacher to whom it is worth our while to listen."[1]

This claim to deity is simple but stupendous. There can be no honest assessment of Christ that does not result in committing ourselves either to the truthfulness or falseness of those statements.

The Incarnation

The second part of verse 28 is an expression of the truth known as the incarnation, for Jesus said, "And [I] entered the world." There are several interesting aspects to this sentence. First, Jesus speaks of having "come" and "entered" rather than of having been "sent." It is true that Christ also was sent. Elsewhere he speaks of "the Father who sent me" (John 12:49). But this is not the point Jesus is emphasizing here. The point he is emphasizing is the voluntary nature of his incarnation. In other words, he did not have to be born. He was born because he wanted to be. This too is unique, because no one else can say that.

But this raises an even bigger question, for if Jesus chose to be born, if he assumed our human nature voluntarily, we immediately want to ask why he did this. *Cur Deus Homo?* Why did the eternal Son of God become man? There are two main answers. First, he became man in order to be our Savior, in order to die in our place and thereby pay the penalty of our sins so that we might be saved from the penalty and power of sin for heaven.

This is the point of that passage from Hebrews from which I quoted earlier. I quoted the verse, "I have come to do your will, O God" (Heb. 10:7). But that verse is prefaced by others that speak of the way in which the sacrifice of Christ perfected the ineffectual sacrifices of animals under the Jewish sacrificial system: "It is impossible for the blood of bulls and goats to take away sins. Therefore, when Christ came into the world, he said, 'Sacrifice and offering you did not desire, but a body you prepared for me; with burnt offerings and sin offerings you were not pleased" (vv. 4–6). The passage says further on, "He sets aside the first [sacrifice] to establish the second. And by that will, we have been made holy through the sacrifice of the body of Jesus Christ once for all" (vv. 9–10).

Once, when Donald Grey Barnhouse was talking with some students about the atonement, he used the illustration of a judge who saw his son come before him, accused of reckless driving. The charge was clearly proven, and the judge fined the young man the full amount permitted under the law. Then the judge adjourned the court, stepped down from the bench, and paid his son's fine. A girl who had been listening very intently objected, "But God cannot get down off the bench!"

Barnhouse's answer was, "You have given me one of the best illustrations of the incarnation that I will ever have. For Jesus Christ was no more or less than God, come down off the bench to pay the fine which he had imposed upon us."[2]

There is a second reason why the Son of God became man, and it is this second answer that the Gospel most emphasizes. It is that Jesus came into the world to reveal God.

We see this clearly simply by examining the occasions on which Jesus speaks of his having "come" into the world or of his having been "sent" into the world by God. Here is a scattering of such sentences just as one is likely to find them by reading quickly through the Gospel. "I tell you the truth, we speak of what we know, and we testify to what we have seen, but still you people do not accept our testimony" (3:11). "The one who comes from above is above all . . . He testifies to what he has seen and heard . . . The man who has accepted it has certified that God is truthful. For the one whom God has sent speaks the words of God, for God gives the Spirit without limit" (3:31–34). "My teaching is not my own. It comes from him who sent me" (7:16). "I am telling you what I have seen in the Father's presence" (8:38). "As it is, you are determined to kill me, a man who has told you the truth that I heard from God" (8:40). "I did not speak of my own accord, but the Father who sent me commanded me what to say and how to say it. . . . Whatever I say is just what the Father has told me to say" (12:49–50). "These words you hear are not my own; they belong to the Father who sent me" (14:24). In the great prayer of John 17, Jesus addresses the Father directly saying, "I gave them the words you gave me" (v. 8) and "I have given them your word" (v. 14).

The point of this is that Jesus has firsthand information about God the Father and that he should therefore be trusted and believed when he speaks of spiritual things.

A Voluntary Departure

The third part of verse 28 deals with Christ's voluntary departure from this world; for he says, "Now I am leaving the world." This throws a great deal of light on the nature of his crucifixion, because if we take it seriously, it means that the crucifixion was not something thrust upon Jesus against his will (as it might well have been were we in his place) but rather that to which his entire ministry was directed and which he joyfully embraced. It was he who said, "I lay down my life—only to take it up again. No one takes it from me, but I lay it down of my own accord. I have authority to lay it down and to take it up again" (John 10:17–18).

We hear much about love today, and God is assumed to be love. But it is only at the cross of Christ, in his voluntary death for us, that we learn that God truly is love. Love is seen at the cross. For this reason there is hardly a verse in the Bible which speaks of God's love that does not in the same context, often within the very verse itself, speak of Christ's voluntary sacrifice. John 3:16, "For God so loved the world that he gave his one and only Son, that whoever believes in him should not perish but have eternal life." Or, Galatians 2:20, "I have been crucified with Christ and I no longer live, but Christ lives in me. The life I live in the body, I live by faith in the Son of God, who loved me and gave himself for me." First John 4:10 declares, "This is love: not that we loved God, but that he loved us and sent his Son as an atoning sacrifice for our sins."

Christ's Destiny

The final section of verse 28 deals with Christ's heavenly destiny: "And [I am] going back to the Father." What is the significance for us that Jesus has returned to the Father, having come to this earth and having died for our salvation? There are several answers. First, it shows us that the work of redemption is completed and that we can be confident as we come to God on the basis of Christ's finished work. If the work was not done, Christ should still be here completing it. But it is done. Hence, he has returned to heaven, where he has sat down at the Father's right hand. The author of Hebrews discusses this in the same passage referred to earlier, for those verses go on to say, "But when this priest had offered for all time one sacrifice for sins, he sat down at the right hand of God. Since that time he waits for his enemies to be made his footstool, because by one sacrifice he has made perfect forever those who are being made holy" (Heb. 10:12–14).

Second, the fact that Christ has returned to heaven shows us that he is now in a place where he is able to impart all spiritual gifts and blessings to us as he sees we have need of them. The first of these gifts was the Holy Spirit, for Jesus said, "It is for your good that I am going away. Unless I go away, the Counselor will not come to you; but if I go, I will send him to you" (John 16:7). There are other gifts also. Thus, we read in Ephesians, "But to each one of us grace has been given as Christ apportioned it. This is why it says: 'When he ascended on high, he led captives in his train and gave gifts to men'" (Eph. 4:7–8; cf. Ps. 68:18).

Third, Christ's present position at the right hand of the Father is one from which he intercedes for his own. Paul speaks of it in Romans saying that Christ "intercedes for us" (Rom. 8:34). The author of Hebrews says, "Therefore, he is able to save completely those who come to God through him, because he always lives to intercede for them" (Heb. 7:25). Thus we sing,

> Arise, my soul, arise,
> Shake off thy guilty fears:
> The bleeding Sacrifice
> In my behalf appears:
> Before the Throne my Surety stands,
> My name is written on his hands.

It is Jesus' present position in heaven that makes us confident both of salvation and in our approach to God in our prayer and worship.

Finally, Christ's present position in heaven is a token that he is coming to earth again, this time in great power and glory and with his holy angels. Jesus is coming. This is as sure as the fact that he has come once to die for our salvation. Will you be ready to meet him? Will you greet him as your Savior, or will you have to greet him as one whose love you have spurned, whose sacrifice you have repudiated?

You say that you believe in Christ as a great man, a great teacher. Good! That is better than nothing. But it is not enough to save you. Why stop there? Why stop with Jesus the man? Why not have the whole Christ as he is here presented? Maclaren has well written, "These four facts—the dwelling in the Father; the voluntary coming to earth; the voluntary leaving earth; and, again, the dwelling with the Father—are the walls of the strong fortress into which we may flee and be safe. With them it 'stands four square to every wind that blows.' Strike away one of them, and it totters into ruin. Make the whole Christ your Christ; for nothing less than the whole Christ, 'conceived of the Holy Ghost, born of the Virgin Mary, . . . crucified, dead, and buried, . . . ascended into Heaven, and sitting at the right hand of God,' is strong enough to help your infirmities, vast enough to satisfy your desires, loving enough to love you as you need, or able to deliver you from your sins, and to lift you to the glories of his own Throne."[3]

That is precisely the case. May you find that One and come fully to trust him for your own soul's good and the praise of the glory of his grace.

204

Christ's Disciples Scattered

John 16:31–33

"You believe at last!" Jesus answered. "But a time is coming, and has come, when you will be scattered, each to his own home. You will leave me all alone. Yet I am not alone, for my Father is with me.

"I have told you these things, so that in me you may have peace. In this world you will have trouble. But take heart! I have overcome the world."

There are two reasons why the Lord Jesus Christ was not as impressed by his disciples' professions of faith as they themselves were. First, their faith had been a long time coming. Second, it was about to evaporate. In the verses that close the sixteenth chapter of John, Jesus had been answering the questions of the disciples without their having actually asked them, and this had led them to exclaim, "Now we can see that you know all things and that you do not even need to have anyone ask you questions. This makes us believe that you came from God" (v. 30). This claim was honest, but really quite pretentious. They claimed to believe. They said that they were sure in their belief, but they were actually weak in commitment. Thus, instead of being impressed with his disciples' faith, Jesus goes on to foretell their confusion and scattering at the time of his crucifixion.

This whole exchange should be a lesson for Christian people, for we are often quite confident in our faith, and yet are not as strong as we imagine ourselves to be. We say, "Now I believe; now I am sure." But in a short while we find ourselves doubting the very thing we affirmed.

A Realistic Appraisal

A number of years ago my first assistant at Tenth Presbyterian Church told me something that he had remembered from his early childhood. He had been helping his father put some things on the dining-room table, and he had asked to carry something that his father judged to be too heavy for him. He argued with his father, making many protestations. "Please, Father, I know I can carry it. I am sure I can." At last his father let him try. He started out confidently and carefully, but suddenly he dropped the container and the liquid spilled. He told me that he learned one of the great lessons of his life that day as he stood staring down at the spilled mess and the broken container. He felt absolutely chagrined; he had been so sure of himself. But his father had been right after all, and he was wrong.

Everyone has had such experiences, and it is these that will help us understand the profession of the disciples and their feelings as Jesus gently revealed the future to them. They were so sure of their faith. But in a short while—in fact, within hours—their faith would be gone.

Notice three things that Jesus prophesied concerning them. First, he revealed that they would soon be *scattered*. Now they were together, and, as is often the case, there was encouragement in numbers. And, of course, there was Jesus. If they had known the song, they might well have sung, "Give me ten men who are stouthearted men, and I'll soon give you ten thousand more." But they did not really know themselves. So before long, much to their chagrin, they would be scattered. Most scampered back over the Mount of Olives toward Bethany at the time of Christ's arrest in the Garden of Gethsemane. Peter followed the arresting party back into Jerusalem, but afar off. After the crucifixion Cleopas and Mary returned to Emmaus, and the others were undoubtedly making plans for their own departure.

Second, Jesus foretold their *confusion*. This is involved in his questions about their belief, for when he exclaims, "You believe *at last!*" it is as much as to say that the time was coming when they would no longer believe and all would be confusion. Now they were sure that he was the Messiah, come forth from God. But how could they be sure of that following the harsh reality of Christ's crucifixion? Like the Emmaus disciples they would all be saying, "But we had hoped that he was the one who was going to redeem Israel" (Luke 24:21).

Third, Jesus revealed that they would soon be *isolated,* for each would be scattered "to his own." When we read that phrase the first time we find ourselves asking, "Scattered to his own what? To his own house? City? Friends?" Jesus is saying that each would be scattered to his own little world and that each would be isolated in it. With the center gone, there would no longer be any cohesion to the little itinerant band. It is as if the devil, the disrupter, would have his way and that this heroic attempt to bind the sinful and scattered race of Adam into that glorious new unity of the church would come to ruin.

Well, what of it? Surely that is not our case, now that we have understood the meaning of the cross and stand on this side of Christ's resurrection! Is that right? Are we never scattered? Never confused? Never isolated? Of course, we are! We are scattered—sometimes by persecution, sometimes by schism within the denominations, sometimes merely by our suspicion of other Christians. We are confused, for even believers do not always have a sure answer to give to those who ask them a reason of the hope within. Circumstances, sickness, and other troubles rattle us. We are isolated, for Christians are often terribly alone. I have had Christians write to me with problems because of having heard me over the *Bible Study Hour,* and they have said, "I have no one to turn to; there is no other person with whom I can share my problems."

I want you to notice that in all of these respects—scattered, confused, isolated—Jesus is the exact opposite of the disciples. They scattered at the time of his arrest, but Jesus stood firm. He stood firm even to the point of death, as a result of which, after his resurrection, he became a magnetic point about which they regathered. They were confused, but he was strong in faith, as a result of which they recovered faith from him. They were isolated. But he, even though he was abandoned by them, could say, "But I am not alone, because the Father is with me." They emerged from their isolation when he came to them again following the resurrection.

I am glad that the Lord accepts weak, stammering, even ignorant faith. If he did not, what would become of us? Who could be saved? But having said that, let us not imagine that our faith or perception is the crucial thing, for "weak, stammering and ignorant" is an accurate description of it. Our strength is not in our faith but in him who is the object of it. It is in Jesus.

Christ's Legacy

The second lesson of these verses is Christ's parting legacy to his disciples. He had gently exposed the weakness of their supposedly strong faith. But not wishing to leave them with the exposure, he immediately goes on to talk of that which really is strong and which will endure even in tribulations. He talks about peace, his peace. It is the same peace he had spoken of in the fourteenth chapter: "Peace I leave with you; my peace I give you. I do not give to you as the world gives. Do not let your hearts be troubled" (14:27). It was announced of Christ at his birth that he had come to bring peace—"peace on earth, good will toward men." This he did, and he left it behind at his departure.

In 1874 a French steamer called the *Ville du Havre* was on a homeward voyage from America when a collision with a sailing vessel took place. The damage to the steamer was considerable, and as a result it sank quickly with the loss of nearly all who had been on board. One passenger, Mrs. Horatio G. Spafford, the wife of a lawyer in Chicago, had been en route to Europe with her four children. On being informed that the ship was sinking she knelt with her children and prayed that they might be saved or, if not, that they might be willing to die, if that was God's will. When the ship went down, the children were all lost. Mrs. Spafford was rescued by a sailor who had been rowing over the spot where the ship had sunk and found her floating in the water. Ten days later, when she reached Cardiff, she sent her husband the message: "Saved alone." This was a great blow, a sadness hardly comprehensible to anyone who has not lost a child. But though a great shock, it did not destroy the peace that either of the parents, who were both Christians, had from Jesus. Spafford wrote as a testimony to the grace of God in his experience:

> When peace, like a river, attendeth my way,
>   When sorrows like sea-billows roll—
> Whatever my lot, thou hast taught me to say,
>   It is well, it is well with my soul.
>
> Though Satan should buffet, though trials should come,
>   Let this blest assurance control,
> That Christ has regarded my helpless estate,
>   And hath shed his own blood for my soul.

This is the meaning of the Christian's peace. It is not an absence of conflict or any other kind of trial or disappointment. Rather it is contentment and trust in God in spite of such circumstances.

Two Conditions

But it is not automatic. That is, it is not ours regardless of whether or not we meet Christ's conditions for entering into this inheritance. The conditions he lays down in this passage are two.

First, the peace Christ gives is for those who are "in him." This could mean simply that peace is for Christians, for when we become Christians God places us in Christ so that we may properly be said to have died and risen with him and to be sitting now with him in heaven. But this is probably not what Christ is talking about here. We must remember in interpreting this verse that the discourses in which they occur have been full of admonitions to "believe on" Christ and, more importantly, to "remain in" him. This is not the kind of being "in" Christ that corresponds with being saved but rather a conscious dependence on him and staying close to him that is the prerequisite to joy and fruitfulness in the Christian life. It is this that Christ has in mind as he closes these discourses. Jesus gives peace. But the gift of peace is appropriated only by those who depend on him, trust him, and remain close to him in their living of the Christian life.

Moreover, this interpretation of being "in" Christ is reinforced by the second of the two conditions: that the words of Christ might be in his followers. Jesus indicates this when he says, "*I have told you these things*, so that in me you may have peace" (v. 33). What things are these? They are the doctrines of this section of John's Gospel. We previewed these at the beginning of our study of this section.

First, there is the fact of Christ's love for the disciples. Chapter 13 begins with this truth: "It was just before the Passover Feast. Jesus knew that the time had come for him to leave this world and go to the Father. Having loved his own who were in the world, he now showed them the full extent of his love" (v. 1). The chapter that is introduced by that verse contains a great demonstration of the love of Christ for his own, the foot washing, which is at the same time both a true demonstration of Christ's condescending love and an illustration of his humbling of himself in order to be able to die on the cross. Throughout the discourses there is repeated evidence of Christ's concern for his own. He is concerned to instruct them, warn them, and prepare them for his departure.

Second, Jesus spoke about heaven, saying that he was going to prepare a place for his own in heaven and that, if he was going, he would return and take them to himself so that where he was there they would be also (14:2–3). What was new in this teaching was not the mere fact of heaven, but rather that Jesus had an interest in it and would guarantee a personalized place in heaven for his followers.

Third, Jesus had spoken about the coming of the Holy Spirit. This was a tremendously new thing, for although the Old Testament had much to say about the Spirit of God, and although several of the Old Testament prophecies had spoken of a day when the Holy Spirit should be poured forth in power, no one had been associating that with Christ's ministry or gifts. Now the disciples were told that Christ would himself send the Spirit and that he would come to be in them and work through them. According to Jesus, the Holy Spirit would comfort the disciples. He would also perform a ministry toward the world, for he would convict the world "of sin, righteousness and judgment" (16:8).

Fourth, Jesus spoke of a work that the disciples were to perform and for which he was leaving them in the world. He spoke of it in different ways. In the fourteenth chapter he spoke of it in comparison with his own work, saying that it would be even greater: "Anyone who has faith in me will do what I have been doing. He will do even greater things than these, because I am going to the Father" (v. 12). In the fifteenth chapter he spoke of it in terms of his commissioning of them to fruitful service: "You did not choose me, but I chose you and appointed you to go and bear fruit—fruit that will last" (v. 16). Having work to do in this world, their lives would be meaningful.

Fifth, the Lord spoke about prayer, giving us some of the most exciting promises in the Bible concerning it. "And I will do whatever you ask in my name, so that the Son may bring glory to the Father. You may ask me for anything in my name and I will do it" (14:13–14). "If you remain in me and my words remain in you, ask whatever you wish, and it will be given you" (15:7). "Until now you have not asked for anything in my name. Ask and you will receive, and your joy will be complete" (16:24). The Lord also told them that he would pray for them. In the seventeenth chapter, we have a magnificent example of just such intercession.

Finally, even as Jesus reminds the disciples of what he has already taught, he adds another teaching: "But take heart! I have overcome the world" (16:33).

Christus Victor

This is the point at which we should end—the point of Christ's victory. He overcame the world in three areas: in his life, in his death, and in his resurrection. He overcame it in life because, in spite of abundant griefs and temptations, he pursued the course God had set before him without deviation, sin, or error. He said of Satan, "The prince of this world is coming. He has no hold on me" (John 14:30). He overcame the world in death because his death was the price of sin and thus broke sin's hold upon us. He overcame the world in his resurrection because by his resurrection he began his return to the throne of heaven from which he now rules the church and from which he will one day come again to put down all authority and power.

"I have overcome the world." These words were spoken within the shadow of Golgotha, at the very foot of the cross. They were spoken on the verge of what surely seemed a defeat. But they were true then. And if they were true then, it is even more abundantly demonstrated that they are true now. Do you believe them? Is Christ the victor? If you do and if he is, then stand with him in his victory. Possess that peace that he dispenses, and in your turn also overcome the world. Does the world deride Christ's gospel? So much the worse for the world. Do circumstances press us down? He has overcome circumstances. Stand with him then. He is the King. He is God over all, whose name is blessed forever.

205

The Real Lord's Prayer

John 17:1-5

After Jesus said this, he looked toward heaven and prayed:
"Father, the time has come. Glorify your Son, that your Son may glorify you. For you granted him authority over all people that he might give eternal life to all those you have given him. Now this is eternal life: that they may know you, the only true God, and Jesus Christ, whom you have sent. I have brought you glory on earth by completing the work you gave me to do. And now, Father, glorify me in your presence with the glory I had with you before the world began."

In several places in his *Institutes of the Christian Religion* and other writings, John Calvin, the great reformer and theologian, speaks of God's revelation of himself to us in the Bible as baby talk, the kind of speech used by a loving mother communicating with an infant child. What Calvin means by this is that any communication to us by God must be in the simplest and most rudimentary language from God's point of view. His thoughts are not our thoughts. His ways are not our ways. Consequently, God must condescend to speak to us in baby talk if we are to understand him. If the Scriptures are to be of any use to us, they must be a rudimentary revelation.

When we think along these lines, however, it is natural to speculate on what that true and deep communication that exists between the members of the Godhead might be by contrast. It is granted that God must talk baby talk to us, but how profound, deep, and unfathomable must be that talk between the Father and Son and between both of them and the Holy Spirit! Are we right in this speculation? In one sense, we obviously are. Still, the section of the Gospel of John to which we come now is an immediate and abrupt check on any of our thoughts along these lines. For, while it is the purest and most extensive example in all the Bible of a direct, verbalized communication between two members of the Godhead, nevertheless it is expressed in the most comprehensible phrasings, syntaxes, and words.

Compare it with Luke's prose, for example. Luke begins the Book of Acts with beautiful Greek style: "In my former book, Theophilus, I wrote about all that Jesus began to do and to teach until the day he was taken up to heaven, after giving instructions through the Holy Spirit to the apostles he had chosen. After his suffering, he showed himself to these men and gave many convincing proofs that he was alive" (1:1–3). It goes on in that vein. But listen to John 17. "Father, the time has come. Glorify your Son, that your Son may glorify you. For you granted him authority over all people that he might give eternal life to all those you have given him. Now this is eternal life: that they may know you, the only true God, and Jesus Christ, whom you have sent" (vv. 1–3). The prayer goes on: "I pray for them. I am not praying for the world. . . . All I have is yours, and all you have is mine. . . . Sanctify them by the truth; your word is truth. . . . Father, I want those you have given me to be with me where I am and to see my glory, the glory you have given me because you loved me before the creation of the world" (vv. 9–10, 17, 24).

This prayer contains the simplest of sentences, though the ideas are profound. It is proof that the difficulty we have in understanding God's truth is not in the complexity of the truth itself or in the language with which it is conveyed (as if it were logarithms or German philosophy) but in our own ignorance, sin, and spiritual lethargy.

A Priestly Prayer

What a wonderful prayer this is! It has three parts: Christ's prayer for himself (vv. 1–5), his prayer for his disciples (vv. 6–19), and his prayer for all who should follow them in faith in the coming centuries (vv. 20–26). The shortest part is Christ's prayer for his own interests. By contrast, he prays at length both for his disciples and for ourselves as members of his mystical body. The prayer has five main petitions, one for himself and four for us. The second and third parts enumerate six distinctive marks of the church, each of which we will eventually study separately: joy, holiness, truth, mission, unity, and love.

A study of these verses soon shows that this is the true Lord's Prayer. The prayer that begins, "Our Father in heaven, hallowed be your name . . ." (Matt. 6:9–13), should more accurately be termed The Disciples' Prayer. The one in John 17 is Jesus' prayer. It has properly been designated his High Priestly Prayer, for he intercedes for us here as our High Priest before his Father's throne.

Luther said of this prayer, "This is truly, beyond measure, a warm and hearty prayer. He opens the depths of His heart, both in reference to us and to His Father, and He pours them all out. It sounds so honest, so simple; it is so deep, so rich, so wide, no one can fathom it." Melanchthon, Luther's friend and colleague, wrote, "There is no voice which has ever been heard, either in heaven or in earth, more exalted, more holy, more fruitful, more sublime, than the prayer offered up by the Son to God Himself." The Scottish Reformer, John Knox, had this prayer read to him every day during his final sickness, and in the closing moments of his life he testified that these verses continued to be a great comfort and a source of strength for his conflict.[1]

This prayer should be to us something of what the burning bush was to Moses, for here we hear God speaking, and we should put off our shoes and bow humbly, being about to tread on the most hallowed ground.

The First Petition

We turn now to the first of Christ's petitions. It is found in verses 1 and 5. It is the prayer that the Father would "glorify" Jesus, as a result of which Jesus would in turn "glorify" the Father. The verses read, "Father, the time has come. Glorify your Son, that your Son may glorify you. . . . And now, Father, glorify me in your presence with the glory I had with you before the world began."

In understanding this petition we are, however, immediately confronted with a problem, for few words in the distinct biblical vocabulary are less understood than the word "glory." What is more, even a perfectly correct definition—once we have found it—does not always do justice to the passage under consideration. This passage is itself a perfect illustration of this second difficulty, for in the first five verses we are told four apparently conflicting things about Christ's glory. First, Jesus possessed a certain glory with God before the incarnation. Second, this glory was God's glory. Third, Jesus did not possess this glory during the years of his incarnation; he here prays that this original glory might be restored to him. And yet, at the same time and fourthly, there is a sense in which he did possess this glory while on earth, for he revealed it to others by finishing the work God had given him to do. This latter sense is involved in John 2:11, to give just one additional example; for we are told there that the changing of water into wine at Cana was the beginning of those miracles in which Jesus "revealed his glory" and as a result of which his disciples "believed on him."

How can this be? How can the Lord have possessed God's glory, have renounced it, and yet have possessed it even in the period of the renunciation? And what does the phrase "the glory of God" mean anyhow?

The resolution of this problem and the only sufficient basis on which we will ever understand Christ's petition lies in an understanding of the way in which the idea of "glory" was used in ancient Greek and Hebrew literature. In the Greek language the word for glory is *doxa*, which in turn is based upon the ancient verb *dokeo*. In the early days the verb meant "to seem," "to appear," or "to have an opinion." This meaning is apparent in the idiomatic expression *dokei moi,* which means, "it seems good to me." It occurs in the New Testament most clearly in Galatians 2 in which Paul speaks of the Jerusalem apostles as those who "seemed to be leaders" (v. 2), "seemed to be important" (v. 6), and were "reputed to be pillars" (v. 9). It was an opinion that Paul himself apparently did not fully embrace. The noun correspondingly meant an "opinion" or, more precisely, "what one thinks." This meaning is preserved in our English words "orthodox," "heterodox," and "paradox," which mean, roughly, "a straight (or right) opinion," "a different (or other) opinion" and "a contrary (or conflicting) opinion." This early history of the words is documented in the great theological Greek dictionary edited by Gerhard Kittel, from which these details are taken.

Some time after this early history of the words, the noun (*doxa* or "glory") began a development of its own that soon took it from its original meaning. In the early stage it had meant an "opinion," any opinion. But as time went on it came to mean, first, a "good opinion" (as opposed to just any opinion) and, then, "that which merits a good opinion." During these stages the word could correctly have been translated as "praise," "honor," "good standing," "reputation," or "renown." When used of a king or of a divine being, it obviously meant the ultimate in praise or renown, as when we read: "Who is this King of glory? The LORD strong and mighty, the LORD mighty in battle. . . . The LORD Almighty— he is the King of glory" (Ps. 24:8, 10).

The quotation from Psalm 24 introduces us to another feature of the history of the word, however, for it begins to show the result of the Bible's applying the word to God. The glory of God was obviously linked to his attributes, for he could be called the King of glory because he was perfect in all his attributes—love, truth, holiness, grace, power, knowledge, immutability, and so forth—and was therefore truly glorious. Incidentally, this also exemplifies the meaning of the word orthodox, because the person who has orthodox beliefs is the one able to form a correct, or proper, opinion of God's attributes. In this way, God's glory consists of his intrinsic worth, or character, to use a human term. Thus, all that can be properly known of God is an expression of his glory.

At this point we can understand one use of the word glory in Christ's petition, for when he says, "I have brought you glory on earth by completing the work you gave me to do" (v. 4), he is saying that, by his ministry, he had revealed the essential characteristics of the Father. When the disciples beheld his glory, as in 2:11, they actually beheld his character, which was the character of God. It is one way of saying that, if we have seen Jesus, we have seen the Father.

Shekinah Glory

This only explains one use of the word, however. It explains the glory that Jesus obviously retained during the years of his earthly ministry. But what of that glory that he had with the Father before the incarnation, which he renounced and which he prayed might be restored? If this glory refers to God's essential character, it would mean that Jesus was less than God during the days of his ministry, and this is not right. What does the word mean in these more exalted references?

The answer to this question is found in the recognition that there is another, entirely different meaning of the word "glory," which had its origin in Hebrew rather than Greek thought, and which entered the Greek language later only as a result of contacts between Greek and Hebrew culture. Although the beginnings of these contacts are not known, it seems that the major factor was the translation of the Hebrew Scriptures into Greek about one hundred years before Christ. The translation is known as the Septuagint. Later writers, such as the Jewish philosopher Philo (born c. 20–10 b.c.) and Flavius Josephus (born c. a.d. 37), employ the word with both meanings.

In Jewish thought any outward manifestation of God's presence was believed to involve a display of light, radiance, or glory so brilliant that no man could approach it. This idea is involved in the phrase "the light of [his] face" (Ps. 4:6; 44:3). It is in Psalm 104:1–2, "O Lord my God, you are very great; you are clothed with splendor and majesty. He wraps himself in light as with a garment." We have a graphic example in the case of Moses whose face glowed with a transferred light after he had been with God on Mount Sinai, so much so that the people asked that he cover his face with a veil that they might be shielded from the radiance (Exod. 34:29–35; 2 Cor. 3:13–15). Light was also associated with the cloud of glory that overshadowed the wilderness tabernacle during the years of Israel's wandering and that later filled Solomon's great temple in Jerusalem (1 Kings 8:10–11). This idea is so important that it is found throughout the Old Testament. In post Old Testament times, in the Targums and other Jewish writings, a new word, *Shekinah,* more perfectly embodied it.

We now have enough knowledge of the word "glory" to understand Christ's first petition. Before his incarnation Jesus had possessed the glory of God in both these senses. He possessed the fullness of God's attributes and character in the inward sense; he also possessed the fullness of God's outward, visible glory. In the Incarnation Jesus laid the second of these aside; for, if he had not, we would not have been able to approach him. Nevertheless, he retained God's glory in the first sense and indeed disclosed it to his disciples, who received it by faith. Now at the end of his earthly ministry, on the verge of his crucifixion and subsequent resurrection, he prays that he might again enter into this visible glory.

Now Jesus has been exalted. He has been given that glory. Stephen saw it at the time of his martyrdom; so also did John (he wrote about it in the Book of Revelation) and perhaps Paul as well. This fact should be a great encouragement for believers, for it points to the kingly rule of Christ who now rules his church in righteousness and preserves his people.

Christ Our Glory

There is one further thought. It is that we shall share in Christ's glory. In a sense, we share in it now, for, to the degree that we embody Christ's character, we possess his glory in the first of its two important senses. Is not this what Jesus means when he goes on to say, "Glory has come to me through them" (v. 10)? Or again, "I have given them the glory that you gave me" (v. 22)? Moreover, we shall even see Christ's visible, outward glory one day, for Jesus goes on to pray concerning us and of that glory, "Father, I want those you have given me to be with me where I am, and to see my glory" (v. 24).

What shall we conclude then? If we shall one day behold Christ's glory and if we are to be filled with it now, let us strive to glorify him and show forth his glory. And let us pray that God will do that in us, for it is obviously not something of which we in ourselves are capable.

But notice! When Jesus prayed that he might be glorified and that God would therefore be glorified in him, he buttressed his petition with reasons. They are instructive. I see five reasons behind Christ's request. First, that the hour had come (v. 1). This means that the hour of Christ's great work had come, the hour of his crucifixion and subsequent resurrection. To say that the hour had come meant that Jesus had been in the will of his Father throughout his life, that this had brought him to the hour of his most important work, and that he would be continuing in that will until it was done. Second, he prays for his glorification because it would result in the glorification of the Father (v. 1). In other words, the prayer was not selfish but merely that which every intelligence in the universe should desire. Third, he says that God the Father had already given him authority to grant eternal life to each one who had been given to him (v. 2). His glorification followed naturally upon this. Fourth, Jesus argues that by virtue of his death he is the only way to life (v. 3). His glorification would therefore mean the salvation of his people. Finally, he speaks of his finished work (v. 4). The divine pattern is first self-denial, obedience, and suffering, after which the glory follows.

This should be our pattern also. We must seek to glorify Christ while we live by showing forth his character. But this will not happen in some mystical way. It will happen only as, by the grace of God, we walk in his will (as he directs), as we carry out whatever responsibility he has entrusted to us, as we point to Jesus as the only way of salvation, as we finish our work, and as we seek the glory of God in its fullness, rather than our own.

206

God's Gifts to Jesus

John 17:2

"For you granted him authority over all people that he might give eternal life to all those you have given him."

The second verse of the prayer recorded in John 17 gives a reason for Jesus' request that is found in the first verse (the request to be glorified by the Father). The reason is that glorification and the authority over all flesh already granted to him go together. As I read this verse, however, the part that strikes me most is its repetition of the verb "to give" or "grant." It occurs twice of the Father's gifts to Jesus: the gift of power [or authority] over all flesh, and the gift of a people. It occurs once of Christ's gift of eternal life to those whom God has given him. As we study this verse we will find that the three are connected, and will be led into the very heart of the relationships of the Son to the Father and of both to us in salvation.

Gift of a People

I do not know if you have ever had difficulty finding an appropriate gift for someone, particularly for a person who apparently has everything, but I confess that I have. And sometimes it bothers me. I can imagine myself giving a bottle of shampoo to a man who wears a wig, though I did not know it, or giving a recording of the Bach *B Minor Mass* to a person who hates classical music. The fear of doing something inappropriate is what makes us hesitant so much at the counter when buying a present for someone just before Christmas.

I do not think, however, that God the Father had a problem when he was considering the first of these great gifts for his Son Jesus. For what could be more *appropriate* for God the Father to give the Son than a people who should be conformed to his own blessed image and be his brothers and sisters throughout eternity? A mansion would not be appropriate, for all the mansions of heaven already belong to Christ and are going to be prepared by him for those who are his own. A world such as this, even a galaxy of such worlds, is not appropriate, for Jesus shared in the making of the worlds that already exist, and he could make billions more at any time, if he so chose. Nothing that we can possibly imagine would be a more appropriate gift to that One who is himself the Lord of glory than a people of his own—a people who had been created in his image, who had fallen into sin, but who were now to be redeemed by Christ and called to him in faith by the power of the Holy Spirit.

As we read this and the other verses that speak along these lines, we find ourselves facing what the old Reformed theologians called a covenant between God the Father and God the Son, according to which God would give to Jesus in salvation that vast company for whom he was specifically to die.

Moreover, this was not only an appropriate gift for Jesus; it was a *satisfying* one as well, for it is often recorded of Christ that he took joy in or rejoiced over his people. One great example of this is in the Old Testament, in the Book of Isaiah. In Isaiah 53, that great chapter in which the suffering and death of Christ for his own is most clearly spelled out, it is said that the Lord should look upon the fruit of his suffering and be satisfied: "Though the LORD makes his life a guilt offering, he will see his offspring and prolong his days, and the will of the LORD will prosper his hand. After the suffering of his soul, he will see the light of life and be satisfied" (vv. 10–11). The satisfaction was in knowing that his death would secure our salvation.

The theme of Christ's satisfaction is also in the New Testament, as in Hebrews 12, to give just one example. We are told there to look to the example of the Lord Jesus Christ, "the author and perfecter of our faith, who for the joy set before him endured the cross, scorning its shame" (v. 2). In what was Christ's joy to be found? Clearly in the knowledge that by his death he would secure the salvation of all whom God had given him.

Do you think that the promise to Christ that a certain people, given to him by the Father and surely to be saved by his suffering, was also a *comfort* to Christ on the verge of his crucifixion? It must have been. Otherwise, why would the phrase "who you have given me" (twice with slight variations) appear seven times in verses 2, 6, 9, 11, 12, and 14?

We all find ourselves repeating an idea or phrase when we have been faced by something particularly trying or traumatic. Sometimes people facing a dreaded operation keep repeating, "It will all be over in just a few hours," or "I know it will turn out all right." When competing in sports, we sometimes repeat something we should recall in order to perform well: "Keep your chin down," "Keep your forearm stiff," "Remember to breathe deeply," or some such point of personal instruction. It was the same with Jesus. The cross was no easy task for him, particularly since, when he was made sin for us, it involved a real, though temporary, separation from the Father. In the Garden, on this same evening, he even prayed in agony that this cup be removed from him, if such could be the Father's will. This was hard, but in his trial he received comfort in knowing that his suffering would result in the salvation of his people. Of these he had said earlier, "All that the Father gives me" (John 6:37). His death was to provide the objective and judicial basis upon which these who had already been given to him should come.

There is no greater gift, no more appropriate gift, no more satisfying gift for Jesus than this, the gift of the church to the One who would die for it. If you have believed on Christ as your Savior, you should know that you are one who was thus given to Jesus before the foundation of the world and about whom he was thinking and receiving comfort as he died.

Authority

The second of God's gifts to Jesus according to John 17:3 is power or, as the word *exousia* should better be translated, authority. The gift is authority over all flesh to do with as he will. It is a great authority, for it is on the basis of this authority that he can give eternal life to all whom God has given him.

There are several very important things about this authority. First, its scope. The text is speaking of this when it says, "For you granted him authority over *all* people." All means everyone, everyone who has ever lived or who will ever live. It means the rich as well as the poor, the supposedly sophisticated persons of our culture as well as the savage in the jungle, the strong as well as the weak, the intelligent as well as the not-so-intelligent. It means the other person. It means me. No one is excepted from the scope of this universal authority of the Lord Jesus Christ. Therefore he may do with them as he wishes. He is the King of kings and Lord of lords.

Moreover, it is not just all men and women, past and future, who are subject to his authority. It is angels and demons, those in heaven and in hell as well. This truth is clearly taught in that great passage on Christ's exaltation—Philippians 2:9–11. "Therefore, God exalted him to the hightest place and gave him the name that is above every name, that at the name of Jesus every knee should bow, in heaven and on earth and under the earth, and every tongue confess that Jesus Christ is Lord, to the glory of God the Father." Here three distinct categories of intelligent beings are mentioned: those in heaven, those on earth, and those under the earth. This refers to angels (whose natural dwelling place is with God), men and women (who dwell upon earth), and those fallen angels or demons (who were cast out of heaven at the time of their original rebellion and who will one day inhabit hell, which has been prepared for them). There are two different kinds of acknowledgment, of course. The holy angels and those who have been redeemed from among men and women will acknowledge Christ gladly. They will rejoice to confess him Lord. Others, the fallen angels and those who have not believed from among men and women, will not acknowledge him gladly. But they *will* acknowledge him, being forced to this by the sheer fact of his triumph. However the acknowledgment is made, either willingly or reluctantly and with hatred, the acknowledgment *will* be made, and the full scope of the authority and power of the Lord Jesus Christ will be vindicated.

It is wise for us to ask, not how we may escape that authority (for we cannot) but rather in what way that acknowledgement of his rule shall be made by us. Willingly and with joy? Or grudgingly and with hatred? If we do not come to believe in and love the Lord Jesus Christ here, we will not do it on that great day when all are called before him.

The second important thing to note about the authority of Christ portrayed in this verse is its depth, for it is not just that Jesus has been granted authority over all, important as that is, but also that He has been granted authority "over all flesh"(KJV). Flesh is the most recalcitrant thing in the universe.

In common English usage the word "flesh" refers almost exclusively to the fleshy parts of the body and is related to the "skin." Yet this is not what the word means in the Bible. To be sure, it can at times mean "skin." But generally it means the entire individual—composed of a body, soul, and spirit—which since the fall is constantly motivated by a sinful nature. We see the first instance of this broader definition in the early chapters of Genesis when Adam says, after God has brought the first woman to him, "'This is now bone of my bones and flesh of my flesh; she shall be called "woman," for she was taken out of man.' For this reason a man will leave his father and mother and be united to his wife, and they will become one flesh" (2:23–24). This last phrase does not mean that the man and the woman were to be united sexually only, though that was an important part of their union, but rather that they were to be united on each level of their being—body, soul, and spirit—so that they would thereafter be what we might conceivably call one organism. The word "flesh," therefore, denotes the whole of man's being.

In this first case the word "flesh" is used in a favorable sense. But with the coming of the fall in the next chapter this initial and favorable usage changes. Now the word continues to refer to the whole of man's being, but a being that is sadly dominated by man's depraved sinful nature.

Let me give an illustration. We may think in terms of an airplane flying at 35,000 feet. The pilot is the soul. The fuselage is the flesh. The thrust of the engines is the spirit. In that form each part of the airplane is good and is functioning as the designer intended it to function. But if the engines stop, the entire plane is in trouble, for now the fuselage, which was an asset when the engines were running, becomes a liability and will soon draw the plane to destruction. To be fleshly in the biblical sense means, therefore, to be dominated by the body without the ongoing thrust of the spirit. Sometimes it is said that we are dominated by our "old man" or "old nature." Sometimes the Bible speaks of the deceitfulness of our heart.

Here are some texts. "Surely I was sinful from birth, sinful from the time my mother conceived me" (Ps. 51:5). "Put off your old self, which is being corrupted by its deceitful desires" (Eph. 4:22). "The heart is deceitful above all things and beyond cure" (Jer. 17:9). "For from within, out of men's hearts, come evil thoughts, sexual immorality, theft, murder, adultery, greed, malice, deceit, lewdness, envy, slander, arrogance and folly. All these evils come from inside and make a man 'unclean'" (Mark 7:21–23). "Those controlled by the sinful nature cannot please God" (Rom. 8:8).

With this background we can appreciate something of the depth of the authority of Christ over all flesh, for the point of this word is not merely that Jesus has authority over all intelligent beings, though that is true, but also that he has authority even over that stubborn and rebellious nature that now so totally dominates men and women. I am glad that he does, for if he had not had that authority over me to turn me from my path of rebellion and quicken my dead spirit so that I might respond to him in faith, I would never have believed. I would be under condemnation and soon to perish in my sin. But in grace he turned me to himself, as he has countless others.

Universal and Specific

This leads to the third of the gifts mentioned in the text. We are told that Jesus has been given authority over all so that he might in a specific way give eternal life to as many as God has given him. The authority is universal. It cannot possibly be greater either in scope or in depth. Nevertheless, the exercise of that authority in the matter of salvation is specific, for it is shown in the giving of eternal life to those, and only those, whom God has given him.

This is the problem of the verse so far as natural, human thinking goes. We do not really doubt or question the statement that Jesus has authority over all—at least no Christian does—for this is what a Christian confesses when he calls Jesus Lord. But it is quite another matter to say that he gives eternal life selectively and that only to those who have already been given to him by the Father. How can this be? Is God partial? Is this really the way God operates in salvation?

We must be ready to say that we do not fully understand these things, particularly when we are asked the why of God's actions. Nevertheless, we must always say that this is the way God operates and that he is just in doing so, whatever our thoughts in the matter may be.

Jesus faced precisely these objections on more than one occasion during his ministry, and sometimes they were violently expressed. For example, on the occasion of his opening his ministry by a reading of the Book of Isaiah in the synagogue at Nazareth, he got into a discussion of the nature of God's electing grace, and the people who heard him were offended. Earlier he had pointed to himself as the fulfillment of Isaiah 61:1–2, and they were not particularly upset about that. In fact, we are told that they actually "were amazed at the gracious words that came from his lips" (Luke 4:22). But then he explained that God does not always work where we expect him to or according to our standards of justice or propriety. He said, "I assure you that there were many widows in Israel in Elijah's time, when the sky was shut for three and a half years and there was a severe famine throughout the land. Yet Elijah was not sent to any of them, but to a widow in Zarephath in the region of Sidon. And there were many in Israel with leprosy in the time of Elisha the prophet, yet not one of them was cleansed—only Naaman the Syrian" (vv. 25–27). These verses illustrate God's authority over all so that he might show mercy on whom he will. And at this statement, not at the earlier one but at this, the people were "furious. . . . They got up, drove him out of the town, and took him to the brow of the hill on which the town was built, in order to throw him down the cliff" (vv. 28–29).

Which is worse, the fact that we are dead in our trespasses and sins and unable to come to Christ unless Jesus first gives eternal life to us, or the fact that we naturally hate these truths when they are spoken to us? It is hard to say. But what is best is to say that God in his grace has given some to Christ and that Jesus has in turn given them his own life that they might be saved.

Are you such a person? I cannot say that you are or are not, apart from your response to Christ, and neither can you. But I can say that if you find stirrings of spiritual life within you so that you are becoming increasingly aware of your spiritual need and are finding Jesus to be the One who is attractive to you as the Savior, and if you are turning to him, then it is because these great gifts of God have already taken place where you are concerned, and you are being brought inevitably to Jesus. God has given you to him. Jesus is drawing you. Come to him. Find him to be your Savior.

207

Knowing the True God

John 17:3

"Now this is eternal life: that they may know you, the only true God, and Jesus Christ, whom you have sent."

One of the things that has always interested me in my study of the Word of God is the number of ways in which one may speak of salvation. In fact, it has been more than interesting. It is important because it is often the case that Christians get locked into one particular way of talking about salvation and thus cannot change, even when the person to whom they are talking fails to understand their terminology. That needs to be corrected.

In evangelical circles the most common way of talking about the gospel of Jesus Christ is by the words "sin," "atonement," "the new birth," "believing on Jesus," and related concepts. It is no surprise that this is so, for these are the dominant biblical terms, and they are correctly at the heart of our Christian proclamation. But what if these words were missing from the English language? Or what if, which is nearly the same thing, these words and what they mean are missing from the thoughts of someone to whom we are speaking about the gospel? Can other terms be used? My study of the Bible indicates that they can. Thus, to give just one example, it is possible to speak of the will of God, our rebellion against that will, and God's activity in Christ and through the Holy Spirit to get our wills in line with his once again. The rebellion of our wills against God's will is sin; this is what the Bible calls Satan's sin (Isaiah 14). Salvation is that by which God again establishes his perfect and holy will in us so that we are drawn to Christ and begin to seek after holiness. Heaven may be described as that place where the wills of those who are there, after having been disrupted by Satan, are harmonious.

Our text in John gives another set of terms for salvation. It says, "Now this is eternal life: that they may know you, the only true God, and Jesus Christ, whom you have sent" (17:3). Here the operative term is knowledge—"that they may know." Knowledge of God is salvation. By contrast, not knowing God and not wanting to is sin.

True Knowledge

When we speak along these lines we must be careful to define what we mean by that knowledge that is salvation, for there are several uses of the word that are not what the Lord meant in this expression and that, far from suggesting salvation, actually are used biblically to explain why men are guilty for failing to come to God for it.

There are four senses of this word that are inadequate. The first is that sense of knowing by which we actually mean *awareness*. It is what we have in mind when we say, for example, that we know the United States is governed by a president and a congress and that the headquarters for both are in Washington. This is not a very profound kind of knowledge, nor is it necessarily detailed. It is the kind of awareness a child might have as a result of something he or she has been taught in school. The Bible speaks of this kind of knowledge in Romans 1, saying that all who have ever been born into the human race have this knowledge and are guilty before God because, having it, they do not come to him. More precisely, Paul speaks of the wrath of God being revealed against men "since what may be known about God is plain to them, because God has made it plain to them. For since the creation of the world God's invisible qualities—his eternal power and divine nature—have been clearly seen, being understood from what has been made, so that men are without excuse. For although they knew God, they neither glorified him as God nor gave thanks to him, but their thinking became futile and their foolish hearts were darkened" (Rom. 1:19–21). These verses are not speaking of a knowledge of God in the sense intended by Jesus when he linked a knowledge of God to eternal life, otherwise all would be saved. Rather, they speak of the most rudimentary kind of knowledge. It is awareness only, but it makes us responsible.

The second inadequate meaning of the words "to know" or "knowledge" involves *information*. To return to the earlier illustration, we may say not merely that we know there is a president and a congress but also that we know much about them. A reporter covering the Washington beat would have much knowledge. But the type of knowledge would be the same. In spiritual terms this would be the kind of knowledge of God possessed by a theologian who, while he may know much about God, is not necessarily born again.

The third view is knowledge by *experience*. But this, although better than either of the other two, is still not enough. We might think of this as the experience of a person who goes out into the fields around his house on a summer night and looks up into the twinkling heavens and returns, saying, "I have experienced God. Do not give me any of your theology. I don't want words. I have experienced the real thing." We may believe that such a person is imagining his experience, particularly if it has nothing to do with the Lord Jesus Christ; but he is not necessarily imagining it, nor is his experience without meaning. He actually may have experienced something very profound and moving. Still, moving as this may be, it is not what Jesus meant when he spoke of eternal life consisting in such knowledge.

Fourth, even in its highest form this knowledge is *not merely knowledge of God alone,* for it always involves knowledge of ourselves in terms of our relationships to him. Knowledge of God and of ourselves go together.

What is this knowledge? It is a personal encounter with God in which, because of his holiness, we become aware of our sin and consequently of our deep personal need and then, by his grace, are turned to Christ who is our Savior. This knowledge occurs only where God's Holy Spirit is at work beforehand to make it possible, and it always changes us, issuing in a heart response to God and true devotion. This is involved even in Christ's brief statement, for he stresses that the knowledge of which he is speaking is knowledge of the *true* God and of himself as Savior.

The True God

This brings us to the matter of knowing the *true* God as opposed to a false or imaginary God. It causes us to ask: Who is this God? What is the effect on us when we come to know him?

There is a story in the Old Testament that is helpful at this point. It is the story of God's revelation of himself to Moses. Moses was certainly aware of the true God prior to this time. He had been born into a godly home. He had undoubtedly heard of God's calling of Abraham and of His subsequent dealings with him and the other patriarchs. He even believed in God's promises to deliver the Hebrew people from their Egyptian bondage, for he put himself forward as the vehicle of that deliverance by killing an Egyptian. Still it is probably true that Moses had never had a personal encounter with God in any full sense of the term until God revealed himself to him in the burning bush on Mount Sinai.

Moses had been going along minding his own business when he noticed this bush. It was burning, which was unusual but not miraculous. The astonishing thing, which he became aware of gradually as he stood watching, was that the bush did not burn up. He went closer. After a while a voice came to him out of the bush saying, "Moses! Moses! . . . Do not come any closer. Take off your sandals, for the place where you are standing is holy ground" (Exod. 3:4–5).

What is the first thing that God revealed about himself to Moses? The first thing that God revealed about himself was his holiness. Here God was obviously calling Moses and desiring him to come close and listen to what he had to say. But the first words Moses heard were: "Do not come any closer. Take off your sandals." And the reason given was that even the ground was holy by virtue of God being in that place. Holiness! That is the first and most important thing that fallen men and women have to learn about the true God, and accompanying that they have to learn that sin bars their access to him. Moses was apparently aware of this instantly, for we read in the next verse: "Moses hid his face, because he was afraid to look at God" (v. 6).

Let me ask in a personal way: Have you ever had the experience of being afraid to look on God because of his holiness and your sin? I do not mean: "Are you always afraid of God?" or "Do you not know that you should be afraid of God?" If you have also believed on Jesus Christ, you have learned that God has made provision to blot out your sin through Christ's sacrifice and that you can therefore come to him boldly and joyfully on that basis. What I do mean is: Have you *ever* been really disturbed knowing that you must ultimately deal with One in whom is no sin at all, who cannot tolerate sin in any form and who must judge it? If you have not really known God in that way, then I suggest that in a sense you do not know even the first thing about him, at least not deeply. Consequently, you do not really know much about the depth of your sin or the true measure of God's great grace.

God's Knowledge

The second thing that God revealed about himself to Moses was his own knowledge of things or, as we would say in more precise language, his omniscience. In this account God spoke to Moses, Moses hid his face, and then God began to tell what he had seen and heard concerning the condition of the people of Israel in Egypt. "*I have indeed seen* the misery of my people in Egypt. I *have heard* them crying out because of their slave drivers, and am *concerned about* their suffering. So I have come down to rescue them from the hand of the Egyptians. . . . Now the cry of the Israelites has reached me, and *I have seen* the way the Egyptians are oppressing them" (vv. 7–9). "I have seen. . . . I have heard. . . . I am concerned," and therefore, "I have come"—these are the words God uses. They speak of omniscience. And if Moses did not get the point in this declaration—because he was hiding his face and undoubtedly trembling in his shoeless feet—he soon got it later, for God showed that he knew all about Moses too, his strengths and weaknesses—and about what was coming, for God foretold difficulties, saying that Pharaoh would not willingly consent to Moses' demands, in fact, that he would strongly resist them and would let go eventually only after God had done many wonders in Egypt.

Why is it important to know this about God? Why is it important to know that he knows everything? The answer is in two areas. First, we must know that God is omniscient so that we will not be tempted to try to fool him with some exalted portrayal of our own deep devotion or loyalty. If we could, we would try to convince God that we are serious about following him when actually we would be going our own way. We would try to appear good, when we are not; loving, when we are actually motivated by hatred or antipathy; humble, when we are filled with pride.

God is not fooled by such things. He is not fooled by anything. Consequently, we are to learn that, whatever our relationships to others may be, our relationships with God must be based on total honesty, as he is honest. We must know that "everything is uncovered and laid bare before the eyes of him to whom we must give account" (Heb. 4:13).

The second area in which knowledge of the omniscience of God is important to us concerns our trust in him. If God did not know everything, if something could at any moment rise up to surprise him, then God could not be trusted. For however good his intentions, the unexpected thing might cause him to change his mind or actually change him so that he would no longer be the God we knew originally. His promises could not be trusted, for he might decide to break or change them on the basis of this new knowledge. He might even change his attitude toward us, for we might surprise him by the sin we commit and thus cause him to look upon us with abhorrence or even apathy. If God does not truly know everything, any of this is possible. On the other hand, if God does know all things both in the past and future, then nothing unforeseen can change him. He has seen the end from the beginning. He has taken all into consideration. Nothing we can ever do will surprise him. Thus, his promises can be believed, and he can be trusted to remain the same in himself and toward us forever.

Our Sovereign God

The third thing that Moses learned about God was his sovereignty. This was personal too, for it was expressed to Moses in terms of God's demand that he return to Egypt with God's message to Pharaoh: "Let my people go." Moses did not want to do it. He was like the rest of us who do not want to do anything difficult and who often are content only when God blesses us while allowing us to do nothing. Moses made excuses, but they were not valid. He asked for signs; God provided them. At last God intensified the tone of his orders, and Moses, who eventually ran out of excuses, succumbed.

Have you learned this about God, that the God of the Bible, the true God, is a sovereign God who will be obeyed and who will most certainly see his will rather than ours done in the universe? There is no other God. Any god less than this is not God. So why do we fight him? Why do we find this matter of doing the will of God so unwelcome?

Knowing God

Here we come to the true problem in the knowledge of God, for the problem is not that God has not revealed himself in at least a partial way or that we do not have the physical ability to seek after him for salvation, if we would. The problem is that we do not want to do this, and the reason we do not is that we find the true God, who is there to be known, threatening. His holiness is threatening. His knowledge is threatening. His sovereignty is threatening. All that can be known of God is threatening, profoundly so when we are yet in our sins, but also sometimes even after God has brought us to faith in himself through Jesus Christ.

God knows this. He knows that we do not know him and do not want to know him. Therefore, he has taken steps to reveal himself to us in spite of our sinful dispositions against him. He has done three things.

First, God has revealed himself in history. This special revelation is in addition to that general revelation of himself in nature of which all have an awareness but to which none will respond. This revelation consists of direct supernatural interventions in earthly affairs. In the Old Testament this was centered in God's actions on behalf of the nation of Israel, in their deliverance, guidance, and preservation. In the New Testament it centers primarily in Jesus, the fullness of God's personal revelation. This One died for us. He paid the price of our sin. He shows the nature of God to be love, while at the same time he satisfies God's justice.

Second, God has revealed himself in writing. This has two purposes: one, that we might know what God has done and, two, that we might understand it. We would not even know what Jesus had said, as in the case of this particular text, for example, if God had not caused these things to be put down on paper and be preserved throughout the years of church history to our own generation. Nor would we understand these things, even if they were recorded, had God not given an interpretation along with the facts.

Finally, God also reveals himself to us personally, applying these truths to us by the work of his own Holy Spirit. So great is our sin, so warped our knowledge, that even with the interpretation of his acts in Scripture we would not know God or understand his ways, apart from this activity. What light does this throw on our knowledge? It shows it to be God's gift, for notice that in John 17:2–3, Jesus speaks, first of all, of his gift of eternal life to as many as God has given him and then, secondly, that this eternal life is to be found in spiritual knowledge. This makes knowledge itself God's gift. And so it is, for no one would ever know God in the fullest sense unless God first revealed himself and then made the reception of this knowledge possible.

208

A Good Work Done

John 17:4

"I have brought you glory on earth by completing the work you gave me to do."

There are few things in life more truly satisfying to a human being than a job well done. Some people never know this satisfaction, because they never do anything well. But those who do, who really work at something and see it to completion, know. It is the satisfaction of a student who has finished his course with high honors, the satisfaction of a musician who has at last mastered a difficult piece. It is, to give a specific biblical example, the satisfaction of the apostle Paul, who said to Timothy near the end of his life, "For I am already being poured out like a drink offering, and the time has come for my departure. I have fought the good fight, I have finished the race, I have kept the faith. Now there is in store for me the crown of righteousness, which the Lord, the righteous Judge, will award to me on that day—and not only to me, but also to all who have longed for his appearing" (2 Tim. 4:6–8).

In all honesty, however, we must say that although there is often satisfaction for us in a job well done, there is never that satisfaction that we would have if we could say that the job was done perfectly or completely. There is only one human being who ever lived who could say that, and that was the Lord Jesus Christ whose words on this subject we are to study.

What is it we do? We do many things; but most of them are not finished, and none are done perfectly. I am sure that every housewife and mother will admit readily that her job is never finished. We even have a saying for it: "A

1263

woman's work is never done." There are always dishes to wash, cleaning to do, meals to prepare, children to help with their homework, and countless other chores. If she works outside the home, she has these (or some of these) perpetual problems plus others. Husbands, for their part, have the continuing obligations of their job. Our work is never completed, and we never do even the individual parts of what we have to do, perfectly. Yet this was not true of Jesus, for he said of his work, "I have brought you glory on earth by completing the work you gave me to do" (John 17:4).

As we study this verse we find that it has three parts: first, that a work was given to the Lord Jesus Christ by the Father; second, that Jesus completed that work; and third, that the result was the giving of glory to God.

Christ's Work

The first thing this verse tells us is that Jesus was given a work to do by God. What a great work it was! It was the work of all works! It was an achievement before which all other achievements pale into virtual insignificance.

In a sense, everything that Jesus had done was an aspect of the work he was given, and God was glorified by it. We know that Jesus was active in the creation of all the worlds of our universe. Colossians says of him, "For by him [Christ] all things were created: things in heaven and on earth, visible and invisible, whether thrones or powers or rulers or authorities; all things were created by him and for him. He is before all things, and in him all things hold together" (1:16–17). We know too that it was Jesus who, together with the Father and the Holy Spirit, guided the fortunes of the Jewish people during the Old Testament period. He may even have been that mysterious figure, the "angel of the Lord," who appears at such strategic moments in the history of the patriarchs and those who followed them (Gen. 16:7–14; 22:11–15; Exod. 3:2; Judg. 2:1–4; 5:23; 6:11–24; 13:3). Finally, it is true that the work includes the whole of Christ's life and ministry, beginning with his birth in the stable in Bethlehem and including all his teachings, acts, and miracles. Since he is speaking in the past tense in this verse, at the end of this ministry, it is this that is particularly in view.

Yet none of these things can possibly be the heart of what Jesus is speaking about, for the great work that was given to him and that he completed perfectly was the atonement for sin, which he alone accomplished on the cross. Therefore, it is this above all that he declares he has finished.

It is not a real difficulty to this understanding of the verse that Jesus speaks here in the past tense while, in point of fact, the death on the cross was not yet actually completed, for the prayer as a whole looks forward to the death and even beyond it with such assurance that it is as though these things had already been accomplished, as they surely were in Christ's mind. Besides, we have that interesting repetition of the phrase "It is finished" later, when Jesus is actually hanging on the cross just before he bowed his head and gave up his spirit (John 19:30). This second reference fixes the meaning of this early reference precisely. In the same vein, we note that Jesus had said earlier, "And what shall I say? 'Father, save me from this hour'? No, it was for this very reason I came to this hour" (12:27). The meaning of this verse is that above everything else Christ came to die on the cross.

A Finished Work

We must go on to the second point of this verse. The first point is that the Father had given Jesus a great work of salvation to do. It is a great point, but while it is great, the second is even greater, for having been given this work, Jesus did not merely attempt it and then drop it or else carry it forward a little bit and then stop. He finished the work, as a token of which he was subsequently raised from the dead and is now seated at the right hand of the Father.

Do you find that satisfying? I know one person who is satisfied with that work. God is satisfied. We know that God was satisfied by Christ's death by the resurrection of Christ, for the resurrection is God's seal upon Christ's work. Paul writes of this in Romans saying succinctly that Jesus "was delivered over to death for our sins and was raised to life for our justification" (4:24–25). This does not mean that we were justified by Christ's resurrection; it was his death that did that. Rather, it means that by the resurrection God gave notice that Christ's death was that perfect substitution for sin he entered this world to make and that he, the Father, had accepted it in place of the condemnation of the sinner.

Ralph L. Keiper told of the time in his youth when his family lived on borrowed money. They were a poor family and sometimes had to depend on what they called "household finance." It was a bad system, for in the end they paid more interest than principal. As a boy, Keiper had the job of taking the passbook, which contained the record of their borrowings, to the bank and there depositing the amount that the family was able to pay back plus the interest. He did it for eighteen months and felt each time that it was a miserable experience. At last the day came when the final payment was to be made. It was terrific. First, he handed in the book with the payment. Then he watched the teller put in the amount paid, mark the last page with the words "Paid in full," and hand it back. Finally, through the window the teller handed him the bank's book against the family, and it too said "Paid in full." Now the account was paid, and no one had any record against them.

This is what the resurrection is to us. It is God's declaration that the account of our moral indebtedness has been paid, that God is satisfied. This just God will never demand anything else for our salvation.

I know someone else who was satisfied by Christ's death. It was Jesus himself. Can you not hear the tone of satisfaction as he turns to his Father on the verge of his arrest and crucifixion and declares without any wavering, "I have brought glory to you on earth by completing the work you gave me to do"? Let us learn from this that Jesus is not sitting in heaven today wringing his hands, saying, "Oh, if I had just done so-and-so . . ." or "If I had just been a little more conscientious at that point. . . ." He is not even wondering if something has been left undone, because nothing was left undone. When he came into the world he said, "Sacrifice and offering you did not desire, but a body you prepared for me; with burnt offerings and sin offerings you were not pleased. . . . I have come to do your will, O God" (Heb. 10:5–7). While on earth he said, "I have a baptism to undergo, and how distressed I am until it is completed!" (Luke 12:50). Then he accomplished it, fulfilling his Father's will. Now he looks back and is "satisfied" (Isa. 53:11).

What then? If God is satisfied in Christ's death and if Christ is satisfied in his death, should not we, who benefit from it most directly, also be satisfied? Yes, and more than that! We should rejoice in that completed work, knowing that it is our glory. We should sing about it:

> Jesus paid it all,
>   All to him I owe;
> Sin had left a crimson stain,
>   He washed it white as snow.

God's Glory

But perhaps it seems wrong to speak of *our* glory. If so, remember that it is not only our glory. It is the glory of Jesus and of the Father too. In fact, Jesus begins with this emphasis, "I have brought glory to you on earth."

How does the finished work of Christ redound to God's glory? It does so because it reveals God's great attributes clearly. We must remember from our earlier study of the word "glory" (in chap. 42) that to glorify God means to "acknowledge his attributes" or "make them known." It means proclaiming his sovereignty, justice, righteousness, wisdom, love, and everything else that may rightly be said about him. But where are these attributes best known? The answer is: at the cross, for only here is the perfection of God's sovereignty, justice, righteousness, wisdom, and love abundantly and unmistakably displayed. We see God's sovereignty in the way in which the death of Christ was planned, promised, and then executed, without the slightest deviation from the prophecies of the Old Testament. We see God's justice in sin actually being punished. Without the cross God could have forgiven our sin gratuitously (to speak from a human perspective), but it would not have been just. Only in Christ is that justice satisfied. We see God's righteousness in recognition of the fact that only Jesus, the righteous One, could pay sin's penalty. We see God's wisdom in the planning and ordering of such a great salvation. We see his love, for it is only at the cross that we know beyond doubt that God loves us even as he loves Jesus.

Jesus revealed these attributes of the Father fully by his death. Hence, his obedience to the Father's will in dying, fully glorified him. No wonder we sing:

To God be the glory—great things he has done!
So loved he the world that he gave us his Son,
Who yielded his life an atonement for sin
And opened the Life-gate that all may go in.

This is God's glory . . . and Christ's glory . . . and our glory too, for we glory in Christ's death, rather than in any works or plans of our devising.

Conclusions

There are a few conclusions to this study, and they are as obvious as they are inescapable. First, if Christ's atoning work is finished and if it has been accepted as such by the Father, then what folly it is and what ingratitude it shows if we think we can add to it. Millions of people, many of them serious churchgoing people, are doing this. They do not disbelieve in Christ's work especially, but neither do they trust it wholly. Instead, they try to add to it by tears and confessions and charity and by every other kind of supposed "good work." They suppose that by these things God may perhaps be moved to be gracious to them and so save them at last. What an insult to God! It is insulting to suppose that you can add to that salvation that he in his own great love and wisdom planned from before the foundation of the world and then brought to completion in time through the death of his beloved Son, the Lord Jesus.

Will you turn from your work to Jesus? His work is a great work, an all-sufficient work, a certain work. It is all you need. It is all that God will accept. Accept it then, and present it to the Father in place of your works.

Second, if Christ's atoning work is really a finished work and if God has accepted it as the sole grounds of salvation, let us proclaim it as such. We cannot honestly proclaim this truth until we have first entered into it ourselves. But if we have entered into it, having come to God on the basis of Christ's sacrifice, then we have an obligation to make this gospel widely known. It should be joy for us to do so. Many need this word. There are the pagans of our world, those who have neither heart nor stomach for Christ's gospel, who would willingly tread it underfoot if they were able. They need to hear that all that is necessary for our salvation has been done by Christ. He has died, and "it is finished."

The sophisticated, ethical people of our world need to hear it also. They think they are pleasing God by their efforts. But they are not; they cannot. Nor need they try. "It is finished." The work is done.

There are also the highly religious persons, some in other religions—Jews, Catholics, Greek Orthodox, cultists—some in our own. These too need the gospel. They need to know that Jesus has finished his work, the very work they need. Who will tell them? Will you? How can you not tell them if you have yourself found what they so desperately need? The Bible says, "How, then, can they call on the one they have not believed in? And how can they believe in the one of whom they have not heard? And how can they hear without someone preaching to them?" (Rom. 10:14).

Third, it may be that you are quite busy and that you therefore react to what I have just said by replying, "But I cannot tell others about Christ's death for them. If I did that, so many other things I have to do would not get done." Do you say that? If you do, you must apply our text by noting that Christ did, not his own work, but rather that which was given him by God. You must ask, "Am I doing what God has given me to do? All of it? Or have I slipped my own plans in somewhere along the line, for my own bene-fit, and so ceased to serve him?" If you do not have time to tell others about the gospel or work to bring them to where they may hear it, you are *too* busy. Perhaps you are not doing the work God has given you to do at all.

Finally, it may also be the case that you really are doing what God has given you to do. You cannot say as Jesus did, "I have *completed* the work you gave me to do." But you can say, "I am working at the work you gave me to do." If this describes your condition, if you can say that, then the message of this text is simply: Keep at it! Do not quit! Hold to that of which God has made you the custodian! Yours may be a glamorous work but one with heavy burdens, as is the case with many prominent works. It may be an un-spectacular work. Most works are like this; but so was Christ's work, at least from the world's unsanctified perspective. Moreover, receive this encour-agement: while it is true that you and I will never fully finish our work in the sense of having done it to perfection, we can nevertheless finish it in the sense of hanging on to the end, Christ helping us. More than that, we can put a lot of "finish" in it by improving our service constantly by the grace given to us.

"I have finished the work you gave me to do," says Jesus. "I am working at the work you have given me to do," we answer. God give us the grace to do that always.

209

Prayer for Christ's Own

John 17:6

"I have revealed you to those whom you gave me out of the world. They were yours; you gave them to me and they have obeyed your word."

So much of what we do is selfish. William Gladstone, the great English statesman, said, "Selfishness is the greatest curse of the human race." The poet Robert Browning wrote, "Man seeks his own good at the whole world's cost." We see it in our prayers. We pray for ourselves most of the time, and even when we pray for others it is often with a view toward what they can do for us or be toward us ("Help my wife to get better, so she can start doing the dishes again" or "Help my boss to become a Christian, so he won't be so mean").

Jesus is not selfish. Nor are his prayers selfish. It is true that he prayed for himself. In the prayer recorded in John 17 he begins by praying for what concerns himself—"Father, the time has come. Glorify your Son, that your Son may glorify you" (v. 1). But even here the request is never for the Lord's interests as opposed to those of others. He asks to be glorified in order that he might in turn glorify the Father. Nor are these requests improper or even especially magnified. Thus, we have a record of one petition concerning himself, but of four for others. Or, to put it in terms of verses, there are five verses in the first section of this prayer (where Jesus is praying on his own behalf), but twenty-one verses in the next two sections (in which Jesus prays for his disciples, and for all who should inevitably follow them in faith).

Christ's Own

Verse 6 says, "I have revealed you to those whom you gave me out of the world. They were yours; you gave them to me and they have obeyed your word." This verse says four things about Christ's disciples. First, they are (or were) God's. Second, God has given them to Jesus. Third, Jesus has made God known to them. Fourth, they have received or kept the revelation. The importance of this sequence is that it is repeated in the experience of everyone who ever comes to Jesus. First, we are God's. That is, he can do with us as he likes. Second, we are given to Jesus. Third, the gospel is made known to us by Jesus through his Holy Spirit. Finally, we receive this teaching. We cannot help but notice that our response comes last in the sequence.

First of all, Jesus says that the disciples were God's originally. "They were yours," says Jesus. In an important sense, everything that exists is God's, for he made it originally and can do with it as he pleases. This is true of the material world. From the tiniest atom to the greatest star or galaxy, all that exists is God's and obeys the laws that he has set for it. Moreover, we know that this is not some independent existence or some law apart from God, as if God were bound by it, for on occasion he steps in over his natural law to do what we instinctively term a miracle, thus demonstrating that creation is controlled by him and not he by creation.

God's right of possession is true in the realm of persons also. Events seem to go according to the dispositions of men and women; for, like the material world, God does not usually intervene supernaturally. Yet human events are no less ordered by him, and the destiny of individuals is also controlled. All things—whether material objects or persons—are in God's hands, and he can do with them as he likes.

But now, in addition to this general possession by God of all things, there is also a possession by God that is more specific. It is a possession of a holy people, who are his in this special way solely because of his election of them to salvation. In Romans, Paul speaks of this in terms of God's possessive foreknowledge, saying, "For those God foreknew he also predestined to be comformed to the likeness of his Son, that he might be the firstborn among many brothers. And those he predestined, he also called; those he called, he also justified; those he justified, he also glorified" (8:29–30). It is this possession of his own by God about which Jesus is primarily speaking in his prayer, for he sets them off as "those you gave me *out of the world*." This possession anchors our salvation, not in any slight whim of the moment (which we might have), or in any faltering ability on our part to choose or keep choosing God (which we do not have), but rather in God's great purposes and possession, which alone are trustworthy.

Given to Jesus

The second point in the sequence of verse 6 is that those who were the Father's in this special, elective sense were then given to Jesus, so that they became his possession as well.

We do not need to treat this point at as great length as the point preceding, for we already looked at it in part when dealing with the verse in which the phrase "as many as you have given [me]" or "those you have given me" occurs for the first time (v. 2). In studying that verse we noticed that the phrase occurs seven times in all and is therefore somewhat of a continuing motif throughout this prayer. We must remember as we think of this that Jesus had been in the world for more than thirty years (by most estimates) and had probably conducted a public ministry of about three years' duration. What had been the result? He was in the world as the world's light. He was filled with the fullness of God's character. He was sinless, gracious, winsome and as loving as anyone could possibly be. But he was not loved for it. Instead, he was hated. He was about to be crucified. At the time of his arrest, even these who were now gathered about him would be scattered.

Where was any bright point in this picture? The bright point was that, in spite of appearances, these disciples and countless others who should follow them in faith had been given to Jesus by the Father. Because it was he who had given them, and because of his power, these would most surely come to him and would be kept by him through the days of their earthly pilgrimage and eventually be united with him forever in glory.

The knowledge that these had been given was a controlling perspective for Jesus as he went about his earthly ministry. He was confronting the sin-enslaved wills of men and women. So, knowing this, he did not deceive himself into thinking that anything was possible apart from God's purpose and power in their lives. On one occasion we read that, even though many had been impressed with him as a result of having seen his miracles, he "did not commit himself unto them, because he knew all men, and needed not that any should testify of man; for he knew what was in man" (John 2:24–25). On another occasion he said, "No one comes to me unless the Father who sent me draws him" (6:44). Jesus knew the problem. He was under no illusions concerning the outward success of his ministry, as if by doing something spectacular or teaching more palatable doctrines or preaching with just a bit more eloquence, he could perhaps win a few more souls to his side. Jesus did not think like that. Consequently, as he went about preaching he was concerned to conduct his ministry as God had instructed him to conduct it, meanwhile looking about for those persons whom God had given him and expecting such to come to him.

Did they come? A few did. At this point in his ministry there were the eleven collected by him, plus a number of others who had been deeply influenced and who probably believed. They were not many. But these were

God's gift to him, however few their number. Besides, there would soon be others. Jesus rejoiced in these and thanked the Father for them.

The Names of God

We must not think that our salvation operates in a mechanical way, however, for in the same verse in which Jesus speaks of God's activity in giving us to him he also speaks of his own personal activity in time to make the Father known to these people. Jesus is speaking of this when he shows that next in the sequence of God's application of salvation to the disciples is the fact that he (literally) had made the name of God known to them.

"The name of God" is a Semitic phrase for speaking about God's attributes. To make the name known is to reveal the God who possesses those attributes. If we think theologically in light of the full scope of the biblical revelation, then Jesus is saying that he revealed the God of the great biblical names to his disciples. There is the name Elohim, the name occurring in the first verse of the Bible—"In the beginning God [Elohim] created the heaven and the earth" (Gen. 1:1). This name speaks of God as Creator; so we may believe that Jesus told the disciples about this aspect of God's nature. Another—indeed the great name of God—is Jehovah. This has a variety of meanings, but it is used primarily in reference to God's character as Redeemer. Jesus revealed this about God. So with all God's other names: El Elyon, Jehovah Jireh, Jehovah Sabaoth.

Yet this approach to the names is only theological, and it is not the whole story. If by contrast we look at the matter historically, asking, "What is the unique name of God revealed to us by Jesus?" then we must say that the name is "Father."

It is not generally appreciated how unique this name was. Today we are at home with the thought of God as Father, but this was not true in Jesus' day, nor would it even have been thought to be proper. The use of this word (and in most quarters the failure to use it) in referring to God has been documented in recent years by two German scholars: Ernst Lohmeyer, who has written a book called *"Our Father"* (a study of the Lord's Prayer), and Joachim Jeremias, in an essay entitled "Abba" from the book *The Central Message of the New Testament,* and in a booklet called *The Lord's Prayer.*[1] According to these scholars, three things are beyond question: (1) the title "Father" as a designation of God was new with Jesus, (2) Jesus always used this form of address in praying, and (3) Jesus authorized his disciples to use the same word, thereby leaving a tremendous legacy for the church.

It is true that in one sense the word "Father" for God is as old as religion. Even the Greeks spoke of "Father Zeus, who rules over the gods and mortal men." But in this case the word really means "Lord." In Israel God was also said to be the Father of his people: "But now, O LORD, you are our father" (Isa. 64:8), and "As a father has compassion on his children, so the LORD has compassion on them that fear him" (Ps. 103:13). But this is characteristically of the people as a whole; nowhere, either in the Old Testament or in any other document prior to the time of Jesus, does any individual Israelite ever address God directly as "my Father."

Yet this is what Jesus does always. He always called God "Father," and this undoubtedly impressed itself upon the disciples to such a degree that they preserved it in their records of Christ's speech and prayers. Thus, not only do all four Gospels record that Jesus used this address, they also report that he did so in all his prayers (Matt. 11:25; 26:39, 42; Mark 14:36; Luke 23:34; John 11:41; 12:27, 28; 17:1, 5, 11, 21, 24–25). The only exception is one that actually enforces the importance of this title. It is the cry from the cross ("My God, my God, why have you forsaken me?") pronounced at that moment in which Jesus was made sin for us and the fellowship which he had enjoyed with the Father previously was temporarily broken.

The Lord's use of this title indicates his awareness that he was the Son of God in a unique sense. But strikingly, he then revealed that it can be used by those who become sons of God (in a lesser sense) by their union with him. After his resurrection Jesus announced that the disciples could come to the Father as he came to him: "But go to my brothers and tell them, 'I am returning to my Father and your Father, to my God and your God'" (John 20:17). In the Sermon on the Mount he taught, "This, then, is how you should pray: Our Father . . ." (Matt. 6:9).

Is this important? Of course it is, for it means that while God is the great, high, exalted, eternal, self-sufficient, self-existent, and inscrutable God, he is at the same time and in equal measure the Father of all who believe. So we can come to him, not with a prayer that says, "O high, exalted and inscrutable God, far from us in your majesty, unreachable and unknowable. . . ," but rather with that warm and personal prayer that begins, "My Father. . . ."

Is God your Father? If he is, then he will be a Father to you during the days of your spiritual infancy when you are just a babe in Christ. He will teach you to walk, as it says in Hosea: "When Israel was a child, I loved him, and out of Egypt I called my son. . . . It was I who taught Ephraim to walk, taking them by the arms" (11:1, 3). God sets our way before us and helps us in it.

Is God your Father? If he is, then he will be a Father to you in his paternal care. The laws of our country recognize that a father is responsible for the care of his children. God accepts this responsibility also. You need not fear that the great God of the universe, the One who owns and controls all things, will let you down, that he will disappoint you or turn his back on you. This God clothes the lily of the field and the grass. "Will he not much more clothe you, O you of little faith?" asks Jesus (Matt. 6:30).

Is God your Father? If he is, he will preserve you to the end and will permit nothing to change your relationship to him. You may disgrace him. You may be unworthy of your high calling. You may run away from him, as Jonah did. But he will still be your Father.

Christ's Word Obeyed

There is one more step in this verse. First, we have been told that those who are Christ's previously belonged to the Father. Second, we are told that they have been given to Jesus. Third, Jesus has filled his responsibility to them by revealing the Father to them. Now we are also told that they have received this word, or obeyed it.

In Greek the word for "obey" literally means "to pay attention to" or "observe," just as one would pay attention to a traffic law and observe it. But observing Christ's word is the end product of first hearing it and then understanding it to the point at which it makes a difference in our behavior. Some people have never heard that word. That is why we have missionaries, radio programs, Christian books, and all other kinds of gospel communication. Some people have never understood. Indeed, all fail to understand unless the Holy Spirit makes these things comprehensible to them. That is why we pray as we give out the message, for we know that our efforts are wasted unless God intervenes to do this miracle. But at last, there must also be the keeping of Christ's words, involving commitment and change. This had been true of the disciples. Jesus says so clearly. It must also be true of us and of all who would follow him.

What will be the results? There are two of them. On the one hand, those who have not obeyed Christ will not like us. In fact, they will hate us, according to verse 14. "I have given them your word and the world has hated them, for they are not of the world any more than I am of the world." But on the other hand, we will be vehicles for Christ's glory, as it says in verse 10. "All I have is yours, and all you have is mine. And glory has come to me through them." There is no greater privilege for those who belong to Jesus.

210

Christ's Word Kept by Christ's Own

John 17:6–8

"I have revealed you to those whom you gave me out of the world. They were yours; you gave them to me and they have obeyed your word. Now they know that everything you have given me comes from you. For I gave them the words you gave me and they accepted them. They knew with certainty that I came from you, and they believed that you sent me."

How does one tell who are the elect of God? How do we judge who are Christians and who are not? We must admit as we raise the question that there is a sense in which we cannot judge and that the answer is none of our business. We cannot judge in this sense because it is a matter of the heart, and the heart is visible to God only. On the other hand, whenever we admit members to a Christian church or seek out Bible school teachers or church officers we find ourselves having to make a decision in just this area. And so, although we cannot see as God sees, the question remains.

How does one tell who are the elect of God? There are certain ways in which we obviously cannot tell. We cannot tell by the alleged depth of the spiritual experience of the person. There are those who measure reality by the depth of their feelings. In some circles this is even accompanied by a certain anti-intellectualism in which facts and doctrines are neglected and emotion is everything. The difficulty with this approach is that feelings come and go. Consequently, such a person may consider himself or herself a Christian one moment and a non-Christian the next. Which is right? In which frame of mind should the person involved be believed?

Another way in which we obviously do not know whether a person is a Christian or not is by his or her denominational affiliation. All denominations are composed of a mixture of people, some of whom are Christians and some of whom, even by their own confession, are not.

How can one tell who is a Christian? There is only one answer, the answer given by the Lord Jesus Christ when he said of those who were truly his disciples, "I have revealed you to those whom you gave me out of the world. They were yours; you gave them to me and they have obeyed your word. Now they know that everything you have given me comes from you. For I gave them the words you gave me and they accepted them. They knew with certainty that I came from you" (John 17:6–8).

According to these verses, the only way to tell whether one is a Christian or not is to see whether he or she believes and continues in the words of the Lord Jesus Christ.

A Second Sequence

Of the three verses the most important for the theme of this study is verse 8, for it sets the matter of keeping Christ's words in a sequence of actions similar to the sequence in verse 6, which we studied in the last chapter.

In verse 6 Christ presents the matter of salvation from God's point of view, stressing his acts. Thus, we find Jesus teaching: first, that believers were God the Father's initially; second, that the Father gave believers to Jesus by an act of sovereign grace; third, that Jesus exercised his responsibility to those he had been given by revealing God to them; and fourth, that they in their turn received or kept Christ's words. In verse 8, by contrast, Jesus presents the matter from the disciples' point of view, thereby in effect elaborating upon the last two steps in verse 6. Here Jesus says: first, that he has given the disciples the words that the Father gave him; second, that they have received those words; third, that on the basis of those words they have known that he came forth from God; and fourth, that they have believed in him as the One whom God sent. To summarize, the steps are: the giving of God's Word, the receiving of that Word, knowing, and believing. The believer is the one for whom and in whom these things have occurred.

The first step in this sequence, then, is the giving of God's Word, which Jesus indicates by saying, "I gave them the words you gave me." The Word is the only thing that is powerful enough to do what is required in the hearts of fallen men and women if they are to be saved. Nothing else can do it. The Word is God's tool. It is, as the author of Hebrews writes, "living and active. Sharper than any double-edged sword, it penetrates even to dividing soul and spirit, joints and marrow; it judges the thoughts and attitudes of the heart" (4:12). Compared to this the words of men are next to nothing. Luther knew this. On one occasion he said, 'We must make a great difference between God's word and the word of man. A man's word is a little sound, that flies into the air, and soon vanishes; but the Word of God is greater than heaven and earth, yea, greater than death and hell, for it forms part of the power of God, and endures everlastingly" (*Table Talk,* xliv). Peter was thinking of the same thing when he wrote concerning the new birth, "For you have been born again, not of perishable seed, but of imperishable, through the living and enduring word of God" (1 Peter 1:23).

The conversion of an individual is much more than mere persuasion. If persuasion were all that is required, then our words would be sufficient and we could win men and women by argument. This is not enough. Arguments have their place. God uses them. But at its base what takes place in the matter of salvation is something like a resurrection, a miracle. Clearly, only the Word of God, not our words, can accomplish that.

This is why there must be witnesses and missionaries in the Christian church and why a bit farther on Jesus will allude to this need, saying, "As you sent me into the world, I have sent them into the world" (John 17:18), and again, "As the Father has sent me, I am sending you" (20:21). God could save the entire race by a fiat, if he so chose. But he has not chosen to operate in this way. Rather, he has declared that it will be by his Word, preached and shared by his people and applied to the hearts of individuals by his Holy Spirit, that men and women will be saved. We have a share in this great work, for it is by us that God's Word is conveyed to those who need so desperately to hear it.

Receiving God's Word

The second step in the sequence of verse 8 is receiving God's Word, for Jesus said, not only that he had given the disciples the words that God had given him but also that they had accepted them. The Greek word for "accepted" is not the same as the word for "obey" in verse 6. The word in verse 8 means only to "get" something or "receive" it. Thus, in going to a lesser word in verse 8, it is as if Jesus is backtracking in order to explain the harder word he used earlier. To "obey" his Word is, as he now shows, to hear it, receive it, know on the basis of it, and believe on him personally. The fact that Jesus puts in the step of merely receiving his Word indicates that it is possible to have the Word given but have it pass over the head of the one listening. Or, as we say colloquially, it is possible to have it "go in one ear and out the other." More than this is required. In contrast to merely hearing the Word, there must also be a receiving of that Word so that it sinks down into the mind and becomes the basis for our thinking and meditating afterward. It is a way of saying that God must actually communicate with us through another's witnessing or preaching.

Knowledge

Up to this point the sequence of giving and receiving the Word that Jesus gives has been obvious. The word must be given if it is to be received, and it must be received if it is to be of any use to us. But now, as a third point, Jesus goes on to talk about knowledge of certain things followed by believing, and this is not so obvious. We have always been taught that in spiritual things it is the other way around. In fact, Jesus himself taught this. In speaking to Martha just before the raising of her brother Lazarus, Jesus said, "Did I not tell you that if you believed, you would see the glory of God?" (John 11:40). The world says, "seeing is believing." Jesus says, "believing is seeing." How then, in John 17, can he seem to put it backward?

It would be a sufficient answer to this question to note that seeing and knowing are not exactly synonyms as Jesus uses them in these two passages. But the truly significant thing to note is that, while a full apprehension of spiritual realities always follows upon belief, nevertheless there is a proper and necessary kind of knowing that must precede it. Otherwise faith is "blind faith," which is not a true biblical faith at all.

Here we come into the area of Christian apologetics and to the question, "Does faith need reasons?" More specifically, "Do we need reasons to undergird our faith, and do we need reasons to present that faith to others?" On one level, the answer to these questions is no, if by them we are asking whether all doubt must be cleared away before God can save someone. God obviously saves many without resolving their doubts, and some retain a great many throughout their Christian life and experience. But on the other hand, knowledge does play a role in faith, for faith is commitment to One whom we have come to know through the propositional witness of Christian people. We find the apostles giving an account of their belief in the face of critical questioning. Peter encourages those who follow him to "always be prepared to give an answer to everyone who asks you to give the reason for the hope that you have" (1 Peter 3:15).

In the context of John 17, this means that a certain number of convictions concerning Jesus must precede faith in him. These convictions will not embrace all possible areas of religious truth. Jesus does not even suggest that in this prayer. But they will embrace the central questions concerning both the person of Christ and his teaching. Jesus indicates this by saying, "They know with certainty that I came from you" (v. 8) and "They know that everything you have given me comes from you" (v. 7). Before we commit our lives to Jesus we must be convinced that he is divine, that his teaching is true, and that he did what he said he did, primarily in dying on the cross. He died as our substitute, bearing the penalty for our sin. If we are not convinced of these truths, our faith is in a phantom.

Nor is it just for our own personal belief that knowledge of this type is important. It is also important for our motivation to evangelism. One of the great impetuses to evangelism is the conviction, based on knowledge and reinforced by experience, that the facts to which we testify are really true. After Jesus' death, and prior to the resurrection, the disciples were downcast and scattering. After the resurrection they were impelled to tell others. Why? The difference was their conviction that the resurrection had really occurred and that it was important that others know of it. So should we think, if we share those convictions.

Finally, knowledge is important in the proper satisfaction of our minds. Some Christians act as if the mind is evil and so refuse to think, at least deeply. This is not right. Though fallen, the reasoning faculty in man is still one aspect of his being created in the image of God and is to be used by the Christian in thinking through spiritual matters. As this is done there is an element of true spiritual satisfaction and a preparation for being able to deal with whatever problems might come.

Faith and Action

Having stressed the importance of knowledge, we must not, however, fall into the trap of stopping there, as if Christianity were only a process of learning certain things. There was an early heresy of Christianity, a form of Gnosticism, which taught that. But this is not Christ's teaching, for having spoken of the three steps of having given the word, having had the word received, and having had the disciples come to know certain things concerning himself because of it, the Lord went on to talk about the most important factor of all, namely, faith or belief. He concludes by saying, "And they believed that you sent me"

Faith is not blind trust, as we have seen from our study of knowledge. But it is not only knowledge either. Rather, it is a personal commitment based upon that knowledge but going beyond it in the sense that, having come to know the Lord Jesus Christ as God, the one who follows him is thereafter willing to follow him in areas about which he has quite limited knowledge or in which he has doubts. Faith like this involves action. So we often say that in the biblical sense faith is believing God as he is revealed in Jesus Christ and then acting upon it.

Who were they, these few disciples? They understood little of his teaching. True, they believed that he had come forth from God. On one occasion Peter affirmed, "You are the Christ, the Son of the living God" (Matt. 16:16). But even in the upper room on this very night, Philip asked Jesus, "Lord, show us the Father" (John 14:8), and Jesus had rebuked him, saying, "Don't you know me, Philip, even after I have been among you such a long time? Anyone who has seen me has seen the Father" (v. 9). They understood. But then again, they did not understand. At best they understood dimly.

Again, they obviously failed to understand the meaning and necessity of his death. He had tried to tell them. He had prophesied earlier in this week, "We are going up to Jerusalem . . . and the Son of Man will be betrayed to the chief priests and teachers of the law. They will condemn him to death and will hand him over to the Gentiles, who will mock him and spit on him, flog him and kill him. Three days later he will rise" (Mark 10:33–34). He taught that "even the Son of Man did not come to be served, but to serve, and to give his life as a ransom for many" (v. 45). But they missed this teaching. What is more, even after the resurrection they were missing it, for they asked, "Lord, are you at this time going to restore the kingdom to Israel?" (Acts 1:6), indicating that they were still thinking in terms of an earthly messianic reign.

Weakness? Poverty of understanding? Yes, but there was strength too. It was not their own. It was only the result of the words of Christ that had by now entered into them. But the words *were* within them. That is the point. Like a seed planted in fruitful ground, those words would sprout into the fullness of a fruitful spiritual life. They were alive—that is what we really want to say—spiritually alive. Therefore the Lord could be confident, saying, "They have received my words, they have known who I am, and they have believed on me as their Savior."

That is the experience of all God's elect. They may vary in understanding, courage, and many other things, but they have been touched by Jesus. They have his words, and they will inevitably continue to grow in the power of his life and be fruitful for him.

211

Prayer for Christ's Own Only

John 17:9–10

"I pray for them. I am not praying for the world, but for those you have given me, for they are yours. All I have is yours, and all you have is mine. And glory has come to me through them."

I do not doubt that there may be some limited sense in which Jesus prays for everyone. But whatever that may be, it is not what our text is speaking of. On the cross Christ prayed for his enemies: "Father, forgive them, for they do not know what they are doing" (Luke 23:34). But between that (or any prayer like it) and the prayer of John 17, there is a gap so vast that in another sense we may say that Christ's prayer is for his people only. Moreover, this is what he seems to teach in the words that actually begin the intercessory part of this chapter. He says, "I pray for *them*," thereby designating the disciples. "I am not praying for the world, but for those you have given me, for they are yours. All I have is yours, and all you have is mine. And glory has come to me through them" (vv. 9–10).

Spurgeon, with his usual eloquence, says rightly of these verses, "I remark that our Lord Jesus pleads for his own people. When he puts on his priestly breastplate, it is for the tribes whose names are there. When he presents the atoning sacrifice, it is for Israel whom God hath chosen."[1] This is a reminder of the unique position in which believers stand to him and that they must not desecrate by disregard of spiritual things or by sin.

However, the most interesting thing about these verses is not that they are part of a prayer that is for Christ's own only. Rather it is that they tell, from the perspective of our divine Lord, why he prays for them as opposed to praying for others. There are three reasons. First, because they are the Father's. Second, because all that the Father has is also his. And third, because he is glorified in them.

Christ's First Reason

The first of Christ's reasons is that those for whom Jesus prays *belong to the Father,* and this means that Jesus values them simply because they are God's. We can find illustrations of this reasoning in our own experience wherever we have been entrusted with something that belongs to someone else and value it because it belongs to that person.

When I was working in Washington, D.C., for *Christianity Today,* friends whom my wife and I knew lent us their home for the summer. This was a great luxury for us, for we were just students at the time, and their home was in beautiful suburban Washington and had great trees and a large backyard with a garden. We valued the home because of our appreciation for those who had lent it to us. That summer we got busy in the garden on Saturday afternoons and in the late evenings. We mowed the grass. We dug up the garden. We trimmed the flower beds. We did our work so well that I think we dug up the bulbs that were in the garden. If a person can understand our appreciation for that house, he can understand how the Lord Jesus Christ values that which is his Father's, for what the Lord is saying in these verses is: "Father, I am praying for these persons because they are yours, and I am concerned for what is yours." This is wonderful for us and for others, for we are going to see, when we get to the end of this study, that it is also why we should value other Christians.

There is also a second thought involved in Christ's reason, for it is not only that we are valued by Christ because we belong to the Father. There is also the fact that we are valued *by the Father.* Hence, this also becomes part of Christ's argument. It is as though he says, "I pray for them because they are yours and you value them; therefore, your interest in them is as my own."

We would do well to go beyond the use of mere indefinite pronouns ("they" and "them") to put ourselves in Christ's sentence, for only then do we get the full force of it. It is as though Jesus said, "I pray for John Smith (Mary Jones, or whatever your name may be) because he or she is yours and because you value this one even as I do."

Though we have been given to the Lord Jesus Christ, as he says seven times in this chapter, the Father nevertheless has a continuing interest in us. Here we may use the illustration of the church as the bride of Christ. We can imagine a father who gives his daughter to be married and then watches her go off with his son-in-law to a difficult field or work, perhaps in another country. The father is anxious to know how they are getting along, and the son-in-law is concerned with taking care of his wife, both for her sake and for that of her father. Suppose that things go badly for this young couple and that the son-in-law eventually writes back to the father at one point to say, "Father, I am sorry to have to write a letter like this, but business has gone poorly. I have suffered great financial losses. We are in jeopardy of losing our home, and I need some financial help." Do you not think that in circumstances like this the father would readily answer the request of his son-in-law (even if he did not care much for him and thought his business venture foolish) because of his concern for his daughter?

That is the kind of compassion that is involved here. So the argument goes, first that Jesus is interested in us because we belong to the Father, and second, that the Father himself is interested in us and values us because we are his possession.

Christ's Second Reason

Christ's second reason for praying for his own is found in the second half of verse 9 and in the first half of verse 10: "For they are yours. All I have is yours, and all you have is mine." What does this mean? It means that the Lord is speaking of *an interest in us that the Father and the Son share jointly*. It is as though, having said in the first instance, "They are yours," he then acknowledges in the next breath, "but they are also mine; and furthermore, it has always been the case that everything that belongs to you as Father belongs also to me as Son, and that everything that belongs to me as Son belongs to you as Father." Jesus therefore comes, not pleading for a cause that is of interest to the Father only, or to himself only, but for that which is of interest to them jointly.

There is a second level on which we can consider this mutual interest. There is an interest between the Father and the Son. But there is also a mutual interest between the Father and the Son and *ourselves*. We see it in the way the pronouns are mixed up in the sentence: "they," "I," "mine," and "yours." They are literally thrown together. So we have a situation here in which we could say that those who are Christ's are wrapped up in the same ball of life with the Godhead and that the Lord prays for us accordingly.

This means that our concerns, however small, are God's concerns; and God's concerns, however noble and beyond our understanding, are our concerns also. The second half of this can be readily understood—God's concerns are ours in the sense that they are for our good and affect us, just as the decisions of a head of state might affect each citizen of his country. The first half—that our concerns, however small, are God's—is not so easy to understand. An illustration may help.

During the summer of the American Bicentennial, I visited the White House in Washington, D.C., as a representative of an informal group of pastors known as the National Presbyterian and Reformed Fellowship. We had drafted a paper on the spiritual roots of our country and on the need for renewal. We wanted to present it to the President. So the head of our group and I went to submit it. We did not get to see the President. Instead, we presented the paper to one of his deputies. But as we were passing through the basement floor of the White House on our way to the north lawn (where the official presentation was to be made), I became aware of the fact that much life in the White House goes on, on two levels. Up above were the important offices where decisions of state are reached. Below, where we were walking, were people much like ourselves with far less monumental concerns. Moreover, in case I might have missed this, just as we were walking through the lower passageways a volley of trumpets sounded suddenly, announcing the arrival of an ambassador. The soldiers who were on duty on the lower level snapped to attention. I thought, "Here are these soldiers, each with his own problems, going through the motions of a proper honor guard drill, while just a few feet away national affairs will be debated. Each of the two groups is unaware of the other's concerns."

In human affairs this is often so, and we would be surprised if it were any other way. We would be astonished if the President and his cabinet, or the President and the ambassadors, were to spend time looking out the window to the guards below and discuss their problems. "Do you think that guard's rifle is too heavy, Mr. President? Perhaps we should get him another one?" Or, "Mr. Ambassador, are you aware that Private Brown's wife (that's the third one from the left) is expecting a baby this June?" We would think that ludicrous. Yet the Father and Son, while not forgetting or neglecting the other great issues of the universe, are also involved in our concerns—no matter how small—because we are important to God.

Christ's Third Reason

Jesus gives a third reason for his prayer in the last half of verse 10. He says, "Not only do I pray for them because they are yours, and not only do I pray for them because we have a mutual interest in them. I also pray for them because *I am glorified in them.*"

How is Jesus glorified in us? There are several answers. First, he is glorified in us *by saving us.* It is his doing, and the glory of it must rightly and inevitably go to him. Here Spurgeon has written wisely, "When the Lord lays hold upon a drunkard, a thief, an adulterer, when he arrests one who has been guilty of blasphemy, whose very heart is reeking with evil thoughts, when he picks up the far-off one, the abandoned, the dissolute, the fallen, as he often does, and when he says, 'These shall be mine; I will wash these in my blood; I will use these to speak my word,' oh, then, he is glorified in them! Read the lives of many great sinners who have afterwards become great saints, and you will see how they have tried to glorify him, not only she who washed his feet with her tears, but many another like her. Oh, how they have loved to praise him! Eyes have wept tears, lips have spoken words, but hearts have felt what neither eyes nor lips could speak, of adoring gratitude to him."[2]

Second, Jesus is glorified *by our trusting him in this life*. Donald Grey Barnhouse was talking to a man about the gospel. The man said to him in the course of the conversation, "But what does God want. Just tell me, what does God want?" Barnhouse said that the answer came to him in a flash. He shot back: "What God wants most in all the world is to be believed. He wants to be trusted." Do you believe him? Do you trust him? Do you live as though you really trust this God who sent Jesus Christ to be your Savior? Do you trust the Savior himself? You do not trust him if you complain about circumstances. You do not trust him if you always worry about the future. You do not trust him if you are fretting over small disappointments every day. On the contrary, you trust him and thus glorify the Lord when you say, "I am his, and I will go his way. I am glad to let him have his way with me whatever the circumstances, whatever the sorrow."

Third, Jesus is glorified in his own people *to the degree that we live a holy life*. Holiness is the attribute of God most mentioned in the pages of the Word of God. To hear most people talk about God today you would think that the attribute most mentioned about him is love. But this is not true. To be sure, love is a wonderful attribute. It is all the more wonderful because we do not deserve it. There is nothing in us that could possibly call forth the love of God. Yet he loves. This makes the love of God particularly wonderful. But even with this wonder, it is not the attribute of God most mentioned in the Bible. The attribute most mentioned is holiness. So if we would glorify him, we must make his holiness known as, allowing him to work through us, we attempt to live upright and dedicated lives. If we live in spiritual adultery, compromising with the values of our society, if the priorities of our non-Christian culture become our priorities, we are not living in a way that glorifies him. But if, by contrast, the priorities of the Word of God seize upon us and we strive for holiness in our lives, then we do glorify him.

Fourth, we glorify the Lord *by our confession of him before the world*. It is important to believe on Christ as Savior and trust him. It is equally important to live a holy life. But in addition to this, we must also testify to his grace, simply because we are called to be witnesses and have something great to say.

Finally, we may glorify the Lord Jesus Christ *by our efforts to extend his kingdom*, that is, not just by our speech but also by our activity. Many Christians are lazy. They sit around and do nothing, content, as the hymn says, to be "carried to the skies on flow'ry beds of ease," while all around there are suffering people, lonely people, people who need compassion, help, and, above all, the gospel. We need to wake up the church of Jesus Christ. We need to wake up ourselves. We need to sense the calling of the Holy Spirit in the area of our service instead of enjoying our luxury, comfort, and time selfishly, as we so often do.

Prayer for Others

In this passage we see Jesus Christ praying for us and, as he does, giving the reasons for his intercession: because we belong to the Father, because he and the Father have a mutual interest in us, and because he is glorified in us. But it is not only the Lord who has a ministry of intercession; we have a ministry of intercession too. We are to pray for others, and the reasons why we are to pray for others are precisely the reasons Jesus gave when he explained why he prayed for us.

Why should you pray for your fellow Christian? First, you should pray for him or her because that one belongs to the Father and is valued by him. What belongs to the Father and is valued by him should be valued by you as well.

Second, you should pray for others because you have a mutual interest in them in the sense that all Christians are bound up in the life of God together. When the Lord calls an individual to faith in himself he calls him not to an individual relationship alone, but rather he calls him into the church. This might not be the way we would do it, but it is the way God does it. He takes people from every nation, race, culture, and academic level, and he puts them together into one body, the church, to show that the binding principle is the love of the Lord Jesus Christ within them and the power of the Holy Spirit. We are together in this, whether we like it or not. Therefore, we should pray for one another, because the success of the other is our success, and his or her failure is our failure.

Finally, we should pray for others because God is glorified in them. Could it be that you would prefer not to have God glorified in them? I think sometimes, when I hear of frictions that exist between certain Christians and between denominations, that this is precisely what some Christians wish. They do not like the other person or other denomination and hope that these others will do something horrible to show that they themselves are right in having taken the position they have. This is not right. Rather, God has called that one, whoever he is and in whatever circumstances he finds himself, in order that he might do something unique in him that he might bear a valued witness.

212

God's Perseverance with His Saints

John 17:11-12

"I will remain in the world no longer, but they are still in the world, and I am coming to you. Holy Father, protect them by the power of your name—the name you gave me—so that they may be one as we are one. While I was with them, I protected them and kept them safe by that name you gave me. None has been lost except the one doomed to destruction so that Scripture would be fulfilled."

There are many points in John's Gospel at which the great distinguishing doctrines of the Reformed faith are discussed, for it is "a right meaty Gospel," as one of the early Reformers stated, and therefore these doctrines are understandably found here.

They are in chapter 10, in which Christ's enemies asked him to speak more plainly, thereby implying that their failure to believe was due to his fuzziness in preaching. Jesus replied with the statement, "You do not believe because you are not my sheep. My sheep listen to my voice; I know them, and they follow me. I give them eternal life, and they shall never perish; no one can snatch them out of my hand" (vv. 26–28). They wanted the gospel said plainly, so Jesus spoke plainly. Thus, these verses contain a statement of man's hopeless depravity through sin, God's electing grace in salvation, and his keeping power over his saints. The same doctrines are also found in chapter 6, for there Jesus pointed out: (1) no one can come to him unless the Father draws him (v. 44), (2) all whom the Father has given to Jesus will come to him (v. 37), and (3) none of those who come will be lost.

We would be surprised if these great truths did not also occur in Christ's great high priestly prayer recorded in chapter 17, for although they have already been stated, we would expect them to have a place (even a dominant place) in this most intimate prayer of our Lord to the Father for his own. Thus, we have, first, a clear distinction between those who are Christ's and those who are of the world. The implication is that the world cannot come to him for salvation and indeed does not. Second, he teaches that those who come are those who have been given to him by the Father. Third, he speaks of his own special ministry to them for which he is set apart. Fourth, he prays for all who shall come to him later as a result of the disciples' testimony, indicating that these shall believe. Finally, in the verses to which we come in this study, Jesus asks that they be kept by the Father and thus never be lost.

Here then are the great distinguishing doctrines of the Reformed faith again stated: (1) radical depravity, (2) election, (3) definite atonement, (4) irresistible grace, and (5) God's perseverance with his saints. Jesus expresses this last point by saying, "I will remain in the world no longer, but they are still in the world, and I am coming to you. Holy Father, protect them by the power of your name—the name you gave me—so that they may be one as we are one. While I was with them, I protected them and kept them safe by that name you gave me. None has been lost except the one doomed to destruction so that Scripture would be fulfilled" (vv. 11–12).

Christ's Second Petition

These words record Christ's second direct petition of this prayer. It is his first for his disciples. Earlier he had prayed for himself, asking that, having glorified the Father on earth by finishing the work that he had been given to do, he might in turn be glorified (vv. 1, 5). Now he turns to others and intercedes for them. This prayer is for their safekeeping. The remaining petitions are for their sanctification (v. 17), unity (vv. 20–21), and eventual presence with him in heaven (v. 24).

As we look ahead to these other petitions, as well as to the one with which we are now to deal, we cannot fail to notice that they all refer to spiritual things. Marcus Rainsford, one of the most comprehensive commentators on this chapter, has noticed this and has written, "The Lord does not ask riches for them, or honors, or wordly influence, or great preferments, but he does most earnestly pray that they may be kept from evil, separated from the world, qualified for duty, and brought home safely to heaven. Soul prosperity is the best prosperity; and, in truth, all temporal prosperity, as it is so called, is only real when it is in proportion to the prosperity of the soul. Remember how the beloved disciple brings out this thought in his third epistle. 'Beloved, I wish above all things that thou mayest prosper and be in health, even as thy soul prospereth' (3 John 2). Soul prosperity is the index of true prosperity."[1]

The Danger

We turn then to the second petition itself, the petition for God's safe-keeping of the disciples, and the first thing we notice is the danger that calls forth this expression of concern from our Lord.

First, although Jesus was leaving to go to the Father, these were not leaving. In fact, they were to remain *in the world*. This is a serious and almost ominous note in an otherwise joyful and optimistic prayer. Moreover, there is a contrast between himself in the position he was soon to enjoy and these in their position. Rainsford puts it like this, "I come to thy presence where there is fullness of joy, and to 'thy right hand where there are pleasures for evermore.' 'I come'—to where the river of the water of life flows from the throne of God; but *these, these* are in the wilderness. 'I come'—where no enemy can follow me, where no temptation can assail me, where no weariness can distress me; but *these, 'these* are in the world.' 'I come'—to reap the trophies of my great victory. 'I come'—to grasp the scepter, to wear the crown, and to ascend the throne. I have been weary here, but I shall soon be weary no longer; the way has been rough and thorny, but it is all over, my haven is almost reached; yet *these, 'these* are in the world!'"[2] We cannot miss the importance of this contrast.

Do we need an illustration? We find one in that story of the disciples' storm-tossed crossing of the Lake of Galilee. They had been sent across the sea while Jesus remained on the mountain to pray. But a storm had come, and he, looking down from the mountain, had seen their little boat buffeted and had come to them walking upon the water. Yes, he had come to them, but he had also deliberately permitted them to go through the period of struggle. Thus it is now. One day Christ will return for his own, but in the meantime we are in the world and he prays for us.

When he was here Jesus was their first and last line of defense. If they were threatened, he was there to receive the blows. If they were hated, he was there to allow that hate to be expended on himself. Now he was going, and the hate that had formerly been directed against himself would soon fall in equal fury upon the disciples.

Earlier he had warned them of it. He said, "Remember the words I spoke to you: 'No servant is greater than his master.' If they persecuted me, they will persecute you also. If they obeyed my teaching, they will obey yours also. They will treat you this way because of my name, for they do not know the One who sent me" (15:20–21).

Second, we notice that the disciples' danger was very great because *apart from God's perseverance, they would surely be lost*. This is the reason for Christ's mention of Judas at this point. We must not think, although our English translation seems to suggest it, that Judas is brought forward as an exception to God's perseverance with His saints, as though, for the sake of a prophecy, God consented to abandon Judas. This is not the case, for Judas was not one of Christ's originally. This is said elsewhere, and even this passage implies it. The phrase "son of perdition" is in the nominative case, rather than the genitive, which sets it off from the words "of them" which precede it. The true meaning is, "I have lost none of them whom you have given me, none at all. But the son of perdition is lost, as has been prophesied in Scripture." The reference is to Psalm 41:9. No, the case of Judas does not teach that a born-again person can be lost. But it does teach what would inevitably happen if God did not regenerate the individual and then keep in his care the one who has been so regenerated. If it were not for God, who could stand? Who could survive the onslaughts of the world if God did not keep us?

The Lord, Thy Keeper

But God does keep us. That is the point of these verses and the object of our Lord's petition. While Jesus was here, he kept those whom God had entrusted to him, and he kept them well. None was lost. Now he is about to return to the Father, and therefore he recommits those whom he had cared for to the Father's keeping.

This theme occurs many times in the Old Testament, often in rich images. For example, in Psalm 121, the image is that of a divine watchman or protector. In that psalm the words "watches" or "watch over" occur five times.

Another important passage is Ezekiel 34:11–16. In the verses immediately before this, God has been speaking against those who had been the shepherds of Israel, that is, Israel's leaders. They had not done their work. Now, says God, I will myself be a good shepherd to them. "For this is what the Sovereign LORD says: I myself will search for my sheep and look after them. As a shepherd looks after his scatterd flock when he is with them, so will I look after my sheep. I will rescue them from all the places where they were scattered on a day of clouds and darkness. I will bring them out from the nations and gather them from the countries, and I will bring them into their own land. I will tend them in a good pasture, and the mountain heights of Israel. I myself will tend my sheep and have them lie down, declares the Sovereign LORD. I will search for the lost and bring back the strays. I will bind up the injured and strengthen the weak, but the sleek and strong I will destroy. I will shepherd the flock with justice"

In Isaiah 27 God's keeping power is likened to the care of an husbandman for his vines. "Sing about a fruitful vineyard: I, the LORD, watch over it; I water it continually. I guard it day and night so that no one may harm it" (vv. 2–3).

These were the images upon which Jesus was drawing as he prayed for his people. Moreover, he had lived these images himself. We can hardly miss the fact that during the days of his incarnation he had been the watchman, the shepherd, and the husbandman. Now the disciples were to be committed to his Father—Israel's great watchman, shepherd, and husbandman. How could they be safer? True, the danger was great without. The danger was even great within, for they possessed an old nature that would surely drag them down into sin again and again. But over against this was One who was greater even than the danger. And he would keep them, even as he had promised to keep and actually did keep Israel.

"In Your Name"

There is one more point here that must not be lost. Three times in these verses Jesus speaks of keeping the disciples, once in reference to God and twice in reference to himself. But in two of these instances he also speaks more specifically of that by which they are kept. It is by God's name. In verse 11 we read, "Protect them by the power of your name—the name you gave me." In verse 12, we are told, "While I was with them, I protected them and kept them safe by that name you gave me."

What does it mean to be kept in God's name? We have already seen a partial answer to this question in our study of verse 6. There Jesus said that he had revealed God's name to those who had been given to him. We saw in studying that verse that "the name of God" is a Semitic phrase for speaking of God's attributes. To be protected by the name is therefore to be protected by the One who is sovereign, holy, all-knowing, wise, compassionate, and anything else that can properly be said of God. And there is more, for to be kept "in the name" is not merely to be kept by God, as if he were only some distant force that could be called in to defend us if that were necessary. It is rather that we are actually in him, much like being in a fortress. Thus, his power and other attributes surround us constantly. Proverbs 18:10 catches this exactly by saying, "The name of the LORD is a strong tower; the righteous run to it and are safe."

Indeed we are! Can anything touch us when we are safe in that fortress? Harry Ironside came from a background that caused him not always to be entirely happy with some of the distinguishing tenets of Calvinism, but he knew that the believer's security was with God and readily perceived it to be affirmed by these verses. He wrote, "You may be sure that whenever the Father gives any one to Jesus, he gives him for time and eternity. Such an one will never be lost. 'Being confident of this very thing, that he which hath begun a good work in you will perform it until the day of Jesus Christ.' People call this the doctrine of the perseverance of the saints, but I rather like to think of it as the perseverance of the Savior. He says, 'Those that Thou gavest me *I* have kept.' If I had to keep myself, I would be hopeless of getting through. I would be sure that something would happen some day which would cause me to lose my hold on Christ and be lost. But it is his hold upon me on which I rely. None can pluck the believer out of his hand. I receive great comfort from these words. When he gives his account to the Father, when the last believer of this dispensation is safely arrived in heaven, he will be able to say of the entire elect Church, 'Those that thou gavest me

I have kept, and none of them is lost.' You may think you know of exceptions to this; but it will be made manifest in that day that these apparent exceptions were like Judas himself, never really born of God."[3]

I like that, because Ironside had it right regardless of what terms he used. We are safe, not because of ourselves (for we are weak), but rather because we are kept by the Lord Jesus Christ and the Father.

God for Us

And what of us? How shall we react to these teachings? Some say that if we believe in God's keeping power with his saints, we will go out and sin. "Why not sin," they argue, "if we are sure to be saved anyway?" How little such people understand spiritual things! Do we feel free to sin, because God is for us? Of course not! Rather we choose to go his way and seek to please him because he, and only he, is for us. Who else is for us? No one! No one at all! The world is not for us. Satan is not for us. Even our friends are not for us when it gets right down to it, for all are for themselves in the final, grim analysis. Only God is for us. And lest we doubt it, we have the death of Christ on our behalf, the impartation of the Holy Spirit, and then the vast number of promises of God's perseverance, of which this is just one.

Shall we sin then? Not at all. Rather we will seek to please God. And what is more, we shall seek to persevere also, since we have learned perseverance from him. We will persevere in our work. It is often discouraging; we often see few results. But we will keep at it, for God has given it to us, and we must be like him in faithfully fulfilling this responsibility. We will persevere in our witness. Again we often find this disheartening. Men and women do not want the gospel. They hate the gospel, and they hate the God who gave it. Still, we will keep at it, knowing that the same God who is able to keep us in the world is able as well to save some out of it. He may use our witness as one means of doing so. Finally, we will persevere with our families. They are a special area of our responsibility, and we are often cast down when a son or daughter or wife or husband will not walk in God's way. Sometimes the situation seems hopeless. But it is not hopeless to God, and therefore we will not allow it to be hopeless for us. We will not give up. We will not quit. God is faithful. He is our keeper, and with God all things are possible.

213

The First Mark of the Church: Joy

John 17:13

"I am coming to you now, but I say these things while I am still in the world, so that they may have the full measure of my joy within them."

What do you think should be the distinguishing marks of the church of Jesus Christ? Or, to put it in slightly different terms, what do you think should be its most important characteristic?

I think that if that question were asked of me a number of years ago, I would have replied that the most important characteristic of the church is doctrinal faithfulness. And after that I would have listed holiness, unity, and love. Well, I do not want for a moment to suggest that holiness, unity, and love are not important; they are. But I have been impressed, as I have studied the great seventeenth chapter of John, containing Christ's prayer for his church, that the characteristic of that church with which Jesus begins is joy. The prayer has three parts: a section dealing with Jesus himself, a section dealing with the disciples, and a final section dealing with those who were to follow them in faith. In other words, the prayer moves by stages from the Lord to the Lord's church. Verse 13, the verse to which we have now come, is halfway through the prayer; so it, not surprisingly, introduces this first characteristic. The others are: holiness (vv. 14–17), truth (v. 17), mission (v. 18), unity (vv. 21–23), and love (v. 26).

The Early Church

That most of us do not think of joy as a primary characteristic of the church probably indicates both how little we regard it and how far we have moved from the spirit of the early church, for if anything characterized the early church it is that it was a joyous assembly.

We see this immediately when we begin to study the subject of joy, for the New Testament is a book of joy. In the Greek language, in which the New Testament was written, the verb which means "to rejoice" or "be joyful" is *chairein;* it is found seventy-two times. The noun, which means "joy," is *chara;* it occurs sixty times. Moreover, as we study these instances, we find that joy was not a technical idea, as if we were to find it only in highly theological passages. Rather it occurs most often simply as a greeting, meaning "Joy be with you!" To be sure, *chairein* is not always restricted to the speech of Christians. It is used, for example, in the letter to Felix about Paul by the Roman officer Claudius Lysias (Acts 23:26). But in Christian hands it obviously meant much more than it did with pagans and is used more frequently.

We notice, for example, that the angel who announced the birth of Jesus to the shepherds said, "I bring you good news of great joy that will be for all the people" (Luke 2:10). This obviously meant more than "Greetings!" Again, we notice Jesus saying, "I have told you this so that my joy may be in you and that your joy may be complete" (John 15:11). The things he had spoken were great promises. So the joy in this verse relates to the fullness of the Christian life.

When the Jerusalem church sent a letter to the churches of Antioch, Syria, and Cilicia after the first church council, they began their announcement of the momentous decision regarding gentile liberty from law by the word *chairein*—"Greetings" (Acts 15:23). James begins his letter in the same manner—"Greetings" (James 1:1). In Paul there are many such greetings. Thus, when in a letter literally flowing over with joy, the apostle wishes to give final admonitions to the Philippians, he writes, "Rejoice in the Lord always. I will say it again: Rejoice" (4:4). As Barclay says in his treatment of this term, "This great greeting, 'Joy be with you!' rings triumphantly through the pages of the New Testament."[1]

Need for Joy

But is the church today joyful? Are Christians? I do not doubt for a moment that we are all far more joyful than we would be if we were not Christians, nor do I doubt there are places where joy is particularly evident. It is often very evident in new believers, for example. But across the board in most churches, if one were to observe them impartially week after week, I wonder if the joy that obviously characterized Jesus and the early church would be visible.

No doubt we think of joy as something that should characterize the church ideally and will doubtlessly characterize it in that day when we are gathered together around the throne of grace to sing God's glory. But here? Here it is often the case that there are sour looks, griping, long faces, and other manifestations of a fundamental inner misery. The story has often been told—I am sure it is a true one—of the church in Scotland in which someone had obviously been bored by the sermon and had begun doodling. He had started drawing pictures of the preacher and then had gone on to writing verses. When the service was over the janitor found this bit of doggerel:

> To dwell above with saints I love,
> Aye, that will be glory!
> To dwell below with saints I know,
> Now that's a different story.

That is the difference between what we profess and know we ought to be, and what we really are. We should be joyful, but often we are not. We are depressed. Circumstances get us down. Instead of the victory we should experience, we know defeat and discouragement.

God's Remedy

Since I am certain that none of us wants to remain gloomy—at least I hope we do not—let us see what we can find as a remedy. Is there one? There must be; for if there were not, what would be the point of Christ's prayer for just this characteristic? That he does pray for it indicates that he was aware of the problem that we so easily develop. That he prays in the way he does indicates that, in addition to merely recognizing our need, he also knows the way by which our depression can be overcome.

The first remedy for a lack of joy is obvious, for it is on the surface of the text. Jesus says clearly, "I say *these things* while I am still in the world, so that they may have the full measure of my joy within them." This means that the basis for joy is sound doctrine. When I first began to handle this subject in connection with my exposition of the Book of Philippians, I was surprised to find how many times joy is associated with a mature knowledge of God's Word. David said, "The precepts of the LORD are right, giving joy to the heart" (Ps. 19:8). Psalm 119 reads, "I will rejoice in following your statutes as one rejoices in great riches" (v. 14). Earlier in these final discourses Jesus declared, "If you obey my commands, you will remain in my love, just as I have obeyed my Father's commands and remain in his love. I have told you this so that my joy may be in you and that your joy may be complete" (John 15:10–11).

Someone may remember that at the beginning of this study we denied that doctrine in itself was the most important mark of the church, and you may feel that we are now reintroducing it dishonestly through the back door. But this is not the case, for what we are talking about in this area is not doctrine in and of itself but rather that experiential knowledge of God's character and commandments that we receive from his Word.

It is rather, to put it in other language, what Francis W. Dixon has called the "establishing" of the hearts and minds of God's people. This particular phrasing of the matter occured in an address by Dixon given at the great English Keswick in 1962, entitled "God's Happy People." It was based on Psalm 34:8, 22, which he translated, "Happy is the man that trusteth in him. . . . None of them that trust in him shall be unhappy." He made the point that happiness (his word) or joy (my word) consists in having settled all our thoughts on God, his dealings with us, and his purposes with and through us. So long as we are unsettled, we are in a quagmire of doubt and inner turmoil. When we are settled in our knowledge of God, his will, and his ways, we can trust him peacefully and joyfully whatever the circumstances.

Dixon gave a number of illustrations. One of them concerned the wife of C. T. Studd, the well-known missionary to Africa. Mrs. Studd was an invalid and could not go with her husband when he returned to Africa for what proved to be the last time. As he left she knew that probably she would never see him again on this earth. She knew that she might have to face years of loneliness. But she did not complain; nor did she become cast down. Rather she said, "I will bless the LORD at all times; his praise shall continually be in my mouth." It was not easy for Mrs. Studd to rejoice in these circumstances, but she did. Dixon observed, "That is what I mean by having our thoughts established. Some Christians are only happy when everything pleases; when they can trace in some measure, or think they can trace, God's dealings with them. But others, like the psalmist, know that because he is their gracious and loving heavenly Father, who is planning their life for them, all things are working together for their good and for his glory; and so they praise the Lord and bless his holy Name at all times."[2]

Another illustration concerned the hymn writer Fanny Crosby. Fanny Crosby went blind when she was just five years old, and she lived to be ninety-five—ninety years of blindness. Yet she did not complain. Instead, she resolved the problem at a very early age, for when she was just eight years old she wrote:

> Oh, what a happy soul am I!
>   Although I cannot see,
> I am resolved that in this world
>   Contented I shall be.
> How many blessings I enjoy
>   That other people don't!
> To weep and sigh, because I'm blind,
>   I cannot, and I won't.

Does someone say, "Oh, but that was easy for Miss Crosby; for she was just a child and probably didn't know how important sight was. My case is different. I am trying to support a large family on an inadequate income, and no matter how we try to save we never seem to have enough." Another says, "But you don't know my circumstances. I am thirty-two years old and unmarried. My parents are dead, and I am lonely. I don't know what I'll do if I have to go on this way for thirty or forty more years." Another says, "But I'm an invalid. I can't get about. My circumstances are so hard." If you are speaking this way, you are indicating your practical ignorance of the sovereignty of God and are confessing that your thoughts are not really settled in him. Instead of this, recognize that he has planned those circumstances and look for his purposes in them.

Let me say something about circumstances, which we often think are so bad. Circumstances refer to things that are without. The word itself is based on two Latin words: *circum,* which means "around" (as in the word "circumference"), and *stare,* which means "to stand." So circumstances are the things that are standing around us. They are external. But where is the Lord in this picture? Is he without? No, he is within. It is a case of "Christ in you, the hope of glory" (Col. 1:27). So why worry about what is without if Christ is within? To know that he is within and that he is directing us moment by moment, day by day, is the secret of that supernatural joy that is our rightful birthmark as God's children.

Fellowship

The second remedy for a lack of joy in the believer's life is fellowship, and that in two dimensions. There is a vertical fellowship: fellowship with God. And there is a horizontal fellowship: fellowship with one another. Jesus is the pattern for us in both cases.

One thing we are going to notice as we continue our study of these six marks of the church is that Jesus is the pattern for each one. And that is certainly the case here; for he was joyful, even though we call him (rightly, but perhaps one-sidedly) "a man of sorrows, and acquainted with grief." We know this from our text, because he speaks here, not just of "joy," but of "*my* joy." It is this that he holds out to us. What was his joy? Well, there was a future joy centered in the completion of his work upon the cross, for we are told that Jesus "for the joy set before him endured the cross" (Heb. 12:2). But that is not the joy referred to here. Instead, it is the joy of moment by moment contact and fellowship with the Father. This is what sustained him in this prayer and on the cross.

It will sustain us as well, if we will only enter into the reality of that fellowship. Do not say, "But that is for Jesus; he was the Son of God, and I am just I." Are we not also sons of God? Is it not Jesus himself who has taught this to us? He taught that we could be born into God's family (John 3:3, 7). He taught that God could become our Father (John 20:17). Paul, who knew this truth well, declared forcefully, "Because you are sons, God sent the Spirit of his Son into our hearts, the Spirit who calls out 'Abba, Father'" (Gal. 4:6). Clearly we are sons of God also. Therefore, we can enter into the joy of Christ even as he entered into it—by constant fellowship with the Father.

Moreover, we can enjoy it on the horizontal level also. In fact, we must enjoy it on the horizontal level, for fellowship with the Father and with one another always go together. We remember how John stated the relationship in the preface to his first letter. He wrote, "We proclaim to you what we have seen and heard, so that you also may have fellowship with us. And our fellowship is with the Father and with his Son, Jesus Christ. We write this to make our joy complete" (1 John 1:3–4). These verses indicate that fellowship with the Father and fellowship with other Christians go together. So if you are not joyful, it may be that you have cut yourself off from other Christians, perhaps even with the thought of establishing your own private fellowship with God. It does not work that way. You need other believers, and they need you. Without them your fellowship with God will be diminished and your joy will not be full.

Righteousness and Peace

There is one final part to God's remedy for lack of joy. It is that we must live holy lives, for sin will keep us from God, and the fellowship with him that we need will be broken. In John 17 this thought is suggested by the sequence of the verses, for immediately after speaking of our need for joy, Jesus goes on to speak of our need for holiness, adding, "Sanctify them by the truth" (v. 17). The same thing is suggested by Paul: "The kingdom of God is not a matter of eating and drinking, but of righteousness, peace and joy in the Holy Spirit" (Rom. 14:17).

Many Christians lack the joy they ought rightly to have, because they do not have the peace about which Paul speaks. That is, they are not resting in God—the point first made about having our thoughts established in him. That is one reason. But it is also true that often they do not have joy because they do not have righteousness. They go their way, rather than God's. They disobey his commandments. They have their own way up to a point, but the Spirit's fruit evaporates. How much better to go God's way in holiness, to rest in him, and thus allow him to "fill you with all joy and peace as you trust in him" (Rom. 15:13).

214

The Second Mark
of the Church: Holiness

John 17:14–17

"I have given them your word and the world has hated them, for they are not of the world any more than I am of the world. My prayer is not that you take them out of the world but that you protect them from the evil one. They are not of the world, even as I am not of it. Sanctify them by the truth; your word is truth."

It may be the case—indeed it is, as I pointed out in the last chapter—that the first mark of the church is joy. But immediately after it, in fact, so close that it might rightly be thought to be competing for first place, is holiness. Holiness is the characteristic of God most mentioned in the pages of the Word of God and is therefore, rightly so, that which should characterize God's church. We are to be a "holy" people (1 Peter 2:9). We are to "follow after" holiness. Indeed, without it "no one will see the Lord" (Heb. 12:14). Jesus speaks of this characteristic of the church in our passage by praying—it is his second petition combined with the third—that God would keep it from the evil one. He says, "My prayer is not that you take them out of the world but that you protect them from the evil one. They are not of the world, even as I am not of it. Sanctify them by the truth; your word is truth" (vv. 15–17).

What Is Holiness?

What is holiness? Some people have identified it with a culturally deter-mined behavioral pattern and so have identified as holy those who do not gamble or smoke or drink or play cards or go to movies or do any of a large number of such things. But this approach betrays a basic misconception. Actually, although it may be the case that holiness in a particular Christian may result in abstinence from one or more of these things, the essence of holiness is not found there. Consequently, to insist on such things for the church is not to promote holiness but rather to promote legalism and hypocrisy. In some extreme forms it may even promote a false Christianity according to which men and women are justified before God on the basis of some supposedly ethical behavior.

Paul had found this to be true of the Israel of his day, as Jesus had also found it previously. So he distinguished clearly between this kind of holiness (the term he uses is "righteousness") and true holiness which comes from God and is always God-oriented. He said of Israel, "Since they did not know the righteousness that comes from God and sought to establish their own, they did not submit to God's righteousness" (Rom. 10:3).

The biblical idea of holiness becomes clear when we consider words that are synonyms for it in the English language, namely "saint" or "sanctify." Christ uses the second one in verse 17. What is a saint? A saint is not a per-son who has achieved a certain level of goodness (which is, nevertheless, what most people think), but rather one who has been set apart to himself by God. It follows from this that in the Bible the word is therefore not re-stricted to a special class of Christians, still less a class that is established by the official action of an earthly ecclesiastical body. Rather, it is used of all Christians, as is particularly clear from Paul's use of the word in his epistles (cf. Rom. 1:7; 1 Cor. 1:2; 2 Cor. 1:1; Eph. 1:1; Phil. 1:1, etc.). The saints are the called-out ones who make up God's church.

The same idea is also present when, as in Exodus 40, the Bible refers to the sanctification of objects. In that chapter Moses is instructed to sanctify the altar and laver in the midst of the tabernacle. That is, he was to make saints of them. The chapter does not refer to any intrinsic change in the nature of the stones obviously—they are not made righ-teous. It merely indicates that they were to be set apart to a special use by God.

In the same way, Jesus prays just two verses farther on in this great seven-teenth chapter of John, "I sanctify myself, that they too may be truly sancti-fied" (v. 19). The verse does not mean that Jesus makes himself more righ-teous, for he already was righteous. Instead it means that he separated himself to a special task, the task of providing salvation for all men by his death. If holiness is to be understood at all, it must be understood in this framework.

A Worldly Church

Now we need to ask this question. If holiness has to do with separation (or, better yet, consecration) and if believers are already holy by virtue of their being set apart to God by himself, why does Christ pray for our sanctification? Why pray for that which we already have? The answer is obviously that although we have been set apart to God we often clearly fail to live up to that calling. We are indeed separated unto God but, to paraphrase Wordsworth, it is nevertheless "trailing clouds of old commitments, sins and loyalties that we come."

We are worldly in the sense that the world's values often remain our values and the world's priorities our priorities. I once prepared a series of studies on "The Secular Church," by which I meant the worldly church. I pointed out that the impact of the world's system on the church may be seen in four crucial areas, the areas of the world's wisdom, the world's theology, the world's agenda, and the world's methods. Each is readily observable.

First of all, there is the matter of the *world's wisdom*. The old wisdom of the church, in every age and in every denomination, was the wisdom of the Scriptures. Christian people stood before the Word of God and confessed their own ignorance in spiritual things. They even confessed their inability to understand what is written in the Scriptures except by the grace of God through the ministry of the Holy Spirit who opens the Scriptures to us. Christian people confessed their resistance to spiritual things and the fact that, if left to ourselves, we always go our own way. But what has happened in our time is that this old wisdom, the strength of the church, has been set aside for other sources of wisdom with the result that the authoritative and reforming voice of God through the Scriptures is ignored.

Once I was taking part in a conference in which a theology professor disagreed with everything I had said. I had expected this from some source, of course, but the words this man used were so forceful they stuck in my mind. I had spoken of the historical Christ in rather moderate terms, I thought. But this professor violently disagreed with my position. He said, "We must understand that each of the Gospels was written to correct the other Gospels. So it is impossible to speak of the historical Christ." Then, since I had also said something about Jesus' return, he added, "We must get it into our heads that things are always going to continue as they are now and that Jesus Christ is never coming back." I knew what to think of that! Peter had warned long ago that in the last times scoffers would come saying, "All things continue as they were from the beginning," and he encouraged us to continue in the things we have learned. But I tell the story to illustrate the problem we have. It is secularism in the area of the church's wisdom.

Nor is this an isolated incident. A pastor told me that after he had spoken to a particular issue at one of his denominational meetings, another minister came up to him and demanded, "Why are you always talking about the Bible when you stand up to argue a point? Don't you know that nobody believes the Bible anymore?" Then, because he had referred to the apostle Paul on this occasion, his critic added, "After all, the apostle Paul was not infallible."

A rejection of the Scriptures as the wisdom of God has serious consequences. One result is that another authority, a poorer one, inevitably comes to take the Scripture's place. Men and women cannot operate without authority. So if you put out one authority, another will come in. If you reject the authority of God, human authority will emerge. The authority that we have in the large denominations today is the authority of the consensus of the people who make up that particular body. In other words, it is the authority of the 51 percent vote.

A second result of the church's abandonment of God's wisdom is that the church becomes irrelevant to life. This is being seen widely, and not just by evangelicals. A number of years ago, speaking at a meeting of the Consultation on Church Union in Denver, Peter Berger of Rutgers University criticized the lack of authority in the churches today which leads to their irrelevance. He argued, "If there is going to be a renaissance of religion, its bearers will not be people who have been falling all over each other to be 'relevant to modern man.' . . . Strong eruptions of religious faith have always been marked by the appearance of people with firm, unapologetic, often uncompromising convictions—that is, by types that are the very opposite from those presently engaged in the various 'relevance' operations. Put simply: Ages of faith are not marked by 'dialogue' but by proclamation." He then added, "I would affirm that the concern for the institutional structures of the church will be vain unless there is also a new conviction and a new authority in the Christian community."[1]

Second, it is not only in the area of the world's wisdom that we are faced with secularism; we are also faced with it in the area of the *world's theology*. The world's theology is easy to define. It is the view that man is basically good, that no one is really lost, and that belief in Jesus is not necessary for salvation.

One consequence is that the theological terms that we have always used and which the church continues to use (because they are part of its heritage) are redefined. We still find people speaking of sin, salvation, faith, and many other biblical terms. But having adopted the world's theology, they no longer mean by these terms what evangelicals mean when they speak biblically. Thus, "sin" means, not rebellion against God and his righteous law, for which we are held accountable, but rather ignorance or the kind of oppression that is supposed to reside in social structures. Since sin is located in the system, the way to overcome it is clearly not by Jesus' death but rather by changing the structures through revolution.

In a similar way, "Jesus" becomes, not the incarnate God who came to die for our salvation, but rather the pattern for creative living. We are to look to Jesus as an example, but not as the Savior. In some forms of this theology he is even considered to be what we might call the evolutionary peak of the race, a peak that we are all supposed to attain.

"Salvation" is defined, not as the old theology would say, as "getting right with God" or even "God moving to redeem us in Christ," but rather liberation from the oppression of this world's structures.

"Faith" is no longer believing God and taking his Word at face value, because his Word is not believed or taken at face value, but rather awareness of the situation as we see it. This approach is closely related to Marxism, because Marxists say that commitment to communism arises from becoming aware of oppression and beginning to do something about it.

"Evangelism" is also redefined. It no longer means carrying the gospel of Jesus Christ to a perishing world, but rather working to overthrow injustice.

The second result of adopting the world's theology is an apparent contradiction to what I have just said, but it is still true. It is a tendency to ignore theology entirely. This is seen primarily in the church's preoccupation with the *world's agenda*. In the third century of the Christian church this meant the concerns of the Roman Empire under Constantine. In the Middle Ages it meant the Crusades in which religious zeal was exploited in behalf of political expansionism. Today? Well, what is the world interested in? We are told that the world is concerned with problems of hunger; therefore, that should be a major concern for us too. The world is interested in the problems of Third World, underdeveloped countries. That should therefore be one of our primary concerns. The world is concerned with racism. So should we be. Ecology! The energy crisis! Aging! Alcoholism! Anything you can read about in the evening paper should be a primary concern of the church.

I do not want to deny for a moment that these are legitimate concerns. But what I want to deny emphatically is that they are the primary concerns of the church. For what happens when the church makes these items its primary concerns? First of all, she begins to look foolish in the eyes of the world, because the world knows that she is attempting to speak about something for which she has no particular competence. The offices of the church know no more about world hunger than the great relief agencies or government spokesmen. They probably know much less. Second, in emphasizing these other items as priorities, the church inevitably neglects that about which it really can speak, namely, the moral climate of our day and the remedy for it found in Jesus Christ. Worse than this, the moral climate of our country is endorsed in the sense of approving divorce, homosexuality, pornography, and other items.

Finally, secularism in the church is seen in the *world's methods*. God's methods are prayer and the power of the gospel, through which the Holy Spirit moves to turn God's people from their wicked ways and heal their land. That has always been the strength of the church of Jesus Christ. But today that power is despised by the great denominations. It is laughed at, because the methods that those laughing want to use are politics and money.

Years ago, when I was in college, I spent some time studying the plays of George Bernard Shaw, and I learned that one of Shaw's beliefs was that the religion of the future would be politics. The idea is in several of his plays. It is in *Caesar and Cleopatra,* for instance. Caesar is a religious figure in these terms. You find it most explicitly in *Major Barbara.* Barbara is a major in the Salvation Army, and she is converted in the play from Salvation Army religion to political activism. Politics is the new religion. This is what George Bernard Shaw, that old rebel, was saying years ago. But that is the philosophy of the church today: politics and money.

God's Church

The secularism of the church is bad, and I have taken space to describe it, first, because it is important to see how true worldliness works and, second, because we are going to be considering the cure for it at greater length in our study of the church's next distinguishing characteristic: truth. But we must notice the cure even now. Jesus makes it clear in his prayer by saying at the beginning of this section, "I have given them *your word*" (v. 14), and then again at the end, "Sanctify them by the truth; *your word* is truth" (v. 17). It is by means of the Bible, then, by the Word of God, that we are to become increasingly separated unto God and grow in practical holiness.

Without a regular, disciplined, and practical study of the Bible, the church will always be secular. It will fall into that state described by Paul when he warned that "there will be terrible times in the last days. People will be lovers of themselves, lovers of money, boastful, proud, abusive, disobedient to their parents, ungrateful, unholy, without love, unforgiving, slanderous, without self-control, brutal, not lovers of the good, treacherous, rash, conceited, lovers of pleasure rather than lovers of God—having a form of godliness but denying its power" (2 Tim. 3:1–5). That is the secular church—"having a form of godliness but denying its power." On the other hand, by means of the Bible, God's people will become the opposite, for if the secular church employs the world's wisdom, the world's theology, the world's agenda, and the world's methods, the true church will invert it. It will employ the wisdom of God, the theology of the Scriptures, the agenda of God's written revelation, and the methods that have been given to us for our exercise in the church until the Lord Jesus Christ comes again.

215

The Church That Is Not Holy

John 17:14–17

"I have given them your word and the world has hated them, for they are not of the world any more than I am of the world. My prayer is not that you take them out of the world but that you protect them from the evil one. They are not of the world, even as I am not of it. Sanctify them by the truth; your word is truth."

We live in the midst of a divided church, but the division is not along the lines that are most talked about. Some say that there is a gap between laymen and clergy. I sometimes hear that the major division in the church is between those who believe in the mission of the church as evangelism and those who believe in the mission of the church as social action. I believe the real division lies between those who regard the church in purely secular terms and those who still regard the church as being based upon and as testifying to supernatural realities.

The danger that confronts us, even as evangelicals, is that worldliness takes hold, and the concern for the biblical gospel and spiritual priorities vanishes. In theory evangelicals object to the secularism of the church, but in practice we often are quite secular ourselves. Therefore, when we point the finger at others (and we must do that rightly in order to uphold the teaching of the Word of God), we must, nevertheless, at the same time examine ourselves. In other words, we must pray as David did: "Search me . . . and . . . test me . . . and see if there is any offensive way in me, and lead me in the way everlasting" (Ps. 139:23–24).

Rampant Materialism

What are the areas in which the evangelical church, in spite of its theology, adopts the philosophy and outlook of the world? Where do we begin? The point at which it is necessary and obvious to begin is with our materialism.

Many persons point to this problem, and the fact that they do so should make us sit up and listen. *World Vision* magazine in its issue of January 1976, quoted a number of evangelical leaders who had been asked to write upon Western civilization and the mission of the church. Most of them, in one way or another, pointed a critical finger at our materialism. J. D. Douglas, editor of the *New International Dictionary of the Christian Church* and editor-at-large for *Christianity Today,* wrote: "Pervading our society is an even more insidious materialism which makes Christians short of breath through prosperity and ill-equipped to run the race that is set before them." Horace L. Fenton Jr., General Director of the Latin America Mission, wrote: "In the Western Church we ought to cut back immediately on all unnecessary expenditures—including the elaborate building programs which have obsessed us far too long. It is just as much a sin for a Church to lay up treasure on earth as it is for an individual Christian." Frank E. Gaebelein, Headmaster Emeritus of the Stony Brook School and General Editor of *The Expositor's Bible Commentary,* wrote: "Negatively the growing materialism in the more affluent western nations is detrimental to the total Christian discipleship essential to the faithful mission of the Church." Each of these men puts his finger on something that is not just a characteristic of our country or of the liberal church, but that is characteristic of evangelicals as well.

This is not a philosophical materialism. A philosophical materialism would be a materialism similar to that of communism. Evangelicals most certainly are not adopting materialism in that sense. As a matter of fact, there is even a negative argument that would go to this effect, namely, that because we are not Communists and Communists are materialistic, therefore we are not materialistic. But that does not necessarily follow. True, we do not have a philosophical materialism, but if we are honest we must admit that nevertheless we have a very practical materialism that is no less detrimental to the advance of the gospel in our age.

Francis Schaeffer analyzed our materialism rightly by saying that it is not so much the desire to be millionaires as it is to have two things: (1) *personal peace* and also (2) *affluence* to the degree necessary to enjoy our peace. Personal peace is the goal that causes us to say, "I don't really care much what is happening in the world so long as it doesn't bother me." The desire for affluence is not necessarily the desire to be a Rockefeller or an Astor but simply to have enough money to enjoy life to the full. That is the kind of materialism we have. And if our goals place both of these items high on our list of priorities, then we have an example in our own lives of the insidious encroachment of secularism.

If you are inclined to say defensively, as we naturally do, "But that's not true of me," let me put the question in this form: Is it true of you in respect to your desire for your children? What do you really want for your children, those of you who are parents? Is your first desire that they might be comfortable, that they might have a home, that they might be happily married? Is that what you put at the top of your list of priorities? If you do, this is materialism in every sense of the term. Rather, you should desire first that they might be men and women of God, obedient to his will and doing without those things that are necessary if his work is to be done.

This World's Fads

Second, we become secularized in that we so easily follow the fads of this world. I once had a conversation with Dr. Hudson Armerding, former president of Wheaton College. We were talking about the situation on the campuses, particularly of Christian schools, and I asked him what it was that bothered him most about our Christian campuses. He said, "It's the fact that the Christian campuses always seem to be following along behind the world; they have the same concerns, but it's always a year or two later." Then he spelled it out, noting that when the Vietnam war became a concern in the secular schools, it became a concern in the Christian schools too, but several years later. When ecology became the burning issue on the secular campuses, it also became a burning issue on the Christian campuses, but a year or two later. When women's liberation became the issue elsewhere, it also became the issue in the Christian world, but again some time later. What he was saying is that we have a case of the world leading the church rather than the church leading the world. And what is that if not the secularization of the evangelical community?

Let me speak about it in several other areas. We have a fadism in *theology*. We know, if we survey the Christian world, that we have a great emphasis upon psychological analyses in our time, upon small group dynamics, interaction groups, sensitivity sessions, and so on. But this has been popular first of all in the world through secular philosophy. Now it begins to enter the church in such a way that small interaction groups begin to replace the proclamation of the Word of God and a proper kind of Christian counseling. This is widely true in the secular church, and it is increasingly true in the evangelical churches, at least in recent years.

We have the same thing in *liturgics*. Liturgics has become a concern in the secular church, and because it is a concern there it has become a concern in the evangelical church too. So we have a great deal of experimentation in worship, which, unfortunately, in many instances is not worship at all. It has such an undefined content that it is virtually impossible to distinguish it from the revelings of hedonism.

We also see an example of fadism in *universalism*. Sometimes I have an opportunity to visit on Christian campuses, and when I do I ask about the mood and thinking of the student body. I have been told again and again that the one area in which Christian students today seem most to depart from historical Christianity is in adopting universalism, that is, the idea that all men everywhere, somehow or other, because of the grace of God, are going to be saved. Where does this idea come from? It most certainly does not come from the teaching of the Bible. Rather it comes from the secular outlook of our time. The world does not want to look at men and women as basically bad in God's sight, that is, as sinners in the eyes of a holy God, but rather as those who may have a few foibles, but who nevertheless are basically all right. That is not the teaching of the Bible. Yet it finds its way into our evangelical churches and schools.

We also find that the world's outlook is being adopted in regard to *marriage*. We have marriages breaking up at a rate that has never been true previously. And, as I observe it, it seems to me that the unique thing today is that the women are leaving the marriages, not the men. It used to be that a marriage would break up primarily because the man would be unfaithful. He would have an affair. That is not what is happening today. I can point to numerous cases where the wife has simply said, not on the grounds of infidelity but on the grounds of a lack of personal fulfillment, "I have had it; this is not meeting my needs," and then has walked out. Secular values, now given popularity through the women's liberation movement, have begun to impinge upon the thinking of Christian people. As a result, God's norms are abandoned and personal desires are sanctified in the name of biblical freedom.

Madison Avenue Religion

The third area in which we see secularism in our evangelical churches is our Madison Avenue approach to Christian commitment. We see this in certain forms of evangelism. I want to be very careful here, because obviously the greater problem in evangelism is not doing it at all. If through a method we are able to rally people to the cause of presenting the gospel of Jesus Christ to those who have not heard it, it is not altogether bad to do that, even if the method is faulty. But at the same time we have to recognize that secularism can enter in even here.

Sometimes Christians are required to memorize a certain stylized presentation of Christian truth. This is something that in the hands of a person who understands the gospel well can be useful. Certainly it helps to have thought through the kind of questions you might be asked and the answers that seem most helpful to most people. But to present the gospel in a rigid way, where the words are carefully chosen by a kind of popular opinion poll or analysis, is secularism.

We see the same thing in the way in which the gospel and Christian concerns are sold to our constituency; that is, through advertisements in our magazines, direct mail, and so on. It should be said, in defense of this, that it is often the case that this is the only way in which evangelical leaders seem to be able to awaken the concerns of Christian people. But the proper stance from the perspective of the individual is to be ahead of the appeal in one's own commitment as to how to use money. In other words, before the appeal comes, when you are before the Lord on your knees, ask how the resources that he has given you should be used and then determine to do that on the basis of the Lord's leading and not necessarily on the basis of the sentimental pictures that happen to be on the front of the brochure that comes in the mail about three weeks before Christmas. If we are to overcome this in our life, these are the practical lines upon which we are going to have to operate.

Indifference

Finally, we see secularism in the evangelical church in our great indifference. Indifference to what? The answer is: to practically anything and everything worthwhile. Let me spell it out. First, we are indifferent to the *state of the lost*. Indifference is the number one problem in recruiting missionaries and support for missionaries. Short-term projects are well received; but the number of those who would commit themselves to a lifetime of missionary endeavor for the sake of Christ and who would support such persons is dwindling.

Second, there is indifference to the *suffering of the world's poor*. We are often so isolated from the very poor in North America that we seldom see deep suffering face-to-face. We do not know what it is to see someone who is so hungry that he or she can hardly think of anything but food. So we are indifferent to these things.

We are also indifferent to the *needs of our fellow believers*. If there is anything we hear in the evangelical church today, it is that evangelicals do not want to listen to the hurts in the hearts and lives of other Christians. We do not want to be bothered. We do not want to hear these things because they are demanding; they require a response, and we are not prepared to make it. Instead we want to rest in our own personal peace and affluence, as I pointed out earlier, and we do not get involved.

There is indifference to the *leadership vacuum in the churches*. There is work to be done, but the hardest thing in Christian work is to find people who recognize the need and who will step into it and do what is necessary by the grace of God, faithfully, if necessary year after year and at great personal hardship. We do not have much of this commitment. I once was given a little poem on the role of the pastor; its conclusion was:

> Ashes to ashes, dust to dust;
> If the people won't do it, the pastor
> must.

But the problem is that the pastor cannot do it all. Moreover, if he is trying to do it all, a number of things, including the preaching of the Word of God, will be buried by the wayside. If people in the church are indifferent to obvious need and the pastor responds in their place, then the whole church suffers. Each one has a gift. Each one must be willing to use it to the glory of God.

The following question was asked of a number of officials in church circles recently: What is the number one problem in the evangelical church today? "Apathy," said an official of the National Association of Evangelicals. "Lack of discipline," said another. "Not caring enough," said someone who was involved in the Watergate scandal.

I conclude with this question: If these things are true of us, what should be done? The answer to that question comes from the words of the Lord Jesus Christ to the church at Laodicea, a church that he said was "increased in riches," like the church in America. He said, "You say, 'I am rich; I have acquired wealth and do not need a thing.' But you do not realize that you are wretched, pitiful, poor, blind and naked. I counsel you to buy from me gold refined in the fire, so you can become rich; and white clothes to wear, so you can cover your shameful nakedness; and salve to put on your eyes, so you can see. Those whom I love I rebuke and discipline. So be earnest, and repent" (Rev. 3:17–19).

The things that God counsels are these: first, "to buy from me gold refined in the fire." In Psalm 19:10 David uses the image of gold to refer to the Word of God, and in Psalm 12:6 he uses silver to refer to it. He does so because the Word of God is precious, of spiritual value. So what the Lord is admonishing us to do here is to master the Word of God by effort—that is the meaning of the word "buy," by effort, by hard work—in order that this which is the most precious thing on earth, the Word of God, might be ours in a personal way.

The second point of God's counsel is that we acquire "white clothes" to cover our shameful nakedness. Raiment refers to righteousness, and it is plural in this case: righteousnesses. What God is saying is that we should be clothed with acts of personal holiness. We should be zealous for good works.

Third, we must put "salve" on our own eyes so we can see. The counsel here is that we might desire afresh the healing of God's Spirit in order that we might see his truth and walk in it. That truth applies to us in our sin, to God in his holiness, to a world that is lost, and to a work that needs desperately to be done.

216

The Third Mark of the Church: Truth

John 17:17

"Sanctify them by the truth; your word is truth."

In each of the previous discussions of the marks of the church we have touched upon the mark to which we now come, for both Christian joy and holiness depend almost entirely upon how well we know God's truth; that is, how well we know and practice the principles of God's written revelation. It is true that Jesus did not begin at this point in his comments in John 17; he began with joy and holiness. But when we ask, "How can I obtain and keep this joy?" or "How can I be holy?" we come to this point at once, for the answer is always, "Through a study of the Bible and the application of its truths to daily life." Jesus indicates this in our text in regard to sanctification by saying, "Sanctify them by the truth; your word is truth" (John 17:17).

It is a striking thing, which we realize more and more as we grow in the Christian life, that nearly all that God does in the world today, he does by the Holy Spirit through the instrumentality of his written revelation. This is true of sanctification. Sanctification means to be set apart for God's use. So our text tells us that the only way this will ever happen to us is by an appropriation of God's truth as is recorded for us in the Bible.

So far as the truth goes, the world lives by an illusion, and this is an inevitable problem for us unless we have a sure way of countering and actually overturning its influence. Ray Stedman writes correctly of this problem when he says, "The world lives by what it thinks is truth, by values and standards which are worthless, but which the world esteems highly. Jesus said, 'What is exalted among men is an abomination in the sight of God' (Luke 16:15). That is how the world lives. And how can we live in that kind of a world—touch it and hear it, having it pouring into our ears and exposed to our eyes day and night, and not be conformed to its image and squeezed into its mold? The answer is, we must know the truth. We must know the world and life the way God sees it, the way it really is. We must know it so clearly and strongly that even while we're listening to these alluring lies we can brand them as lies and know that they are wrong."[1] Stedman is saying that Christians should be the greatest of all realists, because their realism is that of the truth of God. This by its very nature should lead to their greater and greater sanctification.

Dead Ends to Holiness

If we are to receive the blessings God has for his church, we must receive them in the way God has planned to give them to us, and this means that there are many ways in which holiness will not come to us. It will not come through *preaching* or *listening to preaching*, for instance. Most of us know people who have specialized in Bible conferences and conventions to such a degree that they are fully aware of the points at which one speaker varies from another and even at times of what a speaker is going to say before he says it. One Bible teacher said that "they can readily foretell a speaker's third point while he is still in the midst of the second." But this alone does not produce holiness, as such people often testify. In fact, they are often quite restless and confess to a lack of true blessing in their lives. What is wrong? Simply, they are looking to men for their teaching, rather than to God. And when they do hear the Word of God, they hear it without that full yielding of the spirit to God's truth, which produces growth through obedience.

A second way in which we will not find holiness is through *prayer* or, still less, through *prayer meetings*. Prayer is important, and the Christian who is growing in the Christian life will inevitably find that times of prayer, both public and private, are increasingly precious to him or her. But however valuable prayer is, it is not the God-ordained means for growth in holiness. Prayer is preparation for such growth. But at what point in prayer does God actually speak to us and direct us in the way we should go? It is only when God the Holy Spirit brings the words of Scripture to our minds or directs us to the Bible for the direction we need. Apart from this corresponding reflection on the Word of God prayer is merely a monologue. As such, it may relieve our personal anxieties, but it does not provide direction. On the contrary, when we study the Word and pray over it, God leads us clearly and keeps us from the suggestions of Satan or the kinds of autosuggestion (or wish fulfillment) that all too frequently pass for divine guidance in the lives of some Christians.

Third, we must not expect to find holiness through a *special experience,* sometimes called a *second blessing.* There is nothing wrong with special experiences of God's grace; in fact, it is a strange Christian life that does not have many of them. But the error consists in supposing that sanctification will come through one, or even more than one, decisive experience. It does not work that way. Consequently, whenever you find yourself looking for an experience, you are always on the wrong track and in spiritual danger. Sanctification comes rather from seeking always and increasingly to have the Lord Jesus Christ exalted in our lives. And the way to do that is by discovering what he desires of us and for us in his Word.

At this point we are back to the central point of this message. Growth in holiness is through Bible study alone. Therefore, the third mark of the church must be God's truth.

Distinctly Different

We need to be very practical at this point, for in the preceding studies we talked frankly about how the secular church is characterized by the world's wisdom, the world's theology, the world's agenda, and the world's methods. The true church is not to be like that. But what does this mean practically? It means that the godly church must be distinctly, noticeably, and articulately different in each of these areas. This will involve individuals, for the church is made up of individuals. But it will also involve larger units—congregations, associations of congregations, and denominations.

First of all, we have to be clear as to what *our authority* is. One evidence of the secularism of the large denominations is that biblical authority, the authority of the Scriptures, has been thrown out and the authority of consensus has come in. Things are done in denominations today, not because the Bible says they should be done or even because the creeds say so, but because 51 percent of our people say so. If we are to be distinct in this area, we must do what we do because the Bible says so. We must be men and women of "the Book." In theory we are. We say that we are. We acknowledge that this is what our standard is. But much of the time, in practice, evangelical churches operate exactly the way other churches do.

We have to recover the biblical standard. This means that we cannot say, as I have heard evangelical men say on important issues, "Well, that particular thing just does not bother me." That response is not good enough. Instead, we have to get to what the Word of God says. We have to study it, do our homework, and then we must ask: On the basis of this Word, what does God want for the church in this age?

We will have to do that sooner or later anyway, or else we are going to have to go the world's way entirely. This is so because history does not allow us to stand long in an ambiguous position. Someone has pointed out that in Germany, in the Nazi period, the church went in one of two ways: either it capitulated to the Nazi point of view or it became increasingly a church of the Book. Those who lived by the Book eventually established a communion of their own. They signed documents identifying themselves as the "confessing church." Why did they go this way? They did so because, when the whole drift of society and the culture is contrary to biblical standards, it is impossible to appeal to any external norms. You cannot say, "This is backed up in the area of psychology or science or social relations," because it is not. The things that are being written in all those areas are contrary to biblical truth. So the church must increasingly fall back upon the divine revelation. Has God spoken to God's people in this Book? If so, then we must be clear and say, "Let God be true and every man a liar." Evangelical churches are going to have to recapture that outlook.

Second, we need to be distinct in *our theology*. This pays off, because where it is done those who hunger for the truth of the Word of God will come to it. We see the evidence in our seminaries today. Enrollment at the denominational seminaries, where there is often no clear theology and certainly not an evangelical theology, is declining. But enrollment at the evangelical seminaries is growing. *Time* magazine pointed this out in an article some years ago.

The thesis of a book by Dean M. Kelly, entitled *Why Conservative Churches Are Growing*, is that conservative churches are growing because they know where they stand and, therefore, people know where they stand and turn to them. But the same thesis applies to the seminaries. The seminaries grow for that reason too. They are an illustration of what we need in the area of theology.

We need to articulate the great biblical truths, not just adopt the theology of our culture. We need to speak of the depravity of man, of man in rebellion against God, so much so that there is no hope for him apart from God's grace. We need to speak of God's electing love, showing that God enters the life of the individual in grace by his Holy Spirit to quicken understanding and draw the rebellious will to himself. We must speak of perseverance, that God is able to keep and does keep those whom he so draws. All these doctrines and all the supporting doctrines that go with them need to be proclaimed.

Third, we have to be distinctly different in the area of *our priorities*. The denominations set their agenda. It is the world's agenda. We must say that our priorities are not going to be the world's priorities but the priorities of the Word of God. This does not mean that we will neglect social concerns. That is part of the priority of the Christian life. But it does mean that we will not reject the gospel of salvation through faith in the vicarious atonement of Christ either. And we will make the proclamation of this gospel our number one priority.

At the end of *The Invaded Church* Donald Bloesch talks about what evangelicals must do to change the world, and he says that what is needed is not simply an improved social environment but "a new kind of man." That is entirely right. That is what is needed. Then he goes on to give examples, and he gets into the area of racism and analyzes it like this: "For modern secular humanism, including Marxism, the poison of racism can be removed through social reform and education. Biblical Christianity sees this problem in a different light. The real enemy is racial and cultural pride, not ignorance. And behind this pride is unbelief, hardness of heart, what the Bible calls original sin. . . . Laws are necessary to protect the defenseless, but they can only hold the dike against sin. It is the gospel alone that takes away sin, and this means that the final solution to racism and other social ills is biblical evangelism."[2]

We must be clear then, when we set our priorities, that this is where our emphasis goes—in time, money, and the choice of what we do and say.

A New Lifestyle

Fourth, we need to be distinctly different in the area of *our lifestyle*. This is something that evangelicals have not been too conscious of until fairly recent times, because we have lived in a culture that, although it is not Christian, has nevertheless held on in part to the vestiges of an earlier Christianity. This is disappearing. Laws are changing, and there is going to be more agitation to change in future days. When this comes Christians must be distinct in their lifestyle. We must say that we do not go with the trends of our times, the increasing secularization. Rather we must want to be known as God's people in these areas.

One of the priorities we must have concerns our time. Sports take an enormous amount of time in our day, by means of television and by our own participation. It is what many people do on weekends. There are evangelicals who find their time so taken up with sports that Christian activities are crowded out. Is that right? Is this not an area in which we have to say that the drift of our day is not in the direction we want to go?

A second area is the amount of time spent watching television. Statistics say that the average American watches television over five hours every day. Is the tube worth that time? The Bible says, "Make the most of every opportunity, because the days are evil" (Eph. 5:16). I wonder if many Christians are not missing out here and if the challenge of the age is not going to require us to sharpen up in this area.

How about the use of Sunday? I do not believe that we should have blue laws. I do not believe in proscribing what is proper and improper Sunday activity for anyone. But how do we use Sunday? Do we go to church? Do we want to worship God? Is sixty minutes, seventy or eighty minutes, on Sunday morning the whole of our Sunday commitment? Is it the total of the time we want to receive religious instruction?

I have noticed that the public schools are increasingly scheduling school events for Sunday, and this is having its effect on our children. Our schools have the rest of the week filled as full as they can reasonably expect to make it. So what do they do when they want to establish a new activity? There is a glee club, and they need people to sing. There are sports, and someone wants to get in an extra practice. There is an orchestra, and they need time to rehearse. They set it for Sunday morning. We are going to see more of that, and Christian people are going to be confronted with it again and again. Are these activities more important than having our children in church? We must ask that question. We cannot avoid it. Moreover, we must be Christian people at that point. Even if it means not getting ahead as much as we would like, even if it means not being as popular as we would like, even if it means that our children are not going to be as popular as we would like them to be. We must say, "But as for me and my house, we will serve the LORD" (Josh. 24:15).

When we do that we will have an influence upon the world. I know of cases where Christian parents have said to their children, "You are not allowed to do that on Sunday morning; we go to church at that hour." The children have gone to their teachers and have said, "We are sorry, but we can't participate; our family goes to church at that hour." And the teachers have said, "Oh, we didn't know anyone did that. All right, we'll change the hour." Victories can be won, but we must stand on our convictions.

Perhaps the most pressing area in which we have to be distinct is sexual ethics, particularly in our conception of marriage and the way we conduct our marriages. It is not easy to have a Christian marriage today. Everything in the world works against it. The great and overriding concern of our time is for personal satisfaction, and there is always that in marriage that does not seem personally satisfying. We wish things could be different. But the question is: What are we in the marriage for? Are we in it primarily for personal satisfaction? Or are we there because we believe God has brought us together with our spouse to establish a Christian home in which his truth can be raised high, Christian values demonstrated, and children raised in the nurture and admonition of the Lord? It must be the latter. Furthermore, in our speaking we must make clear distinction between marriages that are Christian marriages and marriages that are simply marriages in the world's sense.

Not long ago I saw a fictitious marriage service on television. I watch these because I am curious as to how the writers are going to handle the vows. The vows, as everyone knows, are Christian. I wondered: Will they use them because they are the traditional vows and they cannot avoid them, or will they doctor them up to make them more secular? In this particular marriage service the couple promised to "live with one another and cherish one another, as long as—" I thought they were going to say, "as long as life shall last." But do you know what they said? They said, "as long as *love* shall last." In other words, "As long as I love her I'll live with her; but if I stop loving her, that's the end of the marriage." It could be a year, a month, a week. That is the viewpoint of secular men and women. A Christian marriage is different. Thus, when we stand to take our vows, we must be made clear that they are for life—"until death us do part"—because that is what God wants. And we must live as Christians within the marriage bond.

Finally, we must be distinct in *our use of money and other resources.* How do we use our money? All of us have money we could use in the Lord's work. Do we thus use it? Are we faithful in that area? Some of us do not even give the Old Testament tithe, let alone our life and soul and all that we have to be used in the Lord's own way.

Dependence on God

I have given four areas in which we need to be distinctly different; the areas of authority, theology, priorities, and lifestyle. These correspond to the areas of secularization delineated earlier. But there is a fifth point we need to add. We need to be distinctly different in our visible dependence upon God.

When I was at the conferences I mentioned earlier, something happened that was very revealing. When I spoke about the lostness of men I got a negative reaction. No one wanted to hear that men and women are lost apart from the grace of God. But there was one doctrine that everyone seemed to agree with. It startled me. After I had spoken of the lostness of men, which they did not like, I stressed the grace of God in calling some to salvation. I said, "We cannot move men; we cannot change the world. If the world is to be changed it must be by God's doing, and for that we must pray and ask him." Surprisingly, they agreed with that just as much as they had disagreed with man's depravity! I began to analyze this, and I think I began to understand the reaction. It was because the people to whom I was talking were working in the social arena—trying to help alcoholics, serving those in the ghetto, looking for improvement. And what had happened? They had looked for improvement, but it had not come. So when I said that change had to be by the grace of God, their hearts said, "Amen." They did not like biblical theology, but they knew that the power of God is necessary if change is to come.

So there is a great opportunity for those who know the Lord to show that in dependence upon him changes will indeed come, not because of who we are, nor even because our theology is better, but because we know God and depend upon him.

Salt and Light

How can Christians change the world? The Lord Jesus Christ gave the answer in the Sermon on the Mount. He did not say that we are to maneuver the world. He did not say, "Get elected to high positions in the Roman Empire. See if you can get an evangelical to be emperor." It could happen, of course. He did not forbid it. But that is not the option he gave. He said,

"You are the salt of the earth" (Matt. 5:13), "You are the light of the world" (v. 14).

Salt does a great deal of good, but it does no good at all if it has lost its saltiness. It is only when it is salty that it is effective. So, if we are those in whom the Spirit of God has worked to call us to faith in Jesus Christ, we really must be Christ's people; and it should be evident that by his grace we are not what we were previously. Our values should not be the same values. Our commitments should not be the same commitments. Our theology should not be the same theology. Rather, there must be a new element in us and, because of us, in the world.

We are also "light." If salt speaks of what we are, light speaks of what we do. The purpose of light is to shine, to shine out. The Lord said, "No one lights a candle and puts it under a basket. It is to be set up on a hill where all will see it." We are to be lighthouses in the midst of a dark world. Being a lighthouse will not change the rocky contours of the coast—the sin is still there; the perils of destruction still threaten men and women—but by God's grace the light can be a beacon that will bring the ships into a safe harbor. That is what it means to be set apart unto God, to be sanctified. We are to be a beacon, knowing that as we are there will be cause for rejoicing, and the evangelical church will be blessed by God and thanked by those who have found the Lord Jesus Christ through its witness.

217

The Fourth Mark
of the Church: Mission

John 17:18–19

"As you sent me into the world, I have sent them into the world. For them I sanctify myself, that they too may be truly sanctified."

A number of years ago, when Ralph L. Keiper was preaching at a missions conference in Deerfield Street, New Jersey, he told about a little girl who had come to see him early in his ministry. She was about eight years old. She had been to the church's daily vacation Bible school, and when she came into his study she asked, "Mr. Keiper, is it all right if I commit suicide?"

The young pastor was startled. But he had learned never to give a quick yes or no answer to a child's question without first discovering why the child was asking the question. So he countered, "Mary, why would you ever want to commit suicide?"

"Well," Mary said, "it's because of what I learned in Bible school this morning."

Keiper wondered to himself, "What was this child told?"

She continued, "We were taught that heaven is a wonderful place—no fear, no crying, no fighting, just to be with the Lord. Won't that be wonderful! We were taught that when we die we will be with Jesus. Did I hear it right, Mr. Keiper?"

"Yes, you did, Mary. But why would you want to commit suicide?"

"Well," she said, "you have been in my home. You know my mother and daddy. They don't know Jesus. Many times they are drunk. So we have to get ourselves up in the morning, get our own breakfast and go to school with dirty clothes. The children make fun of us, and when we come home again we hear fighting and things that make us afraid. Why shouldn't I commit suicide? Wouldn't heaven be better?"

It is clear that Mary did not believe in theoretical theology; she believed in practical theology, and she was facing a very practical problem. What she was really asking was why we are in this world anyway. If this world is such a sin-cursed place and heaven is such a blessed place, why do we have to stay here? Why does God not take us to heaven immediately upon our conversion? Or, failing that, why do we not all take our own lives and so speed up what is an inevitable ending anyway? Keiper answered by saying, "Mary, there is only one reason in God's world why we are here. And that is that through our testimony, by life and by word, we might have the privilege of bringing people to the saving knowledge of the Lord Jesus." He then indicated that, as Mary did this, it might be in the Lord's providence that her parents would come to know the Lord as their Savior. Later, her mother did.

A Missionary Church

Keiper's story is important in light of the fourth mark of the church. Up to this point we have been talking about those things that concern the church itself or that concern individual Christians personally. We have been looking at joy, holiness, and truth. But while these are important and undoubtedly attainable to a large degree in this life, nevertheless it does not take much thinking to figure out that all three of them would be more quickly attained if we could be transported to heaven. Here we have joy; that is true. But what is this compared to the joy we will have when we see the source of our joy face-to-face? The Bible acknowledges this when it speaks of the blessedness of the redeemed saints, from whose eyes all tears shall be wiped away (Rev. 7:17; 21:4). Again, in this world we undoubtedly know a degree of sanctification. But what of that day when we shall be completely like him (1 John 3:2)? Or again, here we are able to assimilate some aspects of God's truth and know truly. But in the day of our final redemption we shall know fully. "Now we see but a poor reflection, as in a mirror; then we shall see face to face" (1 Cor. 13:12). If this is true, why should we not go to heaven immediately?

The answer is in the mark of the church to which we come now, for the church is not only to look inward and find joy, to look Christward and find sanctification, to look to the Scriptures and find truth. The church is also to look outward to the world and there find the object of her God-given *mission*. Moreover, it is for this (at least in part) that the other marks of the church are given.

In the World

Our text talks about mission, and the first thing it tells us about that mission is where it is to be conducted. The word "mission" comes from the Latin verb *mitto, mittere, misi, missum,* which means "to send" or "dispatch." A mission is a sending forth. But as soon as we know that we want to ask, "But to whom is the church sent? Where are we sent as Christian missionaries?" The answer is, into the world. Jesus says clearly, "As you sent me *into the world,* I have sent them *into the world*" (v. 18).

Here is why the evangelical church in America is not as much of a missionary church as it claims to be. We are not saying that the evangelical church does not support foreign missions. In fact, it has probably picked this task up at precisely the point at which the liberal denominations have been dropping it. The problem does not lie there. Rather it lies at the point of the evangelicals' personal withdrawal from the culture. Many seem afraid of their culture. Hence, they try to keep as far from the world as possible lest they be contaminated or polluted by it. They have developed their own subculture. As some Bible teachers have pointed out, it is possible, for example, to be born of Christian parents, grow up in that Christian family, have Christian friends, go to Christian schools and colleges, read Christian books, attend a Christian country club (known as a church), watch Christian movies, get Christian employment, be attended by a Christian doctor, and finally, one may suppose, die and be buried by a Christian undertaker on holy ground. But this is certainly not what Jesus meant when he spoke of his followers being "in the world."

What does it mean to be in the world as a Christian? It does not mean to be like the world; the marks of the church are to make the church different. It does not mean that we are to abandon Christian fellowship or our other basic Christian orientations. All it means is that we are to know non-Christians, befriend them, and enter into their lives in such a way that we begin to infect them with the gospel, rather than their infecting us with their worldliness, which is the wrong way around.

Many years ago now a young pastor in the Central American country of Guatemala went from seminary to a remote mountain area of the country known as Cabrican. Cabrican was unpopular, for it was located at an altitude of about 9,000 feet and consequently was nearly always damp and bone-piercing cold. The church he went to pastor was small, having only twenty-eight members, including two elders and two women deacons. These believers met together on most nights of the week, but they were not growing as a congregation. There was no outreach. So in his first messages to them the young pastor, whose name was Bernardo Calderon, said, "I know God cannot be satisfied with what we are doing." Then he challenged them to this program.

First, they abandoned all the many, dull meetings at the church, retaining only the Bible school hour on Sunday. In their place, home meetings were established. On Monday night they would meet in a home in one area of Cabrican, and all the believers would be invited. Moreover, as they made their way to this home they were to invite everyone they encountered, including those they passed on the streets. Since they came from different areas of the city and took different paths to get there this meant that quite a bit of the city was covered. On Tuesday night another home was chosen, and the same method was followed. Only this time, naturally, different paths were used as the twenty-eight members converged; different villagers were invited. So it was on Wednesday and Thursday and the other days of the week, as the church literally left its four small walls to go into the world with the gospel. Within four years that church had eight hundred members. Moreover, the next year a branch church was started, and within a few more years there were six churches in that area of Guatemala, two of which had nearly one thousand members. There was even an agricultural cooperative in which church members buy land for their own poor and buy and sell the produce their own people supply.

The other story is also of a mission to the world in Guatemala, told to me by Mardoqueo Munos of the Central Church in Guatemala City. A young pastor went to the country's coastal plains, where the people are literally worked to death during the eleven months of the year that are the growing season, but where they have one month with nearly nothing to do between the end of one growing season and the beginning of the next. This church decided to use this month for evangelism.

Some time before the beginning of this period each year, teams of two or three people would be sent out into neighboring villages to investigate the state of the Christian witness in those villages. If the town had a strong church, they reported that it was taken care of. If not, they recommended it as one village to which their church could take the gospel. From these reports one village was selected. Then when the month of vacation came the entire mother church—pastor, elders, deacons, Sunday school teachers, husbands, wives, children, everyone—simply moved to the area of the target village and set up housekeeping. For the next weeks the members went from door to door throughout the entire village witnessing; the elders and deacons sought out a piece of property on which a church could be erected and bought it; the young people went to the nearby rain forests to cut down trees from which a simple church could be constructed. Finally, they placed their converts in the new church, commissioned the most promising convert as pastor, and then went home leaving the new church to disciple its members and multiply its witness on its own. Unorthodox? Yes, even for Guatemala! But it was a successful strategy for that area. For in the eleven years that the young pastor has been in the plains area, eleven churches have been established; and some, including the mother church, have grown to nearly 1,000 members.

The point I am making is that these two churches were not content to carry on in a Christian subculture but rather knew that their mission was the world and that they were in the world to carry out that mission. For us this may simply mean getting to know our neighbors better or infiltrating those with whom we work with the gospel. Again it may mean a whole new approach to our church's outreach or that of our denomination.

To Be As Christ

The second thing the text talks about is the nature or character of the ones who are to conduct this mission, which means our nature or character as Christian people. The point here is that we are to be *as Christ* in the world. This is made clear in verses 18 and 19, for Jesus compares the disciples to himself both in the area of his having been sent into the world by the Father and of his being sanctified or set apart totally to that work. He says, "*As* you sent me into the world, I have sent them into the world. For them I sanctify myself, that *they too* may be truly sanctified." In other words, we are to be in our mission as Jesus was in his mission. We are to be like the One whom we are presenting.

Here may be our second problem as far as the mission of the evangelical church is concerned. Let me illustrate by another story told by Ralph Keiper. Quite a few years ago, before Weight Watchers, there was a product for those who were overweight called "Weight Right," and Mrs. Keiper was trying to sell it. She was not successful. On one occasion she came to her husband and asked, "Darling, why do you think I'm not able to sell this product?"

Keiper looked at it. He saw that it was well packaged; in fact, it was very attractive. He said, "Let me hear your speech." This was good too, for Mrs. Keiper was filled with enthusiasm. "May I see the brochure?" he asked. She gave it to him, and as he was looking at it he said, "Oh, oh!"

"Why are you saying 'Oh, oh!' at a time like this?" she asked. He said, "Shall I be polite or truthful?"

"Truthful, of course."

"Well, dear," Keiper answered, "you look like the picture before, not the picture after."

Perhaps that is our problem. We are tying to sell a product, but although the product is excellent and our pitch may be well done, the world can see that we are not using what we are selling. If we were, we would be more like Jesus. Are you like Jesus? Are you as he was in this world?

Perhaps you are saying, "I do not know if I am like Jesus or not. In what areas should I be like him?" Obviously we are to be like him in every way. But in trying to answer briefly we can hardly do better than point out that we are to be like him in precisely these marks of the church that he is citing. Earlier I pointed out that Jesus is our pattern in each case. Certainly we need to remember that here. In other words, as his life was characterized by joy, so is our life to be characterized by joy. As he was sanctified, so are we to be sanctified. As he was characterized by truth, so are we to be. So also are we to be united, as his body on earth, and to be filled with his love both to one another and to a perishing world.

We can readily see how each of these characteristics is important. First, there is joy. This is important because, if we do not have joy, we can hardly commend the "good news" of salvation to anyone. Someone once said to Hannah Whitall Smith, author of *The Christian's Secret of a Happy Life,* "You Christians seem to have a religion that makes you miserable. You are like a man with a headache. He does not want to get rid of his head, but it hurts him to keep it. You cannot expect outsiders to seek very earnestly for anything so uncomfortable."[1] This is true. So rather than being miserable all the time, we ought to find ourselves becoming increasingly like Jesus who, I am convinced, was the best of company and a joy to be with. Moreover, our joy should be contageous and unending. A former archbishop of Canterbury, Geoffrey Fisher, is reported to have said just before he died, "The longer I live the more convinced I am that Christianity is one long shout of joy."

Second, we must have holiness or sanctification. In fact, it is this that Jesus most emphasizes in our text. He says, "For them I sanctify myself, that they too may be truly sanctified" (v. 19). In what sense was Jesus sanctified? As we saw earlier, he was sanctified in the sense of being set apart totally for the work God had given him to do, the work of dying for our salvation. The parallel in our case is to be set apart totally for the work we have been given to do, which is the work of carrying the gospel of the crucified but risen Christ to all men everywhere. If we do not do this, or if we are halfhearted about it, the world will know it and will hardly consider our message to be earth-shattering.

The third area is truth, by which we are concerned both with our message and with our wholehearted commitment to it as a way of life. Jesus was committed to the truth of God and he was "the truth" (John 14:6). In the same way, we should be based firmly upon this rock and should live by it to such a degree that the world will point to us and say, "Those people are certainly characterized by the truth they claim to preach."

If this is not the case, we will not win anyone, for the world will hardly be attracted to a church that does not seem to know even its own mind on religious matters. There was once an essay by Leo Rosten in the *Saturday Review and World,* in which Rosten quoted a number of revealing statistics (July 12, 1976). A recent poll had shown that 75 percent of the American people think that "religion is losing its influence." Another showed that only 50 percent of Roman Catholics attend church during an average week, a significant drop. Only 37 percent of Protestants attend. The Protestant figure used to be up around 50 percent. Then, having given a few more statistics such as this, Rosten declared, "I cannot help concluding that the fortresses of faith are experiencing the most profound alterations in centuries.

Church authority is being challenged on a dozen fronts. . . . It is not hyperbole to say that we are witnessing a remarkable erosion of consensus within the citadel of belief." That is true, of course, so we are hardly surprised to learn that the churches are losing members and that the church's missionary effort is being increasingly curtailed.

Next, we are to be like the Lord Jesus Christ in our unity. In fact, this is precisely the way in which Jesus introduces the subject in the next verses of the prayer, for he goes on to pray, "that all of them may be one, Father, just as you are in me and I am in you. May they also be in us so that the world may believe that you have sent me" (v. 21). The world is fractured in a million ways. It is the logical outcome of the work of Satan, one of whose most revealing names is the disrupter *(diabolos)*. If Christians would win the world, they must show a genuine unity that is in itself desirable and winsome and that at the same time points to the unity within the Godhead, which is its source.

Finally, the church must be marked by love, if it is to be as Christ in the world. Jesus loved the world. It was out of love for it that he died. Consequently, if we would win the world, we must love the world too—not the world's system or sin, of course, but rather those who are in it.

Once my family was eating in a restaurant, and my youngest daughter knocked over her glass of coke for about the thousandth time. I was visibly annoyed as I always was (since we never seemed to get through a meal without the identical accident). But we cleaned up and shortly after that left the restaurant. My daughter walked along in silence for a while; but then she said, "You really hate it when we spill our cokes, don't you?" I replied that I certainly did. She looked serious, but then she brightened up as if a particularly happy thought had just passed through her mind. She threw her arms around me in a big hug and added, "But you *love* me!"

She knew the difference between love of the sinner and hatred of the sin. And so will we if we look to Jesus. We must be like him in love, knowing that if we are, the world will see it and be drawn to him.

Drawn by God

How will they be drawn? By God, of course, for however much and however carefully we strive to actually show forth the character of the Lord Jesus Christ in the world, it is still he and not we ourselves who must move men and women to turn to him for salvation. The description of the early church in Jerusalem, recorded in Acts 2, gives us an indication of this, for having told us that these early believers "devoted themselves to the apostles' teaching [that is, the truth] and to the fellowship [that is, unity], to the breaking of bread and to prayer [which suggests true worship leading to sanctification or holiness]" and "selling their possessions and goods, they gave to anyone as he had need [an evidence of their deep and unique love] and that "every day they continued to meet together in the temple courts.

They broke bread in their homes and ate together with glad and sincere hearts, praising God and enjoying the favor of all the people," it adds as a result, "the Lord added to their number daily those who were being saved" (Acts 2:42, 45–47). The Lord did it! And he will do it for us as we accept that task for which we have been sent into the world and live like him.

218

The Fifth Mark of the Church: Unity

John 17:20–23

"My prayer is not for them alone. I pray also for those who will believe in me through their message, that all of them may be one, Father, just as you are in me and I am in you. May they also be in us so that the world may believe that you have sent me. I have given them the glory that you gave me, that they may be one as we are one: I in them and you in me. May they be brought to complete unity to let the world know that you sent me and have loved them even as you have loved me."

Considering all the divisions that have plagued Christendom for two thousand years, it is amazing that God has continued to use the church to extend his kingdom."[1]

This statement by John White, an InterVarsity Chrisitian Fellowship worker and writer, introduces us to the subject of Christian unity in two important ways: first, by portraying the unfortunate lack of unity that has plagued the church throughout its history and, second, by suggesting why Jesus asked that the church might be marked by unity at this particular point in his high priestly petition. The divisions that exist today are too obvious to need comment. They lie both on the surface and within. Battles rage. Highly praised church mergers not only fail to heal these divisions but also usually lead to further breakups involving those who do not like the new union. So far as Christ's reasons for praying for unity go, it is simply that he foresaw these differences and so asked for that great unity that should exist among his own in spite of them.

Another way of pointing to Christ's interests is to note that all the marks of the church concern the Christian's relationship to some thing or some person and that unity is to be the mark of the church in the relationships that exist between its members. Joy is the mark of the Christian in relationship to himself. Holiness is the mark in relationship to God. Truth is the mark in his relationship to the Bible. Mission is the mark in his relationship to the world. In this mark, unity, and the last, love, which in some sense summarizes them all, we deal with the Christian's relationship to all who are likewise God's children.

What Kind of Unity?

But what kind of unity is this to be? This is an important preliminary question, for if the unity is to be an organizational unity, then our efforts to achieve and express it will be in one direction while, if it is to be a more subjective unity, our efforts will be expended differently.

One thing for sure—the church is not to be is a great *organizational unity;* for whatever advantages or disadvantages may be involved in massive organizational unity, this in itself obviously does not produce the results Christ prayed for, nor does it solve the church's other great problems. Moreover, it has been tried and found wanting. In the early days of the church there was much vitality and growth but little organizational unity. Later, as the church came to favor under Constantine and his successors, the church increasingly centralized until during the Middle Ages there was literally one united ecclesiastical body covering all Europe. But was this a great age? Was there a deep unity of faith? Did men and women find themselves increasingly drawn to this faith and come to confess Jesus Christ to be their Savior and Lord (for that is what Christ promised, namely, that if the church were one, men and women would believe on him)? Not at all! On the contrary, the world believed the opposite. Spurgeon once wrote, "The world was persuaded that God had nothing to do with that great crushing, tyrannous, superstitious, ignorant thing which called itself Christianity; and thinking men became infidels, and it was the hardest possible thing to find a genuine intelligent believer north, south, east, or west."[2]

Certainly there is something to be said for some form of outward, visible unity (at least in most situations). But it is equally certain that this type of unity is not what we most need, nor is it that for which the Lord prayed.

Another type of unity that we do not need is *conformity,* that is, an approach to the church that would make everyone alike. Here we probably come closest to the error of the evangelical church, for if the liberal church for the most part strives for an organizational unity—through the various councils of churches, the Consultation on Church Union, denominational mergers, and so forth—the evangelical church for its part seems to strive for an identical pattern of looks and behavior among its members. This is not what Jesus is looking for in this prayer. On the contrary, there should be the greatest diversity among Christians, diversity of personality, interests, lifestyle, and even methods of Christian work and evangelism. This should make the church interesting, not dull. Uniformity is dull, like rows upon rows of Wheaties boxes. Variety is exciting! It is the variety of nature and the character and actions of our God.

But if the unity for which Jesus prayed is not an organizational unity or a unity achieved by conformity, what kind of unity is it? The answer is that it is a unity parallel to the unity that exists within the Godhead; for Jesus speaks of it in these terms—"that all of them may be one, Father, just as you are in me and I am in you . . . I in them, and you in me. May they be brought to complete unity" (vv. 21, 23). This means that the church is to have a spiritual unity involving the basic orientation, desires, and will of those participating. Paul points to this true unity in writing to the Corinthians, saying, "There are different kinds of gifts, but the same Spirit. There are different kinds of service, but the same Lord. There are different kinds of working, but the same God works all of them in all men" (1 Cor. 12:4–6).

This is not to say that all believers actually enter into this unity as they should. Otherwise, why would Christ pray for it? The actual case is that, like the other marks of the church already considered, unity is something given to the church but also something for which the body of true believers should strive. There is a sense in which we already are one in Christ. But there is also a sense in which we must achieve that unity.

Brothers and Sisters

Here we are helped by the various images used of the church throughout the New Testament, one of the most valuable being that of the family. Christians belong to the family of God, and therefore they are rightly brothers and sisters of one another.

The unique characteristic of this image is that it speaks of relationships and therefore of the commitments that the individuals must have to one another. The relationships are based upon what God has done. Salvation is described in the verses that use this image as God begetting spiritual children, who are therefore made members of his spiritual family through his choice and not through their own. John even says this explicitly in the preface to his Gospel, when he writes of our having become children of God "not of natural descent, nor of human decision or a husband's will, but born of God" (1:13). There is a tendency in the world to talk about all men and women as brothers and sisters, but while this is true in a certain humanitarian sense it is nevertheless not what the Bible is talking about when it speaks of Christian brotherhood. This is something that God has intervened to establish among his own regenerated children.

This fact has two important consequences. First, if the family to which we belong has been established by God, then we have no choice as to who will be in it or whether or not we will be his or her sister or brother. On the contrary, the relationship simply exists, and we must be brotherly to the other Christian, whether we want to be or not.

The second consequence is related to this, simply that we must be committed to each other in tangible ways. We must be committed to helping each other, for example, for we all need help at times, and this is one clear way in which the special bond among believers can be shown to the watching world. A number of years ago I walked into the bathroom in our home and found one of my children sitting on the floor with a large pile of unrolled toilet paper beside her. She had been spinning the roll and watching it pile up in intricate patterned layers as it settled. I took one look at her and said, with a note of astonishment in my voice, "What in the world are you doing?"

"I'm unrolling the toilet paper," she answered. There was no questioning the truthfulness of that.

"Why are you being naughty?" I countered.

She said, "Nobody helps me to be good." I suspect that her answer was a carefully worded excuse (and also not nearly so truthful as her first statement.) But whatever her reasons, the statement did at least point to a true need. We do need help as Christians, and we need it from Christians. Moreover, we must be ready to give help, just as we would to a needy member of our own human family.

A Fellowship

The second important image used to portray the unity of the church of Christ is a fellowship, which the New Testament normally indicates by the Greek word *koinonia*. Unfortunately, neither the word "fellowship" nor the word *koinonia* is very helpful in conveying what we mean. This is because the English word commonly means only a loose collection of friends, and the Greek word has become something of a theological cliché. Actually, the word has to do with sharing something or having something in common. The common Greek of the New Testament period is called Koine Greek. Partners, as those who hold property in common or share in a business, are *koinonoi*. In spiritual terms *koinonia*, or fellowship, is had by those who share a common Christian experience of the gospel. In this respect the New Testament speaks often of our fellowship with the Father (1 John 1:3), with the Son (1 Cor. 1:9), which is sometimes described as a fellowship in the blood and body of Christ (1 Cor. 10:16), and with the Holy Spirit (2 Cor. 13:14). This obviously involves the totality of our experience of God's grace.

But fellowship is not only defined in terms of what we share *in* together. It also involves what we share *out* together. And this means that it must involve a community in which Christians actually share their thoughts and lives with one another.

How is this to be done practically? It will probably be done in different ways in different congregations depending upon local situations and needs.

Some churches are small and therefore will have an easier time establishing times of sharing. Here church suppers, work projects, and other such efforts will help. Larger churches will have to break their numbers down into smaller groups in various ways. At Tenth Presbyterian Church in Philadelphia, which I serve as pastor, we have tried to do this in three ways simultaneously. First, we have tried to divide the congregation according to age levels. Thus we have a fully graded Sunday school, and on the upper levels we have tried to establish groups for college students, postcollege students, young couples, other adult classes, and meetings for senior citizens. Part of this is an adult elective program. Second, we have tried to divide the congregation geographically. Tenth Church members come from a large and scattered metropolitan area. Some of them drive twenty, thirty, or more miles to get there. Midweek meetings at the church are impractical for most. Therefore we have established area Bible studies, where people can meet weekly with those in their area. They meet to study the Bible, share concerns, and pray together. These area groups are probably the least structured but also the most profitable of all the church activities. Finally, we have also begun to divide the church according to professional interests. In this area there are regular meetings by groups of artists, musicians (we have a chamber orchestra), medical students and nurses, and ministerial candidates and young pastors.

My own experience in this area conforms to that of John R. W. Stott, who experimented with similar groups in his own London parish. He has written on the grounds of his experience, "The value of the small group is that it can become a community of related persons; and in it the benefit of personal relatedness cannot be missed, nor its challenge evaded. . . . I do not think it is an exaggeration to say, therefore, that small groups, Christian family or fellowship groups, are indispensable for our growth into spiritual maturity."[3]

Once again, this is an area in which Christian unity can become a visible and practical thing, and its unique and desirable qualities can be made known to the world.

The Body

The third important image used to stress the unity of the church is the body. Clearly, this image has many important connotations. It speaks of the nature of the Christian union—one part of the body simply cannot survive if it is separated from the whole. It speaks of interdependence. It even suggests a kind of subordination involving a diversity of function; for the hand is not the foot, nor the foot the eye, and over all is the head which is Christ. Paul speaks of this in 1 Corinthians saying, "The body is a unit, though it is made up of many parts; and though all its parts are many, they form one body. So it is with Christ. For we were all baptized by one Spirit into one body—whether Jews or Greeks, slave or free—and we were all given the one Spirit to drink. Now the body is not made up of one part but of many" (12:12–14).

However, the one function of the body that is unique to this image is service, for just as the family emphasizes relationships, and fellowships emphasizes sharing, so does the body emphasize work. The body exists to do something and, since we are talking about unity, we must stress that it exists to enable us to do this work *together.*

In the book from which I quoted earlier, Stott speaks of this service flowing out of the small groups that his church emphasizes. "It must be admitted that several have been unsuccessful—through lack of time or of enterprise," he writes. "Others, however, have offered their practical services as a group. . . . Certainly without some such common concern and service, the fellowship of any Christian group is maimed."[4]

Your Part

The question we end with is simply: What is to be your part in this area? What will you do? Obviously you cannot change the whole church, but, as one writer puts it, "You can begin in your own life to be an answer to the high priestly prayer of Christ. You can become a small focus of change."[5] First, you can become aware of that great family, fellowship, and body to which you already belong, and you can thank God for it. Second, you can join a small group, where the reality of Christian unity is most readily seen and experienced. Third, you can work with that group to show forth Christian love and give service. If you are willing to do that, you will find God to be with you, and you will be overwhelmed at the power with which he works both in you and in others whom he will be drawing to faith.

But perhaps you are not a part of that family, the family of God, in the first place. You may be a Baptist, a Presbyterian, a Roman Catholic, a Pentecostal. But you have never been born into God's family. If so, do not let pride of denomination (or of anything else) keep you from the reality of Christianity. Run to Jesus and enter in through him, the only true door.

219

Impartial Love

John 17:23

"I in them and you in me. May they be brought to complete unity to let the world know that you sent me and have loved them even as you have loved me."

We pause in our study of the marks of the church presented in John 17 to deal with a most extraordinary sentence. The sentence is the last part of verse 23: "You . . . have loved them even as you have loved me." It means that God's love for us is in the same measure and is exercised in the same way as his love for Christ. There have been attempts to avoid this meaning, no doubt because it is so tremendous. Some have treated the sentence casually, as though it were saying, "You have loved them *because* you love me." Others have seen it in terms of the mystical union of believers with Christ, as though we are loved as Christ only because we are actually in Christ. These statements are true, but they miss the full force of the sentence because they do not take the key word at full value. That word is *kathōs,* which means "just as" or "to the same degree that." Thus, we are told that God loves those who are Christ's to the same degree and in the same way that he loves Christ.

This is extraordinary, for none of us loves like that, and even though it is true that God can love like that, to claim that he does would be presumptuous and arrogant were it not that he himself tells us so in these verses. Actually our love is quite partial. It is partial in our preference for our friends over against those who are not our friends. It is usually partial in preference for our family over our friends. There is even partiality within the family, for if we were to ask those who are parents about their love for their children, most would admit that while they try to be impartial and in many cases almost succeed in being impartial, nevertheless they do not love each of their children equally. Perhaps it is the grace and accommodating ways of one child in comparison to the other children. It may be the drive and natural ability of another child. It may be some other characteristic. Something causes us to love the one slightly more than the other or at least be more naturally drawn toward that one. But God, we are told, has no favorites and thus loves us with the same love that he loves his own Son. God does not love one of his children more than he loves the others.

The Scope of God's Love

We see the nature of this in the love of the Father for Jesus. So we naturally turn to it and ask, "But what is this love like? What is the scope of the Father's love for Jesus?"

The first answer to this question is that God's love is *infinite*. God is infinite; therefore, he is infinite in this as in all his other attributes. This means that there are no limits on God's love. We always have limits, even though we sometimes pretend we do not. In *A Place for You* by the Swiss psychologist Paul Tournier, I came across a story from the experience of Tournier that is helpful in this area. A woman had come to see him for the first time. She had hesitated for several years before coming, but she had come at last. Now the time had come for her to leave. Her home was far away, and it would be some time before she could come again. She stood at the door obviously reluctant to go. After a pause she asked, "Can I at any rate write to you?"

"Of course," Tournier answered.

There was a further silence. Then she said, "May I write often?"

Tournier's response was, "There is no limit!" The Swiss psychologist indicates that as he said this he spoke in a somewhat extravagant tone as if to indicate that, although he would certainly do everything in his power to help this patient, he was aware (as she was also) that he did have limits and that no one but God could actually provide this limitless support.[1]

But God does supply it. This is Tournier's point and the point of Christ's statement in his high priestly prayer. Can we imagine any limits on the Father's love for the Lord Jesus Christ? Can we imagine him saying, "Well, it is true that I love you, but after all there are limits upon everything and at this particular point even I must draw the line"? Can we picture him saying, "I'll help later, but don't bother me now; I'm busy"? Of course not! No limits are to be placed upon the Father's love for the Son or upon the love of the Son for the Father. So then, in precisely the same way, no limits are to be placed upon the Father's love for us. We can go to him at any time with any need and know that he stands as ready to help us as he did to help the

Lord Jesus Christ in Gethsemane. He is as close to us as to Jesus, whether or not we know it or feel it practically.

Second, the love of the Father for the Lord Jesus Christ is *eternal* which is, we must note, not the same thing as being infinite. An infinite love is, as we said, a love without limits. An eternal love is a love without end. Can we think of the Father ceasing to love Jesus Christ, his beloved? Can we think of the infinite affection that existed between the first and second persons of the Godhead from eternity past up to and including the present time suddenly ceasing? Far better to imagine the dissolution of the universe we know, far better to say as did Othello, "Chaos is come again," than to imagine such an impossible possibility. God's love for Christ will not cease. Therefore, his love for us will not cease. It will not cease because of changes in him, for he does not change: "I am the LORD, I do not change" (Mal. 3:6). It will not cease because of changes in us, for God has foreseen all change. Indeed, he has ordained that the overriding and ultimately prevailing change shall be, not our conformity to sin, but rather our conformity to the image of his own dear Son: "For those God foreknow, he also predestined to be conformed to the likeness of his Son, that he might be the firstborn among many brothers" (Rom. 8:29).

The consequence of this is that nothing, not even sin, can separate us from God's love. As the passage in Romans goes on to say, "Neither death nor life, neither angels nor demons, neither the present nor the future, nor any powers, neither height nor depth, nor anything else in all creation, will be able to separate us from the love of God that is in Christ Jesus our Lord" (8:38–39).

The third characteristic of the love of God the Father for Christ is perfection. His is a *perfect* love. Consequently, his love for us is perfection as well. We do not love perfectly, as we well know. That is why marriages break up, friendships dissolve, children so often rebel against parental authority. It is not always that we cease to love. It is rather that we do not love well. We overindulge, or we do not give of ourselves, or we act inconsistently. Sometimes we spoil a child through love; we give him or her too much. Sometimes we do not give enough; so the child spends a lifetime trying to find what he should have found at home but did not get there. Again, we say we will do something, but then we fail to do it. This is the nature of our love, but it is not the nature of God's love. He loves perfectly with a wisdom and consistency that has only our best at heart.

If we believe that—if we believe that God loves us with the same perfection of love he has shown to Jesus Christ—then we will not be gripers because plans do not turn out the way we would like them to. We will not be despondent because of some undesirable circumstances. On the contrary, we will be encouraged, knowing that indeed "in all things God works for the good of those who love him, who have been called according to his purpose" (Rom. 8:28).

Does God So Love?

Is it really the case that God loves us like this? Can we really believe that we are loved with that same infinite, eternal, and perfect love with which God the Father loves the Lord Jesus Christ? Is there evidence that we are really beneficiaries of so great a love?

The answer, as any Christian knows, is yes. And the proof of it is not some abstract reasoning in regard to God's nature, but rather the historical manifestation of God's love at Calvary. How do we know that God loves us with such a great love? John 3:16 gives the answer, "For God so loved the world that he gave his one and only Son, that whoever believes in him should not perish but have eternal life." We know that God loves with the greatest of all loves because of the supreme gift of his Son to die for us on Calvary. I have frequently said that it is almost impossible to find a verse in the Bible that speaks of God's love without finding that it also speaks (in the context, if not in the very verse itself) of the proof of that love by Christ's death for us. Galatians 2:20—" I have been crucified with Christ, and I no longer live, but Christ lives in me. The life I live in the body, I live by the faith in the Son of God, who loved me and gave himself for me." First John 4:10—"This is love: not that we loved God, but that he loved us and sent his Son as an atoning sacrifice for our sins."

How do we know that God loves us? We know because God sent Jesus; and the reason God sent him is that he might die for us. It is on this basis that God even commends his love to us. For "God demonstrates his love for us in this: While we were still sinners, Christ died for us" (Rom. 5:8).

Security

At this point we must turn to the consequences of such love. What are they? First and most important, such love gives us great security. Love should always give security, a security that is either greater or less depending upon the quality of the love supporting it. Husbands need support from their wives. Wives need support from their husbands. Children obviously need the support of their parents. But often this security is lacking because the love that should support it is lacking. Insecurity results.

By contrast, we have great security in God's love. For one thing, we have security as we look toward the future, to the day of judgment. This, I am convinced, is the meaning of that exceedingly simple (but often puzzling) statement in 1 John 4:17—"In this world we are like him." So far as words go, the sentence could hardly be simpler. It is composed of only seven words. All are monosyllables—"In this world we are like him." But what does this mean? Does it involve obligation, as though it said, "In this world we *ought to be* like him"? Can it refer to the future, as though it could mean, "*We will be* like him when we depart from this world"? No, it obviously refers to life now. Can it refer to some actual moral perfection? The answer is that it refers to our stance before God in view of the final judgment, for that is what is being talked about in the context. The verse reads, "In this way, love is made complete among us so that we will have confidence on the day of judgment, because in this world we are like him (v. 18).

Because of the identity of the love of God for Christ and the love of God for me, my relationship to the final judgment is the same as his. Will Jesus be judged? Will he be forced to give an account of the sins laid upon him as he hung upon the cross? Of course not! He bore our sins in order that they might be judged once for all and be removed from him and us forever. Then we shall not be judged for those sins either. "There is now no condemnation for those who are in Christ Jesus" (Rom. 8:1).

But perhaps you are thinking that this is all a bit too remote. It refers to future events, to the events of God's judgment, and what you are concerned about is life now. Is there security now because of God's love? Yes, there is, in precisely the same sense that there is security for a child in a parent's love, though the child may grow up and move far from home. Or, to give an illustration, it is the security of a seaman who fixes his course by the North Star, knowing that this star, in contrast to all other stars, is not variable. One hymn writer wrote:

> O love of God, our shield and stay
> Through all the perils of our way!
> Eternal love, in thee we rest,
> For ever safe, for ever blest.

Tournier had been counseling a woman who had come back, after a period of several weeks, around the Christmas holidays. "The nail has held," she said as she came in.

"What nail?" asked the Swiss doctor.

"The nail I am hanging on," she explained. "I feel like a picture hanging on a wall. If the nail comes out, the picture falls. My nail was this appointment that you gave me for just after my holidays." The holidays, as Tournier knew, were always difficult times for her. She always approached them in fear that they would be times in which her problems would emerge once more. So she said, "All the time during the holidays I have been watching the nail so as to hold on, and everything went all right." She added, "I don't feel at all that I am hanging on you emotionally; I hang on you existentially."[2]

The love of God is that upon which we can hang. Indeed, we can hang upon it existentially and emotionally and in every other way as well, knowing that it will not budge, even though the wall and everything else in heaven and earth should be shaken. I will be even more graphic. That nail is the nail (or nails) placed through the hands of Christ on the cross; for they are the proof of God's love, the only fixed point in a revolving and chaotic universe.

Love for Others

There is one more consequence of the truth that God loves us as he loves his Son. It is that we should love others and that we should love them, as best we can, impartially. We must not pick whom we will love for Christ's sake. We must not love with an angle. We are not infinite. We will not be able to love everyone with an inexhaustible love. We will not love perfectly. But, God helping us, we can love impartially in the sense that we can love the unlovely for Jesus' sake.

I have been amused by a story along these lines told by Ralph Keiper. Keiper had become a Christian in his senior year of high school, in part through 2 Corinthians 5:17, which says, "If anyone is in Christ, he is a new creation; the old is gone, the new has come!" Having become a new creature he immediately began meditating on the second half of the verse, which says, "the old is gone," because he had a problem in the person of his geometry teacher and sincerely wished that *she* would pass away, which she did not. He says, "She was a witch, the kind of person to whom on Halloween you would give a broom and say, 'This is your night, kid; do your stuff!'" At last the problem drove him to its solution, because he recognized that the new creature of the verse was to be himself and not his teacher, and that the things which were to pass away were his own old attitudes. Recognizing that he was to be like Jesus Christ, he came to the conclusion that if God could endure his teacher then perhaps he could too. He could even love her for Christ's sake. With this attitude he not only finished the course; he even went on to study trigonometry.

God has loved us greatly even as he has loved Christ. But the matter does not stop at that point. It is not meant to. True, the Father has loved us as he loves Christ, but he has loved us so that, as one result, we might love as Christ. If we do, we will become one among ourselves and then by God's grace also win those for whom Christ also died.

220

With Jesus Forever

John 17:24

"Father, I want those you have given me to be with me where I am, and to see my glory, the glory you have given me because you loved me before the creation of the world."

I once talked to a Christian woman who was dying. She had cancer, which by then had spread throughout her body, and as she talked to me about her condition she described her physical state as "sinking." She was sinking physically. But as we spoke of spiritual things we reminded ourselves that such sinking, though painful and difficult, is actually ascending into the presence of God.

I was reminded of a paragraph I had recently read in *Blind Ambition,* John Dean's book on his White House years, for it made a great contrast. Dean had written of his rise to positions of increasingly greater prestige and power in the White House, but he pointed out that, unknown to him at the time, it was actually a descent to corruption and eventual crimes. He wrote, "I soon learned that to make my way upward, into a position of confidence and influence, I had to travel downward through factional power plays, corruption and finally outright crimes. Although I would be rewarded for diligence, true advancement would come from doing those things which built a common bond of trust—or guilt—between me and my superiors. In the Nixon White House, these upward and downward paths diverged, yet joined, like prongs of a tuning fork pitched to a note of expediency. Slowly, steadily, I would climb toward the moral abyss of the President's inner circle until I finally fell into it, thinking I had made it to the top just as I began to realize I had actually touched bottom."[1]

In this assessment of his political career, Dean was not talking about death, but he might well have been; for what he was describing in regard to political or secular morals is true as well of every part of a life that is not linked to God. Millions spend a lifetime striving to arrive at positions of great influence and power, only to find that everything they have worked for is taken away by death. By contrast, a Christian may actually bury himself or herself in God's service, having no outward earthly rewards, and in the end pass through death in obscurity. Yet that burial is actually a resurrection. And that sinking is actually an ascension into the presence of the Lord of life forever.

Triumph, Not Tragedy

Why is the experience of a Christian so different from that of a non-Christian at this point? It is not because of something meritorious in the Christian, of course. Still less is it due to some intrinsic change in him. The difference is to be found only in the will of God, who has decreed that the death of a Christian shall not be a tragedy, but a triumph.

This is declared many places in Scripture, as anyone who knows the Bible well is aware. Paul spoke of his willingness "to be away from the body and [thus] at home with the Lord" (2 Cor. 5:8). He called death "gain" (Phil. 1:21). He shared his indecision as to whether he most wanted to remain on earth to serve other believers or "to depart and to be with Christ, which is better by far" (Phil. 1:23). In Romans he wrote of nothing being able to separate us from God's love (Rom. 8:35–39). In the Old Testament Job spoke with this confidence, saying, "For I know that my Redeemer lives, and that in the end he will stand upon the earth. And after my skin has been destroyed, yet in my flesh I will see God; I myself will see him with my own eyes—I, and not another" (Job 19:25–27). John 17 moves in this same sphere of triumph, for in it Jesus declares his will that all who have been given to him by the Father be with him in glory after both his and their passage through this life: "Father, I want those you have given me to be with me where I am and to see my glory, the glory you have given me because you loved me before the creation of the world" (v. 24).

Here then is an important fact. The triumph of a believer in death is often spoken of in Scripture. But in this verse it receives, as it were, its only proper foundation and true emphasis. Its foundation is seen in that it is based on the express will of God the Son and God the Father (for their wills are one). Its emphasis is seen in that this is the last of Jesus' great petitions to the Father just before his crucifixion. The last thing he asks—indeed, the last thing he wills—is that we might be with him where he is.

Where Jesus Is

Let us think about where Jesus is. Can there be doubt about Christ's meaning? I hardly think so; yet there may be in some minds, due to the fact that he speaks in the present tense ("where I am") rather than in the future ("where I will be"), which we would use if we were thinking of heaven. Does he mean "where I am now," that is, in the upper room or on the outskirts of Jerusalem on the way to the Garden of Gethsemane—depending upon where one imagines this prayer to have been given? No, because if this were the case, there would be no need for Christ so to pray; the disciples were already with him. Besides, in this section of the prayer he is thinking, not just of the disciples, but also of those who would later believe on him through their witness.

So Jesus is not thinking of where he then was but of where he was soon to be, and he is thinking in such confident terms that he actually uses the present tense to express this confidence. In other words, he is so certain that he is soon to be once again in heaven with the Father that he speaks as though it has already occurred, just as he also does in verse 11, where he prays, "I will remain in the world no longer, but they are still in the world, and I am coming to you." Clearly, in both these verses he means that he is about to leave this world and thereby return to glory.

That is precisely where Christ is at this moment. How do we know? We know because of his own statements, of course. But in addition to that we have the fact of the ascension, witnessed by the disciples and testified to by the angels—"Men of Galilee, why do you stand here looking into the sky? This same Jesus, who has been taken from you into heaven, will come back in the same way you have seen him go into heaven" (Acts 1:11). We also have the visions of Christ in glory—seen by Stephen (recorded in Acts 7) and by John (recorded in Revelation).

Of all the pictures of heaven given to us in the Bible, I like the picture in the fifth chapter of Revelation best. However, I know as I read it that the words obviously do not convey the full glory of that place. They talk about a throne upon which God the Father is seated. They speak of the Son, described as a Lamb. There are angels and elders and an additional great host, all of whom are engaged in singing the praises of Jesus Christ. There are harps and bowls of incense. There is a scroll of prophecy that no one but the Son of God can open. But these are images designed to portray something beyond our wildest imagination. Or again, even if they are meant to be literal, they still obviously do not convey the full glory of heaven.

Are we poorer on that account? We may think so, but that is not the impression this great chapter and the other chapters that speak of heaven leave with us. On the contrary, they are rich and reassuring. And the reason they are is that they focus rightly on the most important thing about heaven, namely, upon the fact that God the Father and God the Son are there.

This is the focal point of Revelation 5. It is true that it speaks of the three groups of beings I mentioned earlier: the four and twenty elders, the angels, and a vast host of other creatures from everywhere in the universe. But these are brought forward, not to give us a description of them, but because each of these is bearing a testimony to Christ and thus serves to show how he is prominent. The four and twenty elders praise him. Their praise is this song: "You are worthy to take the scroll and to open its seals, because you were slain, and with your blood you purchased men for God from every tribe and language and people and nation. You have made them to be a kingdom and priests to serve our God, and they will reign on the earth" (vv. 9–10). Then the angels give their testimony. They say, "Worthy is the Lamb, who was slain, to receive power and wealth and wisdom and strength and honor and glory and praise" (v. 12). At last the remaining creatures join in: "To him who sits on the throne and to the Lamb be praise and honor and glory and power, for ever and ever" (v. 13). Heaven is where God is, and it is his presence (and not some high concentration of golden streets or jewels) that makes it heaven.

Do you know that? Do your children know it? My six-year-old daughter was in a first-grade science class. They were discussing the universe—how big it is and of what it is composed. Do you know what the conversation of these six-year-old children drifted around to? Heaven! They wanted to know where heaven fit in. Was it between the stars? Was it beyond them? The only valid answer and the one we gave when our daughter came home and told this to us is that heaven is where God is. It is this that makes it heaven.

Where We Shall Be

So the first thing we note about this particular text is that Jesus is now in heaven in the presence of the Father. It is what he means by "where I am." We must also note that this is where we shall be, if we have truly been given to him. This is the major point of the verse, for Jesus mentions his departure to heaven only to say that it is his desire that we join him there after our work here has been completed.

This is what makes heaven real to us, too, and it is what makes it a comfort. One of the Bible personages who had a vision of heaven was the apostle Paul. He describes it obliquely at one point, using the third person as though he were describing the experience of someone else, but there is little doubt that he is speaking of himself. He says, "I know a man in Christ who fourteen years ago was caught up to the third heaven. Whether it was in the body or out of the body I do not know—God knows. And I know that this man—whether in the body or apart from the body I do not know, but God knows—was caught up to paradise. He heard inexpressible things, things that man is not permitted to tell" (2 Cor. 12:2–4). Here is a man who saw heaven and who could have described it for us. But he does not, for as Paul comes to speak of death later, as he does in Philippians and in some other books, it is always the presence of Christ in heaven that overshadows these other matters and is his comfort.

We shall be with Jesus! That is the promise and the glory. It is what should fill our minds as we think of the life to come.

It is also the thing that should fill our speech as we talk with dying people or with those who have lost a loved one. Most of us do not have great contact with death, because our culture has devised ways to isolate most of us from this reality. But pastors face it many times each year through the experience of those in their congregations. Here is one dying from cancer. The body is wasting away; so the evidence of approaching death is immediately evident to anyone who enters the dying person's room. It is evident to the person himself. What comfort is there? You cannot say, "You are certainly looking better this morning," because it is not true; and even if it were, it would only be temporary. You cannot bring comfort by asking how the person feels. He is in great pain. Where is the comfort? Only here: in knowing that the dying one will soon be with Jesus and that (before long) we too will be there and will be reunited with our friend.

Take another case. A child has died, and you are going to visit the family. The loss is great beyond measure. The family is in a near state of shock. What can you say? The only comfort is that the child is now with Jesus, having completed that span of life to which God called it, and that we will see the child again one day, at the moment of our own homegoing.

Several years ago, when I had been speaking on death, someone sent me a newspaper clipping containing excerpts from the writing of Pearl Buck, who had died just a few months before. Not having the Christian's hope, she had approached death, not in the comfort and assurance of the believer in Jesus Christ, but in the resignation of the Eastern mystics. She had written, "There are times in sleepless nights when I ponder upon this planet to which we cling. I meditate upon how utterly lost we are in space. We bear the total isolation as we must, for however we may hope there is a God we do not hear his voice and we do not see him and, while faith is a valid emotion, it is not confirmed except through hope" (*The Philadelphia Inquirer,* March 7, 1973). I would maintain that the Christian faith is confirmed twice over: first, objectively by Christ's resurrection and ascension, and second, subjectively by the application of these truths to our minds and consciences by the Holy Spirit. Most important, it is this that gives comfort as we contemplate our own passage from this life into eternity.

Like Jesus

I said that the only comfort in death is to know that we will soon be with Jesus. But while it is true that this is the great and only ultimate comfort, I am not sure that this statement is entirely true, for there is at least one other fact that is comforting. The additional fact is that we will not only be with Jesus, we will also be like him. John writes in his first letter, "We know that when he appears, we shall be like him, for we shall see him as he is" (1 John 3:2).

There are many ways in which we shall be like him. We shall be like him in respect to his character, for in that day all the sin, ignorance, and folly that characterize our lives here will be gone. We will be like him in love, holiness, knowledge, wisdom, truth, mercy, and all his other attributes. Then again, we shall be like him in respect to his body, for we shall receive a resurrection body patterned after his own.

I think this is what was in Paul's mind as he wrote those important words on death that are recorded in 2 Corinthians 4 and 5. There is an unfortunate chapter break in this passage, as there is also occasionally at other points of the New Testament. But if we begin reading with verse 15 of chapter 4 and continue through verse 4 of chapter 5, we will receive the full meaning of the apostle. "All this is for your benefit, so that the grace that is reaching more and more people may cause thanksgiving to overflow to the glory of God. Therefore we do not lose heart. Though outwardly we are wasting away, yet inwardly we are being renewed day by day. For our light and momentary troubles are achieving for us an eternal glory that far outweighs them all. So we fix our eyes not on what is seen, but on what is unseen. For what is seen is temporary, but what is unseen is eternal. Now we know that if the earthly tent we live in is destroyed, we have a building from God, an eternal house in heaven, not built by human hands. Meanwhile we groan, longing to be clothed with our heavenly dwelling, because when we are clothed, we will not be found naked. For while we are in this tent, we groan and are burdened, because we do not wish to be unclothed but to be clothed with our heavenly dwelling, so that what is mortal may be swallowed up by life" (2 Cor. 4:15—5:4).

As I read this I sense that Paul was not in good health and that he was, moreover, speaking from a sense of real pain. A chapter later he is to speak of the physical trials he had endured in Christ's service—beatings, imprisonments, riots, hard work, sleepless nights, hunger (6:5). In chapter 11 he will detail this suffering yet further—"Five times I received from the Jews the forty lashes minus one. Three times I was beaten with rods, once I was stoned, three times I was shipwrecked, I spent a night and a day in the open sea, I have been constantly on the move. I have been in danger from rivers, in danger from bandits, in danger from my own countrymen, in danger from Gentiles; in danger in the city, in danger in the country, in danger at sea; and in danger from false brothers. I have labored and toiled and have often gone without sleep; I have known hunger and thirst and have often gone without food; I have been cold and naked" (vv. 24–27). These sufferings were not imaginary for Paul. They were real perils. Luke describes many of them explicitly in the Book of Acts. These had certainly left their toll on Paul. So it may well have been as a nearly broken man that he wrote 2 Corinthians.

But what does he say? Does he complain? Does he bemoan his suffering? No. Rather, he looks beyond it, admitting that although our body is in a state of decline and although physical groans are wrung from us through our suffering, yet we still look up, knowing that a new body awaits us and in that body we will soon stand face-to-face before Jesus. It is after this moving acknowledgment of the problem and its solution that he says convincingly, "We are confident, I say, and would prefer to be away from the body and at home with the Lord" (5:8).

Like Jesus Now

There are some for whom these words are already meaningful. They are old or sick, some close to dying. The thought of being with Jesus forever and being like him is itself a great blessing. On the other hand, there are others who are not in this position and for whom this study therefore does not seem timely. What of these? I could point out that we are all dying, some only nearer to that point than others. Again, I could point out that no one knows the moment of his or her death. It could be thirty years from now; it could be tomorrow or tonight. Instead of this, let me make an application in two other areas.

First, if it is true that you will eventually be with Jesus, if you are a Christian, then why not spend time with him now? This you may do through times of your own personal Bible study and prayer. What would we think of a couple who are about to be married but who do not seem to feel the need to spend time together before the marriage? They say, "Oh, we will be together a lot after we are married; we have other things we want to do now." We would think that a marriage like that would hardly be promising, and we would be right, for if a couple is going to spend their lives together, they should rightly want to get to know one another better even before the marriage ceremony. In the same way, we should want to get to know Jesus better if we are indeed looking forward to being together with him in heaven one day.

The second application is to our moral conduct. If we are going to be like Jesus one day, as John tells us so clearly in his first epistle (1 John 3:2), then why not strive to be like him now? This is John's own conclusion, for having said that we will be like him in glory, he immediately adds, "Everyone who has this hope in him purifies himself, just as he is pure" (v. 3).

Each winter for many years, after the pressures of the Christmas and New Year's services at Tenth Presbyterian Church in Philadelphia, my family and I took a four-day vacation in the Pocono mountains in eastern Pennsylvania. The place where we vacationed is an immense lodge, beautifully situated on a large mountain estate. We looked forward to this greatly as the vacation days approached each winter. Thinking of it actually helped us do our work better. When the time eventually came that we were to make the trip, we started off, drove for about three hours, and then arrived normally in the evening as dusk was settling over the mountain landscape. We parked, approached the door, and as we went in, the magnificent doormen, some of whom had been there for twenty or thirty years, came up to greet us and take our bags. And they said—this is the point for which I tell the story—"Welcome home! Welcome home!" Well, it was not home (unfortunately). It is only a clever device on the part of the lodge to make its guests welcome. But one day we are going to glory where those words will be rightly spoken by no other than our own blessed Lord, the One who has himself prepared our rooms for us. "Welcome home!" he will say. And we really will be home—forever.

Anyone who has this hope in him will try to be like Christ now, and he will work faithfully in Christ's service.

221

The Sixth Mark of the Church: Love

John 17:25-26

"Righteous Father, though the world does not know you, I know you, and they know that you have sent me. I have made you known to them, and will continue to make you known in order that the love you have for me may be in them and that I myself may be in them."

What is the greatest mark of the church? I do not mean by this: What is the first mark of the church, or even, What is the mark that we perhaps most lack? Joy is the first mark mentioned, and the mark most lacking is something that has to be answered differently in different periods of history and in different situations. I mean: What is the greatest mark, the one that holds the others together? What is the one that gives meaning to the others, the one without which the church cannot at all be what God means it to be? There is only one answer. The greatest mark of the church is love.

Paul talks about this in 1 Corinthians 13. After having spoken about love in that chapter and having come to the end in which he looks at the Christian life under the categories of faith, hope, and love—faith that looks back to the cross, hope that looks forward to the Lord's second coming, and love that looks about at the world and other Christians—Paul concludes that while all three are great and abiding virtues, nevertheless "the greatest of these is love."

It is with the same thought in mind that the Lord Jesus Christ, having spoken of joy, holiness, truth, mission, and unity as essential marks of the church in his high priestly prayer of John 17, nevertheless concludes by an emphasis upon love. It is the new commandment of 13:34–35 once again—"Love one another. As I have loved you, you must love one another. By this all men will know that you are my disciples, if you love one another." Here Jesus says that he has declared the name of God to the disciples in order that "the love you have for me may be in them, and that I myself may be in them" (17:26).

When Love Is Gone

We see the preeminence of love readily if we look at it in reference to the other marks of the church. What happens when you take love away from them? Suppose you take joy and subtract love from it? What do you have? You have hedonism. You have an exuberance in life and its pleasures, but without the sanctifying joy found in relationship to the Lord Jesus Christ.

Subtract love from holiness. What do you get? You get self-righteousness, the kind of virtue that characterized the Pharisees of Christ's day. By the standards of the day the Pharisees lived very holy lives, but they did not love others and were ready to kill Christ when he challenged their standards, and actually did kill him. They were hypocrites.

Take love from truth, and you have a bitter orthodoxy, the kind of teaching that is right but that does not win anyone.

Take love from mission, and you have imperialism. It is colonialism in ecclesiastical garb. We have seen much of that in recent history.

Take love from unity, and you soon have tyranny. This develops in a hierarchical church where there is no compassion for people nor a desire to involve them in the decision-making process.

That is one side of it. On the other hand, express love in relation to God and man and what do you find? You find all the other marks of the church following. What does love for God the Father lead to? Joy! Because we rejoice in God and in what he has so overwhelmingly done for us. What does love for the Lord Jesus Christ lead to? Holiness! Because we know that we will see him one day and will be like him; therefore "everyone who has this hope in him purifies himself, just as he is pure" (1 John 3:3). What does love for the Word of God lead to? Truth! Because if we love the Word, we will study it and therefore inevitably grow into a fuller appreciation and realization of God's truth. What does love for the world lead to? Mission! We have a message to take to the world. Again, where does love for our Christian brothers and sisters lead us? To unity! Because by love we discern that we are bound together in that bundle of life that God himself has created within the Christian community.

Is it any wonder that Jesus ends his final discourses and prayer (undoubtedly spoken within the hearing of the disciples) with this emphasis? Hardly! Rather, we expect it, for it is as though Jesus, in anticipation of the writing of the fourth Gospel, could go back to the beginning of this fourth section (where we read, "Having loved his own who were in the world, he showed them the full extent of his love") and then conclude, "Yes, and here at the very end of my discourses and prayer I am going to talk about precisely that, for love is the most important characteristic."

Love's Source

What can we say about love on the basis of these verses? First, we can say that it has its source in God. This is the kind of love we are talking about. We are not talking about the kind of love the world invents, aspires to or imagines, but rather the love of God that is revealed in Jesus Christ and that we come to know as we come to know God. It is obvious that Jesus has precisely this thought in mind, because verse 25, the prelude to verse 26, talks about knowledge. In it Jesus says, "Righteous Father, though the world does not know you, I know you, and they know that you have sent me." It is after this that Jesus goes on to say, "I have made you known to them [that is, I have made you known in your essential nature], and will continue to make you known *in order that* the love you have for me may be in them and that I myself may be in them." What Jesus is saying is that, if we know God, we will know God's nature as being characterized by love and that, if we do not know love, we do not know God. John later clearly makes the same point in his first epistle (1 John 4:7–8).

When Jesus says the world has not known God, he means, besides everything else, that the world does not know God as a God of love. This was demonstrably true in Jesus' day. No Greek, no Roman, no Egyptian, no Babylonian in Christ's day, or in any of the centuries before, had ever thought of God's nature as being essentially characterized by love. It is just not there. Read all the ancient documents, and you simply do not find this element. At best, God was thought to be impartial. Or, if one chose to think optimistically, God could sometimes be said to love those who love him; meaning that he might be favorable to them for their service. But this is a tit-for-tat arrangement (you serve me, and I will take care of you), not the benevolent, unmerited love of God disclosed in the Bible. It simply does not exist in antiquity, apart from a preparatory form within the pages of the Old Testament.

With the Lord Jesus Christ an entirely new idea entered history, for he taught, not only that God is loving, but also that he loves with an extraordinary love, entirely beyond all human imaginations. That love had sent Christ to die. Moreover, on that basis it would now draw a host of redeemed men and women into an extraordinary family relationship with God.

It may be seen linguistically that a new understanding of love entered history through God's revelation, first in the Old Testament and then preeminently through the teaching of Jesus Christ. To begin with, we note that the Greek language, in which the New Testament is written and into which the Old Testament was translated about one hundred years before Christ's birth, is rich in words for love. Yet when the translators of the Old Testament and the writers of the New came to talk about the love of God, they found that they could not draw upon any of the common Greek words for "love," but instead had to choose a word that previously had been little used and change it, thereby infusing it with an entirely new character.

French has only one word for love, *aimer.* A Frenchman uses it for whatever he wants to say. He loves his wife; he loves his country; he loves his house; he loves his bouillabaisse and crepes suzette, anything, in fact, for which he has the slightest liking. The English language is a little better; we have "love" and "like."

French has one word. English has two words. But ancient Greek had three words, plus this indefinite word that could hardly be used for love at all. The first word was *storge.* It referred to general affection, particularly within the family. The closest English equivalent would be "fondness." The Greek would say, "I am *fond* of my children and my relatives." The second Greek word is *philia* from which we get the English words "philanthropy" and "Philadelphia." It refers to friendship. Jesus used this word when he said the person "who loves father or mother more than me, is not worthy of me" (Matt. 10:37). The third Greek word is *eros,* the word for sensual love. From it we get our English word "erotic."

When the translators of the Hebrew Bible came to put the Old Testament texts into Greek, none of these common words was adequate for conveying the biblical conceptions. The translators of the Septuagint might have used *storge,* the word for family affection; but how could they then have conveyed the idea of graciousness that is inherent in God's love? We like things because they commend themselves to us, but God commends his love toward men while they are yet sinners. Again, the translators might have used *eros,* noting that God's love for Israel is portrayed as sexual love in Hosea and in the Song of Solomon. However, this translation would have introduced the idea of an unrighteous love, for *eros* was associated as much with prostitution as with a proper love in marriage. *Eros* had almost no moral content. In a similar way, *philia* was also inadequate, for friendships come and go, but the love of God is eternal. God told Jeremiah, "I have loved you with an everlasting love" (Jer. 31:3).

What were the translators to do? The answer was simple. The translators took another word entirely, one without strong associations, and used it in nearly all cases where the love of God is mentioned. By doing this they created a word that came in time to convey the type of love they wanted.

At this point let me interject an illustration to show how this also happened in the New Testament period. When Jesus appeared in Israel announcing his mission, he avoided a number of messianic titles. The people were expecting the Messiah. But Jesus did not proclaim himself the Messiah, at least not openly, for to the Jews that would have meant a king strong enough to drive out the Romans. The title "Messiah" would have meant an earthly king and would have suggested an earthly kingdom. Nor did he call himself the Son of God. The Greeks knew all about "sons of god," but that title would have put him on the same level with Hercules or Alexander the Great. Instead Jesus called himself the Son of man. This title occurs in Daniel and describes a messianic figure. But in the intellectual climate of Jesus' time it was no longer precise and could have meant almost anything. Hence, Jesus used that title more than any other, allowing his teaching and ministry to paint a proper picture of himself as God's true Messiah and Son—the One who came to die, rise again, and return one day in glory to judge mankind and reward those who have believed on him.

It is the same with the several words for "love." Neither *storge,* nor *philia,* nor *eros* conveys the proper biblical ideas. But *agape* could. It was vague, but it could be made to convey the right ideas. Does God love with a righteous, holy love? Yes. That love is *agape.* Is God's love gracious, sovereign, everlasting? Yes, that too. That love is *agape.* By this means *agape* became the supreme word for speaking about God's love, a new love revealed initially by God through Judaism and then disclosed in its fullness in Jesus Christ through biblical Christianity.

By Revelation

This leads to a second point, the revelation itself. We ask: Where does the revelation of God's love occur? Again, it is a somewhat complicated answer. Certainly God had revealed himself to be a God of love in the pages of the Old Testament. God indicated there that he had set his love upon Israel even though there was nothing in the people to merit it. Again, God is revealed to be a God of love in Christ's teaching. He called him Father, indicating that his was a father's love. All that is true. Yet the best truth is that God is declared to be a God of love by the cross of Jesus Christ. "For God so loved the world that he gave his one and only Son, that whoever believes in him should not perish but have eternal life" (John 3:16).

This is what Jesus is looking forward to in the words that close his prayer, for he says, "I will declare it," meaning the name of God. What is he thinking of here? We could understand the phrase if it had occurred in the past tense, for it would then clearly refer to the previous teaching in the Gospel. But why the future tense? What is Jesus thinking about? It must be the cross itself, for it is as though Jesus is saying, "That which I have been speaking of in years past I am now going to demonstrate in a dramatic and tangible way through my crucifixion."

There has never been—there never will be—a greater demonstration of the love of God. So if you will not have the Cross, if you will not see God speaking in love in Jesus Christ, you will never find a loving God anywhere. The God of the Bible is going to be a silent God for you. The universe is going to be an empty universe. History is going to be meaningless. It is only at the cross that you will ever find God in his true nature and learn that these other things have meaning.

Love in Action

There is something else in this text, for Jesus does not merely show where we can find love. He also shows where we can demonstrate love, for he goes on to pray that "the love you have for me may be *in them,* and that I myself may be *in them.* " Love is to be shown in us personally.

Why is Jesus concerned about this? I am sure he is concerned about this simply because it is only in his followers that anyone in this age, or any other age save his own, can see this great love. Jesus was aware that he was about to die. Following his death, there would be a resurrection and an ascension into heaven. Therefore, this One who was himself the perfect manifestation of love, the only one in whom this world had ever seen what true love really is—this one would be gone. He would not be here for men and women to contemplate. So he says as he closes his prayer that this love is now to be in us, even as he is in us, and that the world is to see it there. It must be love in action.

A Practical Question

As we draw to the end of this volume (and this section of John's Gospel) a person may be saying, "But I have a practical question. I can see the importance of love, as you have outlined it. I recognize that if we leave love out of the equation for Christian living, we have distorted it all. I can even understand the doctrinal points: that love comes from God, that love is demonstrated at the cross, that it must be seen in Christian people. But how do we do it? That is the most important question. How do we love one another? How do we put this great love of God into practice?" Let me share a few practical ways.

First, we need to love one another by *listening* to one another. We live in an age in which people do not listen to each other. We talk to one another, and others are constantly talking to us. But this is a hard world in which no one really listens. So one of the things we need to do, if we are truly characterized by the love of God, is to listen. God listens to us.

I saw a movie in which the dominant male character and the dominant female character were talking to one another. The man was older. He was a product of his generation. The woman was younger; she had grown up with television and was so much the passive product of the television age that she was unable to relate deeply to anyone. She was unable to listen. In this scene they were talking together, and the woman said something like, "What do you want from me?"

He answered, "I want you to love me."

This demand was something she could not cope with and did not really understand. She said, "I do not know how to do that." Then they stood staring at each other, and as they did, one became increasingly aware of how fragile their relationship was and that there was ultimately nothing to hold them together. Finally, the telephone rang. What would happen now? Could the girl transcend the interruption and deal with the pressing personal matter? For a moment she seemed to try. But then, while still facing him, her eyes darted sideways to the telephone and the moment to listen was gone. After this the scene dissolved, because the glance told it all. She could not listen.

Here is another story told by theologian Carl F. H. Henry. On one occasion in his travels he was seated in a diner at breakfast time next to a family who had a small boy. The waitress came to their table and began taking the order from the boy. "What will you have for breakfast?" she asked.

He said, "I'll have a hamburger and french fries with lots of ketchup."

"Oh, no, you won't," his mother said. "You'll have a scrambled egg and toast."

That seemed to settle the matter, so the waitress went on to take the other orders. But when she was done she turned back to the boy and said, "I guess it's going to be a scrambled egg and toast." He nodded. Then she said, "But with lots of ketchup!"

After the waitress had gone to the kitchen the boy exclaimed, "I like that waitress; she thinks I'm real." He liked her because she had listened to him and had learned what he had to say. So should we, if we really love one another.

Second, we should *share*. That is, we should let others share, and we ourselves should share. We are not to be like some professional counselors, listening but never interjecting ourselves. We are brothers and sisters in the Lord. We have a family relationship. So we do not sit like computers, analyzing what we are told and then coming back with answers carefully based upon social science surveys. We come back as people who are on the same level as the ones to whom we are talking, and we say, "Yes, I've gone through that. God has done this and this for me."

Our problem at this point is that we do not like to share ourselves. And the reason we do not like to share ourselves is, if we put it frankly, that we are ashamed of ourselves because we are sinners and are afraid that if we really did tell what is down inside, the other person would turn away and be disgusted. We would lose the relationship. How do we get to the point of being able really to share? There is only one way, and that is to know deep in our hearts that before God we are fully known as we are, with all our blemishes, sins and shames, and that, nevertheless, Jesus Christ has loved us, died for us, and that we are now fully accepted in the beloved. If you can know that you are known and yet loved, then you can share your true self and love others.

Third, we must *serve*. We must listen, share, and serve. If anything has been taught in this section of the Gospel, it is that we must serve. The section began with a reference to service as the outworking of Christ's love: "Having loved his own who were in the world, he showed them the full extent of his love" (13:1). In the thirteenth chapter it contained a demonstration of what this love means in the washing of the disciples' feet. Jesus concluded, "Now that I, your Lord and Teacher, have washed your feet, you also should wash one another's feet" (13:14). Later Jesus goes on to teach what this love means and what the Holy Spirit will do in enabling us to love. Finally, in this prayer, he lists the special marks that should characterize the church in every age: joy, holiness, truth, unity, mission, and love. The last of these involve service.

And quite rightly! For the Christian church is not in the world to be served; she is in the world to serve in order that the love of God in Christ might be increasingly known through the testimonies and specific loving acts of Christian people.

Notes

Chapter 165: Having Loved, He Loved

1. H. A. Ironside, *Illustrations of Bible Truth* (Chicago: Moody, 1945), 67–69.

Chapter 166: Love on Its Knees

1. Ray C. Stedman, *Secrets of the Spirit* (Old Tappan, N.J.: Revell, 1975), 13.
2. Ibid., p. 20.

Chapter 168: A Classic Prophecy

1. William Barclay, *The Gospel of John,* vol. 2 (Philadelphia: Westminster Press), 165–66.

Chapter 170: Christ Glorified Now

1. One major question of the textual criticism of this Gospel is whether or not we have the original order of chapters 13–17 as John has given them to us. The questions arise largely from the fact that the words at the end of chapter 14 seem to suggest an immediate departure from the upper room but that, in spite of this, the discourses actually go on for chapters 15 and 16 and are then followed by the prayer of John 17. In trying to remedy this some have suggested transposing chapters 15 and 16 to this point, allowing them to break into 13:31 after the words "Jesus said." Bultmann is one who does this (although he also includes chap. 17, placing it before 15 and 16), and there are others.

As is often the case with such rearrangements, the original difficulty is solved only by creating others. For example, the "new commandment" of 13:34 does not sound like it was spoken after 15:14. Undoubtedly, this alleged problem comes only from our unjustified desire to have the material conform to twentieth-century standards for neat, logical arrangement. In the absence of any manuscript evidence, it is best to take chapters 13–17 as they stand (cf. Leon Morris, *The Gospel According to John* [Grand Rapids: Eerdmans, 1971], 629–30).

2. Arthur W. Pink, *Exposition of the Gospel of John,* vol. 2 (Grand Rapids: Zondervan, 1945), 338.

Chapter 171: The New Commandment

1. Alexander Maclaren, "Gospel of St. John," *Expositions of Holy Scripture,* vol. 7 (Grand Rapids: Eerdmans, 1959), 227–28.

Chapter 172: Marks of a True Disciple

1. Francis A. Schaeffer, *The Church at the End of the 20th Century* (Downers Grove, Ill.: InterVarsity Press, 1970), 133.
2. Donald Grey Barnhouse, *The Love Life* (Glendale, Calif.: Regal Books, G/L Publications, 1973), 167.
3. Ibid.
4. Schaeffer, *The Church at the End of the 20th Century,* 137.
5. Barnhouse, *The Love Life,* 171.

Chapter 173: Darkness before the Dawn

1. Barclay, *The Gospel of John,* vol. 2, 175–76.
2. Pink, *Exposition of the Gospel of John,* vol. 2, 327.
3. Ibid.

Chapter 175: A Place for You

1. Donald Grey Barnhouse, *God's River,* "Studies in the Epistle to the Romans," vol. 4 (Grand Rapids: Eerdmans, 1959), 49–50.
2. Paul Tournier, *A Place for You* (New York: Harper & Row, 1968), 9.
3. Ibid., 12.

Chapter 176: Heaven

1. Dwight L. Moody, *Great Pulpit Masters,* vol. 1 (New York: Revell, 1949), 211.

Chapter 177: "I Am the Way and the Truth and the Life"

1. Charles Haddon Spurgeon, "The Way" *Metropolitan Tabernacle Pulpit,* vol. 16 (Pasadena, Tex.: Pilgrim Publications, 1970), 412.
2. Pink, *Exposition of the Gospel of John,* vol. 2, 356.

Chapter 179: How to See God

1. *Spurgeon's Illustrative Anecdotes,* ed. David Otis Fuller (Grand Rapids: Zondervan, 1945), 44.
2. Donald Grey Barnhouse, *Let Me Illustrate* (Westwood, N.J.: Revell, 1967), 106–7.

Chapter 180: Greater Things Than Jesus' Things

1. Pink, *Exposition of the Gospel of John,* vol. 2, 362–64.

2. Leon Morris, *The Gospel According to John* (Grand Rapids: Eerdmans, 1971), 646.

3. H. A. Ironside, *Addresses on the Gospel of John* (Neptune, N.J.: Loizeaux Bros., 1942), 617–19.

4. R. A. Torrey, *The Power of Prayer and the Prayer of Power* (Grand Rapids: Zondervan, 1955), 24.

Chapter 181: Praying in Jesus' Name

1. Torrey, *The Power of Prayer and the Prayer of Power,* 126.

2. Ibid., 138–39.

3. Ralph L. Keiper and James M. Boice, *Is Prayer a Problem?* (Philadelphia: The Bible Study Hour, 1974), 21–22.

4. Ibid., 23.

Chapter 182: "Keep My Commands"

1. Maclaren, *Expositions of Holy Scripture,* vol. 7, part 2, 315, 317.

2. Torrey, *The Power of Prayer and the Prayer of Power,* 131–32.

Chapter 183: That Other Comforter

1. J. I. Packer, *Knowing God* (Downers Grove, Ill.: InterVarsity Press, 1973), 60.

2. R. A. Torrey, *The Person and Work of the Holy Spirit* (Grand Rapids: Zondervan, 1970), 8–9.

3. George Smeaton, *The Doctrine of the Holy Spirit,* original ed. 1882 (Carlisle, Pa.: Banner of Truth Trust, 1961), 109.

4. Packer, *Knowing God,* 63.

Chapter 184: The Role of the Holy Spirit

1. Barnhouse, *The Love Life,* 187.

Chapter 185: The Fullness of the Holy Spirit

1. John R. W. Stott, *The Baptism and Fullness of the Holy Spirit* (Downers Grove, Ill.: InterVarsity Press, 1964), 28.

2. Ibid., 46.

Chapter 186: Gifts and Fruit

1. William Barclay, *Flesh and Spirit: An Examination of Galatians 5:19–23* (Nashville: Abingdon Press, 1962), 127.

2. William Fitch, *The Ministry of the Holy Spirit* (Grand Rapids: Zondervan, 1974), 28.

Chapter 187: What about Tongues?

1. Fitch, *The Ministry of the Holy Spirit,* 60–61.

2. Francis A. Schaeffer, *The New Super-Spirituality* (Downers Grove, Ill.: InterVarsity Press, 1972), 24.

3. John R. W. Stott, *Your Mind Matters* (Downers Grove, Ill.: InterVarsity Press, 1972), 10.

Chapter 188: Four Promises

1. Pink, *Exposition of the Gospel of John,* vol. 2, 378.

Chapter 190: Peace Casting Out Fear

1. Ironside, *Addresses on the Gospel of John,* 637–38.

Chapter 191: "I Am the True Vine"

1. The other "I am" sayings are: "I am the bread of life" (6:35); "I am the light of the world" (8:12; 9:5); "I am the gate" (10:7, 9); "I am the good shepherd" (10:11, 14); "I am the resurrection, and the life" (11:25); and "I am the way and the truth and the life" (14:6).

2. Morris, *The Gospel According to John,* 670–71.

3. Charles Haddon Spurgeon, "Without Christ—Nothing," *Metropolitan Tabernacle Pulpit,* vol. 27 (London: Banner of Truth Trust, 1971), 600–601.

Chapter 192: Remaining and Not Remaining

1. Ray G. Stedman, *Secrets of the Spirit* (Old Tappan, N.J.: Revell, 1975), 81.

2. Charles Haddon Spurgeon, "The Secret of Power in Prayer," *Metropolitan Tabernacle Pulpit,* vol. 34 (London: Banner of Truth Trust, 1970), 20.

3. Pink, *Exposition of the Gospel of John,* vol. 2, 408.

Chapter 193: God Glorified . . . in You

1. Charles Haddon Spurgeon, "Love at Its Utmost," *Metropolitan Tabernacle Pulpit,* vol. 33 (London: Banner of Truth Trust, 1969), 506–7.

2. Ibid., 507.

Chapter 195: Fruit, More Fruit

1. Andrew Murray, *The True Vine* (Chicago: Moody Press, n.d.), 23–24.

Chapter 196: Hated for No Cause

1. William Barclay, *The Gospel of John,* vol. 2, 217.

2. Ironside, *Addresses on the Gospel of John,* 684–85.

3. See "Why Miracles?" in volume 2.

Chapter 197: He Will . . . You Will

1. Torrey, *The Person and Work of the Holy Spirit,* 86–87.

2. John R. W. Stott, "Jesus Is Lord," in *Our Sovereign God,* ed. James M. Boice (Grand Rapids: Baker Book House, 1977), 22.

Chapter 198: No Strange Trial

1. *Luther's Works,* vol. 24, tr. Martin H. Bertram (St. Louis: Concordia Publishing House, 1961), 303.
2. Ibid., 314.
3. See Boice, *The Sermon on the Mount* (Grand Rapids: Zondervan, 1972), 66.

Chapter 199: Witness for the Prosecution

1. Morris, *The Gospel According to John,* 698.
2. Torrey, *The Person and Work of the Holy Spirit,* 84–86.
3. Ibid., 90.
4. Charles Haddon Spurgeon, "The Holy Spirit's Threefold Conviction of Men," *Metropolitan Tabernacle Pulpit,* vol. 29 (London: Banner of Truth Trust, 1971), 127–28.

Chapter 200: More Words to Come

1. Barclay, *The Gospel of John,* vol. 2, 226.
2. Ibid., 228.
3. Torrey, *The Person and Work of the Holy Spirit,* 247–56.

Chapter 202: Another Prayer Promise

1. R. A. Torrey, *How to Pray* (Westwood, N.J.: Revell, 1900), 7–31.
2. Ibid., 49–50.
3. Stedman, *Secrets of the Spirit,* 121.

Chapter 203: Great Origin, Great Destiny

1. Maclaren, *Expositions of Holy Scripture,* vol. 7, part 3, 161.
2. Barnhouse, *Let Me Illustrate,* 170.
3. Maclaren, *Expositions of Holy Scripture,* vol. 7, part 3, 168.

Chapter 205: The Real Lord's Prayer

1. The quotations and other information in this paragraph are from Pink, *Exposition of the Gospel of John,* vol. 3, 90.

Chapter 209: Prayer for Christ's Own

1. Ernst Lohmeyer, *"Our Father": An Introduction to the Lord's Prayer,* trans. by John Bowden (New York: Harper & Row, 1965); Joachim Jeremias, "Abba," in *The Central Message of the New Testament* (London: SCM Press, 1965) and *The Lord's Prayer,* trans. John Reumann (Philadelphia: Fortress Press, 1964).

Chapter 211: Prayer for Christ's Own Only

1. Charles Haddon Spurgeon, "Christ's Pastoral Prayer for His People," *Metropolitan Tabernacle Pulpit,* vol. 39 (Pasadena, Texas: Pilgrim Publications, 1975), 505.
2. Spurgeon, "Christ's Pastoral Prayer for His People," 510–11.

Chapter 212: God's Perseverance with His Saints

1. Marcus Rainsford, *Our Lord Prays for His Own: Thoughts on John 17* (Chicago: Moody Press, 1950), 173.
2. Ibid., 175.
3. Ironside, *Addresses on the Gospel of John*, 754–55.

Chapter 213: The First Mark of the Church: Joy

1. Barclay, *Flesh and Spirit*, 77–78.
2. Francis W. Dixon, "God's Happy People" in *The Keswick Week: 1962* (London: Marshall, Morgan & Scott, 1962), 12.

Chapter 214: The Second Mark of the Church: Holiness

1. Peter L. Berger, "Needed: Authority," *The Presbyterian Journal*, (October 20, 1971): 10.

Chapter 216: The Third Mark of the Church: Truth

1. Stedman, *Secrets of the Spirit*, 147–48.
2. Donald G. Bloesch, *The Invaded Church* (Waco, Texas: Word Books, 1975), 99.

Chapter 217: The Fourth Mark of the Church: Mission

1. Hannah Whitall Smith, *The Christian's Secret of a Happy Life* (Westwood, N.J.: Revell, 1952), 15.

Chapter 218: The Fifth Mark of the Church: Unity

1. John White, *The Fight* (Downers Grove, Ill.: InterVarsity Press, 1976), 137.
2. Charles Haddon Spurgeon, "Unity in Christ," *Metropolitan Tabernacle Pulpit*, vol. 12 (Pasadena, Tex.: Pilgrim Publications, 1970), 2.
3. John R. W. Stott, *One People* (London: Falcon Books, 1969), 70–71.
4. Ibid., 87.
5. White, *The Flight*, 150.

Chapter 219: Impartial Love

1. Tournier, *A Place for You*, 197–98.
2. Ibid., 195.

Chapter 220: With Jesus Forever

1. John W. Dean, *Blind Ambition: The White House Years* (New York: Simon and Schuster, 1976), 30–31.

Subject Index

Aaron, 1071, 1088
Abraham, 1034, 1035, 1055, 1067, 1071, 1183
Absalom's rebellion, 1020
Adam, 1240; conduct reversed by Jesus, 1033
Adam and Eve, 1034, 1066, 1076
Affluence, 1306
Agenda, world's, 1303
Ahithophel, 1020
Amen, 1018
Angels, 1253
Antinomianism, 1106
A Place for You, 1066
Apologetics, 1278
Apostles, 1094; taught by the Holy Spirit, 1147
Apostles' Creed, 1111
Arianism, 1233
Aristides, 1190, 1191
Armerding, Hudson, 1307
Arminius, and Calvin, 1210
Assurance, 1036, 1200; completed, 1264–66
Augustine, 1003; and Pelagius, 1210
Authority, 1313; given to Jesus, 1253–55; substitute, 1302
Authorized Version, 1059
Awareness, 1258

Baptism, ix; of the Spirit, 1124, 1125
Barclay, William, 1021, 1049, 1165, 1190, 1191, 1217, 1294
Barnhouse, Donald Grey, 1043–45, 1066, 1092, 1236, 1285
Beatitudes, 1018, 1027
Believing is seeing, 1090, 1091, 1278
Berger, Peter, 1302
Bethany, 1053, 1240

Bible, 1204; disciplined study of, 1304; importance of studying, 1231; inspired, 1118, 1119, 1196, 1197, 1220; reveals Christ, 1144; study, 1345; unlike other books, 1196; Word of God, 1152. *See also* Scriptures, Word of God
Bible Study Hour, 1240
Blessing, second, 1313
Blind Ambition, 1339
Bloesch, Donald, 1314
Born again, 1011
Bride of Christ, 1282
Brotherhood, Christian, 1039
Brothers and sisters, 1329, 1330
Browning, Robert, 1269
Buck, Pearl, 1343
Burning bush, 1259

Caesar and Cleopatra, 1304
Cain, homeless, 1066
Calderon, Bernardo, 1321
Calvary, 1034
Calvin, John, 1245; and Arminius, 1210
Creation, 1264
Christian faith, confirmed, 1343
Christianity, exclusive claims of, 1081; historical, 1219
Christianity Today, 1043
Christians, fruitful, 1131, 1132, 1185, 1186; identified with Christ, 1205; in the world, 1321–23; mark of true, 1043; must be different, 1313–15; not of the world, 1190; realists, 1059; servants of Christ, 1016, 1017; sons of God, 1297, 1298; unity of, 1124
Christ Jesus, absent, 1156, 1157; and Peter, 1010, 1011; and his word, 1167;

1361

Scripture Index

James Montgomery Boice is president and cofounder of the Alliance of Confessing Evangelicals, the parent organization of *The Bible Study Hour*, on which he has been the speaker since 1969. He is the senior pastor of Philadelphia's historic Tenth Presbyterian Church.